BROTHERS IN LIBERTY

The Forgotten Story of the Free Black Haitians Who Fought for American Independence

PHILLIP THOMAS TUCKER

STACKPOLE BOOKS

Essex, Connecticut
Blue Ridge Summit, Pennsylvania

STACKPOLE BOOKS

An imprint of Globe Pequot, the trade division of The Rowman & Littlefield Publishing Group, Inc.
4501 Forbes Blvd., Ste. 200
Lanham, MD 20706
www.rowman.com
Distributed by NATIONAL BOOK NETWORK

British Library Cataloguing in Publication Information available

Library of Congress Cataloging-in-Publication Data

ISBN: 978-0-8117-7061-3 (cloth)
ISBN: 978-0-8117-7062-0 (electronic)

♾️™ The paper used in this publication meets the minimum requirements of American National Standard for Information Sciences—Permanence of Paper for Printed Library Materials, ANSI/NISO Z39.48-1992.

Contents

ACKNOWLEDGMENTS

I would very much like to thank Mr. David Reisch, the expert senior history editor of Stackpole Books, who made this special project possible by believing in its worth and merits from the beginning. He early embraced the core concepts of this fascinating subject that has resulted in this unique book of rare distinction. This important and timely book simply would not have been possible without Dave's wisdom and foresight.

Introduction

After nearly 250 years, it is certainly time to take an entirely new look at different and unique aspects of the American Revolution, especially the most forgotten ones, because new perspectives are badly needed in this notoriously stale field of study long dominated by seemingly endless excesses of nationalistic perspectives, traditional views, and romantic myths. Unfortunately, too often even the best Revolutionary War books, especially those about the lives of the Founding Fathers—including the most popular works from generations of admiring American historians—have been dominated by a sense of awe and reverence, in the nationalist tradition.

In consequence, it is finally time for a less biased, truly relevant, and more meaningful look at the American Revolution, especially in regard to racial aspects and dimensions, for our time in the twenty-first century. *Brothers in Liberty* has been written for today's America, which has been so badly divided on issues of race, especially in regard to the forgotten, but relevant, connections and bonds between Blacks and whites, not only long overlooked and ignored, but also erroneously thought not to exist, especially in terms of the races coming together to fight for America.

The dramatic events of the American Revolution—and the members of America's *actual* greatest generation—have seemed distant and remote for far too long. They have been shrouded in mystique and romantic legend, seemingly so obscure as to be irrelevant on any and every possible level in the minds of modern Americans in the twenty-first century. Complicating this situation, in which the Founding Fathers seem as distant in American minds as those nationalistic stone idols perched on Mount Rushmore in the Black Hills of South Dakota, has been the fact that the American Revolution—America's original creation myth—has been by far the most mythological chapter in the annals of American history.

Unfortunately, some of the most fascinating chapters of the American Revolution have long been absent from the story of America's founding saga, especially in regard to the role of Black patriots and their forgotten contributions during America's struggle for life. It's as if they played no role whatsoever in the making of America—one of the great myths of the American Revolution. In fact, nothing could be further from the truth.

What has long been needed in this static field of American Revolutionary War historiography—the most unfertile of historical fields, or so it would seem—has been something well beyond the repetitious rehashing of the old familiar stories of British taxation, the Boston Tea Party, the early clashes of arms at Lexington and Concord, the lives of the same old cast of political and military leaders, and the best-known battles. These same topics have been endlessly studied generation after generation in great detail by a large number of American writers, historians, and scholars.

Brothers in Liberty is dedicated to taking an entirely new approach to looking at the Revolutionary War, from the perspective of race, in the context of one of the major battles of the American Revolution. The Battle of Savannah, which took place on October 9, 1779, has been one of the most neglected and forgotten major engagements in the annals of Revolutionary War historiography, just like its participants, both Black and white, even though it was bloodier than the famous siege of Yorktown.

Part of my unique approach is the synthesis of Revolutionary War history with certain aspects of today's racial politics in America, in order to better understand the overlooked connection between past and present in regard to race over the span of nearly two and a half centuries. In this way we will investigate the complex factors of America's most vexing historical dilemma and contradiction—race—while providing new relevancy to the American Revolution in connection with today's complex and convoluted racial environment in the United States.

This unprecedented approach of looking more closely at the complexities, nuances, and legacies of various and seldom-explored racial aspects of the American Revolution is important if we want to achieve a better understanding not only of America's struggle for independence, but also today's America in terms of race. Race has long held such a central place in America's story, as much today as it did in 1779. It's almost as if nothing has changed in the past two and a half centuries.

By exploring the deep-seated complexities and complications of race—historically, the most vexing and insolvable dilemma in the nation's history—within the broad framework of the cycles of history, especially in regard to the American Revolution and America's creation story, we can learn not only about the central contradictions and paradoxes of America's past, but also about the present and future issues of race in the United States.

During the last few decades, America has become more divided and polarized along racial lines than ever before, largely because of the self-serving political agendas of politicians and heated rhetoric from both the Democratic and Republican Parties. Fueling today's racial divide in the United States, the shameful, blatant race-baiting of both sides of the political spectrum has been deliberately calculated and orchestrated by American society's elite in order to divide everyday Americans, Black and white, of the middle and lower classes. This severe polarization of American society is not only unfortunate but tragic, largely artificially manufactured by the political radicalization of both the Left and the Right for self-serving reasons in the games of partisan politics and racial politics, rather than from the actions and thinking of average Americans, Black and white.

As a result, by the third decade of the twenty-first century, the racial divide in America has become so great that it seems it will never be closed. Although exaggerated by the politically driven modern media in the United States in an effort to further divide the American public, today's ugly racial realities only reflect the fundamental truth about the centrality of race throughout the course of American history. It has played a key role from the very beginning, in 1619, when the first Africans were brought in chains to Jamestown, Virginia, recently recognized and emphasized by historians and in academe, especially in *The 1619 Project*.

At long last, it is now the right time to take a detailed look at a forgotten "feel good" story of Black and white united as one on a major Revolutionary War battlefield, fighting for America and liberty—the kind of close unity and comradeship not seen anywhere in today's partisan media or popular discourse about race. Such positive perspectives about Black and white interactions and unity have seldom been presented, in the past or the present, for political and racial reasons. In consequence, *Brothers in Liberty* focuses specifically on what has not been written about in history books in the past: the unity that existed between the Black and mixed-race fighting men of the Chasseurs-Volontaires de Saint-Domingue from the French colony of Saint-Domingue and their white allies, Americans and Frenchmen, during the most overlooked battle of the American Revolution, the Battle of Savannah George during the Savannah Campaign of 1779. In an unprecedented development not seen before or after throughout the American Revolution on such a scale, soldiers of different colors served together to battle a common foe in the name of freedom and equality against a European monarchy's imperialist domination and rule, as true brothers in liberty.

Most significant, what the Black and mulatto troops achieved at Savannah was nothing less than the most distinguished Black contribution on American soil before the Civil War, not only in the annals of Black history but also in the American Revolution and overall American history—coming to the rescue of the mauled American and French armies, which had been decimated in the failed attacks on Savannah's strong defenses, by a timely counterattack that helped to save the day and the Franco-American alliance.

In an earth-shaking development that stunned the world, the American Revolution was the first revolt of the common people of the New World that successfully threw off the shackles of European imperialism and colonialism of the mother country, when Great Britain possessed the most powerful empire in the world. Black and mixed-race fighting men from Saint-Domingue and white soldiers, both Americans and Frenchmen, were united in this noble goal of achieving the great dream

4

of equality for the common people of America—a true people's revolution—during the siege and then the Battle of Savannah when the climax of the struggle came on October 9, 1779, the bloodiest single hour of the American Revolution during what was one of the three bloodiest battles of the Revolutionary War.

Often forgotten in the annals of Revolutionary War historiography has been the distinguished role played at the Battle of Savannah by the Black and mulatto fighting men from France's most prosperous colony in the Caribbean, Saint-Domingue, today's Republic of Haiti. In much the same way, the impressive contributions and sacrifices of Black patriots, including the excellent fighting men who served in General George Washington's Continental Regiments, have long been overlooked by Americans, doomed to an undeserved obscurity to this day.

The enduring legacy of these soldiers of the Chasseurs-Volontaires was significant because many of these men were part of the two greatest revolutions in the history of the Western Hemisphere—the American Revolution and then the Haitian Revolution, more closely connected than has been recognized by generations of historians. Indeed, the revolutionary legacy and heritage of these Black and mulatto soldiers of 1779 never died, resurrected on Haitian soil by veterans of the Savannah Campaign less than a decade and a half later, in their own homeland.

Located only six hundred miles from the southern tip of Florida, the former slaves of the prosperous Colony of Saint-Domingue, the prized colonial possession of France because of its lucrative sugarcane cultivation, designed to satisfy the world's sweet tooth, rose up against the French occupiers of Napoleon Bonaparte, who attempted to restore slavery and enslave free people less than a generation later. After the dramatic showdown at Savannah in October 1779 and the success of a people's revolution whose lessons were never forgotten, the people of Saint-Domingue broke away from Napoleonic France to establish the Republic of Haiti on January 1, 1804, which was the second successful revolution in the Western Hemisphere, thanks in part to the inspiration of American revolutionary ideals of equality for all men, which sparked the French Revolution and then the Haitian Revolution.

Significantly, the Haitian Revolution succeeded in part because of the key influences of the Black and mulatto veterans of Savannah, who became the primary leaders of the Haitian Revolution. In this regard, the Battle of Savannah was a truly pivotal event in not only American history but also in Haitian and world history, especially in the fight for freedom. In Haiti, its legacy of 1779 provided an inspirational example that paid dividends in the creation of the world's first Black republic.

Because this bloody showdown at Savannah on October 9, 1779, was such an embarrassing disaster in regard to top French leadership having made the mistake of ordering the assault against a powerful network of British fortifications, generations of American and French writers and historians have avoided writing about what happened at Savannah—an extremely dark chapter of the patriot war effort—to focus on what has been deemed more important subjects of America's creation story, especially the famous victories and glorified leaders. But this is precisely the reason for the need today to explore and understand the distinguished contributions of the Chasseurs-Volontaires de Saint-Domingue, because this volunteer unit of Blacks and mulattoes saved the day by rescuing both the American and French armies and saving them from destruction during the midst of a disaster of unprecedented proportions for the allies, after their repulse.

While Americans have long focused excessively on the decisive Franco-American success at the siege of Yorktown, Virginia, that won the war to ensure an infant republic's independence, the significant and equally fascinating story of the siege and Battle of Savannah has been forgotten, almost as if the first close allied effort after the signing of the crucial Franco-American alliance of 1778 had never existed—primarily because it had proved to be such dismal failure by the end of 1779. However, the Savannah Campaign of 1779 was crucial for a host of valid strategic reasons, including the fact that Great Britain's "Southern Strategy" for winning the war and securing its thirteen wayward colonies was at stake. British control of the strategic port of Savannah would open the door for the conquest of the entire South, including all-important Virginia, leading to a decisive British victory if everything went according to plan.

Although a true American tragedy, in overall strategic terms, what happened at Savannah was one of the most important showdowns in the course of the American Revolution. Generations of historians have lavishly celebrated the remarkable story of the great success at Yorktown, where the unprecedented close coordination of the last major allied effort was the antithesis of the Savannah Campaign. This situation has understandably obscured the first major allied offensive effort at Savannah and its equally riveting tale of fate, hubris, and folly, in the tradition of the heroic story of the siege of Troy, when Greeks and Trojans waged their legendary war during the Bronze Age, as so masterfully described by Homer in the pages of *The Iliad*.

Precious little glory except an exceedingly grim one was achieved by the allies during the strategic Savannah Campaign in the fall of 1779, which was America's fourth year of war, when the Americans and French committed the folly of assaulting Savannah's powerful network of fortifications and paid a fearful price. Because the campaign was nothing less than a monumental disaster on almost every level, most historians and scholars have simply decided to ignore it, focusing instead on General George Washington's campaigns to the north and glorious American victories, such as at Saratoga, New York, in October 1777, which guaranteed the signing of the Franco-American alliance of 1778 that ultimately culminated in the victory at Yorktown in the fall of 1781, when the alliance finally worked to near perfection to win the most decisive victory of the war and ensure American independence.

For a number of reasons, I believe it is most important today to tell the fascinating story of the siege and Battle of Savannah largely from the French perspective, by relying more on quotations from America's Gallic allies on the scene, especially because one distinctive combat unit of the French Army and from the French West Indies saved the day for America in the end. While the Chasseurs-Volontaires de Saint-Domingue, consisting of Black and mulatto volunteers, left no accounts of the battle, fortunately French soldiers wrote about their invaluable contributions and timely achievements on that ill-fated day of October 9.

With British-Hessian-Loyalist victory in the defense of Savannah after the repulse of the uncoordinated and ill-conceived American-French assaults, during the bloodiest single hour of the American Revolution, the door was finally open for British strategists to focus their attention on invading and conquering the South. Capitalizing on the Savannah success, this phase of the British Campaign to win it all began with the attack on Charlestown, South Carolina (the bustling port city would be renamed "Charleston" at the end of the American Revolution), in May 1780, which easily fell to the invaders after an amphibious landing that caught the patriots by surprise.

What began so brilliantly at Charlestown shortly led to what appeared to be the complete conquest of South Carolina, with additional British successes. However, subsequent small-scale American victories in the South Carolina Piedmont, or backcountry, especially the Battle of Kings Mountain, South Carolina, on October 7, 1780, resulted in a dramatic reversal of fortunes. The bloody campaigns in the South paved the way and ultimately led to the entrapment and surrender of Lord Charles Cornwallis's army at Yorktown on October 19, 1781, just two years after the crushing allied defeat at Savannah—the war's end, and American independence.

By any measure, the long-overlooked Battle of Savannah was one of the most unique and crucial major showdowns of the American Revolution for a wide variety of reasons that have been seldom explored by American or French historians, especially in regard to race and ethnicity. For one, it pitted a good many distinctive ethnic groups against each other in America's most ethnic-based battle of the American Revolution. Both sides had Scotch-Irish, Irish, Germans, Blacks, Welsh, and Scots, fighting against each other in what were essentially mini civil wars among these ethnicities. A large number of slaves helped to defend the fortifications of Savannah. Indeed, no major battle of the war has more thoroughly revealed how the American Revolution was actually America's first civil war, in which all colors, races, and ethnic groups were involved.

The turning point of the Battle of Savannah was played out in bloody fashion at the strategic Spring Hill Redoubt, the main target of the allied assaults on October 9. The primary defenders were South Carolina Loyalists, who played a key role in thwarting the attackers, which included the Continentals of the 2nd South Carolina Regiment. This well-trained command of South Carolina Continentals was led by the future "Swamp Fox," Lieutenant Colonel Francis Marion. Regimental members had planted its battle flag on the parapet of the powerful fortification, and the South Carolina silk banner was captured by the British during the brutal hand-to-hand combat that swirled over the Spring Hill Redoubt.

Most important, the Battle of Savannah featured the largest unit of Black and mulatto troops serving on the battlefield during the eight years of the American Revolution, the Chasseurs-Volontaires de Saint-Domingue. These fighting men from the French Colony of Saint-Domingue saved the day at the last moment when all seemed lost near the battle's conclusion, when both the French and American armies were on the verge of destruction after their bloody repulse from the strategic Spring Hill Redoubt. At that critical time, it was the Chasseurs, serving as the strategic reserve, who rushed forward with flags flying and drums beating to stop the British counterattack that had swept beyond the redoubt and threatened to destroy the beaten allied armies. It seemed that the British troops were about to win it all by striking the routed American and French contingents in their vulnerable rear when the men from Saint-Domingue charged in their own sweeping counterattack and even threatened to recapture the strategic Spring Hill Redoubt.

The Black and mulatto soldiers of the Chasseurs were mostly the sons of French planters and their African mistresses—and wives, in some cases—in Saint-Domingue, according to the colony's longtime tradition of widespread interracial mixing. Despite having faced discrimination and prejudice from white French troops, they suddenly emerged as key players on October 9, when everything was at stake for the reeling allies that lay on the verge of destruction. This is a most revealing true story long ignored, partly because of the different positions and roles held by Blacks in the United States as opposed to Blacks in Saint-Domingue at the time. While America, both North and South, had been dominated by a robust system of slavery since the early days of English colonization, including across New England, which served as a key foundation of economic development for each English colony in North America, the situation in the French Colony of Saint-Domingue was quite the opposite in terms of providing greater social mobility for free blacks. Despite the fact that they had a thriving slave regime in a robust agrarian society based on cash crops, much like the American South, Saint-Domingue possessed a large class of free Blacks and mulattoes, some of whom were wealthy and owned slaves themselves. This highly mobile society of free people of color were primarily the sons of French planters and slave women. This vibrant class of free men of mixed race made up a large percentage of the colony's overall population—nearly one-third by the time of the American Revolution. They had risen up on their own initiatives and merits as a distinctive class, to a degree not seen anywhere else, especially in the United States. Appropriately and symbolically, these young men of mixed race dominated the finely uniformed ranks of the Chasseurs-Volontaires de Saint-Domingue, when they saved the day at Savannah on October 9, 1779, not only for the French army, but the American army, as well, just as they were about to be destroyed.

The large free Black population had thrived for generations on their own land, on the western third of the island of Hispaniola, known as the French Colony of Saint-Domingue. They had mostly inherited their land from loving white French fathers, while a lesser number of mixed-race individuals had bought their own property themselves. They had converted this fertile land of Saint-Domingue, especially in the south, into profitable sugar and coffee plantations, while other free Blacks and mulattoes, who later served in the Chasseurs, worked as merchants and skilled artisans in major port cities, especially Cap-Français (today's Cap-Haïtien, also called "Le Cap," which was founded in 1670).

In general, the free Black and mixed-race class was insular and mostly independent from the white world around them, which was still hostile to people of a darker shade. Ironically, they nevertheless faithfully duplicated the white world around them to a remarkable degree, and with outstanding success, reflecting the paradox of racial realities and the complexities of race relations in Saint-Domingue. This included slave ownership by the wealthiest planters of color who owned their own plantations, especially in the colony's southern portion.

While a good many free Blacks and mulattoes possessed wealth and lands, they still lacked equality in the colony because of the white government's racial discrimination against people of color, and a strict racist society based on an extremely brutal regime of slavery. However, to their credit, these people of color had still managed to obtain high status in Saint-Domingue society and an amazing amount of success because of their own initiative, taking advantage of the available economic, social, and physical mobility, which they exploited to the fullest. Despite facing the ugly aspects of discrimination, racism, and hostility, generations of free Blacks and mulattoes also solidified their elevated status by service in the free colored militia of Saint-Domingue, including military service as officers and noncommissioned officers, although only whites could serve as officers at the time of the American Revolution.

The free Black and mulatto militia had long protected Saint-Domingue and performed internal security, while also protecting the vast sugar plantations from attacks by escaped slaves. This group, often called maroons, performed guerrilla raids from their strongholds in the mountains, which were often the tops of former volcanos. A variety of militia duties provided invaluable experience to these mulatto and Black men, and this lineage and tradition paid dividends for the Chasseurs-Volontaires de Saint-Domingue at Savannah during the fall of 1779.

The Chasseurs who rose to the challenge of Savannah in magnificent fashion hailed primarily from two distinct upper strata groups in Saint-Domingue society by the time of the American Revolution—the elite planter class; and the military leadership group, which was part of the Saint-Domingue militia tradition. In general, the young Blacks and mulattoes of the Chasseurs felt a considerable degree of patriotism for Saint-Domingue and France during the American Revolution. France had officially entered the war in 1778, when King Louis XVI officially recognized the independence of the United States and openly provided all manner of invaluable financial and military support to change the revolution's course—a guarantee of war with England and the eventual allied victory in the end.

But equally important, these young men of a darker hue had early seen service in the Chasseurs as a path toward greater social advancement. Their fundamental rights as free Blacks and mulattoes had been denied them by the governments of France and the Colony of Saint-Domingue. They believed that demonstrating courage on the battlefield would result in their winning full and equal rights as French citizens, proving to whites that they were every bit as equal in regard to courage and character.

This was the racial situation that resulted in a highly motivated soldiery, which made for a disciplined and cohesive military command in 1779. Consisting of 545 men, the Chasseurs-Volontaires de Saint-Domingue, the largest Black unit that fought on either side during the American Revolution, would serve with distinction at Savannah, and in the process, overturn traditional racist stereotypes. This unique command of Black and mulatto fighting men from the Caribbean was completely unimaginable to Americans, especially slave-owning Southerners at the time. Despite the political rhetoric and heady idealism of the Founding Fathers, equality for "all men" was primarily for just white men.

As noted, the Chasseurs hailed from France's richest and most pros-perous sugar colony, known as the "Pearl of the Caribbean." The jewel of France's colonial possessions, Saint-Domingue thrived as a bustling slave colony that produced the world's best sugar, experiencing a huge boom after cheaper French sugar from the West Indies had replaced British sugar from the West Indies. The Chasseurs would fight at Savannah in the name of liberty and its spread in the New World, including eventually in the Caribbean—a timely and invaluable egalitarian lesson they would apply in their own upcoming struggle for universal liberty for people of all colors during the Haitian Revolution, which continued on a bloody course until independence was won on January 1, 1804, with the birth of the Republic of Haiti.

As much as possible, I want to present the human side of this remarkable untold story of the Chasseurs, about a time when Blacks and whites were truly brothers in liberty during the righteous, moral struggle for the heart and soul of America, when the life of the infant United States of America and the very existence of a people's republican govern-ment were at stake. What happened at Savannah in the fall of 1779 was quite unlike anything seen on American soil throughout the course of the eight years of the American Revolution, and up until the Civil War, more than three-quarters of a century later when large numbers of Black troops served the Union. As mentioned, it was a rare development simply unimaginable to white Americans at the time of the war's beginning, four and a half years earlier, in April of 1775: More than five hundred free Blacks of the largest contingent of Black and mixed-race troops to ever serve on American soil during the American Revolution rescued thousands of white troops, both French and American, by preventing their systematic destruction from a fierce counterattack by the best troops of the British-Hessian-Loyalist garrison of Savannah.

By any measure, the citizen-soldiers of the Chasseurs were quite remarkable in their own right, long before they enlisted during the summer of 1779. As noted, they were not slaves but free men, both Black and mulatto, from the tropical island where the largest and most prosperous free Black and mixed-race population existed in the world. These men of African descent, more mixed-race than Black in the ranks of the blue-uniformed Chasseurs, were among the elite of Saint-Domingue's robust free Black and mulatto society. They owned large plantations, some growing sugarcane, but mostly coffee in the south, whose lands were located at the foot of towering mountains. Despite the official discrimination and racism that free Blacks and mulattoes had faced all their lives in the colony, in a somewhat bewildering paradox, some of these men owned slaves themselves—a reality that was striking and contradictory on multiple levels.

Compared to hundreds of thousands of slaves who labored endlessly in the sweltering sugarcane fields of the richest West Indies colony of any European nation, the elevated social status of these free Blacks resulted in part because they possessed white ancestry. Proud of a dual racial heritage, they were usually the sons or grandsons of white planters and slave women in the world's most successful Caribbean colony, whose unprecedented prosperity came from sugarcane and coffee production on an industrial scale to feed the world's demand.

Despite facing discrimination, prejudice, and segregation like the much smaller free Black population in the southern United States, the free Blacks and mulattoes of Saint-Domingue enjoyed far greater prosperity and success. They possessed sizable landholdings, especially coffee plantations in the rural areas, and they also benefited immeasurably from their ability to move even higher in free Black society, with greater opportunities to reap brighter futures for themselves and their families.

This was something worth fighting and dying for as young and idealistic volunteers of the French expeditionary force, sent to America to assist the amateur revolutionaries in the South during their struggle for liberty.

The enterprising members of this new and unique society of free people of color represented a rare synthesis of divergent cultures, from pre-colonial Africa, the West Indies, and France. These free men of color were mostly Creoles, fighting at Savannah not only for their own future aspirations in the hope of gaining complete equality as French citizens in the Colony of Saint-Domingue, but also for the freedom of a new nation, conceived in liberty—the United States of America.

For such reasons—especially on the eve of the 250th anniversary of the American Revolution, in an America that has become more racially polarized and divided than ever before in the twenty-first century—it is time to tell the forgotten story of the political, emotional, and philosophical unity that existed between Blacks and whites during their distinguished participation in the Battle of Savannah when they were truly brothers in liberty.

Because America is now so severely divided along racial lines, largely due to polarizing, agenda-driven politics and self-serving politicians of both parties, where heated racial discourse has become the norm, this remarkable untold story of how Blacks and whites served together, fought together, and died together in the fall of 1779 is an important one, on multiple levels. Unity between the races in a common righteous cause for the overall good of America is rarely mentioned or even known today, in an era where growing anti-Americanism has become both trendy and popular among political elites and fringe segments of the US population.

Ironically, Americans are familiar with how US soldiers of a large expeditionary force sailed to France in 1918 ("Lafayette, we are here!") to fight on the Western Front during World War I, to "save democracy," serving beside French soldiers, and then repeating the same patriotic duty in Europe, including France, during World War II. The story of how the French allies, especially the Chasseurs of Saint-Domingue, came to America in another large expeditionary force and fought at Savannah two years before the final decisive showdown at Yorktown has been long forgotten and overlooked largely because of the miserable results, and the fact that the soldiers were Black and mulatto. Indeed, the story of Savannah was nothing less than a shameful and quite embarrassing tale—except for the distinguished role of the Chasseurs of Saint-Domingue—of the overall failure of the Franco-American alliance during their first major land operation together, when true unity of the two divergent command structures proved elusive.

The fact that free Blacks and mulattoes from Saint-Domingue rescued the allied armies also helped to ensure that the dramatic showdown at Savannah, even though a major battle of the American Revolution, would be obscured and misunderstood to this day. In part, this is because generations of Southerners—at the time, and well into the twentieth century—succeeded in silencing stories about Black heroics, like so many other distinguished aspects of Black history that have been forgotten to this day. They were determined to preserve the myth that Blacks lacked courage and character, in keeping with the popular racial stereotypes upon which slavery and then Jim Crow oppression rested.

The significance of unprecedented Black and white unity and valor in 1779 is especially needed today, in part to hopefully help counterbalance some of the animosity and division that exists between the races in today's racially torn United States. Black and white Americans have been artificially divided by elitist agendas and the heated rhetoric of self-serving politicians, Black and white, who have embraced the overall goal of separating the races by fueling mutual antagonism and misunderstanding for their own benefit—an unfortunate and tragic situation that sees America today divided by race to a degree not seen since the 1960s.

Today's deep racial divide in America ignores a good many fundamental truths about shared sacrifices throughout American history, including the positive achievements of Blacks and whites working together for generations in the overall making of America. All Americans, Black and white, share a history of unity and achievements, especially during the Civil War, but also, to a lesser degree, during the American Revolution—America's most forgotten history of racial unity that has been buried and silenced not only by racism, but also by divisive racial politics in the twenty-first century.

Unfortunately, America's artificially enhanced divide between the races has been made possible in part by the lack of knowledge about positive racial aspects and shared experiences in the course of American history—the Battle of Savannah, for instance—beyond the one-dimensional, obsessive focus on slavery, racism, and Jim Crow, which is only one chapter, albeit, the most tragic one, of America's story. In consequence, *Brothers in Liberty* fills a giant void with its rare focus on the forgotten unity and bond of Blacks and whites in America's creation story, finally presenting a positive chapter of race relations—something virtually unheard of today in a thoroughly politicized modern America.

The overall unfortunate lack of Black historical accounts, especially when it comes to examples of Black and white unity like what was demonstrated at the Battle of Savannah, has been most evident in regard to the historiography of the American Revolution. Approximately seven thousand Blacks fought for America, including within the ranks of General Washington's crack Continentals, who were the regulars of the young American army, and the central foundation of the resistance effort against England.

Contrary to the views of today's America and its racially and politically polarized population, Blacks and whites in America actually are more alike than they are different. Black and white Americans share the same hopes, dangers, and fears, generation after generation, while reading the same Holy Bible, worshipping together, and drawing strength from the wisdom and mercy of the same God. All of these factors, including working-class values, have long unified Blacks and whites throughout the course of American history because they were the shared experiences of the common people, like the shared enlightened ideals of the American Revolution at Savannah in the autumn of 1779.

Brothers in Liberty provides notable examples of these significant points of unity and bonds between Blacks and whites by looking more closely at the most forgotten aspects of America's Revolutionary War, especially the fact that Black and white common people, for the most part, have been members of the working class to this day, and have far more in common with each other—especially the daily struggle for survival as they raise their families—than generally understood in the twenty-first century.

Brothers in Liberty also demonstrates that it was an intercultural and interracial fusion between Black and white, both Americans and Frenchmen, that led to the birthing of America, especially in terms of the American Revolution. However, this fundamental truth is not understood or appreciated today in the United States because of the racial polarization largely created by the political climate and the politicized modern media machine that has long spewed divisive propaganda. Unfortunately, in some ways Black and white Americans today have become pawns of political demagoguery and propaganda—in this case, an artificial manufactured divide imposed from the outside, largely by elitists and self-serving politicians who have shamelessly employed the race card at seemingly every opportunity for their own gain; by the extreme Right and Left; and by the agenda-driven modern media, which have excessively played this racial card to fulfill their own political agendas.

In the United States today, the common people of America, both Black and white, are caught between two extremes, the radicalized racial rhetoric of both the Left and the Right. They have continued to live their lives, hoping to survive as best they can in today's challenging environment and struggling to get ahead in an America of ever-diminishing returns and expectations, attempting to provide the best for their children who face an uncertain future. Black and white Americans today have shared a lengthy common heritage, beyond today's much-emphasized stereotypical master-and-slave oppressor-victim relationship. What has been forgotten is that it's a most distinguished heritage of Black and white unity in regard to the American Revolution and the Battle of Savannah, including Washington's Black Continentals and the large number of Black seamen who served on American naval, privateer, and merchant vessels.

During this overlooked Georgia campaign for possession of Savannah in the fall of 1779, Black and white soldiers were very much revolutionary brothers of the same mother, because they were united as one in fighting for the common cause of liberty and a common ideology of egalitarianism. This common mother that bound Black and white men together as one throughout the American Revolution was at America's core and at the center of the young republic's belief system: the enlightened concepts of freedom and equality for all, the very essence of the great dream of America for all people, regardless of color, background, social standing, wealth, or class, to pursue a bright new future in the New World. For the millions of migrants who come to America from around the world, this golden dream of America's promise is still true to this day.

Like white soldiers serving in the ranks of Washington's army, the Chasseurs-Volontaires de Saint-Domingue were also fighting against the ancient racial prejudices and hatreds of the Old World that denied them full rights as French citizens. Both France and England were ancient monarchies, and during the American Revolution were at war with each other in a traditional Old World imperial rivalry that was all about the struggle for empire. In this sense, both white Americans and Blacks and mulattoes from Saint-Domingue were basically fighting for the same lofty egalitarian goal based on republican ideology and idealistic concepts entirely unknown and unseen in the Old World, uniting them as one in this regard—true *Brothers in Liberty*.

The Albion Isle enemy of an Old World monarchy across the sea represented something truly insidious to both Americans and the young Black and mixed-race fighting men of the Chasseurs. At this time, Great Britain was the leading slave nation in the world, and its wealth rested heavily on slave trafficking. This powerful mercantile empire—the world's wealthiest—had firmly planted and nurtured slavery in its thirteen American colonies for generations, from the beginning, and long before the start of the American Revolution. In this sense, the institution of slavery was not one of America's original sins, as has long been alleged and assumed, especially today; rather, it was inherited from the mother country. Bringing most slaves to America by the time of the American Revolution, thousands of British slave ships had flown the Union Jack with pride, reaping lavish profits, especially at Charlestown, South Carolina, which became the center of the Southern slave trade, and the import destination of British slave ships for generations. Quite simply, there would have been no widespread slavery in America without the dominance of the mother country in the slave trade that enriched the major port cities of England, like Liverpool, London, and Bristol, and the nation in general.

Brothers in Liberty explores the rare and long-forgotten unity and bonds that existed between Blacks and whites who were emboldened by the popular ideology of the American Revolution and the Age of Enlightenment, including the popular concept that all men were created equal. They, both Black and white, sought to make the world anew by battling together at Savannah against the world's leading slave-trading power to overturn the dominance of the Old World and all of its sins, including slavery. The story of Black and white soldiers fighting side by side at Savannah, in both offensive and defensive roles, provides the best example of this remarkable development of an interracial revolutionary brotherhood, bonded together in a color-blind commitment and sacrifice for liberty. This is the loftiest goal of revolutionaries of different colors and backgrounds, and truly utopian and idealistic in the Age of Enlightenment tradition, as the shared love of liberty and battling against the perceived evils of the Old World superseded the artificial divisions of color of both American and French societies before the war.

Significantly, no other example can be found in the annals of Revolutionary War history of large numbers of Black and white soldiers serving and fighting together in the cause of liberty than during the siege and attack on Savannah. This bloodiest and most costly assault of the war in the South was destined to fail, through no fault of the French and American troops, who attacked a powerful array of defenses and displayed considerable heroism. The courage of the Black and mulatto troops of the Chasseurs could not have been more impressive on October 9, 1779, when so much was at stake for the future of the Franco-American alliance, after the failures of both the French and American armies in breaking through the defenses, especially at the strategic Spring Hill Redoubt.

As noted, what has been most forgotten about this first major battle for the allies in the South during the American Revolution has been the fact that it was the free Black and mixed-race soldiers, serving as the strategic reserve, who saved the day by coming to the timely rescue of the badly defeated white American and French troops in the midst of a disastrous rout, after they had been repulsed from attacking the British network of defenses that ringed Savannah—the forgotten story and thesis of this current book.

The Black and mulatto men of the Chasseurs-Volontaires de Saint-Domingue launched their timely offensive at the most critical moment, to break the back of the British counterattack and to drive crack enemy troops back to the safety of the Spring Hill Redoubt, when the British had believed the day had been decisively won. The rescue of the routed French and American troops by the counterattacking Chasseurs was important because the British counterattack by some of their best troops in North America would have destroyed what remained of the decimated allied commands—a development that would have destroyed the delicate Franco-American Alliance and King Louis XVI's fragile support for the American revolutionaries, which would have changed the course of not only the American Revolution but also world history. These commands of both nations had lost hundreds of men in the doomed assaults, after which they were consumed by chaos and panic, leaving both armies extremely vulnerable and ripe for destruction until the charging Black and mulatto Chasseurs intervened in a timely manner and saved the day.

Today, unlike the dramatic story of the Chasseurs at Savannah, most Americans know about Crispus Attucks, a free Black seaman, and the first patriot killed in the American Revolution during the so-called Boston Massacre, on March 5, 1770. He has become an iconic figure in the annals of Revolutionary War history, thanks to the growing interest in Black history since the 1960s and greater recognition of the Black role in America's creation story. Before this era, most Americans incorrectly believed that there was no shared heritage of a distinguished nature between Blacks and whites, especially in regard to the American Revolution. American historians also know about Lord Dunmore's "Ethiopian Regiment" of escaped slaves, mostly from Virginia, who fought in Virginia with the motto of "Liberty or Death" on their uniforms. However, what has been most forgotten, including by many American historians, is the fact that Blacks, both slaves and free men, served in virtually every regiment, including Southern units, in Washington's army, and especially in the ranks of the crack Continental regiments, including Southern commands. In total, an estimated seven thousand Blacks fought for America from 1775 to 1783, America's most forgotten patriots to this day on the eve of the 250th anniversay of the American Revolution.

However, the largest number of Black and mixed-race soldiers who fought during the eight years of the Revolutionary War served in an all-Black unit (except for the officers, who were white), and it was not part of the American army. This unique distinction belongs to the forgotten Chasseurs-Volontaires de Saint-Domingue, who achieved glory at Savannah—not unlike the story of the Black and mulatto soldiers of the 54th Massachusetts Regiment, which was the first Black regiment from the North, in the bloody assault on Fort Wagner, South Carolina, during the Civil War, as vivedly captured in the award-winning 1989 film, *Glory*.

The Chasseurs have been the most forgotten and overlooked Black players in America's creation story, even more so than the Black patriots who served under General Washington, including at Yorktown and especially in the 1st Rhode Island Infantry Continental Regiment. They fought in an all-Black and mulatto unit, unlike on the American side, and they made a major contribution toward preserving the Franco-American alliance by saving the two allied armies at Savannah. Too often, the Chasseurs have been omitted entirely from the histories of the war in the South, although they represented the largest Black command that fought on either side in any theater of operations during the war, and with unparalleled distinction. If remembered at all, these young men have been unfairly relegated at best to an obscure footnote, where often the most fascinating facts can be found in works of history.

Revolutionary War historiography—and American history overall— has long been dominated by the traditional and nationalist narrative, which has had no place for Black soldiers. The American Revolution in particular has been excessively romanticized and mythologized, like no other conflict in American history. America's longtime white version of the war has omitted Blacks for blatant racial reasons, based on ugly racial stereotypes that have no basis in reality or fact.

The distinguished contributions of the Black and mulatto fighting men from Saint-Domingue have been forgotten for a wide variety of reasons to this day:

1. Black history in general—and no chapter more so than the story of Haiti—has long been the most ignored field of study in the annals of American history, especially in regard to the American Revolution, which has been excessively romanticized because it was America's creation story.

2. These men of a darker shade from Saint-Domingue risked their lives and fought in the South, which has been the most forgotten theater of operations despite its crucial importance, and long ignored by generations of American Revolutionary War historians. Many of these talented historians have been from New England, and they have primarily focused on Washington's famous campaigns to the north, while overlooking and minimizing the supreme importance of the Southern Theater, where ironically the war was ultimately won in key victories like the Battle of Kings Mountain, South Carolina, on October 7, 1780, which ultimately led the way to Yorktown.

3. The Civil War of 1861–1865 stained the overall patriotic image of the Revolutionary War in the South, and Southern patriots, because most Southerners became traitors to the country when the South Carolinians opened fire with their rows of cannon on Fort Sumter, Charleston, South Carolina, on April 12, 1861. In consequence, the historical record has been distorted and the key contributions of Southern patriots have been tarnished and even silenced in some cases.

4. Generations of white historians, from both the North and the South, have long ignored the contributions and sacrifices of Black soldiers on American soil, from the beginning of America's story, because of prevalent racist attitudes and perspectives that have long dominated in the United States.

5. There is an excess of romantic patriotic myths that have long defined the field of Revolutionary War historiography, to the point of approaching fantasy and fiction, ignoring even some of the most

basic historical facts and fundamental truths to a profound degree, more than is found in any other single chapter of American history.

6. The young Black and mulatto men of the Chasseurs-Volontaires de Saint-Domingue hailed from a tropical land—the richest Caribbean colony of France—and, hence, were not considered part of American history, or part of a story for white Americans, which was certainly not the case, as demonstrated at the Battle of Savannah.

7. The inspirational story of the Chasseurs has been silenced for more than two centuries, partly because America had continued to be a slave nation (the world's largest slave democracy) during the American Revolution and long afterward, for more than three-quarters of a century, in an outright betrayal of the Declaration of Independence's lofty, idealistic words of equality for all men, until more than halfway through the next century. Consequently, because of racial priorities, the distinguished story of Black heroics on the battlefield at Savannah and on other fields of strife needed to be ignored and forgotten in order to maintain the institution of slavery and ensure its safety in the South, and to justify Jim Crow oppression in the twentieth century.

8. The Chasseurs faced a double handicap, because they were both Black and Catholic, which garnered resentment and hostility from the mostly Protestant Americans, then and long afterward, even though they were fighting for the American people and their infant republic at Savannah.

9. The Battle of Savannah, the darkest day for the Franco-American alliance, resulted in the most disastrous American-French defeat of the American Revolution and fostered considerable discord between allies, which was the antithesis of the glory reaped by the allies at Yorktown, where they successfully worked together in perfect harmony to win the war's most decisive victory in October 1781.

10. Veterans organizations in both the nations of France and the Republic of Haiti failed to promote the distinguished "saving the day" role of the Haitians at Savannah, relegating the Chasseurs of Saint-Domingue to the status of the war's most forgotten fighting men, claimed and honored by no one, although their memory has been kept alive by only a few Haitian historians (without publications in the United States) over the years.

Brothers in Liberty not only reveals one of the most forgotten chapters of America's story, and that of the American Revolution, but also provides Americans today with an inspirational and classic example of how it took the efforts of both Blacks and whites together, both on and off the battlefield, to make America during its creation story, and to achieve the ultimate victory, including at Yorktown, in a people's revolution. Indeed, as they fully demonstrated on October 9, 1779, at Savannah, the dark-hued soldiers from Saint-Domingue were brothers in liberty with their white comrades, both Frenchmen and Americans, when they fought and died for the same lofty egalitarian principles of America at Savannah, in a most symbolic example of a righteous revolutionary brotherhood that transcended race, because they sacrificed together in the hope of fulfilling the same dreams.

Significantly, after nearly 250 years, this is the first book that has ever been devoted to this fascinating and long-silenced subject, in an effort to enlighten Americans at this late date about one of the most intriguing aspects of the American Revolution. This remarkable saga about forgotten Black courage and sacrifice during the bloody showdown at Savannah needs to be told, especially now, given the unfortunate racial situation and climate in today's America by presenting an invaluable lesson of the importance of racial unity.

Most important, and as noted, in an example of the timeless cycles of history, a good many of the young members of the Chasseurs took the egalitarian values and lessons they learned from the American Revolution back with them to Saint-Domingue. There, led by a former young drummer boy of the Chasseurs named Henri Christophe, they became the dynamic Black leaders of the most radical and egalitarian revolution in the Americas, with the loftiest of goals—true equality for everyone, regardless of color. Quite unlike the United States during the American Revolution, when egalitarian rhetoric and theory never lived up to fundamental racial aspirations when it came to race, the Haitian Revolution led to true freedom for everyone. The veterans of Savannah played leading and stirring roles in winning their freedom on the battlefield and establishing the first free Black republic in history, based on the first-ever concept of universal liberty. In the end, this was the most enduring legacy of the siege and Battle of Savannah in egalitarian terms.

Brothers in Liberty reveals how these lofty egalitarian values and enlightened principles were equally shared by Haiti and America, from the beginning of their respective people's revolutions for liberty—one Black, and one white. The story of the Savannah Campaign is especially important because it represents one shining example of the shared revolutionary and egalitarian bonds and unity of two sister republics that have been long forgotten. Without the American Revolution, there might not have been a Haitian Revolution, just as there would have been no French Revolution without the American Revolution, all earthshaking historical events that forever changed the world.

Indeed, the bloody tragedy played out in full at Savannah on October 9, 1779, was important because in some fundamental ways, it marked the nascent beginning of the revolutionary spirit of the Republic of Haiti. Here, in the French West Indies, the enlightened ideals of the American Revolution were infused into the hearts and minds of a new generation of young men of a darker hue who were destined to become the future leaders of Haiti's greatest generation. This love of freedom and egalitarian spirit inspired and fueled the Haitian Revolution against France, and then the invasion force of Napoleon Bonaparte in 1802-1803 by members of Haiti's greatest generation and the rise of a corps of new revolutionary leaders: experienced and savvy Savannah veterans who had fought for America's liberty and later evolved into distinguished freedom fighters and liberators, who battled to free their invaded homeland from European domination in the late 1790s and the early 1800s, just like the American patriots had done in the 1770s. *Brothers in Liberty* reveals that the shared humanity of Blacks and whites struggling together as one helped to create a new world and a new birth of freedom, fulfilling the great promise and enlightened dream of America and creating the egalitarian link that connected the American Revolution to the Haitian Revolution in fundamental ways.

These Haitian men of different shades of black faced the same kind of Old World oppressors and obstacles when risking their lives during the high-stakes showdown at Savannah as during the Haitian Revolution, battling for the same Age of Enlightenment and egalitarian principles. The core republican concepts were even more enlightened and inclusive in Haiti than they were in the United States from 1775 to 1783. In this sense, it was a natural transference of revolutionary ideology and idealism from America to Saint-Domingue, which then resulted in the creation of the world's first Black republic, Haiti, by the winning of a bloody revolution against some of Napoleon's finest troops. The inspirational story of the Chasseurs-Volontaires de Saint-Domingue at Savannah serves as the best example in the annals of American history of the rare unity of Black and white soldiers in the eighteenth century, battling together, dying, and sacrificing as one to achieve the same common egalitarian goals against an Old World power and system of oppression.

Most of all, I hope that this book might provide a measure of renewed faith and hope for greater racial harmony in America, at a time when it appears there is none whatsoever. We need to begin the process of healing today's extensive racial divide that now seems insurmountable on every level. If used properly, these fundamental historical truths—as opposed to the modern political falsehoods and agenda-driven propaganda spewing from the modern media and politicians—hold the potential to begin to heal America's deep racial wounds. The current polarization and misunderstandings between the races stem largely from the endless promotion of the wrong historical lessons, based more on political agendas and propaganda than today's actual racial realities in America, creating in essence two distinct nations, one Black, one white.

In today's popular mind, ironically, the United States and the Republic of Haiti could not seem more dissimilar in every possible way—the very antithesis of each other, especially in regard to race, history, culture, and economics. After all, the United States is the richest nation on Earth, while Haiti is the poorest in the Western Hemisphere, thanks to the lingering ugly legacies of slavery, racism, imperialism, and colonialism. But these two sister republics in the Western Hemisphere have a shared revolutionary heritage and rich tradition that has revealed a hidden egalitarian bond, including in the case of the Battle of Savannah.

Whereas the United States had been an unparalleled and remarkable success story with its seemingly endless prosperity and good fortune throughout history, having friendly borders and the ample protection of oceans on either side, the Republic of Haiti was seemingly cursed by God, but even more so by the follies of man, resulting in seemingly endless bloodletting, revolutions, excessive poverty, and an unparalleled amount of human suffering and tragedy. In fact, the historic tragedy of Haiti, which has continued to this day, has been unmatched anywhere else on Earth, ensuring that the Haitians have long been some of the most stoic and longest-suffering people in the world.

The American people rose up in revolt in April 1775 because the colonists believed that they were equal to Western Europeans in every way, in keeping with Age of Enlightenment ideology, and deserving of the equality long denied them by an autocratic king across the sea. The people of Haiti, who were former slaves, rose up in revolt for fundamentally the same reasons against another European imperialistic nation, because they believed they were equal to whites in every possible way, and deserving of equal rights just like the white colonial Americans before them. Both America and Haiti shared these fundamental truths of the human experience during the Age of Revolution, a bond born of violent revolution and shared ideology.

The close bond between the United States and Haiti has existed for more than three centuries, including vibrant trade connections, religion—especially Catholicism—and conservative values. The thirteen English colonies traded heavily with Saint-Domingue long before the American Revolution, and France secretly supplied the American revolutionaries with European arms and munitions through its Caribbean islands, especially Saint-Domingue from an early date.

In a chain reaction, the lofty egalitarian ideals of the American Revolution were ultimately resurrected in Saint-Domingue during another common people's revolution against the day's mightiest empire, Napoleonic France, which resulted in a new birth of freedom with the establishment of the Republic of Haiti. The Battle of Savannah's Black veterans evolved into dynamic leaders for the united front of former slaves and free Blacks and mulattoes who joined together to drive the French out of their country during the world's most enlightened revolution. These veterans of the Battle of Savannah played a major role in leading the way toward winning the bitter struggle against Napoleon's invaders in 1802–1803, and creating the Republic of Haiti on January 1, 1804—a bright new day in world history that also had a profound impact on the United States and, ironically, one that has been largely forgotten today.

The fate of Haiti during the course of the bloody Haitian Revolution was of vital importance to the future of the United States for a variety of reasons. If not for the heroics and sacrifice of hundreds of thousands of Black and mulatto freedom fighters, including the veterans of Savannah, the United States of America would be much different today in significant ways. By 1801, with the establishment of the Treaty of Amiens that negated the powerful British navy, Napoleon Bonaparte had been freed to make his imperialistic move in a bid to create a vast New World Empire, ensuring that the people of today's Haiti would become the ultimate tragic victims of geopolitical developments and his endless ambitions of the former artillery officer from Corsica.

Napoleon had laid careful plans to invade and take control of Saint-Domingue, which had become semi-independent after being left on its own by the central government in Paris, France. During this turbulent time France was fighting for survival during its wars against major European powers, since it was the only republic—seen as a threat by the monarchies—in Europe. The fulfillment of Napoleon's grand imperial vision first required restoring slavery across Saint-Domingue by forcing the former slaves back into servitude. This was to enable the colony to regain its lost prosperity, providing its former agricultural riches to fuel the French economy and Napoleon's war machine, for future conquests in Europe and elsewhere. This ill-fated decision of the French ruler in Paris led to the disastrous failure of the French expeditionary force and the next round of vicious fighting in what became a racial war—a true

Caribbean Holocaust—directed against the Haitian people. Thanks also to the ravages of malaria, Napoleon's once-mighty expeditionary force was all but destroyed by the freedom-loving revolutionaries, both Blacks and mixed-race fighting men, by the end of 1803, after some of the most vicious combat ever seen in the Western Hemisphere.

The primary reason why Napoleon's 1803 loss of Saint-Domingue was so crucial to the future of the United States was because the native Corsican's ambitious strategic plan had called for utilizing the western third of Hispaniola (Saint-Domingue) as a staging area for a New World empire, based in Louisiana. Napoleon planned for New Orleans, Louisiana, to serve as the headquarters for future conquests in North America. If Napoleon's grandiose dream—based on retaining Saint-Domingue and restoring slavery, and the colony's prosperity—had come true, it would have stopped the American people's historic push west into the Mississippi Valley, and all the way to the Pacific's shores.

Instead, the remarkable success of the ex-slaves and mulattoes, including leaders who had served at Savannah, in defeating Napoleon and establishing the world's first Black republic forever ended Napoleon's intoxicating dream of empire in America. This resulted in the United States doubling in size with the Louisiana Purchase in 1803, when President Thomas Jefferson purchased 828,000 square miles of prime lands from France—today's centerpiece of the United States, located just west of the Ohio Valley and just east of Spain's historic border lands of the Southwest, leading to the Pacific. This vast land in the Southwest was later taken by the United States from Mexico as the result of the Mexican-American War of 1846–1848.

In the end, the immeasurable heroic sacrifice of the former slaves of Saint-Domingue ensured that the people of the United States were placed well on the road not only to the Pacific, but also to superpower status and an eventual rise to globalism in the twentieth century. In this regard, the United States owes an extremely heavy debt to the people of Haiti to this day. One respected American historian has appropriately asked the key question: "Did Haiti save the United States?," because of everything that Haiti accomplished and sacrificed for America, including at Savannah in the fall of 1779. It is clear that the American nation

would look much different today without the unprecedented contributions of the freedom-loving ex-slaves of today's Haiti during the world's
first revolution based upon the concept of universal liberty for people of
all colors.

The achievements of the people of the Republic of Haiti provided
an inspiring example to the world of the moral necessity of abolishing
mankind's most evil institution, which the United States finally achieved
more than half a century later, during the Civil War. The longtime paranoid fear of Southerners about the possibility of slaves rising up in revolt
across the South and concerns about the political influence of Northern
abolition played a large role in the South's secession from the Union and
the outbreak of the Civil War in April 1861. A generation of Southerners
viewed secession as the way to avoid another Haiti-like slave revolt that
might devastate the South.

These two neighbors were sister republics dedicated to the freedom
of the common people and close neighbors in the Western Hemisphere,
whose New World experiences in revolutionary struggle against their
European masters across the sea were closely intertwined from the beginning. This included the fact that Washington's army early on gained muskets, black powder, cannon, and other supplies from French ships sailing
out of the major ports of Saint-Domingue, especially Cap-Français,
also known as "Le Cap," located on the north coast. But the ideological
connection between the two republics was even greater because they
were sister experiments in democracy, which reached its egalitarian peak
in Haiti, unlike in the United States. In regard to the overall history of
human progress, enlightenment, and the pursuit of liberty, the Haitian
Revolution was a truly earthshaking event, after which the world—especially the United States—would never be the same.

Often forgotten is the fact that there would have been no United
States of America today without the vital intervention of the French,
from the beginning of the American Revolution to the establishment
of the 1778 Franco-American alliance and then all the way to ??. This
was especially the case in regard to France's powerful navy, which had
been significantly strengthened after the hard lessons learned from the
disastrous Seven Years' War (the French and Indian War, as it's known

in America), but also its army, as demonstrated during the Yorktown Campaign, when the team of often-bickering and dysfunctional allies finally worked together flawlessly, unlike at Savannah. In this sense, the Savannah Campaign can be viewed as an example of the inevitable growing pains of an immature and fragile allied relationship in 1779 that blossomed during the Yorktown Campaign.

Many books have been written about the British mistakes that led to American independence, but no books have been written that have focused on the mistakes of the Franco-American alliance, which almost lost the war before the miracle at Yorktown, costly errors emphasized in this book. This long list of mistakes committed by the blundering allies, especially at Savannah, has been largely overlooked because of the eventual decisive victory at Yorktown and the winning of independence. But had the allies performed at Yorktown like they did at Savannah, America would not have won its independence.

A close exploration of the overall functioning of the crucial Franco-American alliance at Savannah is important for a variety of reasons, especially in regard to a case of history having come full circle when tens of thousands of American troops went to the aid of France in both World War I and II during the twentieth century. Then, the United States and France remained close allies during the Cold War, including in Southeast Asia, when the Americans basically took over for the French in Vietnam and paid an extremely high price for its own march to folly.

Most important, King Louis XVI, who was beheaded by his own citizens during the French Revolution in January 1793, and the French nation, including the fighting men of a darker hue from Saint-Domingue, became the saviors of America in the end. Indeed, the long life of the United States was ensured by the French, whose widespread domestic unrest and deplorable financial situation resulted in the French Revolution. King Louis XVI lost both his country and his head to a people's uprising, in no small part because he had so wholeheartedly assisted America's revolutionaries at great expense, embarking upon a disastrous war against their ancient Protestant enemy in pursuit of global supremacy, and to seek vengeance after having lost the Seven Years' War and key possessions like Canada (New France). Despite his good intentions, the king would pay the ultimate price of national bankruptcy and social revolution, which devoured him.

From the vital ports of Saint-Domingue—especially Cap-Français on the north coast, but also Port-au-Prince on the west coast—flowed the primary sources of French aid that were invaluable for the American war effort, even before the official French Alliance of 1778. Brisk trade, especially with New England traders, had existed between the colonies and Saint-Domingue for decades before the American Revolution. But America's French West Indies connection ran much deeper, in what was most crucial to eventually winning the war: The warships of the French West Indies Squadron, centered in Saint-Domingue, paved the way for the ill-fated bid to capture Savannah in 1779. In the end, it was the French fleet and another strong expeditionary force dispatched by King Louis XVI, in conjunction with French land forces, that guaranteed decisive victory at Yorktown, and the winning of an infant nation's independence.

Clearly, the dramatic story of the all-important contributions of the Chasseurs-Volontaires de Saint-Domingue at Savannah—the allied campaign was one of severe growing pains, as demonstrated by the extent of the disaster during the fall of 1779—was but one distinguished chapter of the French contributions to the winning of American independence. Even more significant, the distinguished role of the Chasseurs at Savannah was also one of the most forgotten chapters in Black history and the overall struggle to achieve liberty and human progress, because of their close connection to the Haitian Revolution and the struggle for universal liberty in a forgotten symbotic relationship.

In much the same way, the long-overlooked story of the Chasseurs at Savannah is but one chapter of the rich history of the Republic of Haiti and its key contributions to the overall progress and march of freedom around the Western Hemisphere, including the revolutionary heritage of the Haitian people who actively supported General Simón Bolívar's army of liberators against Spanish rule, including in Texas in 1816, and their especially brutal band of slavery across South America.

Unfortunately, and as noted, no nation on earth has been more thoroughly misunderstood or less appreciated by the Western world, both past and present, than Haiti, since its establishment as a new republic, despite its closeness to America in geographical, ideological, and historical terms. This is an especially cruel and tragic fate for a long-ignored place and misunderstood people who played such a leading role in America's story, especially during the American Revolution. To Americans, both Black and white, the seldom-visited and much-feared land of Haiti, shrouded in myth and misunderstanding, has remained a place of mystery to this day. The world's first Black republic has been viewed by many Americans as a cursed land of the devil and evil spirits, a truly sad and most unfortunate development in regard to some of the most vibrant people in all of the Caribbean, and a magnificently beautiful land in natural terms. In consequence, the deep historical roots and close connections of the United States and Haiti as sister republics born in the fire of revolts of the common people against the abuses of autocratic European masters and autocratic Old World monarchies in the name of the same lofty goals, freedom and equality, have been forgotten, until it has seemed that there exists no shared history between the two.

The French Revolution, whose ideological model and roots lay deep in the core egalitarian concepts of the American Revolution, was based on the heady idealism of "Liberty, Equality, Fraternity," regardless of color, like America's struggle—but only in rhetorical and philosophical terms. Unlike in America after the American Revolution—because pressing economic realities and the pursuit of profits overrode egalitarian idealism, especially in the South—the revolutionary republic of France officially abolished slavery in 1794, less than fifteen years after the Battle of Savannah, and in the year that followed the beheading of unfortunate King Louis XVI, who had accomplished so much in the saving of America. This was nearly seventy-five years before President Abraham Lincoln issued his famous Emancipation Proclamation during some of the darkest days for the Union during the Civil War, largely for reasons related to bolstering the sagging war effort during a long war of attrition against the South. By 1801, Napoleon had already betrayed the fundamental and lofty egalitarian principles of the French Revolution, especially in regard to his insidious plan to restore slavery in Saint-Domingue, in an effort to return the colony to its former glory and reap fantastic profits from the sale of sugar and coffee.

More than eighty years before President Lincoln freed the slaves, largely because of crucial wartime requirements—the North was losing the war and faced a manpower shortage, and needed tens of thousands of Black soldiers (former slaves, and a smaller number of free Blacks from the North, as in the case of the 54th Massachusetts Regiment)—and to ensure that England and France never recognized the Confederacy, the true fulfillment of revolutionary France's later ideological concept of "Liberty, Equality, Fraternity" was actually first played out on American soil, when Black and white soldiers were united as one in the desperate effort to capture the strategic port of Savannah in October 1779. Not only was their equality to white troops in terms of character and courage demonstrated in full by the Black and mulatto soldiers of the Chasseurs, but also their moral qualities to the vanquished white comrades, both Frenchmen and Americans, who had been thoroughly defeated and routed after their repulse on the strategic Spring Hill Redoubt.

As the American–French army's strategic reserve, the Black and mixed-race fighting men from Saint-Domingue were the only troops who came to the timely assistance of their defeated comrades after more than one thousand of them had been killed or wounded. The Chasseurs advanced with discipline in the face of disaster and stopped the sweeping British counterattack surging north beyond the strategic Spring Hill Redoubt that might well have destroyed the mauled allied armies. At this crucial moment, the battered allied armies were unable to defend themselves after their failed assaults on the powerful fortification, the Spring Hill Redoubt on the Ebenezer Road, suffering some of the highest losses of the American Revolution. During this emergency situation, the Chasseurs rose magnificently to the challenge when everything was at stake and saved the day by the narrowest of margins, when it seemed that the destruction of the French and American armies was all but inevitable.

The Black and mulatto veterans of the Savannah Campaign, who eventually became primary leaders of the Haitian Revolution, had learned an invaluable lesson that was never forgotten: Even an impoverished people of a backward, agrarian infant republic without adequate war-waging capabilities and with seemingly no chance for success could emerge triumphant over a major imperialist European power.

It was most appropriate that the American Revolution was a people's struggle in which so many future leaders of the Haitian Revolution served in the ranks of the Chasseurs at Savannah, helping to bring forth the shining pinnacle of the Age of Enlightenment in the Republic of Haiti: the freedom and equality of all people, especially Blacks and mulattoes like those who served during the Savannah Campaign of 1779, at the peak of the Age of the Democratic Revolution, regardless of color—the day's most enlightened concept of universal liberty that became more of an egalitarian reality in Haiti than in America.

During the earliest phase of the Haitian Revolution, some of the first voices heard in the rising up of people to gain equal rights and the establishment of an independent Republic of Haiti were from mulattoes, including veterans of the Chasseurs who had fought at Savannah. The vast majority of volunteers in this disciplined and well-trained unit consisted mostly of mulatto soldiers from the large, free, mixed-race community, who had achieved success in life and militia service in Saint-Domingue. As noted, these veterans of the 1779 Savannah experience played a key role in the dramatic rise of a revolutionary leadership class that promoted the concepts of nascent Haitian nationalism and the vision of a new nation, conceived in liberty for all people, regardless of color, which led to the establishment of the Republic of Haiti on January 1, 1804.

After nearly 250 years, and for such reasons, it is now certainly time to take a new and fresh look at the American Revolution, in a stale field of historiography dominated by the nationalist and romantic schools that has left little, if any, room for significant ethnic contributions that were often as important as white contributions in this bitter struggle for the heart and soul of America, as demonstrated at Savannah. Almost every book released today about the American Revolution has inevitably discussed at considerable length the same old topics, much like a musty nineteenth-century textbook, except containing more detailed research, with monotonous and ever-predictable regularity—without new views or fresh interpretations ever changing the basic, standard approaches and themes long familiar to generations of Americans since the war's end: basically, the inevitable winner's version of the American Revolution that was often the antithesis of fundamental truths, including the view of the

Loyalists, who possessed their own vision of what they believed was best for America, which was the blessing of a constitutional monarchy in their minds during America's first civil war.

New approaches are important today because fresh views are vitally necessary in order to truly understand and appreciate the extent of the complexities and contradictions of America's life-or-death struggle for liberty. Such common themes, like the usual focus on the famous leaders and battles of the Revolutionary War, have been endlessly repeated by generations of historians for more than two centuries in ever-predictable fashion, as the nationalist or winner's version of the American Revolution.

Brothers in Liberty is the first book ever written about the complexities of race both in early America and the present day, looking closely at a forgotten chapter not previously explored, long absent from the annals of Revolutionary War historiography. For the first time, and as much as possible, *Brothers in Liberty* presents the full story of the free Blacks and mulattoes, the mixed-race "Creole patriots" born in Saint-Domingue who fought for freedom and liberty at Savannah, while bestowing proper recognition to the long-forgotten Haitian soldiers and their contributions to America.

Brothers in Liberty is also important for a number of reasons that are relevant in today's racially polarized United States. This book will hopefully help in the difficult process of beginning to heal America's extensive racial divisions by emphasizing the remarkable story of shared history and early unity between Blacks and whites during the bloody showdown at Savannah. Hopefully, this very special story about Blacks and whites battling together on American soil in 1779 for the greater good of all men will help to provide a historically based antidote to the existing racial toxicity and divisions and perhaps even help to heal some of America's racial ills to some degree: a lofty vision that hopefully will not be a quixotic quest, because racial healing in America should begin by looking at the positive aspects of America's racial history and not just the negative, such as viewing everything through the simplistic and one-dimensional lens of slavery.

One of the fundamental reasons why the heroics of the Black troops at Savannah had to be silenced by whites for so long—especially

Southerners in a land of slavery—was because it was viewed as a dangerous example that had to be hidden from the large slave population, for fear that they might be inspired to revolt, and even to keep Blacks in a subordinate place well into the twentieth century with Jim Crow oppression. Indeed, after American slavery was abolished in 1865 at the Civil War's conclusion, the story of Black heroics at Savannah had to be ignored for generations because a core tenet of American racism has long been the most outrageous of racial lies and myths, and, hence, a perverse basis for the evils of Jim Crow in the twentieth century—that is, that Black people lacked the moral courage and sterling character, especially on the battlefield, to be deserving of full American citizenship like whites. Of course, the early annals of American history, including in the South, have proved quite the opposite to be true.

The free Blacks and mulattoes of Saint-Domingue shattered this long-standing and popular racist myth, which had long thrived in Saint-Domingue as well as America, because the sheer ugliness of American and French racism was much the same. The bravery of the Chasseurs at Savannah in a key situation on the battlefield had to be silenced by whites, especially in the South, because it provided a shining example of Black equality, character, and courage on one of the bloodiest fields of strife during the American Revolution.

For such reasons, the longtime overall racial situation of the South has played its insidious part in dooming the Chasseurs' distinguished role and even the Battle of Savannah to an undeserved obscurity for more than two centuries. Civil War history has long reigned supreme across the South. In this sense, the American Revolution in the South has been the forgotten stepchild because of the glorification of the "Lost Cause"—an experience far more searing than the Revolutionary War for Southern people in general.

For example, Fort Pulaski, located just east of Savannah, was named after Casimir Pulaski, who was mortally wounded in the attack on Savannah on that fateful day of October 9, 1779. The fort has been recognized by the National Park Service as a national monument and includes a national cemetery, unlike what little has been preserved of the long-forgotten battlefield of Savannah. The much-celebrated 1862 siege of Fort Pulaski by Union forces—which was relatively insignificant compared to the 1779 siege and Battle of Savannah—has become well-recognized, while the far more important field of Savannah has been forgotten by the National Park Service. The National Park Service has preserved no lands, monuments, or cemeteries to the fallen soldiers at Savannah. In striking contrast to Savannah, no significant battle was fought at Fort Pulaski, only a relatively inconsequential siege that played no major role in the war's outcome.

The general interest in Civil War Savannah and Georgia has remained high to this day across the South, while the even more fascinating story of the American Revolution in Savannah and Georgia has been ignored and long-forgotten. If white American soldiers, both French and American, could be overlooked despite their heroics in a major battle in America's struggle for independence, it was inevitable that no participants at Savannah in 1779 would be more ignored and forgotten than the Blacks and mulattoes of the Chasseurs-Volontaires de Saint-Domingue.

This development has also occurred because one of the most forgotten examples of overt racism has been America's historic negative and prejudicial view of the Republic of Haiti and its people, by both the national government and American citizens, especially whites, in general. After a horrific struggle that lasted more than a decade, the courageous people of Haiti finally threw off their colonial yoke, just like the Americans before them in 1783, when they had no powerful allies like the Americans did (not only France, but also Spain, who were allied against England) during the American Revolution. The Haitian people were the ones who heroically fulfilled America's most idealistic and egalitarian promise of the American Revolution—unfortunately, one that was only theoretical and philosophical in the so-called "land of the free"—of equality in their own homeland for people of all colors (Black and mulatto, in this case), which only primarily existed in the idealistic words of Thomas Jefferson's Declaration of Independence, especially in the South.

In one of the great paradoxes of history, no nation has been viewed more harshly by Americans and people around the world for a longer period of time than the Republic of Haiti. Haiti's tragic history has been more torturous and disastrous than perhaps any other nation in the world. Of course, this common negative perspective among generations of white Americans about Haiti and Haitians in general has also developed because of the color of its people, who are all descendants of slaves.

In this regard, the issue of color for generations of white Americans has completely overshadowed Haiti's invaluable assistance to America on multiple levels. Haiti has a most distinguished revolutionary past as the world's first Black republic in history, winning an especially bloody revolution, which was true racial and genocidal war, over Napoleon's French troops. This bitter racial sruggle made the combat of the American Revolution—primarily waged in gentlemanly fashion according to the traditional rules of eighteenth-century warfare (which did not apply to the Haitian Revolution), like at Savannah in 1779—look like child's play.

In this regard, Haiti's dark and tragic past, including the vast destruction caused by years of revolution, condemned its people to an especially miserable poverty to the present day, mocking the unlimited richness of its history and its egalitarian legacies. Haiti's greatest generation of revolutionaries, including the men who fought at Savannah, has made America's greatest generation of the Revolutionary War almost look small by comparison in numerous ways, especially the most famous slave-owning Founding Fathers, Washington and Jefferson, from Virginia—certainly a contrarian view well supported by the historical facts.

During the course of the Haitian Revolution, these Black and mulatto revolutionary leaders—including former slaves like Henri Christophe who marched at the head of the counterattacking Saint-Domingue men on the bloody morning of October 9, 1779—made America's idealized concept that all men were created equal a true reality, and not just flowery rhetoric and hollow words written on parchment, like the Declaration of Independence. Christophe, the teenage drummer boy of the Chasseurs, had mysterious origins, although it is believed he was born on the island of Grenada. He would emerge as Toussaint Louverture's top lieutenant during the struggle against the French in the Haitian Revolution, which was truly an earthshaking event on multiple levels, at the cost of tens of thousands of lives of the so-called Black Jacobins of Haiti, true freedom fighters in fulfilling the unprecedented dream of universal liberty. Christophe would serve as the king of Haiti after the revolution was won.

The Republic of Haiti has long been the poorest and most hard-luck nation in the history of the Western Hemisphere, in part because it had been early devastated by war, especially the Haitian Revolution, and then saddled with a huge amount of reparation payments to France for destroyed property (mostly sugarcane plantations on the vast northern plain), to ensure no new French invasion in the future. No people have been more resilient and resourceful than the long-suffering Haitians, who have consistently endured what would be unimaginable to most people around the world, including Americans. Ironically, the Colony of Saint-Domingue was far richer and more productive and prosperous than America both before and after the American Revolution, until an extremely cruel fate and cycles of history, especially the Haitian Revolution, dramatically reversed the traditional equation for the seemingly doomed people of Haiti.

Contrasting with its sheer natural beauty on a breathtaking scale, like no other tropical land in the Caribbean, and the inner and outer beauty of its ever-hopeful people, who still fondly wish for a better day in the future, Haiti's torturous past and terrible poverty have combined with its seemingly endless natural disasters and catastrophes, from devastating hurricanes to earthquakes, on an eerie biblical scale, to leave the distinct impression that the republic and its people have been cursed by God, man, and fate.

There was intense, racial strife in Haiti at this time—not only between Black and white, but also between Black and mulatto (the product of the intermingling of French planters and female slaves, from lust and love, in the early days of the Haitian Revolution), especially during the bloody "War of Knives" from 1799 to 1800. It led to central racial polarization and division in Haitian society, which exists to this day. This deep historical division, based on different shades of color, brought even greater horror and misery to Haiti decade after decade, thanks to the dark legacies of slavery and a society based on deep racial divisions. Somehow, the Haitians have managed to bravely persevere through it all.

In addition to racial strife, the inordinate number of natural and man-made disasters that have befallen Haiti has also played a role in tarnishing its image in the eyes of the world, especially in the United

States. This is especially ironic, as no nation on earth has done more to fulfill America's promise of equality for all men around the world, from the Battle of Savannah to assisting Simón Bolívar in liberating South America from tyrannical Spanish rule, and even an expedition of anti-slavery Haitian soldiers who fought in Texas against the Royalists of Spain, before Mexico became a nation in 1821 in its own revolution against Spain, before the Texas Revolution.

What has been most forgotten has been the fact that by vanquishing Napoleon's invaders, tens of thousands of Haitians immeasurably assisted the United States in becoming a great nation, when its size was doubled with the Louisiana Purchase because of what they accomplished during brutal combat and at a great cost in lives in their bloodstained Caribbean homeland during the Haitian Revolution. Winning the Haitian Revolution directly led to America's well-being and prosperous future, as it destroyed Napoleon's grandiose New World ambitions of establishing a vast French empire, based in Louisiana, controlling the mouth of the Mississippi River and New Orleans. It also meant Napoleon could not invade farther north up the Mississippi, which would have stopped America's westward expansion toward the Pacific, because Napoleon had been forced to sell the vast Louisiana Territory in 1803.

Then, during the War of 1812, Black and mulatto soldiers, refugees from the revolution in Saint-Domingue, played a key role in their timely service to America in a free Black battalion (like the Chasseurs-Volontaires de Saint-Domingue in 1779) under Major General Andrew Jackson, which helped to stop the mighty invasion of the British at the Battle of New Orleans on January 8, 1815. At this time, the British also possessed the grandiose vision of establishing a vast New World empire comparable to the earlier one warmly embraced by Napoleon, because both the French and British saw thwarting America's ambitions, especially in regard to westward expansion and trade, as in their best strategic, global, and economic interests.

General George Washington and his rustic revolutionaries and those finely uniformed Frenchmen and Saint-Dominguan soldiers who fought at Savannah in 1779 saw America and its egalitarian struggle as blessed by the hand of a benevolent God. They believed that only a kind and smiling Providence could possibly save the young republic—a deep faith shared by Washington and his followers that ultimately proved true, ensuring the winning of the long war of attrition, thanks to the outstanding success of the French and American allies working smoothly together in 1781, unlike during the disastrous Savannah Campaign in 1779.

This deep faith in God having blessed America with a special mission to mankind has continued to this day among history-minded and God-fearing Americans, who fully understand and, hence, rightly appreciate the nation's unique historical mission and proper place in world history—the last great hope of mankind and refuge for the world's impoverished people, long before the American Revolution's beginning at Lexington and Concord, Massachusetts, on April 19, 1775. While the United States has seemingly long enjoyed the blessings of God in regard to its prosperity to this day, its sister Black republic, situated only six hundred miles from the southern tip of Florida, has been the most impoverished in the Western Hemisphere, historically viewed by white Americans as the blighted land of the devil: a pervasive negative stereotype, based largely on race, which has resulted in one of the greatest misconceptions and tarnished images of any nation in history.

By understanding the deep complexities and nuances of the twisting contours of Haitian history, whose zenith became a bright, shining reality when a victorious people established a new republic on January 1, 1804, based on the unprecedented concept that Blacks were fully equal to whites in every way, Americans can better understand the paradoxes of their own complicated and tortured racial history. Most important in terms of race, the dramatic story of the Chasseurs at Savannah has provided but one excellent example of this historical phenomenon, especially the richness of Haitian history on multiple levels and its forgotten connections to American history that have gone largely unexplored to this day.

All in all, the unforgettable story of the Black and mulatto soldiers of Saint-Domingue on a bloody autumn day at Savannah is a most important one because of the centrality of slavery and race, not only throughout the course of both American and Haitian history, but also for America today, when the reeling constitutional republic has never been more in need of racial healing and understanding. This can only happen with an accurate and honest appreciation of the past. If America continues to fail to live up to its loftiest egalitarian ambitions and promises in regard to racial harmony and equality for all its citizens, then it will be fated to forever remain a racially polarized society and a badly divided nation, where hate and misunderstanding dominates. This will ensure the continued decline of the United States in the future—the most tragic of fates for a great nation that was conceived in liberty and equality for all.

Like the United States, the first nation to successfully break the shackles of European imperialism and colonialism, so the people of Saint-Domingue, both former slaves and free mulattoes, finally united as one to drive out Napoleon's forces in late 1803. But only several years earlier, the mixed-race people of Saint-Domingue formed a separate political and mulatto army under General André Rigaud, a veteran of the siege and Battle of Savannah, and slaughtered each other without mercy during the brutal "War of Knives." This crucial union of Blacks and mixed-race fighting men was the real key to decisive victory over Napoleon's invaders. In heroic fashion, the people of Haiti broke the shackles of the most severe form of racial oppression—Napoleon's planned imposition of slavery—to create a people's republic, which was more racially enlightened and progressive than the United States, forming a new nation based upon the novel concept of universal liberty for all.

For the first time, and as much as possible, *Brothers in Liberty* seeks to tell the fascinating, timely, and important story of the Chasseurs-Volontaires de Saint-Domingue, mostly free men of mixed heritage who represented a new vibrant race that had found remarkable success as plantation owners—primarily coffee growers in the hills and mountains in the south—in the rural countryside of the French colony during the years before the American Revolution. Because of the scarcity of documentation and sources in America, France, and Haiti, writing this book has been no small challenge. Over the years, many primary sources have been destroyed during the seemingly endless upheavals that have unmercifully ravished Haiti and its people. Unfortunately, members of this distinctive Black and mulatto command of volunteers who fought for America on Georgia soil did not leave behind any memoirs, diaries, or reminiscences as far as anyone knows at this time, including Haitian scholars and historians, which leaves a giant gap in the historical record.

For such reasons, despite their key role in saving the day for the two allied armies, the Chasseurs from the faraway French West Indies have been the most forgotten players in the dramatic siege and Battle of Savannah, despite having been one of the three bloodiest battles of the entire American Revolution, and the bloodiest single hour of the struggle from 1775 to 1783. One of the most passionate and heartfelt motivations of some of these young men of color was the idea that while free men, they were fighting in part to advance higher in Saint-Domingue society, in the hope that their battlefield achievements might result in freedom for their family members, who were still held as slaves on the sugarcane plantations of Saint-Domingue. This guaranteed that these mulatto and Black men, who proudly represented their colony and their standing as free men, were extremely motivated at Savannah to do their best at the supreme moment of crisis, especially when the lives of a good many French and American soldiers of the two decimated armies were at stake as they retreated from their failed assaults.

Significantly, this book combines the divergent fields of Caribbean, Haitian, and American Revolutionary War history in a unique blend of historiography that seldom, if ever, has been united as one. While the saga of these young Black and mulatto soldiers of the Chasseurs has long been considered exclusively a Caribbean and Haitian story, this is not the case, because it is most of all an American story. These young soldiers were committed to the enlightened concept of the equality of all men, regardless of color, and to fighting on behalf of a largely white nation in the South, where, in a striking paradox, the economy and society were based on a robust system of slavery. After the Chasseurs' triumphant return to their Caribbean homeland, their precious egalitarian ideals and values were eventually implanted on Saint-Domingue soil to fuel the creation of an even more enlightened revolution than the one in America, creating an infant people's republic of former slaves based on the concepts of universal emancipation and liberty, which would change the course of history.

By focusing on the remarkable odyssey of the mixed-race and Black soldiers of the Chasseurs-Volontaires de Saint-Domingue, who rescued the two battered allied armies at Savannah and provided the vital link between the American Revolution and the Haitian Revolution, this book explores the close connections on multiple levels that have long existed between the United States and the Republic of Haiti, providing a rare positive example of Black and white unity and comradeship that transcends race, culture, prejudice, and national boundaries.

—Phillip Thomas Tucker, PhD

Central Florida

March 15, 2022

CHAPTER I

The Thriving Free Black Community of Saint-Domingue

Far richer and more profitable in France's thriving colonial mercantile system than all thirteen of the English colonies for the sprawling empire of Great Britain, the Colony of Saint-Domingue, or today's Republic of Haiti, was the greatest economic success story in the history of European colonialism in the New World. Thanks to ample sunshine, rainfall, and rich soil, Saint-Domingue's immense natural wealth—especially sugarcane cultivation, but also coffee, cotton, indigo, tobacco, and cacao production, to a lesser degree—that poured into the major ports around the world, especially in Europe and America, fed the insatiable appetites of the world.

Decade after decade in the eighteenth and nineteenth centuries, thousands of tons of imported Saint-Domingue sugar fueled the economies of the principal French ports of Nantes, Marseilles, Bordeaux, and La Rochelle, making them prosperous on a scale not previously seen in history. The growing of sugarcane and coffee across the rich lands of Saint-Domingue and other French sugar islands in the Caribbean on an industrial scale ensured that their sugar could be sold more cheaply than the products sold from British merchants, which meant that French growers dominated the market by the mid-1700s. The thousands of sprawling sugarcane plantations of Saint-Domingue, especially filling the great northern plain, which was immensely fertile, created untold riches for tens of thousands of Frenchmen. The cash crops of sugar and coffee fueled the booming French economy, proving the merits of colonialism. Saint-Domingue became the world's leading supplier of sugar and coffee, surpassing all of the British sugar islands, including Jamaica, which was the jewel of England's Caribbean possessions.

Sizable numbers of Frenchmen, who mostly wanted to get rich and then return to France with their fortunes, reaped untold riches and ill-gotten gains from the soil of Saint-Domingue. This is because it was based on the New World's most thorough exploitation of a massive amount of long-suffering and abused human labor—slaves who had been captured mostly on Africa's west coast. French planters had found their fabulous El Dorado in the tropical islands of the Caribbean, while slaves found a hell on earth that had been unimaginable to them back in the tropical motherland. This vast wealth gained primarily from the great sugarcane plantations was built on the blood, sweat, and tears of hundreds of thousands of Africans, who suffered and died in large numbers—an incomparable and unprecedented death rate not found anywhere else in the Caribbean or in the world—on this breathtakingly beautiful and bountiful, mostly mountainous land of Saint-Domingue.

Indeed, when Christopher Columbus first landed on the north coast of what is today's Republic of Haiti in 1492, while exploring the wonders of the West Indies, he saw not only the Caribbean's most mountainous island, but also the most beautiful. Ironically, in a seemingly diabolical correlation of natural beauty having to be compensated correspondingly by man-made horrors in history's bizarre cosmic equation, Haiti was a natural paradise, very close to a proverbial Garden of Eden, and had long been enjoyed by the indigenous Taino people. But this tropical paradise under the sun was lost when Columbus and his Spanish seafarers and conquistadors brought cruelty, reprisals for revolting, abusive labor exploitation in the form of a hellish brand of Spanish slavery, and the ravages of European disease, for which indigenous inhabitants had no immunity, leading the way to the early wiping out of the Taino population of half a million people.

The terrible decimation of the Taino people was just the beginning of genocide on the tropical island of Hispaniola—the French occupied the island's western third, while the Spanish held the island's remainder, in the Colony of San Domingo—that continued unabated as shipload after shipload of African peoples were brought in chains to the French Colony of Saint-Domingue each year. Because Africans were known for their physical toughness and durability when it came to working long hours in the sweltering fields, they became the perfect replacement for the decimated Taino people. There was an exceedingly high attrition among the slaves, who died like flies in this man-made hell. The intense labor of hundreds of thousands of Black slaves transformed Saint-Domingue into the most prosperous colony in Europe's long and tragic history of imperialism and colonialism. The world's sweet tooth was satisfied by what was produced on the vast sugarcane plantations that covered the colony like a carpet, which was made fantastically rich by the blood, sweat, and tears of tens of thousands of African slaves.

Smaller than the extensive sugarcane plantations that dominated the fertile northern plain south of Cap-Français were the highly profitable coffee groves, located on the gradual slopes of the mountains, primarily in the south. These coffee plantations overlooked the endless sprawl of sugarcane plantations in the picturesque valleys and wide plains, including arid regions where complex irrigation systems were needed and cactus grew high under the bright sunshine. These plantations on the southern highlands produced the other most lucrative commodity desired by the booming world market: coffee. This was especially the case when the Americans started boycotting tea by the time of the American Revolution, because of its association with the hated English, and turned to coffee (explaining why Americans are primarily coffee drinkers to this day, unlike the English).

But sugarcane production was the greatest cash cow of Saint-Domingue by far, reaping untold riches. Sugar was so profitable—thanks to cheap slave labor, combined with the insatiable world demand—that the Caribbean sugar islands became primary bones of contention between the major European powers during both the French and Indian War (known as the Seven Years' War in Europe) and during the American Revolution, when France sent large numbers of troops, both infantry and naval, to protect King Louis XVI's valuable moneymaking islands in the sun.[1]

Partly because of the scarcity of white French women, but also because of the natural beauty of the slave women and their easy availability, many plantation owners either sexually exploited or fell in love with their female African-Dominguan slaves, who then became their mistresses in long-term relationships. The widespread racial intermixing that resulted from these relationships led to the creation of a new and separate people, who were neither white nor Black, and they thrived in the Colony of Saint-Domingue by their hard work and industriousness. Without the growth of this ever-increasing class of free people of color from the union of Black and white, there would have been no mostly mixed-race soldiers of the Chasseurs-Volontaires de Saint-Domingue, who served and fought with distinction at Savannah in 1779. Over time, interracial lust on Saint-Domingue grew unchecked like the tall green stalks of the seemingly endless sugarcane fields that covered most of the prosperous colony, especially the fertile Norhern plain.

During the seventeenth and eighteenth centuries, most slaves of Saint-Domingue had been captured people from the rich, vibrant cultures of the Mandinka, Ibo, Arada, Ashanti, and Yoruba peoples of West Africa. Saint-Domingue became the primary destination of the booming Atlantic slave trade and the world's most lucrative colony in the New World, especially for sugar and coffee, but also for cotton and other products that flourished in the tropical colony. In addition, slaves had also been captured by French raiding parties in the incessant early warfare between France and England during the long struggle for possession of the Caribbean islands. The massive slave population of Saint-Domingue produced more wealth in sugar than the legendary silver mines of Mexico or the gold of Brazil, both of which benefited immensely from harsh systems of slavery. Saint-Domingue became the admired zenith of the exploitative European colonializing system, which would prove to be even more successful than the French ever dreamed possible, becoming the source of seemingly endless revenues and profits for the mother country.

The number of slaves grew to new heights with the boom in sugar, resulting in a comparable boom of the mixed-race population across Saint-Domingue. With relatively few white women in Saint-Domingue, and surrounded by large numbers of slaves, including a good many attractive and almost naked young women, ever larger numbers of French plantation owners took slave mistresses to their beds throughout the eighteenth century. During this period, the lucrative slave trade thrived on a massive scale for the first time in modern history. Contrary to common assumptions and stereotypes, from the beginning far more slave women, who were situated at the bottom of slave society, worked in the miserable sugarcane fields, performing the lion's share of the hard labor. In general, slave men were most often placed in skilled artisan positions, such as blacksmiths and carpenters.

As opposed to the lustful types who were obsessed with the pursuit of dark "forbidden fruit" and as many sexual conquests as possible, an increasing number of romantic-minded Frenchmen married their female slaves, both African-born and Saint-Domingue-born (Creole) women, who were noted for their attractiveness. Both love and an unbridled lust resulted in broods of mixed-race children across the breadth of Saint-Domingue, fueling the rise of the class of free Blacks. Because of Gallic cultural standards of beauty that focused on whiteness, French men eventually developed a greater carnal interest in mixed-race women—a distinct proclivity for the "mulatta" woman—than for black women in general, which has continued to exist to this day in some Caribbean countries, including Brazil, which was the last nation to end slavery in 1888. They were drawn to these women not only because of their natural beauty, but also due to the pervasive white stereotype of mulatta women as pleasure seekers, with a heightened sexual process and sensuality—of course, yet another popular myth based more on fantasy than fact about people of color that, unfortunately, has existed for centuries and even to this day.

This extremely high level of interracial mixing caused considerable concern among the colony's officials, who saw this widespread "debauchery" as a serious threat to the establishment of white families and social stability in Saint-Domingue, and resulted in an ever-growing class of free people of color. The free Black population thrived and continued to grow without any serious obstacles on Saint-Domingue, where European morals and sexual codes of conduct vanished to a degree that shocked straitlaced and religious Europeans, especially those from Paris, upon their arrival to this free-wheeling colony in the tropics that was so unlike France in every possible way.

Even French law based on the relatively liberal Black Code had early played a role in leading to widespread interracial marriages that resulted in the rise of a large class of mixed-race people in Saint-Domingue. Incredibly enlightened for its day because it offered a number of protections to slaves, including women, and quite unlike in the United States from beginning to end, the Code Noir (Black Code) of France of 1685, which had been issued by King Louis XIV, specified that if a white planter raped a female slave, then he would have to marry and then free her.

But the greatest cause of the dramatic growth of the free Black population on Saint-Domingue stemmed from the fact that French masters often freed their own mixed-race offspring and their dark-hued lovers out of love, generation after generation. What was most significant about the Slave Code was that French citizenship was bestowed to free mixed-race inhabitants, which also helped to fuel the rise of the sizable free Black community. This free Black community achieved amazing success in all fields of endeavor, especially agricultural, because the freed slaves automatically and officially became French citizens, regardless of their color or percentage of Black-white mixtures.[2]

One of the many Europeans who was shocked by what he saw of the fast-paced sexual activity of seemingly endless interracial mixing at Cap-Français, the colony's most fabled city, poised on the north coast, and noted for its interracial carnal interactions of a freewheeling nature, said "The white are brought [from France] to the worst kind of excess [in the colony when it came to their slaves], and selling them a few years later with their [own mixed-race] children. (Has one ever seen anything more horrible than to sell one's own blood?) Enough about the description of this island, as it could lead to a scandal."[3] Another equally shocked visitor to Saint-Domingue was also appalled by what he saw all around him. In his own stunned words, in which interracial sex seemed to dominate above all other activities in this colony: "Nothing more common than the debauchery that exists between whites and women of color, both mulattresses and negresses."[4]

The widespread racial intermixing in the colony combined with the fact that more slaves were imported to Saint-Domingue than to the United States also resulted in the rise of the large free Black community, amounting to around thirty thousand people of mixed race by the

1790s, which was about equal to the white population. The free mulatto population, who were mostly women and children of white fathers, grew so large by 1775—the year that the American Revolution was ignited by Massachusetts militiamen at Lexington and Concord, Massachusetts, on April 19—that the alarmed French leaders of the colonial government, consisting mostly of rich white planters, took direct punitive action. They made it more difficult for whites to free their slaves because they feared the rising class of free people of color was becoming too large and powerful, even threatening their own lofty standing in a race-based society.

Most significant, by the time of the American Revolution, the thriving mulatto class of Saint-Domingue consisted of unique individuals who simultaneously possessed both a rich African heritage and an equally rich French heritage. This dual heritage from two different continents and cultures placed people of mixed race in a separate and distinctive class all its own, nestled between the upper-class elite of the white planter class and the far larger number of lowly slaves.

On their own, the mulattoes of Saint-Domingue early proved to be a remarkably resourceful and business-savvy people. They had learned well from their mostly white fathers, who kindly bestowed support to their own offspring, especially financial. By the time of the American Revolution, more than six thousand free people of color owned much of the mountainous land in the fertile south of Saint-Domingue, dominating the cultivation of coffee, which was second only to sugarcane when it came to profitability and an insatiable world demand. The well-managed coffee plantations of the mulatto people covered the hillsides, making them prosperous and rich in many cases. This dynamic class of an entirely new people thrived on multiple levels as never before.

The free people of color that evolved into a large separate class on Saint-Domingue were dominated by two leadership groups: the wealthy planter elite, who mostly owned coffee plantations and plenty of slaves, especially in the south; and the military leadership group, which had grown powerful with each passing generation to also become entrenched at the top of free mulatto society. This influential military leadership group had steadily grown from the early militia tradition of Saint-Domingue, when everyone, regardless of color, had been needed to protect the endangered colony by serving in the militia, especially in the beginning, when it was virtually surrounded by enemies in the intense game of European rivalries.

In general, members of the military leadership, eventually including the officers and noncommissioned officers of the Chasseurs-Volontaires de Saint-Domingue, most often bestowed freedom to their slaves for generations, more than in the case of white militia officers and the other leadership class of free Blacks, the planter elite of the men of color, partly because some of these mulattoes had fought at Savannah during the autumn of 1779.

Before the outbreak of the American Revolution, free people of color became some of the French colony's most successful and enterprising planters, especially in regard to profitable coffee production in the hills of the rural countryside, far from the main cities. These large landowners of mixed race, including those who owned prosperous sugar plantations, became rich from their enterprising and industrious ways.

The rapid rise of free people of color was all but inevitable for another reason as well. Many wealthy white fathers had sent their mixed-race sons to some of the finest schools in France, giving them land and money to start their own sugar and coffee plantations, along with gangs of slaves to work their estates in some cases, especially if they possessed sugarcane plantations. The fact that some free Blacks owned slaves to labor in the broad fields of their plantations and to become richer seemed no contradiction in their minds; it was accepted as simply part of the natural order of things, part of everyday life in Saint-Domingue. This was not only an example of white enculturation but also the beginning of the bitter Black-versus-mulatto divide that has cursed Haiti to this day.

Because free Blacks—both mulattoes, who made up the vast majority of men who served in the Chasseurs at Savannah, and some of pure African blood—still faced a good deal of official discrimination, both legal and unofficial, they eventually began to champion equal rights to correct their despised status as second-class citizens, which had long existed because of their color.

The French Revolution erupted on the fateful day of July 14, 1789, when the Paris mob stormed the king's prison, known as the Bastille, the most hated symbol of the corrupt monarchy. The revolution stemmed from years of societal unrest, partly caused by the heavy financial burden of having created the Franco-American alliance during the American Revolution. When the 1789 French Declaration of the Rights of Man and of the Citizen was issued, the most influential mulattoes of Saint-Domingue, including men who had fought at Savannah in 1779, proclaimed that this act gave them their long-coveted equal rights to whites.

In a central paradox of Haitian history, and at the beginning of the outbreak of revolutionary currents in Paris that evolved into the "Reign of Terror" of the 1790s, the thriving class of free people of color in Saint-Domingue became more radical and revolutionary than the lowest class (Black slaves), which had the most to gain by rising up against the existing social order that so severely oppressed them.

In an even more striking paradox, the mulatto population opposed Black slaves in their initial bid for freedom, just like the white upper-class elite who ruled the colony, because everything was based on class and shades of skin color. The mulattoes desired to obtain equal rights in a segregated and discriminatory Saint-Domingue at the expense of the slaves in the fields—a true Faustian bargain, and an early division based on varying degrees of color.[5]

THE RISE OF THE FREE BLACK MILITIA OF SAINT-DOMINGUE

The early arming of slaves in Saint-Domingue, which began long before the French Revolution, was meant to protect the colony from European invaders, especially the English sea rovers. This was nothing new in the course of history. Since ancient times, slaves had been armed by people around the ancient world to protect the state and the general population. Even the most elite and legendary warriors of the ancient Greek world, the Spartans, enlisted their "Helot" slaves to fight beside them in emergency situations, including in the famous 480 BC showdown at Thermopylae, in the defense the strategic pass by King Leonidas and his elite bodyguard of 300 men against the invading Persians, to protect the other Greek city-states. The ancient Romans followed suit in arming slaves to counter major threats to their way of life, and to protect their global empire when they were at risk and crisis situations arose.[6]

Although the wealth and personal prestige of the free Blacks of mixed race had grown over the years, reaching lofty levels in Saint-Domingue by the time of the American Revolution, so had their simmering discontent, as racial discrimination and segregation from the state still existed. The white planter–dominated government wanted to keep them in their place as second-class citizens, for racial, social, and economic reasons. Quite simply, the rise of a large and prosperous free Black community threatened the entire slave system upon which the colony was based in the minds of the ruling elite, and whites in general, because of its considerable size and continued growth and prosperity. They also believed this ever-growing mixed-race community would set a bad example to the large number of enslaved people, causing greater discontent and encouraging them to seek their own freedom. The sizable ratio of free Blacks to the white population was evident in the 1754 Royal Census, when nearly one thousand free Blacks, mostly mulattoes, were counted among less than three thousand whites in Saint-Domingue. This percentage of mixed-race people in the prosperous colony would only grow larger in the decades ahead.

The sweet taste of success and power that former slaves and free mulattoes experienced in their private lives, including militia service, became intolerable to many whites of all classes. Indeed, the continued rise of free Blacks of mixed-race and their impressive rapid ascent in Saint-Domingue society threatened the position of not only poor whites, but also middle- and upper-class whites. Therefore, by the mid-1750s, the colonial elites had rallied around the racist concept of "white purity," like whites of the lower-classes, to protect their lofty status by enacting restrictions to exclude free Black people of mixed race from becoming equal citizens in Saint-Domingue society. The elites considered them to be non-white, even though they possessed a large percentage of white blood in their veins—basically, the so-called "one-drop rule," in which one drop of Black blood makes a person officially Black, as is the case in the United States.

This was the racial high card played by the planter elites to maintain their power and privileged positions in colonial society, at the top of the heap, while neatly negating the amazing growth and success of the free Black population and to racially divide the planter whites and mulattoes. Of course, this was a time-proven plan of divide and conquer along strict lines of race and class by the savvy, but increasingly paranoid, French elites, who saw themselves as threatened by the planters, both white and mixed-race, if they decided to unite as one against the colonial government in a possible revolt against their autocratic colonial rulers, who, of course, were all white.

After all, free mulattoes owned a large percentage of not only the land but also the slaves in rural areas in the remote countryside, especially in the south, rather than in the cities, where they worked in more skilled positions. While this situation made them locally prominent among the populace in general, this was not the case in the eyes of the main government, located in major cities in their insular urban world, which made it not only a historic class and racial divide, but also one based on historic urban-versus-rural antagonisms.

For such reasons, before the American Revolution, the planter-class elites of Saint-Domingue imposed greater prejudice and discriminatory laws because of the unprecedented success of free mulatto planters, not witnessed to such an extent in any other slave regime in the world, especially in the United States. The elites also viewed with alarm the increasing closeness between whites and free Blacks and mulattoes, especially by way of interracial marriage—what those in power feared could become the rise of a potential revolutionary leadership class that might eventually challenge their rule. These government-imposed laws to limit their growing influence and success naturally fueled the simmering discontent among the free Blacks and mulattoes.

This potential collaboration of two distinct classes positioned below the upper-class elite was seen as a greater threat because of mutual ties and bonds—a united front that was thought to threaten French loyalty, culture, and societal values of the mother country, centered in Paris, and especially the entrenched privileges of the elites. All in all, what most threatened the French elites who ruled the colony was the

ever-growing power of a new man of a darker hue who had been born
on Saint-Domingue soil, the free Black Creole. He was a proud member
of a new people who possessed a mixture of both white and Black blood
and rejoiced in his success in Saint-Domingue society, experiencing a
measure of pride and independence.

One of the few ways for free mulatto and Black males to strike
back against this sharp official government backlash against mixed-race
people was to serve in the Saint-Domingue militia, which was necessary
to defend the vulnerable colony. This was especially the case because a
good many of the Caribbean islands, especially Jamaica, based on sugar
production but much less lucrative than thriving Saint-Domingue, were
owned by France's ancient archenemy, England, which possessed the
world's most powerful navy and could invade the French islands, if the
right opportunity presented itself.

From the earliest days when members of the French colony first
occupied the western third of Hispaniola, Saint-Domingue was merely
attempting to survive against numerous threats in the dangerous frontier
environment of the Caribbean. The French had been forced to arm Blacks
and mulattoes out of necessity, in order to meet the pressing requirements
of self-defense when the colony's existence was at stake. With its location
so far from Paris, Saint-Domingue was left largely on its own.

For courageous service against the Spanish since the 1690s, some
faithful slaves of Saint-Domingue, including Vincent Olivier, had been
given their freedom, along with awards and pensions, from the thankful
government of Saint-Domingue, and France. To defend Saint-Domingue,
militia units of Blacks and mulattoes had been early integrated as viable
fighting forces because of the shortage of manpower and the extent of
threats throughout the Caribbean from both Spain and Great Britain.

However, racial oppression quickly returned when external threats
receded. By the 1720s, free Blacks and later free mulattoes had faced so
much discrimination and prejudice while serving in the colony's militia
that they had been forced to create their own separate militia companies:
an early genesis of the Chasseurs-Volontaires de Saint-Domingue. This
was a notable development in regard to improving the overall status and
credentials for free Blacks and mulattoes in Saint-Domingue society,

especially when free men of color held officers' ranks, both captain and lieutenant, in commanding their own companies of dark-hued members, while earning the same privileges as white militia officers. In this way, for themselves and for their families, free Blacks and mulattoes who held an officer's rank solidified their free status and earned relatively elevated positions in the all-Black and all-mulatto militia companies, and in Saint-Domingue society—the most brutal of slave societies that supported France's largest and most successful slave regime in the West Indies.

The stern demands of the Seven Years' War, a true global war which began in 1756 between primarily England and France, assisted the free Black and mulatto militia in earning a greater share of responsibility in the colony's protection. In the process, these men of a darker shade gained a lofty and well-deserved reputation of having been "the best" militia troops in all Saint-Domingue, compared to the far less enthusiastic whites, who basically thought they were above the rigors of militia duty because of their color, which automatically bestowed a higher status in the sugar colony. In consequence, white Frenchmen were far more resistant to serving the colony and nation by enlistment in the militia. The desire of whites to get rich as soon as possible superseded their interest in militia service—what they saw as a waste of their time, for low pay.

In general, white Frenchmen detested the dangerous duty of pursuing escaped slaves, often called maroons, and fighting them in the jungles and mountains and the demanding tropical environment. Therefore, the required militia roles against the maroons were mostly filled by the free Black and mulatto militiamen, whose members were not only more obliging but also more capable in this vital mission of providing both internal and external security to safeguard the colony.

For generations, the maroons had waged an especially vicious guerrilla war by launching raids on the sugar and coffee plantations from their mountain sanctuaries and battling to keep their hard-earned freedom. They had to be thwarted for the sake of the colony's agricultural-based economy, which they threatened if unchecked, and the overall security of France's most important overseas possession.

During the first world war between primarily England and France, known as the Seven Years' War, the Chasseurs-Volontaires d'Amérique was formed, which consisted of free Blacks and mulattoes. They served capably until the global war's end in 1763, setting a precedent for the Chasseurs-Volontaires de Saint-Domingue by the time of the American Revolution. The Chasseurs-Volontaires d'Amérique only continued the longtime tradition of the colony's policy of arming of Blacks, which had long been necessary to defend France's invaluable West Indies possessions against English raiders, dating well back to the 1600s. Ample evidence has fully demonstrated that from the beginning of the settlement of Saint-Domingue and other Caribbean islands, these Black and mulatto fighting men in the West Indies were very good and faithful soldiers who were highly motivated in serving God—a Catholic one—their colony, and their country.

As noted, Saint-Domingue possessed a strong militia tradition from the beginning of the colony's establishment, for protection, in the task of guarding its lengthy coastline. This was partly because it was too expensive for France to adequately garrison the colony with regular troops so far from Paris. This overall strategic and economic situation of the Caribbean colony ensured a more important role for the free Black and mulatto militia, first in Saint-Domingue and, later, in America in 1779. But by the time of the American Revolution, the Chasseurs-Volontaires de Saint-Domingue were all volunteers, as their name implied, rather than conscripted or impressed militia, which of course guaranteed a higher level of morale and higher level of patriotism in 1779.

Militia service for some free men of color even opened the door for these mulatto soldiers to marry white wives from good families, including widows of successful French planters, gaining additional wealth and prestige and allowing them to move even higher up the social ladder in a fluid, mobile society—when not restricted by whites. This continued the process of solidifying a new, dynamic class of leading white and mixed-race planters and the unification of an increasingly successful class of people of color, whose growing achievements and prestige threatened the elites financially, politically, and psychologically.

For instance, in Saint-Domingue's Northern Province—the wealthiest province, at the heart of the largest sugarcane production in the colony because of its broad, fertile plain that was ideal for growing the Caribbean's greatest cash crop—the free Laporte family (mulatto, in this case) in the Limonade parish possessed more than two thousand acres of prime lands and three hundred slaves: an excellent representative example of the impressive rise of the free Black population of the ever-growing upper classes of mixed-raced individuals who increasingly mirrored the success of white Frenchmen.[7]

Like its mulatto inhabitants, Saint-Domingue was unique, distinctive in many ways from other Caribbean islands. Many of the rural towns in Saint-Domingue, including those communities from which some Black and mulatto militia members hailed before they journeyed in their new blue uniforms to Savannah in 1779, were denoted by unique names that caught the spirit and essence of this free-wheeling colony that produced so much fantastic wealth for France, especially from the fertile northern plain, which was filled with seemingly endless sugarcane plantations of immense size, situated just south of the booming port of Cap-Français on the north coast.

Like his comrades, a young French soldier, a commoner of German descent named Hans Stiegel—who was fated to die of disease in 1781 while serving in the ranks for King Louis XVI, in America—was amazed and thoroughly enchanted by what he saw when he arrived in the tropical land of Saint-Domingue from France. And a privileged French aristocrat who was equally astounded, wrote: "On the other side [of the mountains to the south of Cap-Français] is the plain in which you find the towns of Limonade and Marmelade. This plain [an economic powerhouse] is beautiful."[8]

But just below the surface of this beautiful colony and its amazing success and prosperity, deep currents of unrest simmered across the land. As mentioned, the rising numbers of free Blacks were seen as a direct threat by the colony's wealthy and aristocratic elites for multiple reasons. In the astute analysis of two noted modern historians, David Patrick Geggus and Norman Fiering, the government's imposition of the concept of "white purity" was calculated to slow the ever-growing progress of the free mulatto class, which had risen too fast in the minds of ruling whites.

Therefore, "as Saint-Domingue's mixed-race planters and merchants passed from the class of 'colonists' into the newly rigid caste of 'nonwhites,' they found themselves in a larger but poorer group of free people. These included artisans, small merchants, ranchers, peasants, and plantation employees, many of whom were former slaves. This enterprising group, which had never belonged to the elite, produced many of the leading military figures of the Haitian Revolution, [Toussaint] Louverture, [André] Rigaud, and Henri Christophe among them," because they hated the discrimination and racism stemming from the white elites of the colonial government.[9]

GENESIS OF THE CHASSEURS-VOLONTAIRES DE SAINT-DOMINGUE

The entry of France on the side of the American revolutionaries in 1778 smoothed over some of the existing internal racial rivalries and simmering unrest in Sant-Domingue, because a rising sense of patriotism led–at least initially–to a sense of unity previously not seen. After returning from his first mission to America at Newport, Rhode Island, to the trand city of France's most prosperous sugar colony, Cap-Français, during the spring of 1779, Vice Admiral Jean Baptiste Charles Henri Hector, comte d'Estaing, went to work, tapping into the colony's manpower, Black and white, beginning the process of creating an expeditionary force for service in America.

Born in Ravel, France, on November 24, 1729, d'Estaing was one of the rare upper-class aristocrats who was open-minded about race. One of his primary earlier missions when he had served as the governor of Saint-Domingue from 1764 to 1766, dictated from the king, had been to reestablish the Saint-Domingue militia. This was cheaper to organize and maintain than France's regular troops, which had been deactivated after the end of the Seven Years' War, in 1763. D'Estaing now possessed a valuable resource pool of experienced Black and mulatto men who had prior militia experience to draw upon, and these free men felt they had much to prove. This was the genesis for the formation of the highly motivated soldiers who would serve in the ranks of the Chasseurs-Volontaires de Saint-Domingue during the spring and summer of 1779, in the expedition that was destined to assist the American rebels in the South at Savannah.

Before the American Revolution, D'Estaing had originally planned for free men of color between the ages of sixteen and sixty to serve as the primary base and foundation for the defense of Saint-Domingue, an ideal solution for the numerous security issues at the time. However, a chorus of white protests arose about giving weapons to the free people of color and elevating their status in Saint-Domingue society. This caused d'Estaing to abruptly end his ambitions of creating a viable free Black militia, which he had correctly envisioned would be more highly motivated and capable than white militiamen, because these Blacks and mulattoes were permanent and lifelong residents—Creoles—who had been born in Saint-Domingue, unlike most whites, who had migrated from France in hopes of getting rich from the sugar boom, which meant that engaging in any kind of civic duty, especially militia duty, was given the lowest of all priorities.

Indeed, in this regard, d'Estaing's thoughtful reasoning was right on target. His vision of a separate unit of Black militia was destined to fnally become a reality in 1779, when America was fighting for its life after four years of war. In the future, including during the Savannah Campaign of 1779, white and Black militia units of Saint-Domingue served separately; no Black man held an officer's rank (no position over the rank of sergeant), which had been the case in the colony since 1769, due to a history of white opposition to any enhanced status of these Black soldiers that would have come with higher ranks, if they had served as officers.[10]

The Franco-American alliance of 1778 and d'Estaing's arrival at Cap-Français had set the stage for the formation of a new Black and mulatto volunteer unit in Saint-Domingue. After his return from the miserable allied failure at Newport, Vice Admiral d'Estaing issued the first call to arms in the spring of 1779 for the expedition bound for Savannah—a destination not known at the time. In theory, this new unit of Black and mulatto fighting men would fundamentally be a resurrection of the old Chasseurs-Volontaires d'Amérique, which had served effectively and won acclaim during the Seven Years' War. But at this point, the mixed-race and Black volunteers enlisted only for the express purpose of joining the vice admiral's fleet for duty and the upcoming expedition outside of Saint-Domingue, the destination still not known to anyone except the vice admiral, for obvious security reasons.

Most important, the new Chasseurs would have no hint of royal connections like its predecessor, while revealing a distinctive pride in the New World and Saint-Domingue. They were officially christened the Chasseurs-Volontaires de Saint-Domingue under the command of aristocratic Laurent François Lenoir, Marquis de Rouvray. He had early embarked upon recruiting young Blacks and mulattoes who made the decision to join as volunteers, as the official name of the new unit implied. The pouring forth of Saint-Domingue volunteers, both Black and mulatto, revealed the rising pride among the inhabitants, especially the free mulatto class that existed in the French colony as part of the French empire, now waging war on its historic enemy, England. This group contributed by far the most volunteers. Fueled by the challenges and rigors of the upcoming Savannah expedition, the nascent nationalism of the French tropical colony was destined to grow in the years ahead, eventually emerging in full flower during the Haitian Revolution, playing a role in the creation of the world's first Black republic, Haiti, which became a beautiful reality with the realization of the unprecedented concept of universal liberty on January 1, 1804.

Significantly, some future leaders of the Haitian Revolution, including Henri Christophe and Jean-Baptiste Chavannes, served in the ranks of the Chasseurs-Volontaires de Saint-Domingue during the fall of 1779 at Savannah, but not as many as long believed by generations of Haitian and American historians. For instance, the mulatto André Rigaud, who emerged as the primary mulatto leader and a dynamic general during the Haitian Revolution, was not a member of the Chasseurs, as long believed and generally assumed, according to the latest evidence. However, popular history has revealed that Rigaud did in fact serve at Savannah in some capacity.

Young Henri Christophe, age twelve and dark in color, revealing his pure-blood African heritage, was destined to serve as a drummer boy in the ranks of the Chasseurs at Savannah, which has been verified by generations of Haitian historians and many years of tradition. But was this actually the case? Some leaders of the first and only successful slave revolt in the Western Hemisphere, and then the Haitian Revolution, have been mythologized, like the "father" of America, George Washington. As a consequence, a great deal of romance and legend has continued to surround primary Haitian revolutionary leaders, especially in Haiti to this day, because historical facts have merged with fiction and lore in the nationalist tradition, as is the case with creation stories of all nations and peoples around the world, including in the United States. Like the American people, Haitians have also naturally idealized and mythologized their history and principal revolutionary leaders, the George Washingtons of their people's republic like Christophe, born of violent revolution. Adding to the considerable challenge, historians researching the Chasseurs have been restricted by incomplete records and documentation, as is the case with any historian working in the frustrating realm of Haitian history, which is notoriously devoid of primary sources and solid documentation.

Historian Stewart R. King, an associate professor in Oregon, presents a contrarian analysis in his 2001 study, *Blue Coat or Powdered Wig: Free People of Color in Pre-Revolutionary Saint-Domingue*. According to King, Christophe failed to serve in the ranks of the Chasseurs-Volontaires de Saint-Domingue, as long claimed by generations of Haitian historians: "Previous studies of the Haitian Revolution have laid great stress on the importance of the Chasseurs-Volontaires as a training ground for the cadre of the revolutionary armies of 1791–1804. Originally, an investigation of this connection was to be an important part of this study. However, the names of only five Chasseurs-Volontaires who were certainly participants in the revolutionary wars have come to light: mulatto rebel Jean-Baptiste Chavannes; [Sergeant] Pierre Augustin, who served as an officer in Toussaint Louverture's army; Black general and later president of independent Haiti, Jean-François L'Eveille; mulatto Limonade innkeeper and revolutionary captain Fabien Gentil [or Genty]; and a mulatto lieutenant colonel in the Santo Domingo [the Spanish two-thirds of the island of Hispaniola in the center and on the east, as Saint-Domingue occupied the island's western third] garrison in 1802 named Gautier.

None of the famous names often cited—Christophe, [Alexandre] Pétion, Rigaud—turned up in the notarial records as Chasseurs-Volontaires."[11]

Jean-Baptiste Chavannes, a natural leader, was destined to lead a key slave uprising in 1790 and emerged as a Haitian revolutionary leader of distinction during the course of the Haitian Revolution. Historian Philippe Girard, one of today's leading experts of Haitian history, emphasized how members of the Chasseurs-Volontaires de Saint-Domingue included "André Rigaud, who would become a general and Louverture's main rival in the 1790s [and the leader of the free mulattoes, while Toussaint Louverture led mostly Blacks, or former slaves, in their separate armies that waged a brutal war, known as the 'War of Knives' (1799–1800) because of its no-quarter qualities, against each other before the arrival of Napoleon Bonaparte's invasion force in early 1802], and Jean-Baptiste Belley, who later served as the deputy in the French parliament."[12]

Clearly, the often heated debate about who served in the ranks of the Chasseurs-Volontaires and who were members of the Savannah expedition in 1779 has continued to this day among both Black and white historians in the United States and Haiti, thanks partly to the lack of accurate documentation and political agendas. Part of the purpose of *Brothers in Liberty* is to clarify as much as possible the seemingly endless confusion and controversy that have persisted to this day, especially in regard to the story of the Chasseurs-Volontaires de Saint-Domingue.

While King has excluded Rigaud and Belley from having participated in the Savannah Campaign, Girard has found documentation that has revealed otherwise. Like the vast majority of other historians, especially Haitian scholars, he also believed that Henri Christophe served in the ranks of the Chasseurs, in accordance with the longtime traditional view of Haitian historians. In the view of this fine author, Henri Christophe might well have been absent from the notarial records, as author King has observed, because of his young age, as a preteen, and the fact of his dark color, without any hint of white blood, as well as his slave status (it's generally accepted that he was not free at this time). Quite simply, the lack of official evidence in this regard should not exclude the possibility that Christophe served at Savannah because so much evidence has indicated otherwise.

Indeed, many other sources, popular Haitian historical tradition, and the research of generations of top historians—Haitian, American, and French—of the Haitian revolutionary experience have revealed that Christophe did indeed serve as a drummer boy in the ranks of the Chasseurs-Volontaires de Saint-Domingue at Savannah in the autumn of 1779, at age twelve, and that he was in fact wounded during the American and French assault on the strategic Spring Hill Redoubt in Savannah's sprawling network of defenses on October 9, 1779. The dark-skinned (of pure African blood) future ruler of the Republic of Haiti was tall for his age, which helped to disguise Henri's extreme youth and allowed him to serve in the ranks of the Chasseurs. This stands in contrast to the recently developed contrarian story, considerably less ennobling, that Christophe had only attended a French military officer as a lowly body servant during the Savannah Campaign.

By the beginning of the American Revolution, when he was owned by a former Black militia member, Christophe worked in a tavern in the Northern Province community of Limonade, founded in 1676, not far from the wealthy port city of Cap-Français, located on the north coast, just to the northwest.[13]

Another point of endless debate about Henri Christophe, who was destined to become the future president of the Republic of Haiti, was whether he had been a slave or had been born free. For instance, historian Norman Desmarais wrote in 2021 of how Christophe had "volunteered as a freeborn infantryman and served as an orderly to a French naval officer."[14] But the traditional view that Christophe served as a drummer in the front ranks of the Chasseurs-Volontaires de Saint-Domingue, like other young musicians, and was then wounded during the spirited counterattack at Savannah has been in keeping with both the traditional and modern views of generally accepted history. Indeed, the fall of young Christophe on the field of Savannah was in keeping with the key role Black and mulatto soldiers played in rescuing the two battered allied armies, when "many Haitians" fell wounded at Savannah on bloody October 9, 1779.[15]

Desmarais also wrote that the following men were veterans of the Savannah Campaign and that they emerged from the ranks of the Chasseurs-Volontaires de Saint-Domingue to become leaders in the Haitian Revolution: "Pierre Astrel, Pierre Auba, Louis Jacques Beauvais, Jean-Baptiste Mars Belley, Martial Besse, Gullaume Bleck, Pierre Cange, Jean-Baptiste Chavannes, Pierre Faubert, Laurent Ferou, Jean-Louis Froumentaine, Barthelemy-Medor Leard, Gedeon Jourdan, Jean-Pierre Lambert, Jean-Baptiste Leveille, Christophe Mornet, Pierre Obas, Luc-Vincent Olivier, Pierre Pinchinat, Jean Piverger, André Rigaud, Cesaire Savary, Pierre Tessier, Jerome Thoby, Jean-Louis Villate, and Henry [Henri] Christophe, future King of Haiti."[16]

Having served as "artisans and urban entrepreneurs [and then] as noncommissioned officers in the colonial militia" and as members of a free mulatto "military leadership class" that shared elite status with the free Black planters, these men of the Chasseurs-Volontaires de Saint-Domingue who became the future leaders of the Haitian Revolution primarily hailed from the Northern Province and its main port city of Cap-Français. Indeed, fifteen "of the nineteen elite free men of color" who rose up and gained an officer's rank during the Haitian Revolution hailed from the North Province, including more than a dozen from Cap-Français. In total, nearly forty of the "forty-four non-elite 'military leaders' lived in the North Province."[17]

BEAUTIFUL LE CAP, THE "PEARL OF THE ANTILLES"

Cap-Français, known as Le Cap, was like no other city in all of the Caribbean. Quite simply, this beautiful city located on the north coast could not be surpassed by any other port city in Saint-Domingue. With a population of around twenty thousand by the 1770s, Le Cap was France's most important naval base in the Caribbean, and had been a focus of bustling trade with the thirteen American colonies long before the beginning of the American Revolution.

Like his comrades, French soldier Hans Stiegel, whose regiment of disciplined French regulars proudly wore the white uniforms of the Bourbon kings of France, was garrisoned in Saint-Domingue during the American Revolution. He was greatly impressed with the sheer splendor of Le Cap, like his comrades, who believed—at least initially—that they had entered a tropical paradise and fantasy land that was the antithesis of Europe in almost every way.

During the American Revolution, one French officer penned with delight and amazement his personal thoughts about this strange but beautiful place in the tropics: "The town of Cap-Français passes for being the most agreeable in the West Indies, and justly so. It is the Paris of the isles. All go there to know the fashions [of Paris]. It is, too, the handsomest, and next to Havana [Cuba], the richest. For its size and commerce, it may be compared to Lyons [France]. Its streets are always full of Negroes . . . Cap-Français is regularly built, all the streets are straight; the houses are low, not over two stories, built of beautiful stone, in spite of earthquakes."[18]

Like generations of French planters before them, the young and healthy French soldiers were astounded by the sheer natural beauty and grace of the shapely Black and mulatto women, who wore colorful and exotic garments like the women of many different cultures in West Africa, especially the brightly colored scarves that they wore around their heads, while walking in a seductive manner and a way not seen among the white French ladies in Paris. For such reasons, Le Cap was seen as the most sensual and sexual city not only in Saint-Domingue, but in the whole of the Caribbean. The enthusiastic pace of interracial sexual activity defined the very essence and lively spirit of this busy port town, which was known for its excesses of every variety, and captured its free-wheeling way of anything goes.

One Frenchman wrote about the wild nightlife of Le Cap—the overabundance of noisy taverns that seemingly occupied every corner, and the "underground" gaming houses, which were natural places for Frenchmen, both soldiers and civilians, to find an attractive Black or mixed-race woman for a night, a few weeks, or even years, depending on the situation and amount of lust—and even love—involved: "These places were usually packed with colored women wearing lace and revealing dresses, their bodies covered with a quantity of heavy voluminous jewelry. They were easily recognizable everywhere with their typical motion of hips and their high hairdos [in the latest Paris fashion] surrounded by a tight veil. These women counted among the most typical clichés of Le Cap."[19]

In 1775, less than four years before the formation of the Chasseurs-Volontaires de Saint-Domingue, a shocked Frenchmen deplored the widespread extent of the "promiscuity produced by slavery" in such a picturesque tropical land, where the degree of lust had long run wild and out of control, producing a seemingly endless number of mulatto children who were seen everywhere.[20]

More important than its beauty and mostly Black and mulatto population, Le Cap, France's vital naval base in the Caribbean, was crucial to the Revolutionary War effort in America, having early fueled the resistance efforts of American armies, including the Continental Army under General George Washington, with all manner of invaluable supplies to keep the people's struggle for survival alive. Even before the signing of the crucial Franco-American alliance in 1778, thanks to its magnificent harbor and King Louis XVI's early desire to aid American revolutionaries in their determined bid for liberty and to strike a blow at the British Empire, Le Cap became the most vital port through which tons of munitions, supplies, and arms were funneled from France to America. This was a continuation of the brisk commerce and thriving trade that had long existed between the colonies and Saint-Domingue before the war, and one of the key connections of a shared revolutionary heritage that exists between Haiti and America.

Of course, this heavy flow of illicit commercial activity of arming rebels rightfully incensed the British government and the officials and residents of the British sugar islands, especially Jamaica, because they realized these clandestine operations under their very noses were fueling the American war effort and making the job of subduing the rebellion more much difficult, if not impossible.[21]

Significantly, the ever-observant Stiegel, the good-natured French regular assigned to duty with his regiment in France's most prosperous colony under the sun, noted the pervasive negative attitude of white colonials and Frenchmen in regard to the local militia of Le Cap and other towns in Saint-Domingue, which would soon incorrectly apply to the Chasseurs-Volontaires when they were organized in the spring and summer of 1779: "The Colonial regiments included a large proportion of black and mixed blood and were considered second-class troops, [like all militia compared to regulars, as in the case of America's soldiers, but especially so because of their color] similar to the militia in France" and in America.[22]

In consequence, the Black and mulatto men of the Chasseurs faced a double handicap from the beginning of their formation: They were widely considered by whites to be nothing more than second-class troops, not only because of their color, but also because they were in the militia at a time when whites hated military duty and viewed it as a most burdensome, if not repulsive, obligation. Most whites in the colony hailed from western and southern France, where the militia system was less important than it was in other parts of France, and especially in Saint-Domingue, where it served as the sturdy foundation of external and internal security in a vast slave regime, and evolved into a central feature of the colony's society.

Based primarily on ugly racial stereotypes and ignorance, the contempt for these Black and mulatto volunteers, held so passionately by whites, could not alter the fundamental truth, which in itself caused even more resentment out of envy and jealousy—that the "free men were recognized as the most competent and least expensive defense force available to the free black population."[23]

Black and mulatto militiamen of Saint-Domingue had become political pawns by this time in regard to the long-awaited bestowing of equal rights for their service to France and the colony, which remained elusive: "As the free population of color grew to almost the size of the white population in the 1780s, some [government] officials [of Saint-Domingue] favored transforming free [Black] militiamen into full-time soldiers and rewarding them with increased civil rights. Yet powerful colonial interests regarded this plan as threatening the very basis of the slave regime and setting an ominous precedent for the white militia" of Saint-Domingue.[24]

What had developed in Cap-Français and the area located mostly in the fertile coastal plain, covered in sugarcane plantations, and the mountains just south of the capital was the emergence of a "regional subculture" of militia members of mixed race from the Northern Province—the fundamental basis of the Chasseurs-Volontaires de Saint-Domingue that served at Savannah in 1779 and paid high dividends to both the French and American armies on October 9, 1779. Here, the militia tradition among free mulattoes was strong and deeply ingrained in the local culture and environment, which played a key role in the successful formation of the Chasseurs in d'Estaing's hour of need.

Indeed, ever since the late seventeenth century, the key northern port of Cap-Français had garnered most of the colony's robust trade with the mother country, both prewar and in wartime. Its foremost location on the north coast closest to France dominated the colony, and "had launched a number of military expeditions in which slaves had won their liberty. It was here, in 1697 [and] after a successful attack on Cartagena [Columbia], that ex-slaves formed a separate free black militia, the first in the colony. . . . Between the revision of militia laws of 1769 and the French Revolution in 1789, the Savannah campaign was the most important example of men of color trying to show their patriotism by adapting the metropolitan ideal of self-sacrifice" for God and country.[25]

THE INCOMPARABLE CAPTAIN VINCENT OLIVIER

For ample reasons, both past and present, Captain Vincent Olivier is seen as the most esteemed Black man among people of all colors in Saint-Domingue—a true local hero who had once been a slave. He was widely known to the common people as Capitaine Vincent, an inspirational legend in his own time. Vincent had risen high in life, mingling with the leading notables, officials, and dignitaries of the colony's elite who welcomed Vice Admiral d'Estaing back to Le Cap when he returned from America, specifically Newport, in early 1779.[26]

In fact, Captain Vincent Olivier, who was distinguished by the darkest of skins that revealed his pure African roots, became the godfather of the Chasseurs-Volontaires de Saint-Domingue. He best represented the rise of the free Black and mulatto leadership class and how the self-sacrificing process of distinguished military service to the colony and France could overcome even deep-seated racial prejudice in an overseas colony dominated by racism and the most successful and vibrant system of slavery in the Western Hemisphere, which fueled the booming sugar economy.

By the time of the American Revolution, the overachieving captain was the most popular and well-known Black militia leader of Saint-Domingue and a hero of the free Black and mulatto community, representing what can be achieved by demonstrating faithful service and valor on the battlefield for France. A former slave who had risen high in life, Olivier had early gained his renown as a young man and distinguished himself during a lengthy military career. He was a veteran of the 1697 campaign that had resulted in the French capture of the rich Caribbean port of Cartagena (named for an ancient city in Spain), Colombia, winning his freedom for demonstrated courage and ability.

By the 1770s, Olivier was a distinguished member of the upper-class free Black elite class, having moved up the social ladder thanks to years of distinguished military service, not only at Cartagena, but also for years afterward for France, including on battlefields across Europe. Captain Olivier's enduring legend was well known in Saint-Domingue, especially in the free Black and mulatto community, because of his self-sacrifice and heroism on behalf of the colony and nation. Instead of returning to Saint-Domingue, he had continued to serve in the ranks of the French army after having been captured during his return from the French victory reaped at Cartagena. He was ransomed for a hefty sum, became a distinguished guest at the court of King Louis XIV, and then won more laurels afterward on fields of strife in Germany for heroism.

Then, in 1716, this remarkable Black man of immense patriotism and seemingly countless abilities was officially appointed the captain-general of all the free Black militia at Cap-Français, after having won widespread respect in France and Saint-Domingue. All in all, Captain Olivier had accomplished a great deal in life for a former slave, especially in providing the inspirational example to future generations of young Black and mulatto men in Saint-Domingue—that faithful military service to France could overcome pervasive racism and discrimination. This was no small accomplishment in a thriving slave regime in the Caribbean based on lucrative sugarcane production, and led to a much better life, including a sizable military pension for his faithful service to king and country. This was the shining example used by both d'Estaing and Olivier in the next five months during the spring and summer, to secure large numbers of Black and mulatto recruits for the forthcoming 1779 expedition.

Not only was Captain Olivier an inspirational role model for the young men of the Chasseurs-Volontaires de Saint-Domingue, but also for other free Blacks and mulattoes throughout Saint-Domingue, and the population at large, including whites. First and foremost, he had achieved what seemed impossible for a man of the darkest color, and an ex-slave, having earned laurels, freedom, and a pension for heroics against the Spanish as early as the 1690s, and rare respect from the highest-ranking whites in the land, including even from the king of France.

In consequence, the Black captain became the primary and best recruiter of the young men, both Blacks and mulattoes, who served in the ranks of the Chasseurs-Volontaires de Saint-Domingue. He represented the remarkable rise from lowly slave to becoming one of the wealthiest and most distinguished members of not only free Black society, but also Saint-Domingue society overall—by any measure, remarkable achievements for an ex-slave of the darkest color. This notable example inspired the young men to volunteer and enlist with enthusiasm in the ranks of this new unit during the spring and summer of 1779.

A savvy agricultural businessman and entrepreneur who had become rich, and the best example of the amazing success achieved by members of the military leadership class of free Blacks, Captain Olivier's remarkable success story began with service in the Cartagena Campaign—a life lesson certainly not lost on the young and ambitious Black and mulatto men of Saint-Domingue, especially in Cap-Français and in the Northern Province, where the aged veteran served as a primary recruiter who met with considerable success. This is because these optimistic young men viewed Vice Admiral d'Estaing's upcoming campaign in much the same light as the legendary Cartagena Campaign.

The ebony captain, who lived in wealth and comfort in the Sainte-Rose Parish and owned a coffee plantation in Limonade, situated just southeast of bustling Cap-Français, was a walking and talking legend and a powerful voice of Saint-Domingue and French patriotism, appealing to the young free mulattoes and Blacks to serve their country in a most effective manner. Providing the example of commitment to the colony and the nation, Captain Olivier continued his tradition of personal sacrifice, sending his own two grandsons, René Olivier, and most likely Maturin Olivier, into the ranks of the Chasseurs-Volontaires de Saint-Domingue without hesitation.

It's almost certain that Olivier's grandsons sought to gain what the captain had secured on his own. The aged captain was a true father figure to the young Chasseurs in the ranks, and now possessed unprecedented power, wealth, prestige, and excellent connections within the colonial government. The fact that a former slave had reached such an amazing level of personal achievement in the most oppressive slave regime in the Caribbean made the captain's call for volunteers extremely effective, beyond the traditional call of French patriotism, reinforcing the great dream of so many young Black and mulatto men of getting ahead in life by way of military service, especially for the lower-class members of the new volunteer unit.

An entrenched figure of Saint-Domingue society, Captain Olivier was very much a part of the colony's economic, social, and political system, especially in the upper ranks of free Black society, having commanded all of the free colored militia of the Northern Province during the years before the American Revolution. By 1779, Vincent Olivier might well have been the last living veteran of the sparkling success at Cartagena in 1697, when he had been a slave and had gone to war beside his master. Most important, Olivier provided the crucial historic link between the colony's first overseas expedition to Cartagena and the American Revolution, with the formation of the Chasseurs-Volontaires de Saint-Domingue. This situation paid nice dividends at the recruiter's office during the spring and summer of 1779, because so many young, mostly mulatto, but also Black, men volunteered to serve.[27]

BONDS OF BLACK BROTHERHOOD

The racial and militia connections that existed between Captain Olivier and the new recruits of the Chasseurs-Volontaires was a powerful one, as most of the free Black and mulatto recruits were drawn from the existing militia companies of the colony. This guaranteed an experienced, well-trained, and disciplined soldiery by the time of the unit's formation, a situation that was invaluable in terms of the overall high quality of the command and the stern challenges that lay ahead. A smaller number of inexperienced men without militia training also joined the ranks of the Chasseurs, however, and they had to undergo an intense training program run by experienced officers who knew how to turn civilians into soldiers. During this recruitment period, Captain Olivier busily gathered Black and mulatto men partly by way of "recalling his past glories to the men of color that were being enrolled for the expedition" of Vice Admiral d'Estaing.[28]

It was primarily patriotism, the bonds of brotherhood, and the desire to advance socially that motivated the Black and mulatto volunteers of the Chasseurs. They enthusiastically joined without receiving any royal recruiting bonuses—a handsome amount of money at the time. The Chasseurs were very much a moral soldiery driven by high motivations, including patriotism, Catholicism, racial pride, and a nascent nationalism, which was destined to emerge and take center stage at Savannah on October 9, 1779.[29]

The popular ideology of the Age of Enlightenment also played a role in securing enthusiastic young recruits to fill the ranks of the new volunteer command. The free people of color in Le Cap and elsewhere rejoiced when America declared its independence on July 4, 1776, based on the enlightened concept that "all men are created equal." This seemed to mark the beginning of an exciting new era in which their rights in a racially restrictive Saint-Domingue were bound to improve, or so it seemed. However, after their heroics in a key situation during the Savannah Campaign, the mulattoes and Blacks of the Chasseurs would learn that because the entire economy and social system of the French West Indies was based on slavery and racism, there was simply no amount of enlightened ideology and patriotism that could possibly alter these fundamental racial realities of life on a Caribbean sugar island, owned by an ancient monarchy that was one of the two major powers in Western Europe.

The role of Saint-Domingue's militia suddenly became more important when King Louis XVI decided to side with the Americans during the centuries-long struggle against their ancient enemy, Protestant England, when Catholic France and the infant United States formed their crucial alliance in 1778. The militia of the tropical colony would now have greater responsibilities, protecting Saint-Domingue and its sprawling coastline, especially if the powerful British navy, which was based in Kingston, Jamaica, launched an invasion in an attempt to capture France's most prosperous colony.

However, because an invasion from the Protestant archenemy of Catholic France thankfully never materialized, and there seemed to be no immediate threat during the spring and summer of 1779, the enlarged militia of Saint-Domingue, especially the Chasseurs-Volontaires, could now be employed on the American mainland in conjunction with their American allies, under the leadership of the much-acclaimed French vice admiral, who was famous for recently winning victories over the hated English in the Caribbean.

The Ambitious Count Jean Baptiste Charles Henri Hector d'Estaing

Indeed, much to his credit, there would have been no Chasseurs-Volontaires de Saint-Domingue, a light infantry command of Black and mulatto citizen-soldiers who volunteered to serve in whatever capacity the king required, if not for the soaring ambitions of a career navy man from France. Without ever receiving specific orders from King Louis XVI, and relying on his own initiative and instincts, Count Jean Baptiste Charles Henri Hector d'Estaing had created his own expeditionary force for a sudden surprise return to America when least expected, to strike a blow for the glory of France and the winning of American independence that he hoped would turn the tide of a lengthy war of attrition.

An elitist, privileged aristocrat, and a "darling of the French court" at Versailles, d'Estaing didn't look much like a fighting man except for his imposing height. He had the common touch that had long endeared him to the average seamen under his command. Dedicated to serving King Louis XVI and a hard worker, he always put duty first. Like a lowly member of the working class of France with no future in a hierarchical feudal society, and much to his credit, the vice admiral toiled hard late into the night, sleeping little, often only dozing briefly in uniform to reenergize his body and mind, closely identifying with his men, like a good commander of character and principle.

D'Estaing was no typical headquarters commander who remained in the rear, safely out of harm's way; rather, he boldly led from the front, unlike so many of the entitled French elite who preferred to casually allow their social inferiors—especially the peasants who had long worked the fields of the rich landowners across France—to die like flies in the mud of a gory battlefield, deemed expendable simply due to their lower station in life and common antecedents.

At age fifty, Vice Admiral d'Estaing possessed the strength, vigor, and enthusiasm of a man half his age. Most of all, he was a glory hunter, his life's blood, which explained his motivations and ambitions to a considerable degree. The war in America now offered him a fresh field of opportunity to reap the glorious victories that he craved, to impress the aristocratic elite and the king at Versailles. As could be expected, given his status among the aristocratic elite of France, d'Estaing's ego was exceptionally large, having won recent victories in the Caribbean in which he had garnered considerable acclaim across France.

Like throwing the dice on a gaming table in a fancy Paris gaming saloon, and with a tradition-based mind that idealized the Greek heroes of antiquity such as Achilles and Agamemnon, d'Estaing was known for taking too many risks—on the battlefield, and even in the quiet of the bedroom during moments of romantic bliss, where he had fathered children with beautiful women out of wedlock. D'Estaing had fought with an enthusiastic zeal in Europe and the Caribbean, almost as if the admiring eyes of King Louis XVI and all of the nobles and ruling elites of France were focused upon him.

A strange destiny seemed to have orchestrated the fate of the vice admiral and his upcoming mission to America. This odyssey that ended at Savannah in disaster and tragedy originally began in a most circuitous manner. D'Estaing's fleet had originally been dispatched by King Louis XVI from the port of Toulon, France, in mid-April 1778, to support the American revolutionaries and their desperate bid to win independence from the world's most powerful nation. Besides the pressing desire to wreak vengeance on England for having lost the Seven Years' War, and all of Canada (New France) and other key possessions, including in the Caribbean, and also for idealistic reasons rooted in the heady egalitarian ideals and philosophies of the Age of Enlightenment, France possessed other valid reasons to deliver Great Britain a stunning strategic blow—all factors eagerly embraced by d'Estaing, with a passion.

Besides valid strategic reasons, a host of economic factors played a large role in King Louis XVI's decision to wholeheartedly support the American revolutionaries and recognize the independence of the United States. This was also a global conflict over which European power would dominate trade with America—England or France? France needed an independent America because the French islands of the West Indies had long depended on the importation of food from America, as almost all of the available land on the sugar islands was devoted exclusively to the vast plantations that were raising a single cash crop to satisfy the world's sweet tooth, thereby accruing massive revenue from sugarcane cultivation.

In early 1779, Vice Admiral d'Estaing and a fleet with thousands of troops had returned from America to Cap-Français, the showpiece and pride of Saint-Domingue, to protect France's most important and profitable Caribbean colony. They also hoped to regain lost Caribbean possessions—lucrative sugar islands—in a roundabout circuit that covered thousands of miles. D'Estaing had not sailed directly from Toulon to Saint-Domingue because of his detour to Rhode Island and a disastrous allied campaign in 1778, which he would have ample reason to regret by the summer of 1779.

The ill-fated Rhode Island Campaign first developed when General George Washington and Vice Admiral d'Estaing had decided to attack Newport, Rhode Island, what had appeared to be a relatively soft target. However, the harsh realities for the inexperienced allies in their first tentative and mistake-filled effort had proved otherwise. True unity between the vastly dissimilar allies proved elusive. Ironically, the allied offensive effort at Newport was a second choice, after Washington and d'Estaing wisely decided against attacking New York City, which was protected by a powerful ring of defenses and garrisoned by too many troops.

This debacle of a campaign in New England during the summer of 1778 resulted in the first dismal failure of the infant alliance. The inability of d'Estaing and General John Sullivan to work smoothly together in their bid to capture Newport caused considerable embarrassment for both the Americans and French, to the delight of London's strategists, who could hardly believe the degree of folly committed by the new allies.

Sullivan had attacked alone without even informing d'Estaing of his offensive effort, because of already-existing tension, misunderstandings, and rivalries, setting the stage for the fiasco and making the concept of an effective alliance look like a fantasy. To the shock of General Sullivan and his men, d'Estaing had then hurriedly departed Newport with the arrival of stormy weather that damaged his vessels, as well as a fleet of powerful British warships from New York City, led by Admiral Richard Howe. In overall terms, the embarrassing lack of unity and understanding between allies at Newport seriously jeopardized the entire Franco-American alliance, upon which America's entire future hinged. D'Estaing actually had no choice but to retire from Rhode Island's waters and sail north to Boston for repairs.

To his credit, d'Estaing's fighting spirit had not disappeared in the least, which has been overlooked and forgotten. After having clashed with British warships in the Atlantic during August outside Newport, he had first returned to the mainland to announce to a disbelieving Sullivan that he no longer supported an assault on Newport and needed to set sail for Boston immediately, to make repairs to his warships, battered from the stormy weather and the recent encounter with the British. Once the necessary repairs were completed, d'Estaing had then headed southeast for Cap-Français, to set the stage for his conquest of Grenada, which he captured on July 4, 1779, along with the islands of St. Vincent and the Grenadines, during the summer of 1779, after having failed to recapture the rich sugar island of St. Lucia.

Vice Admiral d'Estaing's sudden departure from America had dealt a severe blow to the Franco-American alliance, now reeling in consequence. The suddenly abandoned Americans, angry and upset, quickly turned on their departing ally, almost as if they were still the same opponent they had faced during the French and Indian War. An incensed General Sullivan even charged d'Estaing with having deserted his revolutionary army and the American cause, while tarnishing his good name with cowardice.

For all his efforts on behalf of the fumbling amateur revolutionaries who believed that they knew better how to wage war than the European professionals, d'Estaing gained only a stained image in having attempted to assist America. In consequence, by the summer of 1779, he was eager to wipe the stain off his good name by achieving a victory in America when least expected by the British.

The chance to reverse the fortunes of war in America began with the vice admiral's arrival in the friendly waters of the West Indies early in 1779. Here, unlike in America, he enjoyed the luxury of utilizing the ever-cooperative colonial establishment and available manpower of the French islands, especially France's crown jewel of the Caribbean, Saint-Domingue. Almost immediately d'Estaing requested colonial troops to replace the approximately 1,500 men he had recently lost from the ravages of disease during the long Atlantic crossing, in preparation for his return to America for an ambitious new campaign to overturn the severe damage suffered by the fractured alliance, caused by the failed Rhode Island effort.

Vice Admiral d'Estaing was at the height of fame and power from his notable achievements in the Caribbean. Ironically, King Louis XVI considered d'Estaing's successes in the West Indies more important and valuable than whatever could have been won at Newport, because the sugar islands were worth much more than America.

In consequence, d'Estaing's forthcoming expedition in a surprising return to America contained the possibility of resurrecting the overall health and viability of the Franco-American alliance that was now hanging together by a thread—an all-important consideration, because America's future was at stake. Timing was crucial. Since d'Estaing had yet to achieve any significant results in America, the Franco-American alliance was now endangered as never before. D'Estaing realized that after the failed allied effort in Rhode Island, King Louis XVI now desired territorial gains of significance to be achieved in America to strengthen the nearly collapsed alliance, validate his vast expenditures on the war effort, and quell the rising tide of anti-French sentiment in America.

In accordance with the king's wishes, as with the Seven Years' War in Saint-Domingue during the previous generation, d'Estaing acted with confidence in preparing his next expedition to America. In conjunction with the governor of Saint-Domingue, Robert, Comte d'Argout, the vice admiral created a large militia force of Blacks and whites in separate, or segregated, military units to fulfill the requirements of the upcoming Savannah Campaign, including the Chasseurs-Volontaires de Saint-Domingue.

The vice admiral had already achieved glory in the most crucial theater for France and the king in this global conflict, which was the ongoing struggle for the lucrative sugar islands of the West Indies. At this time, Vice Admiral d'Estaing was widely recognized as a conquering hero across Saint-Domingue and France, and his name and lofty reputation alone had secured a good many new recruits for the Chasseurs. At the court of Versailles, all eyes were focused on the French West Indies, because it was the most lucrative theater of war and a central foundation of the French economy. The British had captured the Caribbean sugar island of St. Lucia, so when d'Estaing returned to the West Indies from Rhode Island in January 1779, he went on the offensive, in accordance with King Louis XVI's orders. Although d'Estaing failed to reclaim St. Lucia, he did capture the mountainous St. Vincent, a tropical volcanic island, from a small force of British defenders in June, and then continued his string of successes in the Caribbean.

In July of 1779, d'Estaing decided not to attack his intended target of the British sugar island of Barbados, the oldest and one of the most highly prized of British possessions in the Caribbean, because of contrary winds that disrupted his movements and plans. He continued on the offensive, much to his credit, capturing the rich sugar island of Grenada at the lower, or southern, end of the chain of islands known as the Lesser Antilles. Its isolated English garrison, numbering less than five hundred men, did not stand a chance.

Not long thereafter, the island of Dominica fell to the resurgent French, which meant that strategic Jamaica—England's crown jewel in the Caribbean, and largest sugar island—was now in danger. But the ever-unpredictable Vice Admiral d'Estaing would not be sailing for Jamaica with conquest in his eyes, as expected by the alarmed British. Instead, he would shortly be heading northwest, all the way to the

Georgia coast, and an obscure place that few Frenchmen had ever seen before or heard much about: the vital strategic port of Savannah, and the key to Georgia.[30]

FINAL PREPARATIONS FOR SAILING TO AMERICA

Vice Admiral d'Estaing had made thorough preparations for embarking upon his secret expedition to America during the spring and summer of 1779, including tapping into the manpower resources of the French colonies, especially Saint-Domingue. He even drew colonial soldiers, three full companies, from the French Caribbean islands of Guadeloupe, and two companies from Martinique. If not for the insatiable soaring ambitions of d'Estaing and his determination to compensate for the recent Rhode Island fiasco, the call would not have been made in Saint-Domingue to raise a new regiment of free Blacks and mulattoes for the Savannah expedition, the Chasseurs-Volontaires de Saint-Domingue, which had been created partly through the efforts of government officials and Captain Vincent Olivier.

Olivier, the aged Black Cartagena veteran and a legend in his own time, was known for his imposing size and fiery spirit. He had gained a reputation for having fought in the "German wars" after his first military experience at Cartagena, and was presented with a beautiful sword by the king of France, Louis XIV, for his heroics and service to France. This often-told heroic story filled the young men of the Chasseurs-Volontaires de Saint-Domingue with pride and a sense of awe. It was extremely rare for a Black man to receive such high honors, especially in Saint-Domingue, the most harsh and abusive slave regime in the Western Hemisphere. It was not lost on the young Chasseurs that Olivier had achieved the impossible: a former slave transcending color lines by what he had accomplished on his own, by having repeatedly demonstrated courage and loyalty to God and country on the battlefield. He had been presented to the king and had sat at the table of the white governor-general because he was held in such high esteem. A shining example and an inspiration to one and all, Captain Olivier was the most effective and valuable recruiting tool for the Chasseurs.

By the summer of 1779, Olivier had easily gathered a wide variety of Black and mulatto men of all orders and classes as volunteers for the daunting mission that lay ahead. Most of these young men hailed from the leading mulatto families of Saint-Domingue. They felt pride in themselves, their families, and their colony, which they represented with pride in their new uniforms of navy blue.

Vice Admiral d'Estaing's and the governor's call to arms had proved most effective during the spring and summer of 1779. Significantly, the colonial government and white planter and merchant elites, who had long discriminated against free Blacks and mulattoes, now needed a good many soldiers of mixed race to serve as privates and noncommissioned officers (corporals and sergeants), and they needed qualified white officers, including former militia company commanders, to lead them on the upcoming mission. The leading newspapers of Cap-Français, like the active white recruiters who scoured the streets of Le Cap and the surrounding countryside, especially in the Northern Province, played the patriotic card for all it was worth, calling for men of color to serve God and country. The tireless efforts of white recruiting officers paid nice dividends in Cap-Français and the rural countryside, and they easily secured hundreds of mixed-race fighting men and Blacks, unlike in the Southern Province.

Employing the typical rhetoric of patriotism during the Age of Enlightenment at a time when the people of Saint-Domingue saw themselves as citizens of both the nation of France and the colonial territory of Saint-Domingue, the recruiters in their resplendent uniforms repeatedly emphasized the importance of answering the call of French patriotism by appealing to "the zeal and the good will of [French] Citizens [of Saint-Domingue] of every condition. Good Frenchmen, without a doubt, will not need much encouragement to show their natural valor."[31]

These patriotic words of the recruiters and newspapermen of Le Cap proved as prophetic as they were effective. In total, 941 men of mostly mixed race from the Northern Province, but also Blacks and mulattoes (all free men), volunteered their services by joining the Chasseurs-Volontaires de Saint-Domingue with considerable enthusiasm. Patriotic spirit was strong and vibrant, especially during the spring of 1779. Like eager youths heading off to war since the dawn of time, the young sons of leading free Black and mulatto families in both provinces had stepped forward with enthusiasm for what they viewed as an exciting adventure, one they could not afford to miss.

Filling the ranks of ten companies of the Chasseurs-Volontaires de Saint-Domingue, these young men of varying shades were ready to fight for God and country as part of their patriotic duty to their beloved homeland. Many of these mulatto men were literate, especially the privileged sons of wealthy planters who had enjoyed fancy educations in the excellent schools in Paris. They had learned about the French writers and philosophers of the Age of Enlightenment and their glowing words about individual liberty, which sparked hope for a new day of freedom for the common man of all colors. In addition, these young volunteers had read the patriotic appeals in the newspapers, such as the following that appeared in a Le Cap newspaper in early 1779: "At this moment what Frenchmen does not experience a reawakening of his courage and ardor to [fight] against the enemies of the State?"[32]

Significantly, the heady calls to arms were rooted in the enlightened concept of appealing to the "citizens of every condition," which meant calling on all classes of the free Black and mulatto population, from wealthy planters to domestic servants working in Cap-Français. The heavy hand of existing French racism had failed to curb the enthusiasm of the Chasseurs, even the fact that only whites could serve as officers of the Black and mulatto troops. Blacks and mulattoes could only serve as noncommissioned officers, corporals, and sergeants, whose roles, in fact, were often more important than the most elitist and aristocratic white officers, especially when it came to hard fighting and the stern requirements of the battlefield, where experience, especially in the militia before the war, counted more than color and wealth.[33]

Like so many upper-class French officers, some literate and educated members of the Chasseurs, especially the mixed-race men who had been sent by their wealthy planter fathers to France to obtain educations in the finest schools, had been inspired by the words of the French Enlightenment thinkers, or the popular *philosophes*, who had boldly declared the natural equality of all men—the increasingly popular ideology that served as a theoretical genesis for both the American and French Revolutions. To the Chasseurs, it must have seemed that they had the chance to fulfill the moral promises, idealistic visions, and philosophical obligations of the core ideals of the Age of Enlightenment.[34]

The Chasseurs had been expressly created by d'Estaing for overseas service in America, and the organization was officially deemed a "special expeditionary corps" by the summer of 1779. In total, and exceeding the expectations of Saint-Domingue officials by approximately 40 percent, nearly 950 Blacks and mostly mulattoes from Cap-Français and primarily the Northern Province now filled the ranks of the Chasseurs (although other accounts have emphasized that more than one thousand volunteers had enlisted). By summer, the new volunteer unit of the Chasseurs was commanded by the aristocratic Major General François, Vicomte de Fontanges, one of the elites of France who had played a key role in the recruitment process. He now led both the white officers and the Black and mulatto soldiers, who were the vast majority of the Chasseurs. Fontanges was destined to serve with distinction at Savannah, where he would fall wounded in the nightmarish combat of October 9, 1779.

Fontanges now led two Saint-Domingue volunteer units, one white—the Volunteer Grenadiers—and the other, Black and mulatto, which was "far superior" to the much smaller white command, a fact that would be fully demonstrated during the course of the Savannah Campaign. The two segregated commands of Saint-Domingue volunteers were called the Fontanges Legion, in honor of their aristocratic commander.

Compared to the 941 mulattoes and Blacks who enlisted to serve in the Chasseurs, the white response to the patriotic call was truly pathetic by any measure, revealing a sharp and significant contrast with their darker-hued counterparts, who were more highly motivated and eager to serve in the ranks. Basically, whites of the upper class, unlike the upper class of the mixed-race free population of the colony, utterly rejected the patriotic appeal and call to arms when it came to active service, primarily because they viewed military service as beneath their dignity—the antithesis of the view of the Black and mulatto volunteers, who saw military service as a golden opportunity to excel and prove their worth to one and all.

Like savvy businessmen, which was often the case, the white upper-class elite of Saint-Domingue primarily expressed their patriotism in financial support and flowery words without risking their lives on the battlefield. However, with clear consciences, the older, wealthy white men of high social standing implored young Black and mulatto men to sacrifice their lives for the good of the colony and country. This was unlike the case of lower-class Blacks, who served in the Chasseurs, revealing their superior level of patriotism to the white population in general, especially the upper-class elites.

Nothing short of an embarrassment to the colony, only 156 whites enlisted and served in the ranks of the Volunteer Grenadiers, which consisted of only four companies. This was an extremely poor showing compared to the ten full companies of enthusiastic and committed Blacks and mulattoes of the Chasseurs-Volontaires de Saint-Domingue. Clearly, these men of a darker shade felt a sense of pride in serving in the Chasseurs, considering it a distinct honor and privilege, unlike whites, who viewed serving in their own separate all-white unit as a necessary evil, for a variety of personal reasons.

YOUTHFUL IMPATIENCE CAUSES PROBLEMS FOR THE CHASSEURS

However, not all was ideal in the ranks of the new Black and mulatto command of young volunteers. After spending weeks drilling and learning the ways of a soldier, serving their country began to lose some of its romantic appeal to these young men, who were away from home for the first time. Consequently, some of these recruits deserted during the summer of 1779, partly because of the inactivity and boredom of camp life. Encamped either in or near Cap-Français, some young men of the Chasseurs were tempted by the lures of the many beautiful and seductive women of all colors who filled the streets of the picturesque city on the wide bay of turquoise blue.

To some young men of the Chasseurs, the prospect of duty farther away from home than they had ever been in their lives was not appealing in the least. Relatively few of these soldiers had been at sea before, and if they were city boys, most were only familiar with the city of Le Cap. It is not known for a fact, but the distinct possibility exists that very few of the 545 men of the Chasseurs-Volontaires de Saint-Domingue would have ever boarded ships bound for faraway Savannah, Georgia, on the North American continent if they had known it would be their ultimate destination, so far from their families and home colony.

Even the popular Captain Jacques Mesnier, a wealthy white merchant (all officers of the Chasseurs were white) who led a leading mulatto company of Le Cap, became disillusioned during the boring summer of relative inactivity. Unexpectedly, the revered captain officially submitted his resignation from the Chasseurs. However, with convincing arguments, the governor eventually changed Mesnier's mind, which was important at this time, because his mulatto men "would have all deserted if he had not assured them that he would march with them" to war.[35]

The rash of desertions frustrated white officers and suddenly reduced the ranks of the Chasseurs in the summer of 1779. The need to gain additional new recruits caused the colonial government to take more drastic action to bolster the volunteer unit for the forthcoming expedition, whose destination was still a closely guarded secret that never leaked out of d'Estaing's headquarters, located at a stately mansion in Le Cap. The governor, Robert, Comte d'Argout, was forced to take stern and autocratic steps to ensure there were sufficient numbers of men serving in the Chasseurs' ranks. Consequently, with the stroke of a quill pen, he dissolved several free Black militia units in the Northern Province and near Cap-Français, whose shocked members were ordered to enlist in the Chasseurs within a week's time.

Those militiamen who failed to report within the allotted week faced stiff consequences, including permanent demotion, as threatened by the governor of Saint-Domingue. If the deadline was missed and two more weeks passed, then the free Blacks and mulattoes of the disbanded militia units would be sentenced to serve for a period of three months in the rural police, or constabulary, which was the harshest and lowest form of militia duty, and included the dangerous service of attempting to subdue maroons, escaped slaves who fought with fanatical desperation in the thick tropical rainforests of the most remote mountains.

Evidently these harsh consequences—tough coercive actions from the government that mocked the concept of patriotism and the new unit's proud designation as "Volontaires"—were nothing less than an example of official government "bullying" of free Blacks and mulattoes to fill the ranks of the new command that had been created by the governor and d'Estaing. This was a dismal reality, in striking contrast to the idealistic patriotic and nationalist portrayals of many nationalist Haitian historians, who have long viewed the Chasseurs as patriotic liberators and freedom fighters for America. The actual situation of the command was far less simplistic than has been generally recognized or acknowledged by generations of historians.[36] Clearly, some of the basic and fundamental facts about the Chasseurs have thoroughly overturned the popular myths and legends long put forth by the nationalist writers of Haiti that have overly glorified these Black and mulatto soldiers in the romantic tradition. Regardless of exact motivations, these men were destined to rise to the challenge in splendid fashion at Savannah on October 9, 1779.

A Unique Black and Mulatto Soldiery

Who were the men who served in the Chasseurs-Volontaires de Saint-Domingue, especially those non-white soldiers of the noncommissioned officers' ranks? One capable and experienced noncommissioned officer, Sergeant Pierre Augustin, was one of these forgotten members of the Chasseurs. He represented a distinct minority in the ranks as a Black man, because the unit was primarily composed of mulatto soldiers who were proud of their mixed-race heritage and their status in Saint-Domingue society as free men of color. Augustin was a mature man, in keeping with his elevated rank in the Chasseurs, the highest that could be achieved by a Black soldier in Saint-Domingue because of racist laws and outright discrimination. A resident of bustling Cap-Français, Augustin was married to Marie Janvier Augustin, nee Benjamin, who was of mixed-race, evidently fathered by a Jewish resident, as revealed by her last name. Augustin's background was one of stability and prosperity in keeping with his high status in Saint-Domingue society.

Augustin provides an excellent example of the extent of the mobility in Saint-Domingue for members of the free Black society, which offered opportunities to rise ever higher with an application of hard work, intelligence, and initiative—a striking paradox for industrious and enterprising individuals of color in the midst of the largest and most oppressive slave society in the New World. Augustin had been brought to the colony as a slave, and what he achieved in life was nothing short of remarkable, in the tradition of the legendary Captain Vincent Olivier. It is not known if he was taken from Africa or another sugar island in the West Indies, like Henri Christophe, when Augustin was forced to begin a new life of servitude in Saint-Domingue.

Like Olivier, and by any measure, Augustin was very fortunate. Usually, a pure-blooded African in Saint-Domingue faced a harsh life of misery in the seemingly endless sugarcane fields, one entirely without hope. Somehow, Augustin benefited from a key break that would change his life forever. At some point, he was freed by his master, who had prepared him well for an independent life. To supplement the master's income, Augustin had learned the trade of wig-making, a skilled occupation; his products were worn by both whites and people of color, whose higher-class members dressed like whites. His skill and the high quality of his work guaranteed his success, as wig-makers were in great demand in Saint-Domingue society.

In fact, like quite a few skilled and hardworking slaves in Saint-Domingue, Augustin might have earned enough income to purchase his freedom by paying off his total financial value to his master, or he might have benefited from an enlightened master who freed him for humanitarian reasons, a relatively rare development when the owner was not the father of such a fortunate slave. Almost certainly, Augustin was highly personable, and the friendship between master and slave must have been genuine in consequence, which perhaps also contributed to his good luck in life, especially in eventually gaining his freedom.

Augustin married a free Black woman with some assets, which additionally assisted his rise up the ladder in free Black society, thanks in part to landowning, but also due to his faithful military service, including at Savannah in 1779, as a well-qualified and skilled noncommissioned officer. He became an esteemed member of the military leadership class. His story is one of a dramatic rise, from the lowest order of an African-born slave, to a high standing in the free Black class—an amazing feat that was accomplished by other enterprising Blacks, because of the ample opportunities presented to people of color in Saint-Domingue.

This was the kind of dramatic rise of fortunes in free Black society that was hoped for and believed possible by so many young optimistic Chasseurs during the initial excess of patriotic optimism, when the excitement of enlisting and serving in this new unit was at a high during the summer of 1799. In this way, the enterprising Augustin followed in the footsteps of Captain Vincent Olivier, who had played such a key role in the recruitment of the young men of the Chasseurs-Volontaires de Saint-Domingue.[37]

"Many of [these Chasseurs] were socially prominent" in the insular free Black and mulatto world of Saint-Domingue by virtue of having become successful as landowners and planters, especially in the south, where they owned most of the land and dominated coffee production on the gently sloping hillsides of the mountains. As a result, these soldiers of a darker shade believed they were equal to whites and fully deserving of equal rights because of what they had accomplished in life, as they were about to demonstrate to one and all by their upcoming service in America.[38]

In fact, the majority of volunteers in the Chasseurs were men of property, consisting of many "landowners who had abandoned their fortunes in order to serve the King,"[39] although the finely uniformed ranks of the Chasseurs were composed of both the lower and upper crust of free Black and mulatto society, and also included slaves who hoped to win their freedom by demonstrating their worth and courage on the battlefield, which made them distinctly eager to confront the hated British and any enemies of their beloved homeland.[40]

However, not even the bonds of a revolutionary brotherhood or the fact that they hailed from the same Caribbean colony were sufficient factors to close the wide gap that existed between low-born Blacks and the mulattoes of a higher class—a tragic and fatal divide that has played such a large role in the course of Haitian history. This wide historic divide defines Haiti to this day, and also largely explains how the world's first Black republic has failed miserably as a modern nation-state. This most bitter of divisions was based on race from the beginning, creating a people and a society basically at war with itself because of the seemingly endless friction and antagonism between Blacks and mulattoes.

As early established in the colony, the official racial order of Saint-Domingue society was divided into thirteen subgroupings. It was incredibly strict, and based upon varying shades of black and brown, to an obsessive degree. An individual's standing was solely based on color, and this defined the colony's social order and internal dynamics. Because the men of the Chasseurs-Volontaires de Saint-Domingue left behind no letters, accounts, or memoirs that have been found to his day, the amount of rivalry and animosity that existed between Blacks and mulattoes within the volunteer command can only be left to speculation. Despite its severity, however, this prominent historic divide in Saint-Domingue society was not enough to stop the Chasseurs from rising splendidly to the challenge to save the day at Savannah on October 9, 1779, partly because of this newfound unity between Blacks and mulattoes.[41]

This burning desire of the mulattoes (Creoles) born in Saint-Domingue to obtain equality with whites was in keeping with the fact that this "new and exciting race" possessed sterling qualities, physical, intellectual, and with a distinct business-wise sense that had allowed them to succeed in society. With the same passion they felt for their Catholic faith, the Creoles embraced a sense of Saint-Domingue nationalism and distinctive ethnic pride, along with a measure of French nationalism; it is not known which was actually the most prevalent and pronounced, because of the lack of written records from the Chasseurs. In general, these were the distinctive superior qualities and traits of the mulatto class, including even a more pronounced, in general, physical beauty and more muscular physicality, derived from their often relatively "plain" Black and white parents, who were generally undistinguished by beauty or physicality compared to their offspring.[42]

Although it was an ad hoc military unit that had been hastily formed for Vice Admiral d'Estaing's Savannah expedition, and most important, the Chasseurs-Volontaires de Saint-Domingue was no rookie command that now consisted of mostly mulattoes, members of a "new and exciting race that [united] the best of both worlds." In some significant ways, this unique volunteer command already possessed the qualities of a seasoned military unit, entirely un-militia-like in the traditional sense like a conventional new command, because of the overall high quality of its experienced members, especially among the noncommissioned officers. This was thanks to the long-standing Saint-Domingue military tradition, and the existence of experienced members of both the officer corps and the noncommissioned officer corps. The new unit included many highly capable members of this military leadership group, long positioned at the top of free Black society, along with elevated individuals of the planter elite, both white and free Black.

This new and distinctive ethnocultural group known as the Creoles, who had been born in Saint-Domingue, were highly motivated because they were determined to demonstrate their equality to the arrogant, haughty "blan," or whites, especially the wealthy elites in power. These young men of a darker hue desired to prove that they were deserving of full equality in society by their own behavior and actions, especially on the battlefield, and preferably in a crisis situation, which would certainly be the case on October 9, 1779. Many of these men, both officers and noncommissioned officers, but especially the latter group, like Sergeant Pierre Augustin, benefited from plenty of militia experience that would serve them extremely well in the days ahead—one of the reasons for the outstanding success of the Chasseurs at Savannah during a true crisis situation, when the lives of so many American and French soldiers were at stake, after they had been repulsed from the attack on the Spring Hill Redoubt.[43]

The following members of the Chasseurs all possessed militia experience in the defense of their colony, which proved invaluable during the bloody showdown at Savannah: Pierre Augustin, Alloun, Mathieu Blaise, Jean-Louis Cassagne, Jean-Francis Edouard L'Eveille, Jean-Baptiste Lagarde, Jean-Baptise L'Eveille Riche, and a good many others who were eventually bound for Savannah and an extremely notable battlefield achievement on October 9, 1779.[44]

Six of the white captains who led their companies—the command contained ten companies in total—of the Chasseurs possessed extensive militia experience dating back to 1769. The overall experience of this veteran officer corps was invaluable on every level in the days ahead, especially for those new recruits who possessed no prior military experience. For instance, Captain Charles Dupetithouars, who had married into a planter family of the elite, had long led the free Black militia of his parish. The white captain shared close comradeship with the Blacks and mulattoes of his command.

From the beginning, white officers had been vital to the formation of the Chasseurs. A white Frenchman like Dupetithouars, and over the age of sixty, Captain Jacques Mesnier had early on secured the most recruits for the unit, a total of thirty-two, on the day after the first news of the official formation of the Chasseurs was released. A wealthy merchant of the port of Cap-Français, Mesnier possessed a number of distinct leadership advantages because he had been the captain of the free Black militia of the "Pearl of the Antilles." It was easy for Mesnier to recruit in part because he had freely spent a large amount of money to secure the best equipment and arms for those who did not possess their own weapons. He was an excellent leader and gained the respect and admiration of his mostly mixed-race soldiers, who were ready to follow him to hell and back if necessary, including all the way to Savannah.[45]

As mentioned, and most important, this invaluable militia experience was destined to serve the Chasseurs-Volontaires de Saint-Domingue extremely well in the upcoming ultimate crisis situation at Savannah. The white upper-class officers of the Chasseurs were well-known former militia officers with considerable experience, and their companies included many former members of the militia, from their own parish—hopeful young men who wanted to validate their claim to full French citizenship and equal rights as French citizens of the monarch of King Louis XVI, while also eagerly representing their parish, colony, and Catholic faith.

ANSWERING DESPERATE APPEALS FROM AMERICA

By the summer of 1779, General George Washington had learned that Vice Admiral d'Estaing would be returning to America for the second time, but this time from the warm waters of the West Indies instead of France. The austere Virginian from his vast plantation known as Mount Vernon, which was worked by large numbers of slaves in the tidewater, awaited the opening of a second front by his French allies, upon which so much of America's future and very existence now depended. The commander in chief, who possessed meager French and Indian War experience, fully realized by this time that America would never gain its independence by force of arms on its own.

However, before d'Estaing was able to return to America after his humiliating failure at Newport, responsibilities and opportunities in the Caribbean beckoned. He first had to fulfill the king's desire for conquest of British possessions in the West Indies, including attempts to recover lost territory, like St. Lucia, in the ongoing struggle for possession of the rich sugar islands that were strewn like golden pearls across a turquoise sea. D'Estaing's capture of St. Vincent, Grenada, and the Grenadines, a tiny strand of islands nestled between the two former islands, freed him for his next adventure in America. After the completion of his conquests in the West Indies, the vice admiral was free to answer the urgent calls for assistance from South Carolina's governor James Wright; Major General Benjamin Lincoln, who commanded American forces in the South, now headquartered at Charlestown; and high-ranking French officials in Charlestown.[46]

These frantic appeals for help from the United States were fully embraced by d'Estaing, who fondly envisioned how a great victory on American soil would wipe away the bitterness that existed between the allies and the stain of his failure in Rhode Island. D'Estaing felt sure that with the assistance of Lincoln's forces, combined with a fresh French expedition force and fleet from the West Indies, not only Charlestown but also South Carolina and Georgia could be saved from the British invaders, who now dreamed of the conquest of the entire South after having captured the strategic port of Savannah in late December 1778—an ambitious and bold plan to reverse the entire course of the American Revolution in dramatic fashion.[47]

The French Allies, America's Gallic Saviors

The Chasseurs-Volontaires de Saint-Domingue would never have served at Savannah or anywhere else in America during the course of the American Revolution if not for what happened at Saratoga, in upper New York, in October 1777. In fact, there would be no United States of America today without the bountiful amount of resources, supplies, and manpower of France, which poured into America primarily because of the surprising Saratoga victory, continuing the coveted aid previously forthcoming to the rebels. Quite simply, in the end, King Louis XVI and France were destined to save the infant republic from an early death when the Bourbon monarch decided to support America and its independence on February 6, 1778.

However, contrary to romantic myth, the French did not decide to form an alliance with the American rebels primarily for enlightened and ideological reasons, rooted in the idealistic concepts of freedom for all men, as revealed in the words of the Declaration of Independence; rather, it was for a variety of practical considerations and geopolitical and strategic realities of a pragmatic nature. In addition, hatred of the British was a primary consideration for the establishment of the Franco-American alliance that stemmed from the hostility and long-standing rivalry, including religious, that existed between the two major powers in Europe.

In fact, the French tended to view the American Revolution in broad historical terms as the "Second Hundred Years' War," because England had been an ancient enemy for centuries. The most forgotten reason for the forming of the most crucial alliance in American history was the French desire to save its precious Caribbean jewel of Saint-Domingue, which had to be protected at all costs for economic and strategic reasons. Consequently, the obligations of the alliance obliged America to help protect Saint-Domingue and France's other valuable sugar islands, if they were threatened, revealing the supreme importance of the sugar islands.

The stunning strategic victory at Saratoga was like no other event during the war. It was won by England-born general Horatio Gates over the British, Hessian, and Loyalist forces of "Gentleman Johnny" Burgoyne, who had advanced too far south through the wilderness from Canada for the fulfilling of the overly ambitious plan of attempting to link with the forces of General William Howe at Albany, New York. But in a classic march of folly, Howe never arrived, and Burgoyne, who refused to sensibly withdraw and return north when it would have been extremely prudent to do so, was then forced to surrender around six thousand men at Saratoga, to dramatically change the course of the American Revolution in profound ways—a turning point of the war.

First and foremost, the most significant rebel victory of the war before Yorktown—which thwarted the ambitious British Campaign of 1777 that had been calculated to end it all and conquer America—had sent shock waves that reverberated across Europe, especially in London, but also in Paris, for entirely different reasons. The British realized that this increasingly bitter struggle to regain its American colonies would be far more lengthy and costly than originally imagined. Amid the luxury and splendor of his palace at Versailles, King Louis XVI had awaited just such a golden opportunity to officially join the Americans' struggle for liberty, to exact revenge for the loss of New France (Canada) and other key possessions, including in the Caribbean, won by Great Britain during the Seven Years' War.

Except for the key Mississippi River port of New Orleans, and Louisiana, the French had lost North America in that global conflict, which left a deep psychological scar on the French psyche, which thereafter longed for revenge. Like the French people in general who supported the faraway war in the name of national honor, and to avenge the grievous losses and humiliations of the Seven Years' War, King Louis XVI was determined to decisively change the strategic equation and world balance of power by coming to the aid of the American rebels with massive support, to exploit the vulnerabilities of an old enemy.

With a keen eye toward securing the lucrative British possessions in the West Indies, he knew that direct intervention in America's war would cause considerable damage to the reeling British economy, which was gradually being drained by the long war of attrition in America, while discontent was growing to new highs at home. In addition, King Louis XVI forged his crucial alliance with America because he also feared that the thirteen colonies might reconcile with the mother country, which would come as a severe blow to French interests, especially commercial and economic.

As destiny would have it, the French and Americans were natural allies of convenience against a common foe, on multiple levels. However, a good many deep-seated prejudices, stemming from the searing experiences of the French and Indian War, when New England's settlements had been so often struck by Native American and French raiding parties with devastating results, still existed across America. In consequence, from the beginning the alliance ran into an almost endless series of problems and difficulties, in large part because England and France had been ancient enemies for centuries, and the American people, like the British, were primarily Protestant, while the French were Catholics, during this extremely religious age when faith was far more important in people's daily lives than it is today.

French intervention was not only of extreme importance in the overall final outcome of the American Revolution, but also the most decisive element in the overall equation that separated winner from loser, as events subsequently demonstrated in full. In the representative view of French strategists in Paris and Versailles, the court of King Louis XVI, and even the opinions of top American military men, it became increasingly clear that the Americans "[wouldn't] be able to hold [the colonies that were now states] without a nation that protects them by sea."[1] This was demonstrated in convincing fashion throughout the course of the 1776 New York Campaign, when a befuddled General George Washington had barely managed to survive with his inexperienced army of amateurs.

The weak French navy, which had proved no match for the British navy, had been a primary reason for their defeat in the Seven Years' War, and had led to the recent strengthening of the French navy to more realistically be able to contest England's superiority at sea, especially in North America's waters, that had long gone unchallenged. Thanks to key French bases on its Caribbean sugar islands, especially its colony of

Saint-Domingue, and primarily at Le Cap, the French were in an ideal position to dispute Great Britain's mastery of North America's waters and to provide invaluable assistance to American forces, which were badly in need of everything imaginable, except raw courage. The French were well within striking distance to challenge Great Britain's domination of the seas, thanks to France's excellent naval bases in the magnificent harbors of the Caribbean.[2]

VAST SUGAR RICHES IN THE CARIBBEAN

This most crucial and timely alliance in American history had significantly changed the war into a vast global conflict, when France took the bold step of recognizing the independence of the United States as the first nation to do so, supporting its desperate life-or-death bid to shake off the grip of the mother country.

All of a sudden, with the signing of the Franco-American alliance, England's valuable sugar islands in the West Indies became an even more important area of operations, because they were far more profitable than all of their other possessions on the North American continent. Because the powerful French navy could now openly challenge the Royal Navy, the Caribbean islands became primary bones of contention in the endless rivalry between the two ancient enemies, one Protestant and one Catholic, for global supremacy in a conflict now waged around the world to determine imperial destinies.

America's economy had also centered on the ever-lucrative market of the sugar islands of the West Indies, long before the American Revolution, and the flow of commerce had been brisk and highly profitable for decades. But the French islands were now more important to American merchants because British ports, like Kingston, Jamaica, were closed to the rebels. Consequently, French ports in the West Indies picked up the considerable slack, while becoming the most important source of supplies and munitions sent from France to the American revolutionaries during the lengthy struggle to preserve the life of their infant republic.

Because of the new focus of British strategists on the West Indies and the struggle over possession of the sugar islands, as part of the great international rivalry between European powers, Philadelphia was evacuated by General Henry Clinton during the summer of 1778. This urgent strategic move was done in part to redeploy British troops to the Caribbean to protect the valuable sugar islands and strengthen the garrison of New York City, which served as British headquarters, and the primary anchor of the war effort orchestrated from London. In addition, the British capture of America's capital in September 1777 had accomplished nothing in regard to winning the war.

Earlier in the year, British strategists and King George III had even contemplated abandoning the frustrating and costly war in America to subjugate the resilient insurrectionists, especially now that the conflict had evolved into an extremely demanding global war with France's sudden official entry, increasing the need to protect the rich sugar islands at all costs. The South had suddenly become more important to London, because the major Southern ports, especially Savannah and Charlestown, could serve as key staging areas for future campaigning in the West Indies, where French sugar islands beckoned to British expeditionary forces like a siren's song.[3]

Fortunately for America, Vice Admiral d'Estaing had been extremely receptive to the appeals from not only George Washington, but also South Carolina governor John Rutledge and others, to sail from the French West Indies to come directly to America's aid in the crucial Southern Theater with a sizable expeditionary force. The ambitious French aristocrat now possessed a golden opportunity to stop the fulfillment of Great Britain's ambitious "Southern Strategy," which hinged on retaining the strategic port of Savannah, which had been captured in December of 1778, before conducting future operations, especially in regard to capturing the vital port of Charlestown, to the north.[4]

D'Estaing was eager to sail for the Southern coast of America because he felt "morally obliged to do so," in part because of the humiliating Rhode Island fiasco, but also because he sensed a great opportunity to reap the success he had not obtained at Newport.[5] By the summer of 1779, he badly desired to win laurels, and the best place to do so, it seemed, was in America. General Washington wrote a letter to Conrad-Alexandre Gerard, France's top diplomat in America, which was duly forwarded to d'Estaing, presenting the sweetest of possibilities for achieving glory in Georgia, especially at Savannah: "There is every reason to believe" that the golden opportunity existed to "capture & destroy the enemy's fleet & Army."[6]

After having secured the newly formed colonial militia units, including the Chasseurs-Volontaires de Saint-Domingue, from the West Indies, the opportunistic Vice Admiral d'Estaing now looked to gain the assistance of another group of colonial troops, the Americans, for his next adventure in America, as if the Newport fiasco and his fractured relationship with General Sullivan had never happened. Eager for action, the vice admiral dispatched an envoy directly to Major General Benjamin Lincoln and promised a joint offensive effort against the troublesome General Augustine Prévost at Savannah. Of course, Lincoln readily accepted the invitation, which seemed too good to be true—a golden opportunity to reverse the entire course of the war after the British capture of Savannah in late 1778.[7]

THE SOUTH'S LUCRATIVE PORT OF SAVANNAH

Of all the thirteen colonies on the eve of the American Revolution, the Colony of Georgia, named for King George II, who had given his blessing to the ambitious colonization project, possessed the distinction of having been the most recently settled, in February 1733. It was positioned the farthest south, and was also the most Loyalist during the American Revolution. Parliament had long toyed with the idea of establishing a buffer for South Carolina to the north, from the ominous threat of Spanish Florida, especially St. Augustine to the south, by establishing a new colony on the rich lands vacated by Native Americans, whose power had been broken after the South Carolinians won the Yamasee War of 1715–1717.

The little colony of Georgia was established by Englishman James Oglethorpe, a former member of the English Parliament and an enterprising aristocrat of the upper-class elite. To a group of savvy English investors, he had enthusiastically promoted the idea of a new colony in the wilderness that the Yamasee had once called home, barely four decades before the beginning of the American Revolution. The site of Savannah was ideal for a new city in the New World, the capital of

Georgia, and a future world port of considerable significance by the nineteenth century.

Long before Oglethorpe's arrival would change this remote place forever, this fertile and picturesque area had been inhabited by Native Americans called Yamacraw. This excellent site for a new city was chosen by Oglethorpe because it was situated atop a forty-foot-high sandy bluff located on the south bank of the Savannah River. Well designed and laid out in two dozen wards by its meticulous founder, the town on its high perch overlooked the wide, slow-moving watercourse about eighteen miles before it entered the Atlantic, to the southeast.

One of the South's great cities was founded methodically and systematically, without fanfare, in what would become the last—and the poorest—of England's colonies situated along the Atlantic coast. Thanks to Oglethorpe's foresight, the new city was laid out in specific geometric squares with utopian zeal and considerable enthusiasm. Savannah earned the distinction of having been America's first planned and organized city, with broad streets, plazas, squares, and a checkerboard symmetry not seen anywhere else in America on such a grand scale.

The city was centered on Bull Street, named after Oglethorpe's friend, William Bull, who was South Carolina's governor. The dusty street would run through the center of the frontier community like Broadway in New York City, amid a seemingly endless sea of surrounding pine forests, which were as vast as the Atlantic. Never touched by an ax, this great expanse of virgin timber represented an omnipresent threat as a potential place from which raiding parties of Native Americans and the Spanish could attack with stealth. Beyond the frontier town on the commanding bluff that towered above the Savannah's dark waters, the rich bottomlands along the river and on the coastal plain were soon covered in broad rice fields that spanned as far as the eye could see—the natural resources that made the city prosperous and fueled commercial trade and its growth into a mighty world port.

English entrepreneurs and capitalists had early envisioned a new colony, based on the thriving port of Savannah, where England's poor would develop this rich land and transport its natural products to London to reap a fortune for its savvy investors. A dreamer as well as a doer in a rare combination, Oglethorpe was convinced that "England will grow Rich by sending her Poor Aboard." Most important in overall strategic terms, and to the great relief of South Carolina, and especially Charlestown, Georgia would serve as a buffer colony to protect South Carolinians to the north just across the Savannah River, while blocking the Protestant-hating Spanish—who had centered the power of their Catholic colony in their powerful masonry fort, the stately Castillo de San Marcos, at St. Augustine in northeast Florida, on the Atlantic—from surging north up the Atlantic coast. The strategic genesis for Georgia's birth was partly about the safety of South Carolina and the key port of Charlestown.[8]

The last established of the thirteen colonies, by the time of the American Revolution Georgia was still very much a frontier state, with a population of only around thirty thousand people in a sprawling land mostly covered in dense pine forests. Although constructed on what one observer described as nothing but "a sand heap," Savannah was distinguished by "its graceful name" and a sense of pride. The largest city in the state with around three thousand residents, Savannah served as the capital and mercantile center of Georgia. Surrounding plantations, especially those located in the broad coastal lowlands devoted to rice cultivation, and little towns, like Ebenezer on the Savannah River north of Savannah, all sent their products to the river port for shipment to various corners of the world.

Augusta, located 120 miles north up the Savannah River, Georgia's main artery, was nothing more than a remote frontier village at this time, with trading ties to the Cherokee and Creek people, while Savannah and the coastal economy were dominated by vast rice plantations and large numbers of slaves who worked the land from sunup to sundown. Like the seaport of Sunbury, located on a commanding bluff southwest of Savannah on the Medway River, the town of Ebenezer situated just north of Savannah and on the river of the same name was also strategic, having been settled by mostly German but also Scottish immigrants in a raw and untamed area dominated by a variety of industrious ethnic groups.

For the people of Georgia, the Savannah was a river of destiny that flowed southeast into the Atlantic, becoming one of the South's most strategic waterways and the life-support system of the entire region. As fate would have it, Savannah was initially a largely Celtic community, partly because Oglethorpe had envisioned it as a colony and a haven for England's poor and foreign Protestants, as a safe place of refuge. The first settlers of Savannah were mostly lowland Scots who were proud of their Celtic heritage and culture, demonstrated in the distinctive Scottish bonnets they wore, with the colors and designs of their clans, as if still back in their ancient homeland with its troubled history of British rule and domination.

The aristocratic elites, including the Trustees in England, shortly discovered that the Celts, who were known for their outrageously independent and rebellious spirits, were an unceasing headache to all figures of authority. Outraged leaders thoroughly denounced the outspoken and rowdy Scots as nothing more than "Riff Raff" and "Malcontents." Less troublesome than their lowland cousins but armed with Scottish broadswords and a distinctive independent-mindedness, nearly two hundred Highland Scots, who spoke Gaelic and wore their traditional Scottish tartan, poured into Savannah in 1735, and then settled the town of New Inverness, south of Savannah, and later renamed Darien, Georgia.[9] This town was named after the Scottish Highlands town of Inverness, a Gaelic name that meant "situated at the mouth of the River Ness," located on Scotland's northeast coast.

During the early years after the Crown took over the colony in 1753, shocked righteous men from England saw Savannah as a sinful "Sodom-like" city, like most port and frontier towns, and not unlike Le Cap in Saint-Domingue. Savannah was the cultural, intellectual, and social center of Georgia, like the bustling port of Charlestown, South Carolina.

Growing pains for Georgia could hardly have been more difficult. It earned the well-deserved reputation as England's poorest colony in North America decade after decade, before the American Revolution's outbreak, and Savannah did not hold much promise well into the 1770s. By the time of the American Revolution, Savannah was known as a "sickly hole in the wilderness." It was common at the time for unfortunates with few possessions to be described as "poor as a Georgian," especially the lowly mostly Scotch-Irish Presbyterians, or the "crackers" of the backcountry, dominated by immense pine forests that seemed to have no end. For generations, a good many struggling immigrants from Western Europe discovered that Georgia was in fact "a very bad corner of the world."[10]

By the time of the siege and Battle of Savannah in October 1779, the town possessed only 750 white residents, most of whom were Loyalists or neutrals, and many more slaves who had fled to the safety of the port town from the surrounding countryside with the British conquest of Georgia, or who had escaped from patriot slave owners in South Carolina. During the British occupation, Savannah served as one of the most important Loyalist centers in the South, having drawn British supporters from the rural countryside from many miles around.[11] A disillusioned German Hessian, who served against the American revolutionaries for the coveted right to take the king's shilling, like so many of his Teutonic countrymen, was not in the least impressed by Savannah. In some astonishment, he wrote how the wide streets of the port city "have white sand so deep that it was just like walking through fresh fallen snow a foot deep . . . A man runs no small risk of being chocked [sic] by the clouds of sand and dusts."[12]

But a visiting Englishman, who was reminded of home far away, was more complimentary than the caustic German about what he saw in Savannah, and even felt a measure of enchantment for the place. He wrote how the river city perched atop the "great sand bluff" occupied a picturesque setting in a pristine land of plenty. He felt it had much future potential if adequately developed by a great amount of slave labor, essential to taming this raw land: "Let the English reader picture to himself a town erected on the [white] cliffs of Dover and he will behold Savannah."[13]

SLAVERY'S SURREAL HORRORS IN THE SPRAWLING RICE FIELDS

Although still a remote frontier region and the southernmost English colony in America, Georgia prospered greatly as a land of slavery primarily because of a lucrative cash crop, also the main staple of the Colony of South Carolina: rice. Savannah had been made prosperous by rich planters who always wanted to gain more land and slaves, always the key to fabulous wealth, as well as by merchants and heartless slave traders. This human tragedy for people of African descent was certainly not a feature in the beginning of Georgia's settlement, although some of the first buildings in Savannah were partly constructed by around twenty slaves from South Carolina, located just across the Savannah River, to the north.

Ironically, in the beginning, in true utopian fashion, the English Trustees of the Colony of Georgia had righteously banned slavery in an excess of idealism and well-placed humanitarianism that was not suited for the extensive demands of economic development in a wilderness land that required immense quantities of human labor. As in the case of South Carolina, they feared that slaves would be encouraged to rise up in revolt and run away south to the safe confines of St. Augustine, where the Spanish bestowed free status to escaped slaves and wisely formed them into excellent militia units to safeguard Catholic Florida from the heathen Protestants—a situation that had long presented a direct threat to South Carolina.

In consequence, large numbers of indentured white servants from Germany, Ireland, England, Wales, and Scotland first served as laborers in the dreary fields of this new agricultural colony at the southernmost point of the thirteen colonies. Indeed, this was the first organized system of labor in Georgia, partly because of the fear of slave revolts like those in South Carolina to the north and the presence of Catholic St. Augustine to the south. The Germans proved especially industrious, establishing the outlying town of Ebenezer on the Savannah River, north of Savannah. Liberal Spanish policies, like offering Blacks freedom for serving the Spanish Crown, had long served as a magnet for South Carolina's runaway slaves, posing a threat if slavery were to thrive in Georgia, for which it was ideally suited, especially along its fertile coastal plain that was a natural environment for rice cultivation.

But this shortsighted plan of employing indentured servants in Georgia and not Black slaves only lasted from 1733 to 1755, before large numbers of Africans were finally imported because of the great challenge of transforming the vast Georgia wilderness into a productive colony, ideal for rice cultivation. (West African peoples from the lowlands of their native land also possessed expert knowledge and technical expertise in rice cultivation, including irrigation systems, and they were eagerly sought by white planters.)

After the Trustees' ill-advised (in economic terms) ban on slavery ended when Georgia became a Crown colony in 1753, the number of slaves skyrocketed to become nearly one-third of the population in that same year, long before cotton would become king across the South during the nineteenth century. The number of Blacks toiling in the seemingly endless rice fields of the Georgia coastal plain increased to 3,500 by 1760.[14] Even Georgia's royal governor, James Wright, possessed nearly a dozen lucrative plantations situated along the fertile coast in the Savannah area, and more than 500 slaves worked his rich lands that were highly productive, earning him great wealth and prestige as one of Georgia's leading planters.[15]

Like New England's major port of Boston more than one thousand miles northeast up the Atlantic coast, Savannah became a revolutionary city with a rise in patriotism. This happened despite its sizable Loyalist population, which divided families across the country in what was America's first civil war as much as a revolutionary movement for nationhood. This civil war was especially pronounced and bitter in the South.

The first Liberty Pole was erected in Savannah in June 1775, when the spirit of patriotism reached a fever pitch. The popularity of independence was best represented by the Sons of Liberty, who regularly met at the popular Tondee's Tavern, where South Carolina's Second Provincial Congress was held in 1775, not far from the city's Liberty Pole, which boldly proclaimed the independence of a new man in the New World, the American patriot. All Loyalists were expelled from Georgia in late 1777 in a great patriot purging of America's internal enemies, with a harshness that revealed the unchecked passions and hatreds of an embittered, divided people, torn apart by the Revolution.

Complicating Georgia's overall situation since the end of the French and Indian War in 1763 was nearby Catholic Florida, to the south. St. Augustine was the most vital port located on the Atlantic coast south of Savannah, and served as the center of the royal colony. It presented an omnipresent threat to Georgia's patriots because the British navy controlled the Atlantic coast, since the upstart American revolutionaries possessed no navy at the beginning of the American Revolution.

The Loyalists of Georgia should have expected the worst because of their faithfulness to the Crown, and the aggressiveness of the patriots. To demonstrate early support for the British-closed port of Boston, and long before the emergence of the bitter divide between North and South in the 1860s, Savannah patriots had sent tons of rice to their fellow patriots to the north and up the Atlantic coast, in an impressive display of American unity that was entirely unfathomable to King George III and his out-of-touch ministers in London.[16]

GREAT BRITAIN'S DESPERATE LAST GAMBLE: THE AMBITIOUS SOUTHERN STRATEGY

The year 1778 was one of the forgotten turning points of the American Revolution, when the nature and course of the war began to change forever. The top British strategists and King George III in London faced one of the most daunting of strategic dilemmas that had dogged armies of great powers since ancient times: How can an efficient and well-trained professional military force of a great empire defeat irregular forces of indigenous peoples in expansive foreign lands far from home, especially in an unpopular war when recruitment is increasingly difficult in the homeland during a lengthy war of attrition?

At nearly the midway point of the American Revolution, in late 1778, Great Britain was shackled with this vexing problem. After having been unable to achieve decisive victory in the northern and middle colonies of America—largely because General George Washington, to his credit, had wisely decided against engaging in a major confrontation with a superior war machine led by experienced professional commanders and better-trained fighting men—what was the next best British plan for the conquest of America? In addition, Great Britain also faced political and domestic problems at home for the constitutional monarchy, especially in regard to the growing unpopularity of this long war. Britons had fully expected a swift, easy victory, and they were expressing a growing desire for peace with America, especially those citizens who had originally been against waging war in the first place. There was also a rise of political opposition to the uncompromising hard-line policies of the single-minded King George III. From the beginning, he had been the most obstinate and stubborn of kings, who wanted to crush rebel resistance in America without mercy and regain possession of its thirteen wayward colonies at almost any cost.

The entire British plan of conquest had been compromised by General Washington, who had grown as a savvy commander by this time. He had found success by thinking more like a guerrilla commander, as revealed in his lightning-strike victories at Trenton and Princeton in the winter of 1776–1777, where he waged an irregular brand of warfare rather than foolishly attempting to fight like a traditional British commander, as he had done during his disastrous New York Campaign of 1776. He had learned some hard lessons early in the war that had included disasters like the loss of New York City in 1776, and Philadelphia, America's capital, in the following year. Consequently, he had learned to avoid direct confrontations with the vastly superior British-Hessian-Loyalist army, knowing that saving the Continental Army was all that mattered during a lengthy war of attrition against an opponent more than three thousand miles from home.

The war in America, therefore, had stalemated, to the frustration of King George III and his ministers. It had already lasted far longer than anyone had expected, which naturally led to a decided lack of enthusiasm among ever-growing numbers of Britons for conquest in the faraway land against the descendants of Englishmen, in the final bitter irony. High losses from disease and rebel bullets had made recruiting difficult in England, and dying for king and country thousands of miles from home proved increasingly unappealing to the average Englishman.

With General Washington wisely unwilling to risk decisive defeat with a superior British army, with Canada secure and safe from invasion because of America's failed 1775–1776 offensive effort to win a fourteenth colony (Canada) in the north by force of arms, and knowing that the British naval blockade and American threats on New York City and Canada could be contained, a new British strategy for achieving decisive victory was required by Great Britain in order to prevail in this frustrating conflict that seemed to have no end.

At first, England's top strategists had incorrectly believed the rebellion was a problem inherent only to New England, especially the troublesome Massachusetts port of Boston, before learning otherwise that this was a general national uprising of the common people. Great Britain's initial plan of conquest had only called for isolating and then conquering New England, but that had failed, because the rebellion's roots were much deeper than imagined back in London. The revolutionary spirit in America existed in the hearts and minds of the common people and had nothing to do with isolated regions or parts of the country defined by a map or geography—a fact never completely understood by the British at the highest levels, and especially by King George III.

Even the capture of the young republic's capital of Philadelphia by General William Howe's forces during the fall of 1777 had failed to bring decisive success in the typical European-style manner. Indeed, capturing major cities in the vastness of America meant relatively nothing, since the rebellion and spirit of independence rested deep inside the American people. Quite simply, the patriots no longer believed that America should be part of Great Britain, because a nascent sense of nationalism had risen high, along with patriotic songs, slogans, and Liberty Poles, including at Savannah. British gains in this war had been neatly negated by the surrender of General John Burgoyne's army at Saratoga in upper New York during October 1777, ensuring the entry of France into the war and the emergence of a truly global conflict. It was time for British strategists to begin anew in a final bid for decisive success, or America would be lost forever.

King George III had heard many lofty promises from exiled Loyalists and royal officials in America that the South would be easy to conquer, because of the much-anticipated massive Loyalist uprising that would be forthcoming with the arrival of British troops. He felt they should look to the South for a new strategy to win the war.

After the devastating loss at Saratoga, Great Britain badly needed a bold new plan to achieve decisive victory and win back its former thirteen colonies. George Sackville, better known as Lord Germain, was secretary of state for the American colonies. He had the extremely difficult job of crushing this people's revolution that had flamed out of control, and believed that he knew the way to bring about decisive success. An aggressive plan was developed by the ministry in London, whose amateur members knew nothing of Southern realities and complexities on the other side of the Atlantic. Actually, it was an old plan, resurrected out of desperation, even though it had already failed in the northern and middle colonies early in the war, and in the South in 1776. The new, so-called "Southern Strategy" for winning America was largely devised by Lord Germain, and, of course, King George III.

This extremely ambitious strategic plan called for turning south, away from Washington's stubborn little army that refused to be defeated in a traditional stand-up battle, to a much more lucrative field of operations. The king and his top military minds, especially Lord George Germain, viewed large Loyalist support in the South as the key to winning the war. British strategists desired to utilize the assistance of the slave population along the coast and hostile Native Americans on the west; these groups would be key players in a great resurgence of British fortunes in the South, ensuring that tens of thousands of Loyalists would flock to the ranks at the first sight of the Union Jack. Loyalists, Blacks, and Native Americans were allegedly just waiting for the opportunity to rise up as one when the British army appeared in the South, to settle old scores with the hated patriots because of past abuses in this bitter civil war.

This optimistic new strategy for the South made key assumptions without a sturdy foundation, rooted in a host of failed British efforts in America. The strategists believed that decisive British victory could be won by relying on existing resources, especially British regulars and the Royal Navy, which would serve as the nucleus for the rising up of large numbers of Loyalists in Georgia and South Carolina, thought to be hot-beds of pro-British sentiment among the common people.

Even more, an invaluable flow of Southern supplies that fueled rebel armies to the north, especially Washington's Continental Army, would be cut off by British control of the South, including, eventually, the key state of Virginia, which was the breadbasket of the rebellion and the most populous state. More important, after winning Georgia and South Carolina, and with the Loyalists in control of the newly conquered regions, the British army of regulars, Hessians, and Loyalists could then sweep north from South Carolina to conquer North Carolina and then Virginia, and perhaps even farther north, to strike at Washington's Continental Army and deliver a lethal blow.[17]

After General "Gentleman Johnny" Burgoyne met with disaster in October 1777 at Saratoga, and France had entered into the all-important alliance with America, Lord Germain had been forced to take drastic action. He had become more desperate by this time because of intensifying political pressure from a rising tide of opposition to the king's hard-line policies, since it seemed that the war in America was an unwinnable "political quagmire." Leading voices of Parliament rose up against the war and especially targeted Germain for all manner of abuse, to weaken his power. Legendary William Pitt—the war-wise British secretary of state and brilliant architect of aggressive battle plans for the French and Indian War, who achieved decisive victory by not focusing primarily on Europe—declared, "I know that the conquest of English America is an impossibility."[18]

With usual British optimism and confidence, the Southern Strategy began to be enacted when Philadelphia was evacuated by General Henry Clinton, who had taken overall command of British forces in North America in early 1778, when General William Howe retired. There was a renewed focus on protecting the valuable sugar islands, especially Jamaica, because of the ominous threat of the revitalized French navy.

From Philadelphia, Clinton then marched northeast for New York City, fighting the Battle of Monmouth, New Jersey, along the way to fend off Washington's aggressive pursuit in the last major battle in the North, when Washington attempted in vain to fully exploit a withdrawing army's vulnerabilities during the lengthy retreat. Although unrealized at the time, this showdown in New Jersey on one of the hottest days of the year was the final major clash of the war in the Northern Theater.

From General Clinton's secure defensive bastion of New York City and with the Royal Navy's might at his disposal, the fundamental basis of the Southern Strategy was to target the South's major port cities, beginning with Savannah. If Savannah was captured, this would open the door to Charlestown, just to the north, exposing the entire southern flank of the rebellion.

The French fleet under Vice Admiral d'Estaing arrived back at its home port in the West Indies in January 1779, returning from the disastrous first allied effort at Newport, Rhode Island, in the fall of 1778. At this time, Savannah posed the most tempting target along the Atlantic coast for General Clinton. The most important port city in Georgia was also targeted because of its proximity to St. Augustine, the Loyalist capital of East Florida, with its strong British naval presence. Neither East nor West Florida had rebelled with their sister colonies, which meant they provided excellent land and naval bases for the British to strike north, especially at Savannah, while becoming a safe haven for Loyalists who had been driven out of Georgia and South Carolina.

England had gained East and West Florida from Spain during the settlement of the Seven Years' War, during the 1763 Treaty of Paris. Situated along the Atlantic coast, as the patriots fully realized, Savannah was sandwiched between New York City and St. Augustine, and thus, extremely vulnerable. The city's location near the Atlantic meant that the powerful British navy, which controlled the seas and could land amphibious forces at any point with impunity, could descend simultaneously upon the key Georgia port from two directions, to squeeze the life out of Savannah like a vise. In overall strategic terms, Savannah and Georgia needed to be secured by the British partly because the patriots had already attempted three different offensive efforts, from 1776 to 1778, against St. Augustine, the capital of British Florida, to make Georgia, which shared the border with Florida, more secure.

If Savannah was seized by General Clinton, then the next logical strategic target lay just up the coast: the even more lucrative port of Charlestown. Located approximately one hundred miles to the north, it would be ripe for the taking if Savannah was captured. There were also sound economic objectives for Great Britain to embark upon the fulfillment of the Southern Strategy. By cutting off the key natural exports, especially rice, tobacco, and indigo, that flowed out of Savannah to the outside world, this would eliminate the ample amount of American funds that had long secured invaluable supplies of ammunition, muskets, and cannon, in what had become a logistical and economic war on a global scale by this time.

Quite simply, the Southern Strategy called for rolling up one Southern colony after another in a methodical fashion that would have made
William Pitt proud, especially Virginia, which was the most important
Southern state. These bold British strategies were calculated to make the
middle and northern colonies ripe for conquest after the South had fallen
to the British—that is, if everything went according to plan, and large
numbers of Loyalists rose up to support the relatively small number of
British regulars and their Hessian allies in a united front that could not
be matched by the patriots.[19]

As early as March 8, 1778, Lord Germain ordered Sir Henry Clinton, the overall commander in North America, headquartered in New
York City, to detach an expedition south for the mission of undertaking
the conquest for Georgia—the weakest and most vulnerable state, with
plenty of Loyalists eager to settle old scores because of years of harsh
patriot persecution. This would take place in the fall, with the advent of
cooler weather, to reduce the spread of coastal disease, especially malaria
and yellow fever, among the vulnerable European soldiers.

The major offensive envisioned by the honor-minded Germain—a
former military man known for having possessed sufficient nerve and
spirit to challenge a political enemy to a duel—began in late October,
when Clinton, despite his concerns about the safety of an undermanned
New York City, moved his expeditionary force south along the Atlantic
coast toward Savannah, in mid-December 1778. Unwilling to risk the
loss of too many of the troops at the New York garrison, which would
make it more vulnerable, the naturally cautious Clinton dispatched a
flotilla of a relatively small expeditionary force of Hessians, New York
Loyalists organized in provincial regiments, and the crack Scottish Highlanders of the 71st Regiment of Foot.

Even geography favored the British conquest of Georgia, which was
only lightly defended. The domination of the British navy could not be
matched, with d'Estaing and his fleet now back in the Caribbean to protect the king's precious sugar islands. Overwhelming the motley band of
American defenders of Savannah would be relatively easy, as the expeditionary forces could be landed with impunity by British warships at any
point along the Atlantic, and the Americans could do nothing to stop

them. To separate South Carolina from Georgia, British warships could then ascend northwest up the wide Savannah River, the border between the two states, all the way to Augusta, Georgia, in the untamed frontier of the so-called backcountry.[20]

For these reasons, Lord Germain bestowed a degree of flexibility to the Southern Strategy that allowed Clinton to make necessary adjustments to any tactical situation that he might find on the ground: "I have thus stated the King's wishes and intentions, but he does not mean you to look upon them as orders, desiring . . . that you use your discretion in planning [and] all operations which shall appear the most likely means of crushing the rebellion."[21]

Major General Augustine Prévost, who had been born in Geneva, Switzerland, commanded British troops in East Florida, which had become a safe refuge for uprooted Loyalists who had been forced out of Georgia and South Carolina by patriot persecution. Prévost was destined to command Savannah when the French and Americans laid siege and attacked in the fall of 1779. With ample justification that reflected the best thinking of Lord Germain and other leading London strategists, and with prophetic insight, Prévost described the widespread American weaknesses across the South that seemed to have no end: "I am certain the four southern provinces are incapable of making any formidable resistance; they are not prepared for a scene of war."[22]

For such valid reasons, Lord Germain, King George III's right-hand man in orchestrating the war in America, had emphasized to General Clinton that taking the war to the South was "considered by the King as an object of great importance," and now viewed as the only existing realistic strategy for winning the war.[23]

This was indeed the case, because the South was the soft underbelly and Achilles' heel of the rebellion. Like they had in the North, patriot forces in the South had already demonstrated an inability to conduct successful offensive operations against British regulars and their experienced professional leaders, who had been trained at military academies in Europe. After the Cherokee had been largely eliminated from the war during the 1776 Campaign in the western mountains by coordinated efforts of Southern militias and then sued for peace in early 1777, the backcountry militias of South Carolina had moved into the wilderness above Augusta to gain control of the region.

Emboldened by their success against Native Americans to eliminate the threat to their rear to the west, the backcountry militia had then marched on St. Augustine during the summer of 1778, in what was their third and final attempt to subdue the British bastion. This ambitious effort was launched partly in response to Prévost's raids on patriot plantations in southern Georgia. Of course, the summer was the worst of all times to conduct offensive operations in the sweltering heat and swamps of the uncharted Florida wilderness. As demonstrated on three different occasions, the patriots' pathetic offensive efforts in attempting to conquer St. Augustine failed miserably, leaving the region ripe for the taking with Clinton's targeting of Savannah to exploit a host of patriot failures and weaknesses.[24]

By late 1778, Savannah was protected by a ragtag force of too few men who lacked training and proper discipline, under the leadership of Major General Robert Howe of North Carolina. Because the war had not yet come to the South after the 1776 British repulse at Charlestown, the patriots were ill-prepared for war, and especially for stopping a powerful British invasion of Georgia by water. Even worse, these Americans, imbued with lofty republican and Age of Enlightenment ideology, were supremely overconfident; their naiveté and hubris blinded them to the fact that they were handicapped by almost too many disadvantages to count.

The handsome and charming Howe was not connected to any aspects of the war that were rooted in reality. He was also preoccupied with his romantic pursuits as a voracious "woman-eater that devours everything that comes his way." Like his poorly trained troops, he was hardly up to the formidable challenge of defending Savannah. Revealing the level of his hubris, Howe reportedly boasted how the British troops consisted of nothing more than "raw boys from the [Scottish] Highlands and of [Oliver] DeLancey's [New York Loyalists] green-coats, who would not fight, and that he did not care if there were twice the number" as had been reported to him at headquarters.[25]

After his embarrassing failure to capture Charlestown in the summer of 1776, General Clinton had learned some key lessons about how to properly wage war in the South. He had chosen a highly capable Scotsman, thirty-nine-year-old Lieutenant Colonel Archibald Campbell, with around three thousand veteran troops from New York City to sail south to capture the vital port of Savannah, located on the river of the same name.

Utilizing England's successful seaborne expeditionary strategy of relying on amphibious landings, because America's sprawling coastline was wide open and undefended, on December 23, 1778, Campbell landed his troops on Georgia soil from his fleet of British warships that possessed complete sea superiority. Catching Major General Robert Howe by surprise, experienced and confident redcoats poured inland like a flood and onto Tybee Island, located at the mouth of the Savannah River, around sixteen miles southeast of Savannah, without meeting any serious opposition.

Clearly, Clinton had learned his lesson of not directly attacking a Southern port city after he had failed miserably by reducing water defenses, primarily Fort Sullivan on Sullivan's Island, at Charlestown in late June 1776. During this political war for hearts and minds, he was also instructed by Clinton to reestablish the royal government, not only in Georgia, but also in South Carolina. This would occur after additional conquests were made farther north, if possible, after the capture of Savannah, to set the stage for the expected massive Loyalist uprising, when they would flock to the Union Jack in large numbers.

After pushing northwest up the Savannah River for another unopposed landing closer to Savannah, Campbell then led his men north through the low-lying swamps to catch Howe and Savannah's defenders by surprise. Campbell's troops included two battalions of the elite 71st Regiment of Foot, which consisted of Scottish Highlanders under Scotland-born Colonel John Maitland, who led the vanguard.

The invaders were assisted by a slave and paid informant named Quamino Dolly, who led the task force, which included the two battalions of Loyalists of the New York Volunteers from Oliver DeLancey's Brigade that would defend Savannah during the autumn of 1779. Dolly led the troops "by a private Path through the Swamp, upon the Right of the Americans." Suffering the loss of barely twenty-five men, Campbell easily vanished around seven hundred ragtag defenders, both Georgia militiamen and Continentals under General Howe, in barely a day's time, in a shockingly easy victory that astounded one and all. Howe was forced to evacuate Savannah in short order, and the conquerors in scarlet uniforms took possession of the city on December 28, raising the British flag over Savannah with pride.

Every inch a fighter in the Scottish tradition, and facing a less capable opponent in Major General Howe, Campbell had captured Savannah with a small force of barely 1,500 men, including two battalions of his trusty Scottish Highlanders of the 71st Regiment of Foot. Heady with success, which he felt heralded the fall of all of Georgia, he prematurely bragged to General Clinton in New York City that he was "the first officer taking a stripe and star from the flag of [the Continental] Congress."[26]

Meanwhile, the Union Jack now once again flew in triumph over Savannah after two years of patriot control, sending the patriot government into a hasty exile. Georgia's rebel governor, John Houstoun, fled Savannah for his life, and former royal governor James Wright prepared to return from his own exile in England. For all practical purposes, Georgia had once again become a royal province of extreme importance because of its strategic position, located just south of the vital strategic port of Charlestown, South Carolina, which had suddenly become fertile ground for conquest.[27]

Most important, the Southern Strategy had seemingly been proven successful to British leadership, because the capture of Savannah had been so easy and painless. And as predicted, thousands of Georgia Loyalists—upon which the entire Southern Strategy had been based—poured forth to take the oath of allegiance, making "peace at the expense of their patriotism."[28]

THE PROMISE AND FOLLY OF 1779

The new year of 1779 was destined to be a year of decision for British fortunes in Georgia. This was especially the case after Savannah, an ideal staging base for future operations directed at Charlestown to the north, had been so easily captured. This ensured a permanent British presence in the South for the first time in the war north of East Florida—a most ominous strategic development for the patriot cause, opening the door to the Americans' southern flank while fulfilling the first key requirement of the new Southern Strategy: Savannah would serve as the base of future operations and an all-out British effort to conquer the South, ending the war with a decisive victory—if everything went according to plan.

By mid-January 1779, the experienced and talented Major General Augustine Prévost had advanced north from the port of St. Augustine in East Florida and crossed the border into Georgia. He united with Campbell and then replaced him as the new commander, because he had seniority. Prévost commanded excellent troops, including the 60th Regiment of Foot (known as the Royal Americans), in which he had served during the French and Indian War, Lieutenant Colonel Thomas Brown's East Florida Rangers, and three companies of New Jersey Volunteers, who were Loyalists.

The outspoken Lieutenant Colonel Campbell—who had once served capably with the British East India Company's Bengal Engineers, and was already upset that he had not been promoted to brigadier general—was not happy with the sudden change of command. In a bitter letter to William Eden, and for good reason, the high-strung Scotsman wrote that he still worried Georgia's future would be in doubt if the rebels suddenly became resurgent, something no one else on the British side seemed to expect after the swift conquest of Georgia. Campbell wrote: "[Prévost] seems a worthy man, but too old and inactive for this service. He will do in garrison," and not in active field command, while "I shall gallop with the light troops."[29] Fortunately for the British, Campbell was entirely wrong in his gross underestimation of Major General Prévost's abilities as a commander and leader of men.

Meanwhile, in reaction to the new British threat in Georgia, and influenced by General Washington's glowing words of praise for the New Englander, the Continental Congress belatedly appointed a new commander of the Southern Department in the hope of reversing fortunes in this suddenly all-important theater: They had decided to replace

Howe with Major General Benjamin Lincoln and hoped for the best far southwest of America's capitol Philadelphia.

The rotund Lincoln seemed an unlikely choice for a variety of reasons, including his unmilitary-like appearance. Born in 1733, the former Massachusetts farmer carried excess weight on his large frame, and still appeared to be very much a man of the soil. Lincoln was extremely devout, believing that God was on the side of the revolutionaries, and that a kind Providence had blessed their righteous cause and struggle for liberty. But Lincoln was a fighter and a true holy warrior, a veteran of the decisive victory at Saratoga, where he had been wounded on October 7 in the right ankle, giving him a permanent limp on a leg that already supported too much weight. Most important, Lincoln was highly esteemed by Washington, despite his narcolepsy that appeared at inopportune times, to the embarrassment of one and all.[30]

Now was the time for the opportunistic British to exploit the host of advantages stemming from the almost effortless capture of Savannah. To his credit, Lieutenant Colonel Campbell gained more of Georgia. He was not only ambitious but also possessed an excellent strategic sense that was as keen as that of Prévost, which led him to take the initiative after Savannah's capture. Augusta, located to the north, up the Savannah River on the Georgia frontier, became the next British target in January 1779: an enticing conquest that was calculated to separate British Georgia from patriot South Carolina. This aggressive strategy was based upon securing Georgia's two main population centers—Augusta and Savannah—located at each end of the navigable portions of the strategic Savannah River, in an ambitious bid to win the Georgia backcountry.

Of course, according to their ambitious Southern Strategy, the British envisioned large numbers of Loyalists joining their ranks as soon as Augusta was captured—a dream that failed to materialize as anticipated. This should have raised valid doubts among British leaders and planners in London about the wisdom of basing everything on the Southern Strategy, which was founded on the premise of massive Loyalist support at all levels.

Lieutenant Colonel Thomas Brown, who hailed from the seaport community of Whitby in North Riding, Yorkshire, England, and his

Florida Rangers, who were tough Loyalist partisans and Indian fighters and intimately knew Indian ways, led the way north for Campbell's expedition up the Savannah River to Augusta. The key town on the upper Georgia frontier was easily occupied by the British on January 31. With his second in command, Lieutenant Colonel John Maitland—another talented Scotsman of extraordinary ability who proudly wore a scarlet uniform and was eager to fulfill Lord Germain's ambitious plan—Campbell planned to unite with large numbers of Creeks from the west and Loyalists from the east, which would swell his ranks. Meanwhile, more than one thousand Georgians signed the oath of allegiance and organized hundreds of men into Loyalist militia companies. This number was a considerable disappointment to soaring British ambitions, because they had expected six thousand Loyalists to come forth with enthusiasm, which never materialized. Campbell shortly abandoned Augusta with the approach of resurgent American forces from Georgia and South Carolina on February 14, heading south toward Savannah.

Here in the Augusta area, an ugly incident took place that was destined to fuel the combat resolve and fury of Campbell's red-uniformed Scotsmen, who were already crack troops. It was a tragic incident like so many others that had occurred on the divided frontier of the Georgia backcountry during this bitter civil war in the Southern backcountry.

A paroled rebel major had asked Lieutenant Colonel Campbell—who began his career in the British army as an engineer before becoming the commander of the 71st Regiment of Foot—for protection against the South Carolina raiders, who often struck across the river. Campbell had assigned a Scottish sergeant named MacAlister to this duty. While protecting the American's home, believed to be an easy assignment, MacAlister soon fell victim to the horrors of war when patriot raiders from South Carolina slipped across the Savannah River and "hacked [him] to pieces" with their sharp swords, in what an angry Campbell officially described as a "shameful Act."[31] This led to battle cries of "Remember poor MacAlister" at the Battle of Brier Creek, Georgia, on March 3, 1779, where an impressive British victory was won, and later, during the decisive showdown for possession of Savannah in the fall of 1779.

During the withdrawal south to Savannah, when Captain Thomas Tawes and his dragoons led the way after having abandoned Augusta on February 14, 1779, Campbell had prudently withdrawn in the face of an upsurge in patriot aggressiveness in the Georgia backcountry. This resurgence included a surprising patriot victory on the same day in a remote location, about fifty miles northwest of Augusta, at Kettle Creek, a tributary of the Savannah River.

Lieutenant Colonel Campbell lamented the failure of Lord Germain's ambitious plan of uniting Loyalists and Creeks, whose growing numbers and always menacing threat had united patriots and Loyalists on the frontier. The plan to terrorize the patriots with this sinister strategy backfired, fueling the enlistment of far more patriots across the frontier than Loyalists. The Native American threat only made the patriots more aggressive in their offensive into South Carolina, aimed at the capture of Charlestown, thwarting the ambitious British strategy of employing Native Americans in their timely efforts.

Meanwhile, Campbell named Lieutenant Colonel James Mark Prévost, the younger brother of Major General Augustine Prévost, as temporary acting governor of Georgia. This was before the arrival of Royal Governor James Wright, an attorney and rice planter from England who had served as chief executive of Georgia since 1761. Ironically, both Prévost and Campbell had been wounded during the decisive September 13, 1759, showdown on the Plains of Abraham that had resulted in Quebec's fall and the winning of most of North America for the Crown.[32]

Georgia was now divided, with the patriots in control of Augusta and the upper part of the state while the British held the lower environs of the state. Civil government had been restored in the latter, where Savannah served as the center of the strongest British presence in the entire South, and a future base of operations for the much-anticipated conquest of South Carolina. In early 1779, General Prévost arrived in Savannah to take command, and an embittered Campbell departed without the expected promotion, despite a job extremely well done.

Like so often in the South, politics now came into play. Major General Benjamin Lincoln, who was under increasing domestic pressure, moved his army south from Charlestown in April 1779, in part to support the new provisional Georgia government recently established in Augusta and the rise of the new patriot state of Georgia. Significantly, this also ensured that Lord Germain's plan of uniting Loyalists and Creeks would not materialize.

In addition, Governor John Rutledge, the South Carolina government centered in Charlestown, and other South Carolinians eager for revenge urged Lincoln to unleash a scorched-earth policy against the Loyalists of Georgia. This was just part of the cruelty of the bitter civil war that raged between the predominantly Loyalist Georgia and the predominantly patriot South Carolina. Lincoln targeted Augusta for capture, and hoped to keep the Loyalists and Native Americans in the backcountry from uniting with the British on the coast, to create an overpowering united front and to cut supply lines to the British, as fondly envisioned by Lord Germain.

The chess game for possession of Georgia continued. As spring weather brought warmth to the Georgia–South Carolina border, there was a lack of backcountry supplies flowing south to feed the Savannah garrison. To negate Lincoln's push toward the Georgia backcountry, General Prévost acted boldly to disprove Lieutenant Colonel Campbell's harsh words against him. He was determined to show that his age did not affect his skill or ability to act aggressively.

Prévost knew that Lincoln had departed Charlestown with a sizable force, swelled by militia volunteers, confidently pushing south to gain possession of the Georgia backcountry. With Brown's trusty Florida Rangers—die-hard Loyalists—leading the task force of around 2,500 men, Prévost crossed the Savannah River near the end of April and entered South Carolina. Hoping to draw Lincoln out of the Georgia backcountry, he then marched north to threaten Charlestown near the end of April.

The South's wealthiest city was now commanded by General William Moultrie, Lincoln's second in command, who hastily attempted to defend the vulnerable port city with his small garrison of South Carolina militiamen. With Prévost drawing ever closer, Charlestown was in a panic. Governor Rutledge hurriedly recalled Lincoln before it was too late. But before Lincoln could return to protect the city, the audacious

Prévost demanded the surrender of Charlestown on May 12. However, Prévost was forced to shortly withdraw back south when Lincoln's forces returned in overpowering numbers—his strategic objective, to force Prévost out of the Georgia backcountry, depriving the British of their grip on Georgia.

To his credit, Lincoln decided to strike when he learned from deserters that Prévost's network of defenses at Stono Ferry along the Stono River were weaker than expected, and that Maitland—in charge of this rearguard contingent, and assigned to holding this advanced position to buy time for Prévost to continue south toward Savannah—planned to shortly evacuate to return to Savannah.

The sharp and intense Battle of Stono Ferry, South Carolina, just southwest of Charlestown, erupted amid the low-country heat and humidity on June 20, 1779, when Lieutenant Colonel John Maitland stood firm in typical Scottish stubborn defiance with his rearguard Hessians, North and South Carolina Loyalists of their respective Provincial Regiments, and the 71st Regiment of Foot, while Prévost slipped away with stealth and headed south for Savannah, as planned. Becoming the hero of the day, Maitland was successful in his key delaying action at Stono Ferry, buying Prévost precious time for withdrawing safely south to Savannah, just like the elite Scottish Highlanders at Stono had bought the Scotland-born lieutenant colonel precious time.

While this hard-fought and relatively forgotten battle on James Island, located just southwest of Charlestown, brought no decisive results, it did ensure that Prévost would eventually reach Savannah safely, making Georgia much more secure. The blue-uniformed Hessians of a grenadier German regiment known as the von Trumbach Regiment, which had been participants in Savannah's capture in late December 1778, won distinction at Stono Ferry, when these hard-hit Teutonic warriors were rallied by Maitland and joined the counterattack of the 71st Regiment of Foot. These same resurgent Germans would defend Savannah in the fall of 1779, when they displayed their most sterling qualities as excellent fighting men when on the defensive.

Prévost continued to island-hop south toward his refuge of Savannah, leaving his favorite Highland Scots, the 71st Regiment of Foot, at

Beaufort, South Carolina, on the island of Port Royal. After a remarkable campaign that had terrified all of Charlestown and American leaders throughout the South, Prévost then safely returned to Savannah with his force of disciplined Hessians.

But like the upcoming showdown at Savannah during the autumn of 1779, it was Lieutenant Colonel Maitland's magnificent leadership and tactical skills that saved the day for Prévost's rearguard command, whose crucial mission had been to buy time for the British withdrawal back to Savannah, which had been left on its own on the Stono River, to do or die. Here, at the port of Beaufort, situated around forty-five miles northeast of Savannah, after another job well done, Maitland finally linked up with Prévost, who had early won recognition for courage and skill as an outstanding officer of the 60th Regiment of Foot (the Royal Americans) on July 8, to reunite an excellent fighting team that was truly formidable.

One forgotten patriot loss that went unnoticed by one and all except for his close-knit Scotch-Irish family in the South Carolina backcountry was the oldest brother (Hugh) of Andrew Jackson, who was the teenage son of a hard-working immigrant from Ulster Province, Ireland. Hugh died while campaigning in the sweltering South Carolina lowlands not long after the Battle of Stono Ferry on June 20, 1779, a tragic loss never forgotten by the British-hating Andrew when battling against the invaders of his homeland during both the American Revolution and the War of 1812, especially at the Battle of New Orleans in January 1815.[33]

In conclusion, and most important in overall strategic terms, Prévost succeeded in his strategic objective of drawing Lincoln and his army back to Charlestown and out of the upper Georgia backcountry, which made not only Savannah but Georgia more secure. Meanwhile, General Clinton was not a happy man, primarily because of Lord Germain's unrealistic and "ridiculous recommendations," including the sending of more troops from New York City, Great Britain's most important American possession, to the West Indies. Quite simply, Clinton now possessed too few troops. He had twice attempted to resign in 1779, and now looked foolish because of his anger over the aggressive Scotsman, who had nearly captured Charlestown and disrupted patriot plans for the formation of a Georgia government at Augusta, having made his aggressive advance north without his permission.

While Prévost, who had gained his well-deserved promotion to major general in February 1779, had returned to the Savannah River port to make Savannah more formidable with his main force of around 1,500 troops, Lieutenant Colonel Maitland and his 900-man command remained at Beaufort, in a good strategic position to launch future strikes into South Carolina, which was Lord Germain's next target after Georgia's complete subjugation. It seemed as if Prévost had succeeded on all accounts to ensure a solid British hold on Georgia, but almost prophetically, he was still worried, and desired the arrival of reinforcements from New York City.[34]

The farsighted Major General Prévost had ample reason to be worried by this time. As mentioned, an influential and highly respected Frenchman in Charlestown had been attempting to convince Vice Admiral Charles Henri d'Estaing to sail from the West Indies and head for the American coast to exploit British vulnerabilities. He emphasized the disorganized and confused state of American forces and fortunes, to the point where he indicated that resistance would be feeble if the British struck at South Carolina, beginning at the strategic port of Charlestown. For such reasons—and to his credit, without specific authorization to do so from King Louis XVI and France—Vice Admiral d'Estaing had decided to boldly take the initiative with an aggressive style all his own. He had become convinced that the "American cause was in great peril and that all hopes were based on my early arrival."[35]

By this time the war for the heart and soul of America had changed forever, becoming not only bloodier and grimmer in its fifth year, but also more complex in regard to race. This factor was especially important in the South, because of the implementation of the bold Southern Strategy that had been calculated in London to win it all. In June 1779, consequently, Sir Henry Clinton in New York City issued an emancipation decree that declared that any American slaves who fled to the safety of British lines would neither be sold nor deemed as property, unlike what would happen to a slave slipping into American lines and linking up with men who fought for liberty—their own, and not for Blacks.

This decree, of course, opened the door for former slaves to serve in the manpower-short British army. Instead of having been issued as an enlightened humanitarian decree, as it seemed on the surface and at first glance, Clinton primarily hoped to weaken patriot forces by removing their vital support system of Black laborers and providers in the South. He also hoped to raise the level of fear among whites, encouraging larger numbers of patriots to sign oaths of allegiance and ensuring that Blacks replaced British soldiers in rear-echelon duties, so that white soldiers could be utilized on the front lines. More than six hundred former slaves from the South's small farms and sprawling plantations were destined to play a key role in the upcoming defense of Savannah before the year's end, as both laborers and soldiers, which was an invaluable contribution to the eventual victory in October 1779.[36]

With summer already over and the increasingly shorter Southern nights in the low country becoming cooler and less humid, the British strategic situation had never looked better in the South, thanks to Prévost's recent descent on Charlestown, when it was least expected by the stunned patriot leaders. The entire British southern flank of the Southern Theater was secure and primed for additional conquests along the Atlantic coast, especially Charlestown. British strategists believed that not only Georgia but also South Carolina could be won with minimal cost and effort, and this had certainly proven true in the case of Georgia. Not only Savannah, the key launching pad for future British conquests across the South, but also Georgia had been secured, setting the stage for the next phase of England's ambitious Southern Strategy: a future attack on the strategic port of Charlestown, the greatest prize in all the South.

But everything was about to change, in a conflict full of surprising developments and unexpected changes in the ever-unpredictable fight for domination of America and its untold natural riches of unlimited potential. An entire French fleet under Vice Admiral d'Estaing was shortly to appear off Tybee Island, Georgia, near where the Savannah River enters the Atlantic, when least expected by British leadership on both sides of the Atlantic. Just upriver from the Atlantic, the rich port of Savannah lay ripe for the taking by the French expeditionary force, or so it seemed to the overconfident vice admiral.[37]

Vice Admiral d'Estaing was determined to remove the dark stain of his failure in the allied effort to capture Newport, Rhode Island, during the fall of 1777, when he had been blamed by the Americans for everything that had gone wrong. The vice admiral's sarcastic words revealed the depth of his bitterness that still lingered and haunted him: "Being accused of weakness and timidity, in short, bearing the stigma of cowardice, was nothing; that is one of the rewards of serving a foreign country."[38]

Vice Admiral d'Estaing's bloated pride and ego were about to get a large number of young Frenchmen and Americans killed at a relatively little-known place in Georgia called Savannah in the early autumn of 1779. This vital port city on the Savannah River was considered "the key of the southern provinces, and the Gibraltar of the Gulf [Stream] passage."[39] An American sea captain who had sailed from the port of Cap-Français with d'Estaing's fleet would shortly provide accurate information for a colonial newspaper: "[T]he expedition on which they were going was kept a profound secret, but that it was undoubtably [sic] for this continent [because the fleet was] steering for Georgia."[40]

From the strategic port of Charlestown, French colonel Charles François Sevelinges, Marquis de Brétigny, had earlier written to d'Estaing, promising the easiest of victories in Georgia. If and when d'Estaing arrived, he would easily capture Savannah and its small garrison of ill-prepared redcoat and Loyalist defenders, who never expected the sudden arrival of an entire French fleet from the West Indies in their wildest dreams, especially during the height of hurricane season. "[W]ithout firing a shot d'Estaing could win the victory" was an enticement that the glory-seeking vice admiral simply could not ignore.[41]

The French Invasion Force Suddenly Appears Outside Savannah

Desperate appeals from two respected Frenchmen, especially Colonel Charles François Sevelinges, Marquis de Brétigny, in Charlestown, and influential Americans had convinced d'Estaing that glory could be won in America and that it would all be so easy—almost like taking candy from a baby. Vice Admiral d'Estaing had been convinced that the Americans were about to lose the war in the South, and decided to act on King Louis XVI's long-term wishes, but without his express consent to sail to Georgia. The Franco-American alliance was shaky at best at this time, after the recent Newport fiasco that had caused widespread embarrassment for the allies. The vice admiral wanted to wipe away the stain of this miserable failure in Rhode Island, as did King Louis XVI. The king at Versailles wanted to strengthen the fragile alliance, especially now when it appeared that the Americans were losing the war, especially after the recent capture of Savannah by Campbell. Colonel Campbell's successes had given the British an ideal base for future strikes, not only along the Southern Atlantic coast, but also when it came to capturing some of the all-important French sugar islands in the West Indies.

As noted, it was the height of Atlantic hurricane season, which reached its peak in August in America's southern waters. It was also a risk for the French fleet to leave the relative safety of the French West Indies, which would be exposed and vulnerable to British raids in d'Estaing's absence. Despite these factors, d'Estaing had prepared a mighty expeditionary force of both colonial troops and French regulars to come to the aid of the beleaguered South, which lay open for the taking and tottered on the brink of collapse at this time, especially if Charlestown fell. In the end, to his credit, d'Estaing could not pass up the "prospect of inflicting a decisive blow against the British in North America [which] was irresistible to this proud Frenchman."[1]

Monday, August 16, 1779, was a special day in France's most prosperous Caribbean colony. The fighting men, Black, white, and mulatto, from the Colony of Saint-Domingue were going off to the war, to some still-unknown destination known only to Vice Admiral d'Estaing.

The magnificent port of Cap-Français, known as Le Cap, was like no other in the Caribbean—the "Paris of the Antilles"—the city's splendor reflected in its stately architecture and exquisite Catholic cathedrals, surrounded by towering palm trees blowing in the warm breeze sweeping off the blue-green sea. Located on the colony's north coast and at the foot of imposing mountains covered in bright green tropical rainforests, Le Cap, which had been founded in 1670, was by far the most magnificent city in the Caribbean.

D'Estaing's mighty fleet of thirty-three warships, formidable with more than two thousand cannon, contained some of France's finest and most famous infantry regiments, legendary combat units such as the Auxerrois, Dillon, Agenois, and Cambresis regiments, all aboard and ready to serve God and King Louis XVI. Although the French and colonial troops had yet to learn where they were headed—the vice admiral's entire strategy relied on complete secrecy and the element of surprise, if Savannah was to be captured—they were about to sail for America in support of George Washington's ill-prepared Southern rebels, who had dared to defy King George III with their lofty ideals about the equality of all men—a heady, idealist concept, especially to the Black and mulatto soldiers of the Chasseurs-Volontaires de Saint-Domingue.

D'Estaing's multiethnic army of various colors was an extremely ad hoc and heterogeneous one. This did not necessarily bode well for the upcoming campaign, or so it would seem to the stuffy French traditionalists and old-school elite, especially back in Paris. The expeditionary force bound for America consisted of thousands of enthusiastic young volunteers from the West Indies and French regulars, who had been drafted into fourteen different legendary regiments that were the pride of France.

Vice Admiral d'Estaing and his expeditionary force of approximately 4,450 men assembled under the bright summer sunshine of the tropics, and confidence could not have been higher. The troops included veterans of the great European battles of Minden, Germany, in 1759 and Fontenoy, Belgium, in 1745, which had become legendary across Europe, from three divisions, including those troops under the command of Irishman general Arthur Dillon and Colonel Louis-Marie Antoine Vicomte de Noailles.

Also included were Saint-Domingue's two homegrown units, the white Volunteer Grenadiers and the Black and mulatto Chasseurs-Volontaires de Saint-Domingue, aboard their assigned warships as the white silk banners of the Bourbon dynasty waved in the warm Caribbean breeze. All the while, joyous citizens of all colors lined the shores of Le Cap waved flags and family members shed tears into their white cotton handkerchiefs, knowing they might never see their loved ones again. Where were the flowers of the Black and mulatto youth of Saint-Domingue bound, and for how long? Would these Chasseurs ever return to their beloved homeland with their lives and limbs intact, after fighting on some distant battlefield far from home?

For the young men and boys, most of whom had never been at sea before, the sendoff from Le Cap was spectacular. This was a great adventure to them, and they were excited and supremely confident that they would succeed. As the mighty French fleet sailed out of the expansive harbor of Le Cap with brass bands playing, the soldiers felt they were bound to win glory for France, Saint-Domingue, and themselves, or so they hoped and prayed. The most experienced and savvy veterans of the Saint-Domingue militia, who had battled the ever-desperate maroons in the jungled-covered mountains, knew better than to believe in the heady romance and glory of warfare that intoxicated these young men of considerable innocence. They realized that stern challenges lay ahead.[2]

D'Estaing was wisely keeping their destination secret for the sake of overall security. The savvy vice admiral was determined to maintain the element of surprise, because he knew that it was the key to the capture of Savannah and reversing the war's course in the beleaguered South. He knew he could afford to take no risks, adhering to the wise old axiom: "The unspoken word is a sword in the scabbard, while the spoken word is a sword in the hand of one's enemy." In this regard, d'Estaing was right on target.

However, the most clever French officers of the command reasoned that the secret expedition was headed no farther north than the warm climate of South Carolina. This was certainly not going to be a return journey to cold Newport, Rhode Island, based on their review of the neat ranks of the Chasseurs-Volontaires as they came aboard ship for the journey with disciplined step. These young men, the pride of the Black and mulatto community of Saint-Domingue, still wore their light tropical uniforms of linen rather than wool, like the French regulars, who were uniformed for campaigning in a colder climate.[3]

In his journal, a French officer named Philippe Séguier de Terson, who led a company of grenadiers of the French army later, described the journey, as they all tried to guess at the expedition's ultimate destination, regardless of rank or noble status: "We have maintained a steady course to the northwest. We thought for a while that we were going to [British-held] St. Augustine [Florida, which was the capital of East Florida]. It is obvious, however, that is not M. d'Estaing's intention. We have passed it. We are sailing toward land, but still with the same uncertainty about where we will land."[4]

In his journal, Second Lieutenant François d'Auber de Peyrelongue, of the French artillery, wrote about the turbulent temperament of Mother Nature and the ordeal that cost d'Estaing precious time during hurricane season: "On September 1 we anchored off the Florida coast to the latitude of the St. Johns River. On the second we weathered a squall which lasted thirty-six hours. Most of our ships were dispersed, many lost cannon, and some rudders were shattered. It took us a week to reassemble and make repairs."[5]

Antoine Augustin Aubert Defoix Seigneur Dupetithouars, a white officer without a hint of mixed race, was one of the captains of the ten companies of the Chasseurs-Volontaires de Saint-Domingue. For a mulatto slave named Aman, July 10, 1779, had been the most special day of his life. On this Saturday, he had been freed by his master, the captain, just in time to serve in the ranks of the Chasseurs. Then, on August

4, Captain Dupetithouars had freed another one of his slaves, Pierre Charles dit Floissac, to also serve in the ranks of his company.

For whatever reason, this respected captain of considerable means did not free another one of his slaves who served in the ranks of the Chasseurs-Volontaires de Saint-Domingue—one of the few slaves to have served in the Chasseurs, which consisted almost solely of free Blacks and mulattoes. Captain Dupetithouars, his two former slaves, and his current slave, Fabien Genty (or Fabien Gentil or Gentil dit Tollo, as he is also known) had no idea where they were bound while the long journey continued northwest, toward the colder waters of North America and then up the Atlantic coast.

It was not until early September that the soldiers of the expeditionary force, including the volunteers of the Chasseurs, learned of their ultimate destination. As penned in his journal, an eager Séguier de Terson wrote: "Today the report from M. d'Estaing's ship is that we are to capture the city of Savannah where there are 2,000 Englishmen under siege of the Americans. The rumor is that all the troops with M. d'Estaing will land to attack and take the city. Let it be soon!"[6]

At this time, Vice Admiral d'Estaing was under the delusion that he could capture Savannah in a week by merely sailing his armada of warships up the Savannah River, forcing the city's surrender and scoring an easy, if not bloodless, victory. After all, in d'Estaing's own words, which revealed the extent of his heady overconfidence, "Grenada was taken and Admiral [John] Byron was defeated in less time," or less than a week.[7]

The vice admiral still recalled the encouraging words written by Colonel Brétigny, who had been serving as a French volunteer in the ranks of the Continental Army. They had fueled his ambition to accomplish great things in America, and were part of the inspiration for the genesis of the Savannah Campaign: "Never has this country been in greater need of help. It is necessary to defend it against itself and against the enemy. All here is in frightful confusion; very few regular troops, no help from the north [or from Washington's army], a feeble and badly disciplined militia and the greatest friction among the leaders, [and] in truth to you alone, Monsieur le Comte, to save her from peril."[8]

After having recently won the rich sugar islands of St. Vincent, Grenada, and the Grenadines that were strung out like shining pearls on a turquoise sea in the Lower Antilles, Vice Admiral d'Estaing could not have been more confident of an upcoming victory over France's ancient enemy, the hated English, in his new adventure in America. The pursuit of glory—the vice admiral's central weakness as a commander that lingered at the core of his being—beckoned him to America like a siren's song.

Most of all, the optimistic d'Estaing envisioned another quick and easy victory over the British, like in the West Indies, but this time on the American mainland, before a swift return back to the safety of the Caribbean to protect French's sugar islands, his main priority and responsibility as assigned to him by King Louis XVI. Clearly, maximizing his flexibility and initiative, d'Estaing was a bold gambler in this regard, because sailing north to Georgia on his own without the king's express orders meant leaving the invaluable sugar islands of the West Indies without adequate protection for a period of time, which he hoped to minimize as much as possible, including the key Caribbean islands that he had recently captured. The vice admiral believed that he could force Savannah's surrender in short order to ensure a swift return to protect his top priority.

Indeed, not only would the capture of Savannah be easy, according to all accounts that he had received, but the vice admiral also envisioned it would be swift. This lightning strike was the key to the entire expedition to America. In consequence, Vice Admiral d'Estaing's plan was relatively simple—just a matter of sailing a relatively short distance northwest up the Savannah River to take the British by surprise, forcing the undermanned garrison of Major General Prévost to surrender. Prévost would have no choice in the face of a mighty French fleet with hundreds of cannon and an expeditionary force that consisted of some of France's finest troops.

In fact, d'Estaing was so confident of decisive victory that he allowed only a week to complete the job of subduing Savannah before returning to the West Indies, which he had left defenseless, after which he would hand over the captured city to the Americans in a gracious gesture and reap a measure of glory, thereby fulfilling the strategic objectives of King

Louis XVI and France. He never expected that the British would wisely block the river of approach to the city with two sunken warhips in the nick of time, which would force him to undertake something he had never planned—a lengthy siege of Savannah by land, when time was not on his side, which would cause him to launch a foolhardy assault on powerful fortifications on October 9 that never had a chance of succeeding.

The seasoned admiral had overlooked the fact that this time, everything would be quite different. A remote and faraway Southern campaign on the American mainland would be much more difficult, because Savannah was not an island that could be easily surrounded by French warships, automatically dooming the hapless defenders, who had no hope of reinforcements, like in the Caribbean. The Battle of Savannah would be the exact opposite, posing daunting new and entirely unexpected challenges for which d'Estaing was ill prepared.

To d'Estaing's delight, in early September the French fleet finally reached the coast of Savannah near Tybee Island, at the mouth of the Savannah River where it entered the Atlantic, when least expected by the British, and without opposition. They still believed the much-touted French vice admiral was in the Caribbean protecting the French sugar islands, as should have been the case at this time. Because there was no British fleet nearby to stop the French invasion of the American mainland, Major General Prévost was now left on his own to make the best of a very bad situation at Savannah.

On September 3, the astounded royal governor of Georgia, James Wright, described one of the great strategic surprises of the American Revolution to Lord Germain: "No man could have thought or believed that a French Fleet of 25 Sail of the Line, with at least 9 Frigates, and a number of other Vessels, would have come off the coast of Georgia in the [hurricane-peak] month of September, and Landed [4,000] to 5,000 troops to besiege the town of Savannah, but My Lord, amazing as this is, it is certainly Fact."[9] The majority of the troops of d'Estaing's expeditionary force were from the West Indies, or, in the words of a French officer, "the greater part of whom were obtained from the colonies," including the troops of the Chasseurs-Volontaires de Saint-Domingue.[10]

The immense size of the mighty French armada fostered an even greater hubris about easily and swiftly achieving victory in America, in the mind of not only d'Estaing, but also his equally confident men of all ranks. A French officer, an aristocratic teenager who enjoyed high-placed social and political connections on both sides of the Atlantic, and a privileged member of the French upper-class elite, wrote quite correctly in his journal that "there was nothing lacking in this paragon of success" for the vice admiral.[11]

It was fully expected by almost everyone on the French side that the upcoming conquest of Savannah would deliver a decisive stroke that would reverse the war's entire course and bring glory to France and Frenchmen under arms, both land and naval forces. Indeed, with "the British army in the South destroyed, Savannah again in American hands, and a French [naval] squadron on the coast, Lord Germain's new overall strategy of war [for conquering the South] would die in the borning."[12]

In truth, this glowing vision and automatic faith in an easy victory by forcing a quick surrender of Savannah was very much a fatal delusion. D'Estaing's glorious capture of the valuable sugar islands of St. Vincent, Grenada, and the Grenadines, which had intoxicated the people of Paris and delighted King Louis XVI, hid a dark undercurrent of disturbing realities just below the surface. First, the vice admiral had secured key British sugar islands because of the lack of stiff opposition and absence of a strong British fleet. He had isolated the relatively small British garrisons on the islands to ensure that their capitulation was their only tactical option, in a no-win situation. Those ideal circumstances did not exist at Savannah, as the vice admiral was about to discover, to his dismay and shock.

Despite the string of d'Estaing's West Indies successes that had made him a hero across France, he had displayed an excessive caution to keep his lofty status and reputation fully intact, taking only carefully calculated risks. The vice admiral's excessive caution had already caused one of his top lieutenants to write with disgust regarding the recent campaigning in the Caribbean: "What comfort our indecision, our endless delays and our wasted maneuvers are giving to the enemy!"—unfortunately for the

French, almost the exact situation that was about to raise its ugly head at Savannah.[13]

The people of Paris would later learn about d'Estaing's successful landing of troops on Georgia soil that had caught the British completely by surprise. The pages of the *Paris Gazette* gave rare initial recognition to the Black and mulatto soldiers of the Chasseurs-Volontaires de Saint-Domingue. The leading newspaper of Paris reported how some 2,979 white "Europeans" were eventually landed with 545 "Colored: Volunteer Chasseurs, Mulattoes, and Negroes, newly enlisted at St. Domingo."[14] Vice Admiral d'Estaing had accomplished one of the great objectives of military leaders throughout the ages: Without firing a shot or losing a man, he had succeeded in winning complete tactical surprise over his unaware opponent, when he possessed all the advantages and his unprepared foe was saddled with all the disadvantages, which seemed too great to possibly overcome—a tactical situation that almost ordained either a swift defeat or capitulation.

Here, at this strategic port surrounded by the Georgia wilderness of seemingly endless pine forests, former Native American lands never touched by an ax, Major General Prévost would have to make the best of a very bad, if not impossible, situation with an ad hoc defensive effort, when the stakes could not have been higher. What was now at stake was the entire British plan for winning the war as so optimistically formulated in London on the Thames—the ambitious Southern Strategy of subjugating the South to reverse the war's course, setting Great Britain on the road toward decisive victory. If Savannah fell to the allies, then the very foundation of the Southern Strategy would crumble, along with the lofty visions of achieving decisive victory that had consumed the calculating minds of King George III, Lord Germain, and other optimistic strategists in London.

Despite being a product of the French army before becoming a career navy man, d'Estaing was still most of all a seaman by nature and proclivity; the sea was in his blood. The capture of Savannah, however, located just inland from the coast, required the skills and abilities of an experienced army general. The British blocked the Savannah River, which ended his initial overly optimistic plan of forcing a quick surrender of the diminutive garrison. As mentioned, the vice admiral's past successes in the Caribbean had reinforced his already-existing cautious and slow approach. He did not want to do anything that might cause the loss of his lofty reputation, which meant acting neither too hastily or too aggressively—the origins of his failure at Savannah.

D'Estaing was not the kind of aggressive commander who understood that decisive victory lay in striking quickly and hard—especially at this point, when he was anxious not to repeat his Rhode Island mistakes. The vice admiral was eager to assist America in her bid for liberty, but only to a limited degree, since his reputation was at stake. After all, d'Estaing's top priority in fulfilling the king's desires was to protect the rich sugar islands of the West Indies, which meant he had originally allotted a mere week to serve in America. Although he knew that the element of surprise was the key to victory, d'Estaing simply "lacked the requisite comprehension of the vital importance of speed and surprise in a land campaign, [and he evidently] viewed Savannah as he had a West Indian target; if that was true, then the effort proved flawed from the start, with an attendant loss of the critically important surprise factor, [while perhaps] also, subordinate commanders in the operation failed to make the point that a leisurely landing and advance on Savannah would allow [Prévost] to react."[15]

From the beginning, a host of inherent problems ran much deeper on the French side, even before the landing on the American mainland was initiated. This was because of disorganization that partly stemmed from the recent creation of this ad hoc force of regulars and West Indies volunteers, who hailed from a number of French islands in the Caribbean and had not previously served together.

As Séguier de Terson recorded in his journal, the initial French landing of the first troops on Georgia soil and the vice admiral's overall plans had to be readjusted to a land approach rather than a water approach, because the British had blocked the Savannah River with the sinking of the British Warships H.M.S. *Venus* and H.M.S. Savannah, including with all fourteen of its canons. This unexpected tactical situation had already caused confusion and dissension among French leadership and boded extremely ill for future cooperation and close operations so far from the Caribbean: "We are to begin by attacking Tybee Island [located at the mouth of the Savannah River and lightly defended], which will not be difficult to take since there are few soldiers there. Such is not the case with Savannah, the objective of our expedition. The English are entrenched and in force [and some of the top French naval officers] do not approve of M. d'Estaing's plans [and they] fear that we are at a disadvantage . . . Right now I see little order, and I am afraid a terrible mess of things has been made . . . We proceeded [toward a landing on Georgia soil] without knowing where we are going [which was the mouth of the Savannah River]. Here we are at seven o'clock in the morning, still anchored in the same place we were last night and still not order[ed] to proceed."[16]

In utter frustration, a disgusted Séguier de Terson continued to describe the chaotic landing, when the French finally went ashore at the primary landing spot on the Georgia mainland during the second week of September: "[A]t the [Savannah] river's edge we set up camp [but] no one had a tent or even a cooking kit [while the rain poured]. The place was called Beaulieu [located on a bluff on the Vernon River and on the Sea Island Road, which led inland from the Atlantic coast, barely a dozen miles below Savannah]. Our arms and cartridges are unusable without major refurbishing. That is dangerous under present circumstances, when we will soon be needing our muskets. The troops were in poor condition, the officers not much better, having no more supplies than the soldiers, [and] a quantity of soaked cartridges had gotten too wet to be used."[17]

A frustrated d'Estaing was already guilty of numerous missteps before the first shot had been fired in anger, especially in regard to the wasting of far too much precious time due to the thorough unpreparedness of his ad hoc campaign. In addition, the landing site at the Beaulieu Plantation (symbolically, the name of a French plantation owner) was "very badly chosen" for the French army, so far from home.[18] Nevertheless, the vice admiral still felt supremely confident that they would prevail and achieve an easy success over the small British garrison, having caught Major General Prévost and his troops so completely by surprise, believing that "the resistance of Savannah will be very feeble."[19]

In a compliment to the overall worthiness of the Chasseurs-Volontaires de Saint-Domingue in regard to the ambitious bid to capture Savannah, d'Estaing had been early informed by Colonel Charles François Sevelinges de Brétigny (with distinct racial overtones that revealed shared white attitudes) that "two fifty-gun ships and some mulattoes" were all that were necessary for the job of ensuring that the white Bourbon flags of France flew over the strategic Georgia city located on the Savannah River.[20]

But as fate would have it, the vice admiral, was about to receive the shock of his life about the overall high quality of the much-maligned opponent from the Albion Isle—something he had badly underestimated, in part because of cultural arrogance and popular French stereotypes about the central weaknesses of the character of the British soldier, and the English people in general.

Extremely thankful that d'Estaing had wasted so much precious time in landing and then lumbering inland at a leisurely pace toward Savannah, despite meeting no opposition, Major General Prévost had been even more shocked by d'Estaing's sudden arrival than Governor Wright. To his credit, Prévost adjusted quickly to the sudden arrival of the formidable threat. D'Estaing had initially landed an advance force on Tybee Island, located at the mouth of the wide Savannah and less than a dozen miles downriver from the strategic city, before gaining his permanent landing site at the Beaulieu Plantation.

Immediately squandering the supreme advantage when he had held all the cards, d'Estaing had already made the costly mistake of not hurling his command inland for a rapid march on the city, to completely exploit the element of surprise before Prévost could concentrate his forces from the surrounding area and organize sound defensive preparations. Again, Major General Prévost had been granted too much time, which gave the Savannah garrison a new lease on life from the beginning. The fact that d'Estaing had only landed a small French reconnaissance in force on Tybee Island before targeting the Beaulieu Plantation had galvanized Prévost, who had originally believed it was too late in the year for the French fleet to arrive, especially during the peak of hurricane season.

This situation had allowed d'Estaing's greatest advantage to slip away, especially in regard to allowing the British to block the Savannah River.[21]

First and foremost, wasting no time after having learned of the arrival of the French fleet on September 4, Prévost had immediately called in his troops from their outposts at various small Georgia communities, in the hope that it was not too late for these scattered troops to reach Savannah in the nick of time: Lieutenant Colonel Thomas Brown's King's Rangers, whose experienced Loyalist members now wore new green uniform jackets with crimson cuffs and collars, from the town of Ebenezer, Georgia, located about fifteen miles north of Savannah on the river of the same name, and by way of the Ebenezer Road that led north from Savannah to Augusta, Georgia, where the exiled rebel government had fled when Savannah had been captured by Lieutenant Colonel Campbell; the well-trained 1st Battalion of around 150 men from Oliver DeLancey's New York Brigade of Loyalists, under Lieutenant Colonel John Harris Cruger, who was highly motivated, partly because he had heard rumors that the Americans planned to put his beloved Loyalists to the sword, from Sunbury, Georgia, located southwest of Savannah; and the more than 300 men of the 3rd Battalion of the New Jersey Volunteers, which had been organized in November 1776, from its assigned position on the brown waters of the Ogeechee River that flowed south and southwest of Savannah to enter the Atlantic.

Originally, the New Jersey Volunteers and two battalions of Oliver DeLancey's New York Brigade, which had been one of the first Loyalist commands raised in New York, had been dispatched from New York to East Florida and had participated in the capture of Savannah in late December 1778. In addition, the garrison at the small British outpost at Cherokee Hill was also recalled, with orders from Prévost to rush to Savannah as rapidly as possible.

Because of both the superior quality of its experienced members and its talented Celtic leader, the most important contingent of veteran troops recalled by Prévost, around nine hundred men, were located at the town of Beaufort on Port Royal Island, South Carolina, just to the north. This was the experienced 71st Regiment of Foot, under the highly capable Lieutenant Colonel John Maitland, easily the major general's top lieutenant.

For ample good reason, Maitland was extremely proud of his fellow Scots. They were the army's best and the pride of the Scottish Highlands, an ancient Celtic land with a turbulent history that had long produced exceptional fighting men throughout the ages. As Prévost and his men fully realized by this time, everything now depended on Maitland's arrival from the South Carolina port of Beaufort. If he could somehow reach Savannah—if it was not blocked by either the French or Americans, or both—Maitland's men would nearly double the size of the diminutive garrison of Savannah. Quite simply, this would determine whether the city would be surrendered, or defended to the bitter end.

Now the only British garrison, a lonely and isolated one, located on the coast between New York City and Savannah, Beaufort was hastily evacuated by Maitland, who then embarked upon the long journey south by boat in the hope that the Scottish Highlanders and a contingent of Hessians would be able to arrive at Savannah in time, as Prévost had ordered. Quite simply, the very life of the diminutive Savannah garrison now depended on Maitland's arrival in a desperate race against time.[22]

As the Savannah Campaign would demonstrate in full, Lieutenant Colonel Maitland was an exceptional Scottish officer on every possible level. If anyone could do the impossible, especially reaching Savannah safely despite the seemingly endless obstacles and low chances for success, it was the irrepressible Maitland. Tough as nails and the consummate professional military man, Maitland had served as a Royal Marine during the Seven Years' War. As Prévost fully realized and appreciated, Lieutenant Colonel Maitland could be depended upon, especially in an emergency situation.

Born in Scotland in 1732 and distinguished by his receding red hair that revealed his Celtic heritage, the iron-willed Maitland was a former member of the House of Commons. He looked young for his age when just beyond his mid-forties. He had first become a battalion commander of the Scottish Highlanders of the 71st Regiment of Foot, and then the regimental commander of one of the best regiments in the British army in 1778. Hailing from one of Scotland's most distinguished families and an aristocrat, Maitland was a true holy warrior. Although he had lost his right hand during the Seven Years' War, he never considered retirement from the service he loved. By this time, nothing could stop Maitland's determination and will, as he would demonstrate throughout the course of the Savannah Campaign in which he was destined to repeatedly rise to the fore in magnificent fashion.[23]

Although stricken by malaria during the summer of 1779, Maitland served with extraordinary distinction throughout the grueling Savannah Campaign, and on multiple occasions during the campaigning in both Georgia and South Carolina, before the final dramatic showdown at Savannah. He died not long after his outstanding heroics there and elsewhere across the Southern Theater, breathing his last on October 26, 1779, barely two weeks after the bloody failure of the main Franco-American assault on the array of defenses that protected the city, which he would help to stop.

Capable Loyalist commanders now served under Prévost at Savannah, including the South Carolina Royalists and the recently raised Georgia Loyalists, under Major James Wright. The hundreds of Loyalists who defended Savannah against their fellow Americans, who must have been astounded by the incredible extent of this brothers' war that had consumed the South, revealed that the struggle for Savannah was very much an American civil war, long before Confederate artillery opened fire on Fort Sumter in Charleston Harbor on April 12, 1861.[24]

Ironically, the fact that the fighting men on both sides at Savannah knew they would be facing fellow Americans only raised their morale and fighting spirit to new heights. They already possessed a degree of hatred for each other, which had only grown during the savagery of America's first civil war, especially in the backcountry, especially by the fifth year. In the words of one patriot, the "Royalists, as they termed themselves, were viewed by us with scorn and hatred."[25]

Far too much time had been wasted by d'Estaing from the very beginning, when the first opportunities were squandered almost nonchalantly by the overconfident vice admiral. Between the moment when the first French ships had been sighted by alarmed British pickets stationed off Tybee Island on September 4 and the landing of a sizable number of

French troops on the high ground at Beaulieu Plantation on September 12, more than a week had passed by in leisurely fashion. This leisurely pace was much to General Prévost's and the garrison's benefit at a time when every single day counted. The reality of this situation was not fully appreciated by d'Estaing in the chess game for the possession of Savannah, in which Prévost would prove the undisputed master.[26]

The wasting of so much time by d'Estaing was as alarming as it was costly for French fortunes. After having wasted too many days at Tybee Island, despite meeting no opposition, Vice Admiral d'Estaing had only belatedly begun to land most of his army at Beaulieu Plantation, located on a sandy bluff among the stately pines overlooking the Vernon River, a dozen miles south of Savannah, from September 12 to 14. Far too many rain-filled days had passed, soaking the French soldiers to the bone. They suffered severely from lack of proper clothing and supplies, and they had no tents, and their morale dropped accordingly.

This was well past the originally planned date of September 11 for a joint allied assault on Savannah, which proved to be utterly impractical. It had first been agreed upon by Major General Benjamin Lincoln and the vice admiral's representative, Major General François de Fontanges, who now served as d'Estaing's adjutant and chief of staff.

Of course, Prévost badly needed this extra time because of the incompleteness of the defenses on the land side, or south, southwest, and southeast, from where, in their hubris, the overconfident British had long expected no threat. The entire semicircular network of Savannah's defenses, more than 12,500 feet in length, needed to be improved and strengthened as quickly as possible, because they were in deplorable shape from a long period of neglect. However, Prévost benefited from the fact that each flank on the east and west rested securely on the Savannah River.

From the beginning, Prévost knew that he was in serious trouble, because he possessed only 1,200 British, Hessian, and Loyalist soldiers to man the sprawling defensive line—too few troops to defend such an extended line against thousands of French and American attackers. However, he had a secret ace in the hole that he used to the fullest: Captain James Moncrief of the Royal Engineers. A talented officer whose time had come in a true crisis situation, Moncrief immediately went to work with a zeal and an energy seldom seen. He was ordered to strengthen the defenses on the land side of Savannah, before it was too late, as the enemy was already descending upon Savannah. Making the most of the opportunity, Moncrief immediately began the laborious process of creating a new and more extensive network of fortifications, including the building of an entire series of new redoubts.

First and foremost, three key roads that entered Savannah had to be protected and the defenses strengthened where they entered the expansive network of fortifications: the Ebenezer, or Augusta, Road that led northwest through the seemingly endless pine forests to Augusta and entered the southwestern edge of the defenses at the Spring Hill Redoubt; the Sea Island Road that cut through the malarial swamps and broad rice fields located southeast of Savannah, and the sandy artery that d'Estaing had used to advance steadily northwest along the flat coastal plain, toward the city from the main landing site at the Beaulieu Plantation; and the Ogeechee Road that led south through the low-lying coastal plain, located not far from the Atlantic's cold waters.

By any measure, Moncrief was no ordinary royal engineer. The chief engineer's task was considerable, because when he went to work with enthusiasm on the greatest challenge of his career, only four neglected earthen redoubts were positioned on the land side of Savannah on the south. Fortunately, the Savannah River protected the city on the north and caused Prévost no worry, after prudently blockading the river approach to the city—much to d'Estaing's everlasting grief.

Moncrief now had to make up for a good many past mistakes and miscalculations from months past. After Campbell's easy capture of Savannah in late December 1778, no one had even bothered to order the strengthening of the land side of the city because British confidence in the conquest of all Georgia had been so high and entirely unquestioned. Of course, this was a most glaring omission that now came back to haunt Prévost and his command during this true crisis situation. Another highly capable Scotsman, born in 1741, and a distinguished graduate of the Royal Military Academy, Moncrief came to the rescue at Savannah with his abundant skill and competence, doing the impossible in record time, to the utter shock of the French and Americans.

As a cautious and ever-traditional commander, d'Estaing was already out of his element, far more than he realized: He was worried about not repeating his Rhode Island errors; he was unfamiliar with land operations; and he continued to act on the premise that no haste was required for the successful reduction of the Savannah garrison, and for the strategic city to fall into his lap. The cocky vice admiral was already convinced that the Savannah garrison was doomed and had no realistic choice but to surrender, partly because he mistakenly believed that Maitland had been blocked at Beaufort and would never reach Savannah, which was certainly not the case, as he was about to discover. All the while, Vice Admiral d'Estaing continued to squander his overall chances for success with each passing day by wasting too much time, as if unmindful that the clock was ticking.[27] His ill-fated men were destined to pay a high price for these weaknesses and miscalculations in the end.

The capable aide-de-camp to Major General Prévost, Major T. W. Moore, described how much time it took for d'Estaing to land all his forces, negating the element of surprise, while the British were busily strengthening their fortifications night and day, to present another surprise to the vice admiral: "Count d'Estaing's Fleet appeared off the Bar on the 4th of September, said to be 46 in all—25 of them Ships of the Line; and came to anchor the 9th, and soon began to land their Men and Guns, and were busy in bringing every Force against us till the 16th, when they appeared within 300 Yards of our Lines."[28]

Indeed, four days passed from the time of the initial French landing date at the Beaulieu Plantation to the investment of the city on September 16. Prévost, Moncrief, and his men made very good use of this time, working around the clock to improve the defenses, to make them formidable.[29] Prévost realized that his only hope lay in strengthening the defenses of Savannah as much as possible and in record time, before it was too late. Fortunately, he possessed the brawn, both Black and white, and brains, in his command, especially in the case of his gifted chief engineer, to accomplish the seemingly impossible task.

The brilliant Captain Moncrief was in his element, excelling in masterful fashion. He proved his extraordinary talents by working overtime and with great energy, utilizing at least nearly 530 Blacks (about 250 slaves, 59 Black Pioneers of the British army, and 218 Black volunteers), but almost certainly more, who made significant contributions in a timely manner to create a powerful defensive network.

The slaves at Savannah had come from nearby plantations and had been gained in South Carolina by the British during Prévost's push to Charlestown. These men of African heritage now paid immeasurable dividends by serving as the central foundation for the laborious and time-consuming process of strengthening the earthen defenses, including the four existing redoubts that were made more formidable, and then building new defenses and creating even more sturdy redoubts of immense strength. Before the tough job of adequately protecting Savannah had been completed, hardworking Blacks and whites had added an astonishing total of ten new redoubts, for an impressive total of fourteen, while also connecting them with trenches in an intricate and strong defensive network.

In addition, houses, barns, and trees were cleared by the Black laborers, both slaves and free men, to provide open fields of fire before the line of British trenches and redoubts that circled Savannah in the shape of a giant horseshoe. The Savannah River protected the open end of the horseshoe, on the north. The collection of wood taken from numerous dismantled houses, including the ample timber that had been found on one of Governor Wright's many sprawling plantations, was then used to build gun platforms for the cannon that crammed the redoubts, to make them more formidable. The imposing Spring Hill Redoubt that anchored the British right contained some of this timber, as well as iron and bronze pieces that had been taken from British warships. One amazed British soldier wrote about what had been achieved in short order: "In the meantime Moncrieffe [sic] was indefatigable in putting the place in a proper state of defense."[30]

Loyalist Elizabeth Lichtenstein, who had long called Savannah home, described how the wasting of so much invaluable time by Vice Admiral d'Estaing "gave Colonel Moncrief, our brave engineer, time also to throw up works, [and] such was Moncrief's ardor, skill, and industry that he made the town able to stand a siege of six weeks."[31]

One defender of Irish descent, Captain Kennedy, wrote with admiration about what had been accomplished by the industrious British and their Black allies, who possessed good reason to hate the patriots, who would return them to slavery if captured: "We had for some Time been repairing the four old Redoubts, and making some additional Works . . . Bur now the greatest and most extraordinary Exertions were made by Captain Moncrief . . . [and] between two and three hundred Negroes. [In total] 13 good Redoubts were soon erected round the Town, and 15 Gun Batteries containing about 76 Pieces of Cannon."[32]

Originally, the French had carefully counted only around two dozen cannon in the lengthy line of the British defenses and sensed an easy victory in consequence, if either prudently ordered to attack or initiate a heavy bombardment by the vice admiral. However, like a patch of mushrooms rising from a grassy meadow in a rainy springtime in Georgia, the number of British guns steadily grew with each passing day. Eventually, a remarkable total of 123 bronze and iron guns, whose barrels had been cast mostly in London, appeared like magic, including artillery pieces transported from British warships and manned by experienced seamen. The Gallic onlookers were stunned, especially the vice admiral, who could not believe the sight.[33]

It was clear that the devout and duty-minded General Prévost, who was not unnerved about the prospect of facing superior numbers, was determined to make the most tenacious defense, in his own words, "by the blessings of God, to be vigorous and worthy of British troops."[34]

The forces of nature and geography also came to Moncrief's and Prévost's aid, in the form of a cold rain, the sandy soil composition, and the area's overall topography. These factors presented a far more daunting tactical dilemma to d'Estaing, much more than he had originally imagined while making his grandiose plans in the lavish comfort of his imposing flagship.

First and foremost, the Savannah River had been effectively blocked by the sinking of two vessels and the timely creation of a large boom across the river's considerable width. Of course, this was meant to thwart d'Estaing's naive plan to force the city's swift surrender to his warships by sailing into the wharf area, with rows of cannon ready to fire. The wide, sluggish river protected Prévost's rear on the north, while low-lying swamps secured both sides of the town on the east and west, making Engineer Moncrief's formidable task easier. A thankful and increasingly more confident Prévost wrote how he "had nothing to fear from the rear, or from the right and left . . . It was necessary therefore to provide for the defense only of the front or southern exposure of the city."[35]

Finally, in the tradition of an overconfident upper-class aristocrat who had been seduced by his string of recent successes in the West Indies and an easy life of almost unlimited privilege as a member of France's upper crust, Vice Admiral d'Estaing continued to waste valuable time. From the beginning, he proved to be entirely unimaginative and ill-suited for the formidable task of campaigning on land in America with the goal of capturing Savannah. The vice admiral was far more focused on traditional European protocol and old-fashioned ways of warfare, as if still relying on his winning tactics that had garnered him fame when capturing the British sugar islands of St. Vincent, Grenada, and the Grenadines in the lower Antilles. With courage and audacity, d'Estaing had led his tough French marines up the formidable high ground of "hospital bluff" against the British fort that overlooked the blue harbor of St. George, the primary port of Grenada, and captured the British guns perched on the high ground on the night of July 3–4, 1779.

Compared to attacking the high ground of Grenada, a volcanic island whose mountains towered above the wine-colored sea, facing an extensive network of fortifications on the level plain situated atop the Savannah River bluff looked easy in comparison—but this was a fatal illusion, as d'Estaing would soon learn, along with his unfortunate followers, both Americans and Frenchmen.

PLAYING THE OLD LEISURELY EUROPEAN GAME INSTEAD OF IMMEDIATELY ATTACKING

The distinguished-looking vice admiral would waste even more time by following European conventions and tradition when he issued a formal demand of surrender to Major General Prévost. This happened on

September 16, while d'Estaing was on the march along the sandy road to Savannah, after having finally disembarked all his troops at the Beaulieu Plantation. This old plantation owned by a French immigrant was situated on a picturesque bluff covered in tall, virgin pines that still looked as inviting as when they were first seen by European explorers, who had marveled at the beauty of this new land of boundless promise and beauty.

D'Estaing had fully expected that his overwhelming numbers would induce a swift capitulation of Savannah, much like Colonel Brétigny's prior promise to the gullible vice admiral, who knew nothing at all about the challenges of campaigning in the South or the nature and character of its people, when he said that a decisive victory could be won "without firing a shot" in anger.[36]

D'Estaing's summons for the surrender of Savannah was sent by way of Irish captain James O'Moran of the Arthur Dillon Regiment, which consisted of crack Irish fighting men who were known for their combat prowess and overall toughness. As could be expected, with Lieutenant Colonel Maitland and the Beaufort garrison now making their laborious way south to Savannah, Major General Prévost immediately stalled for time, thankful that d'Estaing had not immediately ordered an all-out assault that would have captured the city with remarkable ease at a small cost in lives. Playing a clever game to exploit d'Estaing's naiveté and overconfidence, which was rooted in traditional European ways of waging war that were now badly outdated at Savannah, Prévost naturally requested specific terms for surrender, as well as more time—now the key to preserving Savannah and the diminutive garrison.

The traditional procedure and protocol ensued, which involved a steady flow of communications between respective commanders. This bought additional time for the small garrison of British soldiers, who were now completely at the mercy of the superior might of the French army and navy. At this time, d'Estaing fully believed that Lieutenant Colonel Maitland and his garrison were still located at Beaufort, far from Savannah. Still believing that time was on his side, the vice admiral leisurely replied to Prévost during their traditional exchange of letters. Many increasingly alarmed French officers considered all of this an unnecessary and "vainglorious display" of proper etiquette and protocol, as if d'Estaing was waging a proper gentleman's war in faraway Europe.[37]

In the words of one proud Loyalist: "[T]hey sent their flag to offer terms [when] our General was told that no quarter would be given if he refused, and that he would have the lives of his men to answer for"—to higher authorities, including God.[38] Proving that he was out of touch with existing realities far from the West Indies, d'Estaing continued to expect an automatic and swift capitulation to his diplomatic summons for the surrender of Savannah, which had been carried by the gentlemanly and diplomatic Captain O'Moran of Sir Arthur Dillon's Irish Regiment, who wore their red uniforms with Celtic pride. The end result now seemed inevitable to the confident vice admiral, who still believed he held the winning hand in this high-stakes poker game.

The French knew a little about the Geneva-born Prévost, but nothing that indicated to them that he was the most cunning and formidable of opponents. Underestimating Prévost like almost everyone else, especially d'Estaing, one French grenadier officer wrote in his journal: "This man, a major general, is a Genevan and has his wife [Anne] and son with him." They may have believed this meant Prévost had more than military matters to think about during this stressful period, when the fate of Savannah and his small garrison had been caught in the grip of a mighty French expeditionary force that had suddenly appeared out of nowhere.[39]

In actual fact, Major General Prévost was an exceptionally tough and seasoned veteran leader who combined competence with a great deal of solid experience. He was not the kind of commander to give in to diplomatically veiled threats from the French, like a typical European commander would have done during the Seven Years' War, by way of a polite exchange of traditional formalities between high-ranking officers and gentlemen. Perhaps Prévost's unique nickname said it all: "Old Bullet Head," only employed in private conversations between his men, well out of his hearing.

Prévost's sobriquet stemmed from a still noticeable dent in his temple made by the glancing blow of a British cannonball. The injury had occurred when Prévost was standing before a lengthy formation of his troops on the Plains of Abraham, just outside Quebec's gates, at the famous Battle of Quebec, Canada, on decisive September 13, 1759, when the French suffered the defeat that had lost North America during the French and Indian War. Prévost had received another wound on May 11, 1745, during a key French victory at the Battle of Fontenoy in the War of the Austrian Succession, which won Flanders for the triumphant French.

If anything, Prévost's popular nickname revealed his toughness and tenacity as a hard-nosed fighter, which did not bode well for d'Estaing, who expected nothing more than a demoralized foe eager to surrender in a bloodless victory that would win him greater fame in the king's court at the luxurious palace of Versailles. Despite his advanced age, Prévost was tactically innovative and flexible, which made him a first-rate commander. He was not bound by the confining rules of traditional protocol and ancient custom, like d'Estaing. Prévost was similar to Maitland, a freethinker who utilized flexibility and unorthodoxy to outwit his elitist opponents and secure victory in crisis situations like the one he now faced at Savannah.

Ironically, Major General Prévost had recently requested to resign for the sake of his family, who were now with him in Savannah. He had even considered that he was too old for active service and vigorous duty. Fortunately for England, Prévost's wise superiors thought differently, and now Prévost had turned from family man to the consummate warrior in an emergency situation. To the major general's credit, the daunting challenge posed by the sudden arrival of the French expeditionary force had energized him and brought out the best in this savvy career army man from Switzerland.

To buy additional time, Prévost wisely requested the establishment of a temporary truce of twenty-four hours to consider the generous terms to capitulate, which Vice Admiral d'Estaing naturally granted, like a proper gentleman and according to time-honored military custom—"in the true style of a Frenchmen," as one British soldier mockingly penned in a letter. All the while, the outnumbered troops of the small, isolated, and now extremely busy Savannah garrison continued to make all manner of defensive preparations. Most of all, they continued to hope and pray for the arrival of Lieutenant Colonel John Maitland, the highly capable

Scotsman in command of the army's finest regiment—the 71st Regiment of Foot, consisting of disciplined and well-trained Scottish Highlanders.

Like Prévost, Maitland was every inch a fighter, and would never capitulate as long as a good fighting chance remained. He had departed Beaufort as soon as possible on September 12, pushing rapidly south from the evacuated port of Beaufort fifty miles away from Savannah in a desperate race against time, knowing he had to reach Savannah as soon as possible.

D'Estaing continued to allow his chances of capturing Savannah to steadily slip away by being outwitted by a clever opponent, a cunning Scotsman of outstanding ability he had grossly underestimated.[40] Significantly, Prévost took full advantage of every minute d'Estaing nonchalantly granted to him like a true gentleman, tirelessly improving his weak defenses that had been sadly neglected since the city's capture by Lieutenant Colonel Campbell in late December 1778. Ironically, d'Estaing was well aware of this fact but basically looked the other way. In a nicely worded and polite reminder that was excessively diplomatic to the point of being ridiculous, so as to not cause any personal offense, d'Estaing told Prévost that the hectic pace of his defensive preparations were not proper gentlemanly behavior during the ongoing surrender negotiations, according to traditional protocol: "It is a matter of very little importance to me," but such improper and impolite conduct during formal talks should cease, for proper "form's sake."[41]

Clearly, unlike Major General Prévost, d'Estaing was simply not dealing with the blunt realities as they existed on the ground at Savannah, in this new kind of war in America that was most often the antithesis of how centuries of warfare had been conducted in Europe. The vice admiral had yet to learn that he was not dealing with an ordinary British opponent. Prévost was definitely not overly consumed with the outdated concepts of proper gentlemanly behavior or the outdated dictates of tradition, as he was.

In many ways, it was almost as if the vice admiral had never left the European or Caribbean theaters of war, and existed in another time and place. He was still awed by memories of the glories of ancient warfare, immortalized by Homer. The vice admiral especially rejoiced in one of his names—Hector, who had been one of the main heroes of the Trojan War. D'Estaing never quite understood that a new kind of war was now being waged in America. This was the unorthodox and challenging New World, and the new rules for waging war were far removed from the traditional ways of conducting war in Europe—a reality that had been fully demonstrated by the later stages of the French and Indian War. This was well understood by Prévost and other resourceful military men, like Maitland, and it would take all their cunning, experience, and skills to save themselves and the strategic port of Savannah from the superior might of the Gallic invader and their American allies during this crucial campaign for possession of the second most important port city in the South.

During this long truce period that was exploited to the fullest by the British, when time was of the essence, the more realistic and common-sense Americans were not saddled by traditional etiquette and protocol from faraway Europe, like their Gallic allies. Consequently, they were shocked that d'Estaing had wasted so much precious time with niceties like exchanging letters, especially with the gracious granting of a temporary truce when the enemy was most vulnerable and ripe for the taking.

Because they were already familiar with the bitterness and horrors of this war, unlike the newly arrived French whose idealism and innocence remained intact, many Americans realized that a golden opportunity was being unnecessarily squandered by these old-fashioned formalities from faraway Europe. Leading the 2nd South Carolina Continental Regiment, an incredulous Lieutenant Colonel Francis Marion, a successful Santee River, South Carolina, planter and Indian fighter who had helped to defeat the Cherokee of western South Carolina in 1776, said it best: "My God! Who ever heard of anything like this before? First allow an enemy to entrench and then fight him!"[42]

A German Hessian officer of the Savannah garrison, which contained the grenadier regiments of von Wissenbach, of 529 men, and von Trumbach, of 293 Germans, was also absolutely amazed by the folly of the French vice admiral that seemed to have no end. This Teutonic officer wrote in astonishment of how d'Estaing had not attacked to take full advantage of the most favorable of situations and reap the benefits of the golden opportunity that would never come again: "Why did he not on the 13th, or at least on the morning of the 16th, storm and take this miserable sand pile with fixed bayonets?"[43]

As throughout the course of this ill-fated campaign, d'Estaing's lack of aggressiveness and tactical astuteness only made him more unpopular among his men, especially among his fellow aristocrats of the upper-class elite, who were jealous of his past successes and rapid rise through the ranks. Dissent and anger were on the rise in all ranks of the French expeditionary force in both the army and navy, which would erode its overall effectiveness and cohesion in this all-important campaign.[44]

JOHN MAITLAND'S TIMELY ARRIVAL

Prévost had already succeeded in winning the master chess game of well-educated and professional military minds, because he had successfully "stalled and d'Estaing did not press [and] the stalling paid off," when a sudden miracle appeared out of the blue: The first of Lieutenant Colonel Maitland's Scottish Highland and German reinforcements marched wearily into the sandy streets of Savannah on a rainy September 16, in the most vital of rescue missions. This now gave the thankful defenders more than a decent fighting chance. With Maitland's timely arrival, an emboldened Prévost decided that "We will defend ourselves as long as we can."[45]

The French were naturally upset, because Maitland's arrival violated the twenty-four-hour truce and the traditional European protocol that had been established between proper gentlemen of the upper-class elite. In the words of one shocked French officer, who was shackled by the past and as custom- and etiquette-bound as Vice Admiral d'Estaing: "The reason they asked for a truce is that they were expecting a small reinforcement of four to five hundred men from a little island named Beaufort. They were afraid that we would harass them, but we by no means have the ability to do so; only about half our troops had landed and not a single artillery piece. The reinforcement entered Savannah by way of the river, much to the elation of the English and to our great regret. It could make the defense of the fortress last longer. The event illustrates how honorable our enemy is."[46]

Adding insult to injury, on the morning of September 17, Lincoln and d'Estaing watched with their field glasses from the high ground of Brewton Hill while the last elements of Lieutenant Colonel Maitland's troops—roughly eight hundred men in total—pushed up the wide waters of the Savannah River in rowboats, after the most harrowing of journeys south from Beaufort by land and water. No longer harboring any lingering doubts or illusions, the two commanders of their respective allied armies realized that they had been badly outsmarted by the wily Prévost. They knew that they now had a serious fight on their hands, and far more than they had bargained for in their gross overestimations of a quick and easy victory.[47]

Feeling disgust and disbelief, Vice Admiral d'Estaing was astounded by the sight of Maitland's arriving soldiers in their bright red coats: "I have had the mortification of seeing the troops of the Beaufort garrison pass under my eyes."[48] These experienced veterans with flintlock muskets on their shoulders poured into Savannah to a chorus of wild cheers.

Capturing the representative mood among the stunned Gallic fighting men, who already knew that victory had slipped away like the recent hot Georgia summer, one French artillery officer was equally bitter, writing that d'Estaing had wasted so much precious time when he "tried to prove to him [Prévost] in a long letter the uselessness of putting up a defense. Prévost prolonged the negotiations for three days, under the pretext of assembling a council of war. He was aware of the forthcoming arrival of Maitland who . . . joined him during the negotiations."[49]

Conveniently overlooking their own colonial allies—the Blacks and mulattoes in the ranks of the Chasseurs-Volontaires de Saint-Domingue—the French were also upset that the opposing major general in a scarlet uniform was simply not waging war fairly. They felt this way because Maitland's force now included "many negroes" who he had prudently armed, because the wily Scotsman knew that every soldier would be needed to defend Savannah.[50] Many aristocratic French elites who were serving as officers in both the army and navy expressed these feelings of astonishment, including the navy's distinguished Louis-Antoine de Bougainville.

A genius and scientist who had written a masterful book on calculus at an early age and freely quoted words from Homer's *Iliad* and other revered writers of the ancient classics, the gifted de Bougainville had served as the brilliant aide-de-camp for the Marquis de Montcalm during the French and Indian War. This high placement had been partly due to the helpful efforts of a fawning Madame de Pompadour, who was blessed with an astute "military mind." The revered Montcalm had been killed on the Plains of Abraham in a futile defense of Quebec during the dramatic final showdown for possession of the North American continent—the so-called Battle of the Plains of Abraham. Bougainville was proud of having long served with distinction as Montcalm's "right hand," and now wore the deceased general's sword on his side in a display of sentimentality and fond remembrance.

The open-minded, thoughtful Bougainville, who was the priviledged son of a talented Paris lawyer, had long deplored the gross mismanagement of the war effort in New France (Canada): "What a country! What a war!" The war in New France had been shabbily supported by the faraway mother country, dooming Montcalm's best efforts to save France's largest overseas possession from conquest. The gifted Bougainville was a famed global navigator, circumnavigating the globe and visiting Tahiti during the late winter of 1766. He had introduced the European world to the beautiful red-flowered tropical plant known as bougainvillea, named in his honor. He also left an enduring legacy in the Solomon Islands in the South Pacific with the tropical island named Bougainville, which he discovered, to the delight of the upper-class elites of Paris.[51]

In an April 21, 1758, letter he had written about the folly of Louis XV in not properly allocating resources to save New France from the might of William Pitt's ever-growing and better coordinated offensive operations. Bougainville lamented "that French bones would cover this battlefield," without ever realizing that a far greater number of French bones would lie in the sandy ground of Savannah by the end of 1779, where they remain undisturbed in an unknown location to this day.[52]

Like so many other high-born members of the upper-class elite of France, Bougainville was a prime example of the dedicated and highly capable aristocrats who served with distinction under d'Estaing from beginning to end during this miserable campaign in Georgia. It would be wrong to think that these wealthy, privileged aristocrats were not determined and hard-nosed fighting men, as was naturally assumed by the British, who looked down with contempt upon their Gallic opponent (albeit, with less contempt than they directed toward the American rebels). The fighting prowess of these French soldiers would be fully demonstrated at Savannah on bloody October 9, 1779, when they rose magnificently to the sternest of challenges.

In truth, "these titled dandies of Old France were no mere carpet-knight warriors. In battle they were bold as lions, ready to die with their men . . . The roster of highborn [officers] reads with the sonorous cadence of Shakespeare's catalogue of the French chivalry at Agincourt [on bloody October 23, 1415, during the Hundreds Years' War]. Besides Comte d'Estaing, Vicomte [Louis-Marie] de Noailles, Comte [Arthur] Dillon, and the Vicomte de Fontanges, there were the Marquis de Pondevaux, a nephew of the great [Comte de] Vergennes; Comte d'Hervilly; Vicomte [Jules-Jacques-Elenore] de Béthisy; Marquis de Rouvray; Comte de Villeverd; Marquis de la Roche-Fontenilles; and Baron Curt von Stedingk."[53]

However, the heightened arrogance and pride of these young aristocratic men from France's most privileged families had already sowed the seeds of an ever-growing amount of discord in this army of regulars and volunteers, including among the men of the Chasseurs-Volontaires de Saint-Domingue. It was inevitable that elitist officers of such a high social class, especially the haughty nobles and counts of France's elite, would ensure not only a lack of cohesion in the army, but also a deep-seated animosity, based largely on jealousy, toward d'Estaing, in regard to almost everything he did to further the interests of France. Hot-headed, opinionated, and temperamental, in keeping with common stereotypes about Gallic aristocrats embraced by the English, these privileged elites of France were truly a "volatile lot," to say the least, which was revealed during the course of this ill-fated campaign in Georgia.[54]

Because these high-born men of privilege were highly capable fighters in their own right, it was no wonder that Vice Admiral d'Estaing had fully expected that "soon the city would be his, a brighter feather in his cap than Grenada."[55] But worst of all, D'Estaing viewed himself as invincible after his string of Caribbean successes that had made him the toast of Paris, convincing him that "Caesar and Alexander [the Great] were nothing [compared] to him."[56]

But when hundreds of Maitland's troops safely arrived in Savannah, the spirits of these entitled counts and nobles were shaken to an inordinate degree, as if they had made a minor mistake in proper protocol for all to see at the court of Versailles. Along with the timely bolstering of British manpower—and thus, firepower—at the last minute, the psychological benefits of Maitland's timely arrival, especially Prévost's elite command, the 71st Regiment of Foot, could not be overestimated. It fueled the defender's once-low resolve and determination to hold firm against both Frenchmen and Americans.

In the words of Loyalist Elizabeth Lichtenstein, who had been caught inside the city with her family like other Loyalists, and rejoiced at what seemed like a miracle sent from heaven with Maitland's timely arrival: "Our men, having few to relieve them, suffered from fatigue and want of rest, but in the height of our despondence [Lieutenant] Colonel Maitland effected a junction in a wonderful manner, crossed from the Carolina side [and] entered Savannah, this giving new life and joy to the worn-out troops."[57]

As could be expected, the Americans, including Major General Benjamin Lincoln, who believed "that it was the French responsibility to prevent the evacuation of Beaufort by anchoring vessels up the [Port Royal] river," blamed the French, and the French naturally blamed the Americans—their favorite scapegoat from beginning to end of this campaign—for having allowed Lieutenant Colonel Maitland and his crack troops to come all the way from Beaufort without meeting any opposition.

D'Estaing had been "entirely convinced that the Americans were blocking" the land route from Beaufort to Savannah, which was the case. The ever-resourceful Maitland had trekked across fifty torturous miles by water, the remote coastal lowlands, and then by land, when near Savannah. Major General Viscount François de Fontanges, who now served as the vice admiral's adjutant, was incensed and accusatory. He heaped so much scorn upon the Americans for having failed to block Maitland from reaching Savannah at one especially heated conference that d'Estaing feared young Lieutenant Colonel John Laurens, known for taking offense at the slightest insinuation, in the tradition of hot-blooded and proud South Carolina aristocrats, would surely challenge Fontanges to a duel.[58]

In truth, the vice admiral was the true culprit, responsible for the embarrassing fiasco that would cost the allies so dearly on October 9. As mentioned, D'Estaing had simply taken too much time landing most of his expeditionary force, moving them inland at such a leisurely pace, as if time was of no concern whatsoever. This was only one reason for the bad feelings that developed between Lincoln and the vice admiral. It certainly did not help matters that Lincoln's army was delayed partly because Charlestown's worried officials had argued against the departure of their guardians on a mission so far south, never forgetting Prévost's recent scare that had consumed the city and its inhabitants during the late spring of 1779. Both d'Estaing and Lincoln had given Prévost too much time before Maitland's arrival; although for different reasons, it caused the same result, which would prove disastrous to France's and America's fortunes in the end.

In fact, d'Estaing had unilaterally issued his surrender summons before Major General Lincoln had arrived overland from Charlestown, which caused the indignant Massachusetts general to strongly protest the unilateral action that was made without American input or approval. This was a violation of proper protocol and unity among allies, and a very bad start to what should have been a close interaction between the allies for the overall benefit of achieving success, especially after the lack of cooperation and hard feelings that had resulted from d'Estaing's failed effort in Rhode Island during the autumn of 1778. These gloomy sentiments regarding the alliance's previous failure still lingered like a dark cloud, and helped to sabotage a considerable amount of unity, trust, and cooperation that was absolutely necessary for success.[59]

In addition, the wide gap in cultural differences that existed between the allies raised its ugly head at Savannah. The spirits and confidence of the finely uniformed soldiers, especially among the aristocratic officer corps, from France and the Caribbean were also considerably lowered when they first caught sight of their American allies, including the over-weight Major General Lincoln, whose appearance was hardly imposing, especially when he periodically fell asleep at the most inopportune of times. A shocked French grenadier officer penned the following in his journal on September 15: "The American army joined us today; it is composed of nearly 2,000 men . . . For the most part these forces do not appear to be in good condition. Of those I saw only the Virginia dragoons are well mounted. The rest are militia who are supposed to be quite good, at least they say they are."[60]

Fearing that his old Saratoga wound might prove fatal with the approaching summer heat, like Major General Prévost, Major General Lincoln had attempted to resign in the spring of 1779, but had been convinced otherwise by Governor John Rutledge of South Carolina. As Lincoln, a New Englander, wrote in a letter: "I have been too long accus-tomed to a Northern climate to think of risquing [*sic*] a seasoning at this time of life [mid-forties] to a Southern one."[61]

To Lincoln's credit—much like General Prévost, who had also desired to resign for personal reasons—he had quickly gone into action, collecting all available troops, including men from the South Carolina backcountry, to answer the urgent call to duty at Savannah. Most import-ant, Lincoln remained eager to work closely with the French in the hope of reaping a turning point victory at Savannah and reversing the course of the war, which was exactly why he had been sent south by Washington and the Continental Congress in the first place.[62]

Like so many other soldiers in the French camp, one exasperated French artillery officer also had harsh words for the Americans, who looked like a bunch of rustic farmers from the remote backcountry: "They never had more than 2,500 men, for the most part [South] Carolina militia . . . Ah, my General, what a disappointment these men are when you see them firsthand; how different they are from the impression they give us in camp! You have no idea of the disintegration of the American army."[63]

Even the three regiments of South Carolina Continentals, under Scotland-born Brigadier General Lachlan McIntosh, were in bad shape overall by this time, and certainly inspired no confidence in the Gallic allies. The arms of these Continentals—America's regular troops—consisted of anything and everything that they could find at home and elsewhere, including fowling pieces and old hunting muskets. The Continentals used Spanish moss that hung down in long strands from the trees as wadding instead of paper to cushion lead bullets against black-powder charges in their musket barrels. Footwear was scarce; leather boots were worn only by officers, when available. Many Georgia Continentals wore moccasins ingeniously fashioned by themselves from any available beef hides, while headgear—contrary to the stereotype of finely uniformed Continentals—consisted of "cocked hats, round hats, beaver hats, leather hats, and straw hats," as worn by common farmers in the rural countryside and the backcountry. Even some uniform coats of the Continentals had been fashioned from deer hides, as if they were still living in the backwoods of the piedmont and on the untamed frontier, before the war. Of course, the raw members of the Georgia and South Carolina militia were in far worse shape than the Continentals.[64]

This was certainly not the case with the men of the Chasseurs-Volontaires de Saint-Domingue, who had been finely uniformed by their white officers, which included some men who had been wealthy merchants of Le Cap. The ragged, undisciplined Americans from the South must have looked in amazement at the almost unbelievable sight of the hundreds of well-dressed and well-trained Black and mulatto soldiers of the Chasseurs—something they had never seen before or even imagined in their wildest dreams.

Presenting a splendid appearance, these young men from faraway Saint-Domingue wore lightweight navy blue uniforms with white cross belts and a white waistcoat. This linen uniform for tropical service was topped with a stiff, high yellow collar to present a sharp look. The Chasseurs also wore navy blue tricorn hats that matched their uniform coats. Meanwhile, French regulars wore tricorn hats and white uniforms in the longtime tradition of the soldiers of the Bourbon kings.[65]

THE REAL TURNING POINT BEFORE THE FIRST SHOT WAS FIRED

Lieutenant Colonel Maitland's timely arrival was not the miracle it seemed. The abundant leadership skills and sheer determination of the fiery Scotsman were the main factors—and not a kind Providence—that ensured Maitland's Beaufort command reached Savannah just in the nick of time. Paradoxically, even though it had not seemed all that important at the time to the French and Americans in the ranks, because confidence was so high, Lieutenant Colonel Maitland's sudden arrival with "the flower" of Prévost's little army was nothing less than the crucial turning point of the struggle for possession of Savannah.

Cut off from proceeding south by land from Beaufort, Maitland had faced the most daunting of challenges from the beginning of what had been a true odyssey. Nevertheless, he had still managed to slip out and reach Savannah by way of cunning stealth, easing through the twisting maze of inland waterways of coastal South Carolina amid a low-lying sea of grass that covered the coastal region before reaching the Atlantic's waters. After a great deal of effort, Maitland and his sojourners finally reached the Savannah River, which was surrounded by swamps and watery grasslands as far as the eye could see. The men rowed and dragged their boats at shallow points through the twisting inland waterways of the flat coastal grasslands and then through subtropical forests on higher ground to eventually gain the city by land.

Lieutenant Colonel Maitland and his men refused to be denied, thanks to their dogged tenacity and Maitland's outstanding leadership. He and his men, including North and South Carolina Loyalists, had been forced to wade through about twenty miles of dense swamps, "often up to the Middle in Mud and Water," which was dark and foul-smelling, like the typical watery Georgia lowlands at this time of year. The final elements of Maitland's command—around eight hundred weary, wet, and mud-streaked men—struggled into Savannah on the evening of September 17, after having accomplished what had seemed impossible to one and all, except the Scotland-born lieutenant colonel, who refused to give up.

They also benefited from the timely guidance of a Black Gullah fisherman, who spoke a distinct Creole language (Gullah) that consisted of a variety of West African languages mixed with a scattering of broken English. Maitland and his troops had met the fisherman by chance, who enlightened Maitland about a suitable route—a narrow passageway and shortcut nestled between tidal creeks of a brackish and shallow saltwater way dug years ago by slaves to connect two wide creeks of sluggish, brown water. This was known as "Wall's Cut," located behind Daufuskie Island, upriver from the stationary French warships that had blocked entry to Savannah, prudently guarding the Savannah River's mouth. Thanks to the Black fisherman, Maitland and his troops reached Prévost just in the nick of time.

Clearly, this remarkable feat was nothing less than Maitland's finest hour. Quite simply, the aristocratic Scotsman had performed a minor miracle to revitalize all of Savannah and its defenders, while dashing d'Estaing's false dream of forcing Savannah's surrender without wasting a good many French lives. As Vice Admiral d'Estaing had learned the hard way, anyone who underestimated Maitland did so at their own peril. Instead of having retired two decades before because of a disability from a wound suffered during the Seven Years' War, fortunately, for the people and garrison of Savannah, Lieutenant Colonel Maitland remained faithful to God and the king by continuing to do his duty year after year. The empty right scarlet sleeve of the Scotsman's uniform coat told the true story of what kind of man he was, still fighting even after having lost his right hand to a French cannonball in the naval fight that was won by the British, at Lagos Bay, located southwest of Cadiz, Spain, during the summer of 1759.

While serving in the Northern Theater, he had specifically requested transfer to the 71st Regiment of Foot. He had proven to be an ideal commander of the Scottish Highlanders, who idolized Maitland, and for good reason. Recently, he had emerged as the hero during the sharp clash of arms at Stone Ferry on June 20, 1779, when he had held the American attackers at bay and bought precious time for Prévost to return to Savannah.

As mentioned, Maitland was fated to die in less than two weeks, but only after the day had been won and Savannah had been made secure for the remainder of the war. He would die on October 26 of overexertion combined with the effects of the so-called "bilious fever" that had long ravished the people of the Georgia coastal lowlands. It had struck Maitland and racked his weakened system during the recent, miserably hot summer on the coast, and would contribute to his death in the fall.

The sudden arrival of Maitland's eight hundred experienced troops, the finest soldiers of the Savannah garrison, could not have been better timed "to the inexpressible Joy of the whole Army," penned one thankful defender. The overconfident d'Estaing, who fully expected a quick capitulation, had just issued his summons in vain for Prévost to surrender. Now, to end the temporary truce, and as noted, an emboldened Prévost defiantly responded with an outright rejection of the surrender summons. Vice Admiral d'Estaing was shocked. He now realized that this frustrating war in America was going to be far different from the war in Europe and the West Indies, where he had won nothing but victory and glory for God and counry.

Clearly, these stubborn men in scarlet uniforms—Prévost, who was described as "brave as Caesar," in the words of an admiring staff officer, and Maitland, who held his Scottish claymore broadsword in his left hand, after having lost his right hand in battle—were quite a formidable team of experienced officers. They were an entirely different breed from the less-determined British leaders, who had been vanquished by d'Estaing with relative ease on St. Vincent, the Grenadines, and Grenada. The vice admiral held in such high esteem by King Louis XVI was learning some harsh lessons even before the serious fighting for possession of Savannah had begun. Now, with a united British and Hessian force of 2,360 men of the two commands against around 5,500 French and Americans, the formidable team of Prévost and Maitland would ensure that "England was to experience at Savannah one of her finest hours" on October 9.[66]

American newspapers reported on how the irrepressible Lieutenant Colonel Maitland and his men had only succeeded in reaching Savannah because they had "plunged through swamps, bogs, and creeks which had never been attempted before but by bears, wolves, and run away negroes."[67]

Bolstered by Maitland's timely arrival and British defiance, Loyalist Elizabeth Lichtenstein described the dramatic scene that set the stage for some of the bloodiest combat of the American Revolution: "When they sent their [white] flag to offer terms [Prévost] refused to capitulate. Captain William Johnston [her future husband and a dedicated Loyalist officer] met the officer, the Count de Noailles, and conducted him to headquarters [in Savannah], and was present when he gave the [surrender summons] in an elegant style, contrasting strongly with our plain, blue Swiss or German [of General Prévost]. The answer the Count received was laconic, 'The King, my Master, pays these men to fight, and they must fight, and we decline your terms.'"[68]

Clearly, Prévost had felt insulted by d'Estaing's letter and almost casual demand for a surrender that he fully expected. It was dominated by Gallic arrogance, which reflected the vice admiral's supreme confidence in a hasty capitulation, without cost to his expeditionary force. One of his officers wrote in a letter how d'Estaing's letter boasted "of his formidable Armament by Sea and Land; the great Feats he had performed with it in the West Indies, and mentioned how much Lord [George] McCartney had suffered by not capitulating Grenada, and that it was in vain to think of resisting his Force."[69]

As if not realizing that a turning point in the struggle for possession of Savannah had already taken place with the arrival of Maitland's full Beaufort garrison of crack troops, d'Estaing had been thoroughly shocked by his opponent's behavior, which he considered unethical. As recorded by French artilleryman François d'Auber de Peyrelongue, when Prévost had "announced that he had decided to defend himself, M. d'Estaing [who was as fixated with pretty women as the celebrated mythical heroes of the ancient Greek classics] had expected a better outcome; he said jokingly that a girl who made compromises was very close to surrender."[70]

Experiencing a degree of frustration that he had not encountered with his victories over the British in the Caribbean, the vice admiral, who had been educated in the ancient classics and greatly admired ancient Greek heroes, later complained how "this strange siege was the work of Penelope," referencing the wife of Ulysses, or Odysseus, who had been absent because of the ten-year Trojan War, and her clever scheme that had deterred her many suitors over the years. D'Estaing was basically blaming his own mistakes and miscalculations on the hands of a cruel fate and the fickleness of the Gods, comparing it to the heroic story of Ulysses in Homer's *Odyssey*, because so many of his well-laid plans had been so effectively thwarted seemingly by the hands of fate.

As noted, even more bad blood bubbled up between the French and the Americans because of Maitland's arrival, which caused inevitable finger-pointing. The cocky vice admiral had mistakenly assumed that the Americans had blocked Maitland's southward route from Beaufort to Savannah, and that he would only need a mere ten days in America to capture the city on the Savannah River.[71] In the bitter words of South Carolina's Major Thomas Pinckney, if only Maitland and his troops had been effectively blocked from entering Savannah unopposed, then "they would have Capitulated without firing a Gun," and the strategic port city would have been easily won, as d'Estaing had originally imagined.[72]

Here, at Savannah, d'Estaing would prove to be more astute in the art of cracking jokes than in cracking the British line and morale during the siege, which officially began on September 23, followed by the frontal attack on the defenses of Savannah on October 9. One of his officers, François d'Auber de Peyrelongue, failed to appreciate the vice admiral's oddly timed sense of humor. He complained in his journal how d'Estaing "always knows how to make jokes in the least amusing circumstances," including at critical moments—especially when they knew a lengthy struggle would now be necessary to subdue Savannah and its tough garrison of determined defenders, who were now more emboldened and confident than ever before.[73]

Other key cultural qualities of the French, especially in regard to the elitist attitudes of the upper-class aristocrats in the officer ranks, boded ill for the outcome of this all-important campaign that centered on whether or not the South would be conquered by the British war machine. As a Mediterranean people, and in general, the French—especially the wealthy elites of the noble class, including d'Estaing—were more volatile and temperamental. These well-known qualities of Gallic nature and personality, including impatience and impetuousness, came into play at

Savannah—factors that also ordained the final outcome of the struggle for Savannah during this eventful fall of 1779.

In general, the "mercurial qualities of these Frenchmen contrasted sharply with the more restrained temperament of their English foes," especially the even-tempered and thoughtful Prévost and Maitland. Even though neither man was born in England, they hailed from fundamentally the same climate, in Western Europe and were dominated by a practical sense and wisdom.[74]

Having bolstered d'Estaing's confidence for easy success, one that he anticipated would be as bloodless as it would be effortless, Major General Lincoln's force contained some of the leading names from Southern society, especially in regard to Charlestown. Charlestown native at only age twenty-four, the dashing Lieutenant Colonel John Laurens was one of Lincoln's top lieutenants, and his top commander of the Continentals. Well-educated and fluent in French, he was the aristocratic son of wealthy planter Henry Laurens, who served as the governor of South Carolina and then as president of the Continental Congress from 1777 to 1778.

Noted for wearing a resplendent blue Continental uniform with a long plume on his tricorn hat, young Laurens had been one of General Washington's favorite aide-de-camps, a best friend of fellow staff memeber Alexander Hamilton, and was an exceptional leader. His only weakness was a brazen aggressiveness that too often caused Laurens to take unnecessary risks on the battlefield. Laurens, totally committed to the cause in his heart and soul, commanded the well-trained Continentals of the Light Corps. The dashing lieutenant colonel was destined to lead the right attack column on October 9, when he went for broke at the head of his South Carolina and Virginia Continental troops in attacking the Spring Hill Redoubt on October 9, in a desperate bid to secure victory at any cost.

For ample good reason, and in a French analogy, the young South Carolina blueblood with a fiery nature had acquired the reputation of "the Bayard of the Revolution." He was destined to lose his life because of an excess of courage and bravado in an insignificant South Carolina skirmish after the great victory had been won at Yorktown. He was shot off his horse while leading a doomed harge on the enemy with only a few men in a backwater sector of South Carolina on the Combahee River on August 27, 1782, because he could not stand the enemy's presence of South Carolina soil—one of the truly tragic and unnecessary losses on the patriot side during the course of the American Revolution.

A little modest and serious-minded man of Huguenot descent named Francis Marion now led the 2nd South Carolina Continental Regiment, which was in Laurens's assault column on October 9. Marion was as unpretentious as he was hard-fighting and determined, including when he battled against the Cherokee in the 1776 campaign to protect the Western settlements and secure the patriots' vulnerable rear, which freed them to now serve in the coastal region of Georgia. Marion hailed from the fertile Santee River country in South Carolina, where he was a successful planter. He would earn fame the following year and thereafter leading a determined band of South Carolina guerrillas as the elusive "Swamp Fox," endlessly evading the British during his sparkling career as the die-hard and wily leader of highly effective partisans. Like d'Estaing's expeditionary force, Lincoln's army now possessed plenty of ethnic diversity, including a good many Scotch-Irish from Ulster Province, North Ireland, and their sons, along with Germans, Scotsmen, Welshmen, and even a "Jews Company" of patriots under the command of Captain Richard Lushington.[75]

The Southern backcountry was also well represented in the ranks of Major General Lincoln's motley army of Continentals and ragtag Georgia and South Carolina militiamen. Brigadier General Lachlan McIntosh was of Celtic descent, like so many of his men, including three South Carolina Continental regiments and around five hundred Georgia and South Carolina militiamen, whose ancestors could be traced back to Ulster Province of North Ireland. There were upcountry militiamen from Augusta, Georgia, located some 120 miles upriver from Savannah. One of these fighting men battling for an infant nation's liberty was the father of the future president of the Confederacy from 1861 to 1865, Kentucky-born Jefferson Davis, who was of Welsh descent.[76]

An aggressive Continental leader like Laurens, McIntosh was every inch a fighter in the Celtic tradition. He had led the second of three failed patriot attempts to capture St. Augustine, Florida, which was the capital of British East Florida, in 1777. When McIntosh and Button Gwinnett, who commanded the Georgia militia, had clashed over seniority in leading the expedition south to Florida, a deadly duel resulted. Near Savannah's cemetery, in the most famous duel in Georgia history, McIntosh had mortally wounded Gwinnett, who also served as the president of the Georgia Council of Safety, in another self-inflicted tragedy on American fortunes and efforts that so often seemed to self-destruct.[77]

Prévost was every bit as tough as Laurens and McIntosh, and defying French threats from arrogant aristocrats came exceptionally easy and natural to him. Of course, the real key to Prévost's change in attitude and heightened defiance toward d'Estaing's overtures had been Maitland's timely arrival. One defender wrote in his journal on September 16, describing the timely rescue of the small British garrison when least expected by the allies: "[Lieutenant] Colonel Maitland and the Troops from Beaufort arrived—71st and New York Volunteers [of Loyalists]; brave Fellows [and now all of] Savannah in the highest Spirits."[78]

With his spirits rejuvenated by the clever buying of additional time by Prévost and the complete befuddlement of Vice Admiral d'Estaing, Major T. W. Moore, one of Prévost's capable staff officers, wrote in a letter how during this crucial period that "General Prévost desired [which was twenty-four hours] to consider [the surrender summons], we were reinforced with 800 Men, under the Command of Colonel Maitland, from [Beaufort, South] Carolina. This made us about 2,000 strong, and very saucy as to refuse to let Monsieur [the French] and Jonathan [the Americans] in."[79]

As could be expected, the British and Loyalists held the French, and especially the "Rebels," in absolute contempt, thanks to long-existing anti-Gallic views stemming largely from the French and Indian War experience. After all, France had been both England's and America's historic enemy in the generation before the American Revolution. And this same kind of utter contempt was felt by the French toward their ancient enemy, the Britons, and even toward the Blacks and mulattoes of the Chasseurs-Volontaires de Saint-Domingue, but, of course, less so in general—only because of the curse of racial prejudice and hatred.

One well-bred French officer of the upper class at Savannah—who considered himself a proper gentleman, unlike the detested English of the Albion Isle—described how "the English are a Parcel of rude, unpolished Savages."[80]

As if this was not enough, still another kind of contempt had raised its ugly head during the campaign, already deeply ingrained among both Lincoln's and d'Estaing's troops—the mutual hostility and distrust between allies that continued to grow with each passing day. François d'Auber de Peyrelongue, an officer of the French artillery, was already bitter and angry about recent developments since having landed on Georgia soil, feeling a sense of betrayal, which was a representative attitude. As he penned in his journal: "[T]he provisions that the insurgents had promised to furnish us [were not forthcoming]. They deceived us on that point and many others. The [original] decision to [go to] Savannah was based upon a letter of supplication which the [South] Carolina Assembly had addressed to M. d'Estaing at Saint-Domingue, on the word of [the French representative in Charlestown], who described the expedition as very easy, and on the pitiful account they gave of their situation. All the intelligence from Charlestown was found to be absolutely false. The English were supposed to be only 1,500 in total in all. We found them well entrenched 425 yards in front of the city in numbers of 4,500, counting militia and sailors under arms. Their regular troops did not exceed 2,500, including three Hessian battalions."[81]

As could be expected under the circumstances, especially in regard to already having been outwitted by the savvy team of Prévost and Maitland, Vice Admiral d'Estaing was naturally even more upset than de Peyrelongue. Rather than from his own ineptitude and the general confusion and disorganization that was epidemic among the French on Georgia soil, he blamed his initial delays and wasting of precious time directly on the Americans, who became the favorite scapegoat of not only the increasingly cynical d'Estaing, but seemingly every Frenchman at Savannah: "I remained at anchor for quite a long time, doing nothing, waiting for the delivery of wood that [the Americans] probably did not want to send us quickly, for our presence was useful to those who furnished it."[82]

Of course, the British eventually learned of the depth of the growing bitterness that existed and continued to grow between the fumbling allies, who only saw each other's worst qualities. As printed in the pages of a Loyalist newspaper in New York City: "Mutual animosities and Revilings have arisen to such a height betwixt the French and Rebels . . . that they were almost ready to cut one another's Throats."[83]

D'Estaing later wrote indignantly: "The enemy, scattered in four different posts, was supposed to be prevented from rallying his troops. We were told that there were only 1,300 men at Savannah, many of them sick. We and the Americans together made up a force of 6,000 men; the numerical ratio between besieged and besieger then was almost exactly correct according to regulations. Singular causes gave us reason to believe that if the British general could capitulate without signal dishonor, he would do so . . . it is certain that if the Beaufort garrison had not joined the one in Savannah, there would have been a capitulation. This reinforcement was not inevitable, could have been prevented; any sort of reinforcement whatsoever was supposed to be stopped [by the Americans, in the vice admiral's mind, without taking any personal responsibility whatsoever, although this was his campaign to win or lose]; it should not have happened. The plan, then, was a good one, and I therefore had the duty of carrying it out; and if I had not done so, I would have been judged culpable not only by others but also by myself, which is much more distressing."[84]

Clearly d'Estaing was self-serving and defensive here, attempting to justify his failure to capture Savannah by indicating that he and his troops had been betrayed by the Americans. As mentioned, in the vice admiral's mind, and in the opinion of the French in general, the American rebels were to be blamed for everything.

In this same biased narrative, written in the interests of himself and the French for the official record, Vice Admiral d'Estaing was more specific, emphasizing in no uncertain terms how to the north the South Carolina port of "Beaufort [was left open], although I was entirely convinced that the Americans were blocking it off by land."[85] Out of touch with reality, the vice admiral had been erroneously "convinced that Savannah's resistance would be very weak," which was certainly not the case, as he was about to discover, to his shock.[86]

In a decisive turn of developments and as noted, the overall situation at Savannah was dramatically changed by Maitland's arrival from Beaufort, when d'Estaing accused Prévost of shameful and dishonorable duplicity. D'Estaing felt the Swiss-born British commander had been reduced to a detested socially inferior status, below the most revered one, of a proper "officer and a gentleman." In his mind, "According to his own letter, General Prévost requested the truce to convince various interests and classes of the town to support a surrender; it was nothing but a trick."[87]

But of course, the clever Major General Prévost actually had no other choice under the circumstances, as he had found himself in a do-or-die situation. According to the proper protocol of the day, he had committed "a cardinal error" by his adroit maneuvering to gain time with a much-needed truce on the premise of considering the surrender summons from the vice admiral, when in fact he was only deliberately buying time, waiting for Maitland's arrival, which he admitted in his report to Lord George Germain in a surprisingly straightforward manner.[88]

In one of the great ironies of the Savannah Campaign, given the situation, d'Estaing was even angrier at the Americans than he was at Prévost. Indeed, throughout his writings, d'Estaing reserved his most bitter contempt for his own American allies, partly a lingering legacy of the Rhode Island disaster, which had badly bruised his ego and left lasting scars. As he penned in a broad generalization based on existing stereotypes that revealed the extent of his bitterness from this ill-fated campaign in Georgia: "It is the nature of Americans to promise much and deliver little; this nation always counts on acquiring whatever it lacks."[89]

Almost as much as for the British, an ancient enemy of the Gallic nation for centuries, the French contempt for the Americans, especially the untrained South Carolina and Georgia militiamen, grew to new heights when their high level of inexperience was shortly exposed more thoroughly, only reinforcing the already-existing anti-American stereotypes and attitudes so pervasive among the French. One French artillery officer could not resist the opportunity to thoroughly denounce the amateur Americans: "I had considered them brave until I saw them take flight, leap out of the trenches, fall on their stomachs because of a few misdirected cannon balls, even though they were under cover. I like to think that the troops from the north are better."[90]

To be fair to the Americans, after the British failed to capture Charlestown in 1776, the absence of war in the South for the past three years had left the Georgia and South Carolina militiamen without combat experience or discipline, in overall poor shape for the demands of the conventional showdown at Savannah. Unlike the French and likie even George Washington, the patriots possessed no experience in siege warfare. Most of all, they were citizen-soldiers of the republic in the truest sense, and still appeared to be nothing more than a motley crew of armed farmers rather than legitimate soldiers, which was largely the case. There was simply no comparison in training, discipline, and experience, not only between Lincoln's militiamen and the British and French troops, but also the soldiers of the Provincial Loyalist commands at Savannah, who were excellent fighting men. Nonetheless, this much-maligned America militia, without proper uniforms or equipment, would rise splendidly to the challenge of the assault on October 9, when it counted the most.[91]

Aristocratic general Curt Bogislaus Ludvig Christopher von Stedingk, a nobleman and one of d'Estaing's top commanders, also had harsh words for the ragtag Americans, who were decidedly unsoldierly-like in almost every way, except for the Continentals. In an insightful and hard-hitting letter to the king of Sweden, von Stedingk emphasized how the Americans were "so badly armed, so badly clothed, and I must say so badly commanded, that we could never turn them to much account. . . . It seemed as if the Americans in general were tired of the war [which was true compared with the newly arrived French]. . . . Their troops were reduced almost to a band of deserters and adventurers from every country."[92]

Bordering on open hostility, the ever-increasing level of internal divisions and dissension had already weakened the moral fiber and morale of the allies, especially among the French officer corps of both the army and navy, natural rivals in the French military. As mentioned, regular French soldiers even felt a degree of hostility toward their comrades of a darker hue, which made the fighting men from Saint-Domingue feel almost as if they had never departed their tropical homeland, whose entire economy was based on racism and a robust system of slavery not seen on such a massive scale anywhere else in the Caribbean, including the British West Indies. One French artillery officer, who was frugal by nature and race-conscious, complained about the soldiers who were darker than himself and his comrades: "600 black volunteers [were] enlisted at great expense at the Cape [Cap-Français]" in Saint-Domingue.[93]

At this time, however, the young men of the Chasseurs-Volontaires de Saint-Domingue "were being treated like musketeers," in d'Estaing's words, revealing that they had gained a measure of equality to the white soldiers in the French expeditionary force during this campaign. Like combat experience in general, the hardships shared by both Blacks and whites together had a tendency to lessen the amount of racism, but only to a degree.[94] Because of matters of class, pride, and honor, and since they hailed from a race-based slave regime and had long felt the sting of discrimination in all varieties, the Black and mulatto men of the Chasseurs were naturally averse to taking any orders from excessively autocratic white officers other than their own, and those who still believed that soldiers of a darker shade were good for nothing but menial labor, like slaves.

For this reason, and to quell the racial sensitivities and discontent simmering at Savannah, and much to his credit, Vice Admiral d'Estaing demonstrated early on that he was not afraid of dirtying his hands to set the proper example for the sake of unity and morale: "I myself had to carry for several yards cast-iron swivel guns with small field carriages, which we were likely to use anywhere [at the front], in order to convince the [white] commander of the mulattoes that yellow and black soldiers . . . could easily perform the same task without dishonoring themselves or tiring themselves too much."[95]

THE GROSSLY INEFFECTIVE SIEGE OF SAVANNAH

Destined to be one of the costliest sieges, counting the October 9 assault, of the American Revolution, and up to the time of the Civil War, for American soldiers and civilians who were Loyalists, the unorthodox and nontraditional siege of Savannah was officially initiated on September 23.

This decision mocked d'Estaing's original ten-day timetable to achieve a swift victory in Savannah, now completely in shambles and utterly impractical, thanks to having wasted so much precious time, as well as Maitland's arrival at the last minute.

Going against the conventional rules of European warfare, the vice admiral planned no traditional siege approaches or parallels that were the usual formula for reaping victory, because they were so time-consuming. In what would prove to be yet another miscalculation on the vice admiral's part, the elaborate French siege works were primarily constructed to support and protect the batteries for the upcoming bombardment. The vice admiral had his own unorthodox plan for capturing Savannah, which called for an unconventional strategy that deviated from traditional siege tactics, because of his ever-growing obsession with returning to protect the sugar islands of the French West Indies as soon as possible.[96]

As the long, hot summer in the South was gradually dying with the advent of fall, so were d'Estaing's chances of reaping a decisive victory. Already, some of the first unmistakable signs of the early arrival of fall in the Savannah River country had been ascertained by men in tune with the subtle nuances of nature. As the oak trees and meadows along the creeks were turning brown, D'Estaing and Lincoln now optimistically believed that victory would come when a heavy bombardment sufficiently reduced the will of the civilian population. Of course, this would take place after the large French cannon were moved into position and they opened fire on Savannah. Then, the inevitable mounting pressure from civilian authorities would pressure the British to surrender to save the community and countless lives.

The town of Savannah consisted of only around 430 houses, almost all wooden structures, and especially vulnerable to hot shot that would start fires. They would be forced to surrender by the rain of falling projectiles that would do extensive damage. The two allied commanders were convinced this was only a matter of time once all hell was opened up on Savannah—basically, it was a means to sufficiently terrorize and demoralize the enemy, both soldiers and civilians, to force a surrender. As noted, the allied commanders were convinced the civilian population of men, women, and children, including Prévost's own family, would apply heavy pressure on military authorities to capitulate. D'Estaing's strategy was clearly the most optimistic of scenarios, based on a tactic of terrorism that was relatively rare in the annals of eighteenth-century warfare, especially during this war in America. If it worked, then it would not have mattered at all that Lieutenant Colonel Maitland and his men had arrived in Savannah, because they would be forced to surrender like everyone else.

While d'Estaing continued to waste valuable time as the early fall weather gradually turned cooler, especially at night, without ever delivering a devastating blow, the extremely energetic Chief Engineer Moncrief continued to work overtime with a zeal that amazed military and civilian onlookers. With considerable professional expertise, ingenuity, and a single-minded doggedness that paid immense dividends, Moncrief made Savannah's defenses much stronger with each passing hour, turning what had been an incredibly weak position into a powerful one. He skillfully improved the original four redoubts and created nine entirely new redoubts, anchoring the lengthy defensive line that was becoming truly formidable, thanks to his tireless efforts. More than one hundred artillery pieces were eventually placed inside the defensive network that ringed all three sides of Savannah.

Organized into efficient work details by Chief Engineer Moncrief, hundreds of slaves, recently freed Blacks, and the 277 Black Pioneers, an official unit of the British army led by white officers, had cut down cedar and tall pines to fashion a massive network of abatis that strengthened all thirteen redoubts. Of course, the sharp ends of the abatis before the earthworks were positioned by Moncrief to point toward any attackers who might dare to cross the open ground that had been turned into a natural killing field, guaranteeing to break up assault formations and thwart the attackers.

Significantly, this talented Scotland-born engineer, whose worthy counterpart in the French army was the respected Captain Antoine O'Connor, created a lengthy span of defensive works that consisted of a combination of dense sand from the bluff overlooking the river and green and spongy pine wood, guaranteed to absorb the iron projectiles, even of the largest caliber of French cannon. Even the sand itself became an asset to the British. After the sand defenses were damaged during the day by bombardment, they would be quickly and easily repaired by the defenders during the night, to negate the damage. The highly skilled Moncrief worked day after day until "he made the town able to stand a siege of six weeks," in the words of one Loyalist woman.[97]

Before Maitland's arrival, the British leaders and men of the small garrison could not have successfully defended the town if d'Estaing had ordered a general assault as soon as possible, as so many French and Americans had clearly ascertained and freely voiced in disgust. A Hessian officer, of either the von Wissenbach Regiment or the von Trumbach Regiment, trapped inside the inadequate and incomplete defenses, yet to be strengthened by Prévost's talented chief engineer, was incredulous. The astonished German wrote how it was almost beyond comprehension that the around five thousand French and Americans had failed to immediately "storm and take this miserable sand pile with fixed bayonets" and easily capture Savannah.[98]

The fate of d'Estaing's mission had been sealed early on when several wooden merchant ships had been shuttled into the main channel of the river below Savannah, to stop French warships from sailing farther north up the wide river to shell the town into submission. Then, the British had smartly erected "a good boom," in Prévost's words, and on his orders, across the river to prevent French fireships—long an effective strategy of European naval warfare—from smashing into anchored British warships and the town's commercial district and wharves along the river, to wreak havoc.

All in all, consequently, such thorough British defensive "preparations meant that whereas the French could have taken the Georgia capital with relative ease if they had moved directly against the town after first coming ashore on September 12, they would now encounter considerable difficulty in breaking through" what had become a formidable defensive network by this time.[99] One distraught French soldier wrote in his diary about the dark realization and haunting feeling that was becoming more pronounced in the increasingly gloomy French army with each passing day: "We regret that we did not attack on the very first day."[100]

François d'Auber de Peyrelongue of the French artillery was awed by what he saw before him. As penned in his journal, he described early in the siege how "the enemy entrenchments consisted of a large abatis along the entire front of their line, which was studded with five redoubts [that were increased to more than a dozen, thanks to Captain Moncrief's excellent and thorough efforts], each of which protected it. In the intervals between the redoubts were the batteries. In front of all of this they had a ditch nine feet deep. Behind it there was a second ditch into which they would probably have jumped if they had been expelled from the first one. The whole defense line was protected by 130 pieces of cannon of all caliber, but mostly 4-pounders. It backed up on the river on two sides, and its flanks were defended by swamps. We had dug our trench facing the center of their line."[101]

Like Vice Admiral d'Estaing, most Americans still remained under the delusion that Prévost would suddenly come to his senses and surrender, once the large French guns were positioned and opened fire in all their fury. Of course, the tough and resilient Scotsman in his resplendent red uniform had no thoughts whatsoever about ever giving up; it was not in his nature, and he believed that he owed his best efforts—and even his life, if necessary—to the king and Crown. Nevertheless, an optimistic and young Lieutenant Colonel John Laurens shortly dispatched a messenger on horseback to General Washington to inform him that Prévost was bound to surrender Savannah in only two or three days. Like so many other soldiers in both armies, Laurens was entirely wrong in his overly optimistic estimation.[102]

Even a journalist of a Charlestown newspaper crowed that once all of the French cannon were positioned in advance locations by capable French engineers and opened fire, then the "town would immediately surrender or be laid in ruins in a few hours."[103] And the *Maryland Gazette*, which was printed in the state capital of Annapolis, revealed the pervasive optimism to its readers: "[E]very body [is] in full prospect of repossessing Savannah, and of having the British general, his troops, and the wrong governor Sir James Wright, prisoners of war within a week."[104]

But young Laurens and other Americans failed to realize exactly how ineffective the siege of Savannah would prove to be, falling far below lofty expectations for a quick capitulation. Why would this be the case? First and foremost, d'Estaing's plan of a steady artillery bombardment to terrorize the civilian population, who would then force a surrender by applying pressure on military authorities, would have no influence on determined men like Prévost and Maitland and the Loyalist residents, who hated the rebels and remained committed to a die-hard defense to the bitter end. In this regard, the French vice admiral had once again badly underestimated his opponent, revealing that he was very far out of his element in waging war in Georgia.

However, other key factors also came into play to thwart Vice Admiral d'Estaing's grand designs and ambitions that had been formulated in the French West Indies.

Trapped in Savannah with her family during the siege, Loyalist Elizabeth Lichtenstein emphasized the faulty tactical and psychological reasoning that lay behind d'Estaing's off-target plan to force Prévost to surrender, from the anticipated pressure from the civilian population, who would be terrorized by the upcoming bombardment. She described how the allies "were opening their batteries, and constantly cannonading and throwing bomb shells [into the city]. Fortunately, however, our men were encamped near the trenches [instead of near Savannah], and these deadly shells went a distance over their heads. The streets being sandy and not paved, the shells fell and made great holes in the sand, which often put out the fuse and prevented explosion. Indeed, the colored children got so used to the shells that they would run and cover them with sand . . . [A]s we were rather scarce of ammunition, they would often pick up the spent balls and get for them seven-pence apiece" from the British.[105]

Ironically, the British defenders at the front were destined to be safer from the upcoming bombardment than the population of Savannah, because it had been chosen by d'Estaing to be targeted—yet another partial reason for the unleashing—and failure—of the October 9 assaults. For safety's safe, even Governor James Wright was destined to wisely depart his comfortable quarters in town on October 4 because of the hail of falling projectiles, moving "to the Camp, having pitched a Tent next to Colonel Maitland's [own tent] on the right of the Line."[106]

To additionally disrupt d'Estaing's overoptimistic timetable in regard to his desire to return to the French West Indies as soon as possible, the British took swiftly well-designed steps to slow the overall progress of the siege. For instance, General Prévost additionally decided to attempt to buy time and to disrupt the siege's progress by launching nighttime sorties to disrupt siege operations that were calculated to choke the life out of the Savannah garrison. On September 24, he initiated the first confrontation of the war between regular British troops and regular French troops on American soil during the American Revolution—certainly a historic milestone for the Franco-American alliance, upon which the entire fate of America now hinged in this war. Then, another British sortie was launched three days later by Major Archibald McArthur, who led a Scottish Highland strike force of the elite 71st Regiment of Foot on the French siege lines, but without significant or lasting results.

Taking a long-term strategic view, Major General Prévost's other top priority of holding out as long as possible was "to detain Mr. d'Estaing as long as possible from (perhaps) attempts of higher consequence on the coast," especially New York City, whose safety was the top priority among British leaders and strategists on both sides of the Atlantic.[107]

Meanwhile, the overall progress of d'Estaing's siege was not moving forward at a pace that held much promise for the much-anticipated capitulation. Philippe Séguier de Terson, a proud French grenadier, was upset like other French officers, and for ample good reason, as the siege's painfully slow progress was turning into a joke. As he penned in his journal during the last week of September: "The night was so quiet that we were able to use it to construct fortifications, both to continue work on the batteries and to improve the trench. But unfortunately there is no one who knows how to oversee the works, and, to our great regret, nothing is finished."[108] On the following day, September 26, the frustrated French grenadier wrote: "The siegeworks are not going forward, but some artillery arrived which we could put into position if we knew how."[109]

Nevertheless, many naive Americans still remained confident and optimistic for success, despite the lack of progress and any tangible positive results. On September 28, Colonel Joseph Clary, of Scotch-Irish descent, and a victim of the optimistic delusions that ran rampant in the American camp, wrote in a letter to a friend: "I hope my next [letter] will Congratulate you on the Reduction of Savannah . . . In a few Days I am hopeful [our efforts] will put us in Possession of [the] Town."[110]

In fact, significantly reducing the defenses and weakening them to make them vulnerable was not a top priority for d'Estaing, as it would be in a typical siege according to traditional methods of forcing a surrender. Therefore, the upcoming planned massive bombardment was destined to be a complete waste of time, because d'Estaing's "artillery was useless against the sand fortifications" and accomplished nothing to break the will of Prévost and his men, or even that of the civilian population.[111]

The vice admiral and his well-trained artillerymen had not realized that the upcoming ineffectiveness of his bombardment would partly be due to the fact that "the ground was all sand in the city and the streets were not paved," like large cities in France, especially Paris.[112] To the wealthy aristocrats and elitist nobles of the French officer corps, Savannah hardly looked like anything worth fighting for, especially when it came to selling their lives for France and King Louis XVI, if necessary, when so far from home. To many of them, the once-popular idea that they might be able to win glory in this bleak part of Georgia seemed extremely far-fetched, and more so with each passing day.

Fated to be killed during the upcoming allied assault on the strategic Spring Hill Redoubt on October 9, Major John Jones was a pious officer of the Georgia militia of General Lachlan McIntosh's command, and a respected aide-de-camp to the general of Welsh heritage. Jones had old scores to settle with the enemy, after having had his Sunbury, Georgia, property confiscated and his plantation, home, and store destroyed by Loyalists. He would write a letter to his wife Polly on a Sunday—certainly no day of rest for either side at Savannah, but one he attempted to keep as holy as possible under difficult circumstances—when the optimism was still pervasive for the most part among both the French and Americans: "[This] afternoon . . . we shall open with twenty-six pieces of battering cannon and thirteen bombs. I am in hopes, in the course of twenty-four hours' plan on their different redoubts, that they will think it prudent to surrender; and if they should not, God knows what will be the consequence. Many valuable lives must be lost in taking the town by storm, the last resource . . . We have the prayers of the Church, and I hope, from the justness of our cause, that God will decide in our favor."[113]

His letter to his beloved Polly would prove prophetic, as one of the lives lost at Savannah would be his own.

The Loyalists in the defenses at Savannah were as highly motivated as Major John Jones, prepared to give their lives so that all America would once again be under full control of the mother country and a constitutional monarchy that they considered superior to a republic. Typical Tory political and moral sentiments were revealed in a Loyalist recruiting effort in Philadelphia that had promised a moral cause and honor to Loyalists serving "in Defence of their Country, Laws and Constitution, against the arbitrary usurpations of the tyrannical Congress" of the young United States of America.[114]

FORGOTTEN BLACK SOLDIERS WHO FOUGHT FOR THE BRITISH

Since the issuing of General Clinton's June 1778 emancipation decree, escaped slaves from South Carolina, Virginia, and Georgia—the vast majority—had poured into Savannah. An estimated total of 620 Black soldiers, including 277 men of the official British army unit known as the Black Pioneers, served in the trenches of Savannah, including the "many negroes" who Maitland had armed out of necessity. Prévost had followed Maitland's smart example by arming even more former slaves; these men made fine soldiers because of their high motivation and hatred of slave-owning patriots that knew no bounds.

Meanwhile, a good many Black women and children likewise supported the British in rear-echelon roles, freeing up manpower, Black and white, to serve in the front lines. Most Black women served as cooks and laundresses for primarily British officers, often also the case in regard to patriot officers from the South in a striking paradox, because Blacks viewed the redcoats as liberators. Major General Prévost later paid a lofty tribute to these Black soldiers, who were a worthy counterpart to the Chasseurs-Volontaires de Saint-Domingue. These former slaves from the South were mostly darker in color compared to the mulattoes from the West Indies serving in the ranks of the Chasseurs. Prévost wrote with priode: "They certainly did wonders . . . in fighting [and] they really shewed [sic] no bad countenance."[115]

Born a slave in Virginia around 1740, David George and his wife Phyllis, who was half Black and half Native American, and their three children, Ginny, Jesse, and David, had escaped the surreal horrors of slavery, including whippings by an angry master, to find what they believed to be safe refuge in Savannah. But the siege and entrapment in the city had jeopardized the family's existence each day, for what seemed like an eternity.[116] David George was described as "a free Negro" and faithful "good subject to King George."[117]

Former slave Scipio Handley was another one of the Black fighting men of Savannah who battled for the British. A former fish seller from the cobblestone streets of Charlestown, Scipio had escaped not only slavery but also patriot reprisals for having carried dispatches for the royal governor. He had then joined the British navy, but was stationed at Savannah by the time of the siege. Here, he worked in the Savannah armory in the manufacturing of grapeshot for the British cannon. During the siege, Scipio ran ammunition, including grapeshot, to the cannon of a redoubt, which might well have been the strategic Spring Hill Redoubt located on the Ebenezer Road. During one risky mission, he was hit in the leg by a bullet, which nearly resulted in amputation of the damaged limb.[118]

The notable fact that Maitland and Prévost possessed the wisdom to utilize Black soldiers, who had been former slaves, appalled the patriots, especially slave owners, who saw this utilization of Black manpower as the worst of all horrors, unimaginable to the typical slave-owner mentality. These sentiments were put into print in colonial newspapers, including the pages of the *Maryland Gazette*, which deplored the "negroes and other rubbage [*sic*] which general Prévost had seduced to join him."[119] Of course, Americans in general refused to admit that Blacks in arms were battling for liberty, just like themselves, because of the obvious irony of color that mocked the lofty concepts of the Age of Enlightenment and the Americans' cause.

The Loyalist editor of the *Georgia Gazette* of Savannah, Georgia, was forced to defend the decisions of British leadership to arm former slaves in this campaign for possession of Savannah by emphasizing that it had been the French who "had started it by bringing" Blacks and mulattoes from the West Indies, especially the large Black and mulatto unit, the Chasseurs-Volontaires de Saint-Domingue, of the expeditionary force.[120]

What the indignant patriots of the South had conveniently forgotten was the fact that Major General Lincoln—an enlightened Massachusetts man to the core—had written the Continental Congress regarding the urgent need to form a Black regiment to fight for America's liberties. This bold and novel idea was quickly rejected, especially by Southern politicians,[121] many of whom, like slave owners, were imbued with regional prejudices and customs when it came to race.

The civil war between Blacks who fought for England and the Blacks and mulattoes of the Chasseurs-Volontaires de Saint-Domingue, and also free Blacks who served in the ranks of Lincoln's army, was played out in full during the showdown at Savannah. For instance, Private Shadrach Battles, who hailed from Albemarle County, Virginia, in the Piedmont, served in the 10th Virginia Continental Regiment. He had fought in some of the war's major battles in the north, including at Monmouth, New Jersey, when Clinton evacuated Philadelphia and escaped across the country to New York City during the summer of 1778.[122]

Born around 1746, before the French and Indian War, Shadrach Battles "enlisted in Amherst County in the State of Virginia for the term of three years in the Company commanded by Capt James Franklin of the 10th Reg't of the Virg'a. [Continental] line [and] he was in the Battles of Brandy Wine, Monmouth, and Germantown, and at storming the fort [the Spring Hill Redoubt] at Savannah," on bloody October 9.[123]

Ironically, Blacks on opposing sides, victims of all manner of discrimination, faced much the same kind of racism and prejudice for basically the same reasons: ignorance and ugly racial stereotypes that were prevalent and accepted unquestioningly as fact by so many white Frenchmen. To his credit, Vice Admiral d'Estaing was more open-minded about race than most Frenchmen, reflecting his Saint-Domingue experience, having long admired the excellent performance of Black soldiers on both sides during the battles for the Caribbean sugar islands. After all, he had warmly welcomed the Chasseurs-Volontaires de Saint-Domingue into the ranks of his expeditionary force from the beginning, almost as if knowing they would play an important role in the future—perhaps in a crisis situation when the lives of many of his soldiers were at stake, which would be the case in the days ahead.

D'Estaing had therefore emphasized in a written order to the army that the Black and mulatto soldiers—who consumed meager rations of confiscated rice day after day, like d'Estaing's white soldiers, because there was no bread and supplies were low—were to "be treated at all times like whites," since they sought to gain "the same honor" as white troops. D'Estaing firmly believed that "they [would] exhibit the same bravery" on the battlefield at Savannah, something that ultimately proved true on October 9, 1779, fortunately for him and his army.[124]

By this time, the Black and mulatto soldiers of the Chasseurs-Volontaires de Saint-Domingue had suffered severely in their new environment of Georgia. It was much colder this far noth than what they were used to in their tropical homeland, especially as the season changed to autumn. The Chasseurs' thin linen uniforms, ideal for campaigning in the tropics, were ill-suited for the cold, blustery fall weather along the Atlantic and the lapli?? in Haitian crede spoken by he Chasseurs.

In a journal entry, François d'Auber de Peyrelongue wrote: "The soldiers [from the tropics] had to be content with linen uniforms in a climate which was very cold or foggy at night. The water in Georgia is detestable, and so there are many sick," including some of the Chasseurs,[125] who suffered more severely in general than white French, American, and British troops. In a letter that he penned on October 7, Major John Jones complained to wife Polly about his personal situation, similar to that of a good many of the Blacks and mulattoes of the Chasseurs: "The want of thick clothes has been the means of my taking a great cold. We have been very unlucky with respect to weather—a continued rain, and now very cold."[126]

In keeping with their cultural background, the men of the Chasseurs-Volontaires de Saint-Domingue had a decided preference for wine—the drink of choice among the French, unlike the British, who generally preferred rum. Like other members, Black and white, of the upper ranks of Caribbean society, the Chasseurs found this was one of many aspects of waging war in America that ran contrary to their high-class status, epicurean tastes, and cultural sensitivities. In the words of Vice Admiral d'Estaing: "Our black soldiers from Saint-Domingue would not drink the mixture of sugar, water and fermented molasses which makes up the nectar the Americans call grog. Unfortunately it was wine for most of our officers and all our soldiers," including the Chasseurs, who enjoyed dinking the diven (wine in Haitian Creole that is about 80 percent French).[127]

Although they suffered more from the elements in September, the Black and mulatto soldiers from Saint-Domingue proved to be far more durable during this campaign than the much-touted white regulars from France, including the men from some of the finest regiments in the French army. This made the Chasseurs an ideal strategic reserve for the army that was demonstrated in full on October 9.

In consequence, a valuable lesson was learned by French leadership, including d'Estaing, about the overall high quality of the Chasseurs-Volontaires de Saint-Domingue: The amount of "sickness and hospital costs of white troops quadruple the value of the local [Saint-Domingue Black and mulatto] infantryman. White troops from France are too weak to deal with the local climate. [In consequence, a] standing corps of Chasseurs-Volontaires would save the lives of French soldiers and the king's budget . . . [A]ll persons of color wishing to be freed should be required to serve for eight years."[128]

Their demonstrated superiority as soldiers on multiple levels meant the Chasseurs generated a certain degree of resentment among the white troops—especially the Southern militiamen from Georgia and South Carolina, but also among the soldiers from France. This was due to the popular racial concept that only whites should serve in wartime, to reap the glory reserved exclusively for them, as they were deemed far superior to Blacks and mulattoes, according to the common racial perspective. It is likely that the Chasseurs' impressive navy blue uniforms with their long-tail jackets also caused some envy and resentment, especially among the Americans, who possessed few such resplendent uniforms, and must have viewed the dark-colored fighting men from the tropics with complete astonishment.

Vice Admiral d'Estaing had given specific orders to his white troops, especially the aristocratic officers of the French elite, regarding the treatment of Black and mulatto troops: "[T]he people of color [are] to be treated at all times like whites [because] they aspire to the same honor [and] they will exhibit the same bravery" in battle.[129] It is not known if General Prévost issued comparable orders to his white soldiers about the Blacks serving the British. The garrison included not only Black soldiers who had been former slaves, but also around eighty Creek and Cherokee warriors, whose leaders, including Scotland-born Captain William McIntosh, had allied with England in the hope of stopping the endless transgressions of American expansionism on ancient tribal lands.[130]

Unfortunately, because the men of the Chasseurs-Volontaires de Saint-Domingue left behind no letters, diaries, or memoirs that have been found to this day, very little is known about their exact roles and responsibilities on a daily basis during the siege. However, because of the racial attitudes of upper-class French officers—d'Estaing was a shining example of a notable exception to the rule—from the campaign's beginning, the Frenchmen had naturally expected that men of a darker hue would perform menial labor, because of their color. This led to the vice admiral's official order to his army that the Chasseurs from Saint-Domingue were to be treated the same way the white soldiers were treated.

The aristocrats, counts, and nobles who made up the officer corps of the French army could not have been more elitist. Even in this wartime environment and like at home, however, the Blacks and mulattoes of the Chasseurs still felt themselves equal to whites, partly because they were members of the elite free Black population of Saint-Domingue. They were also imbued with the core concepts and egalitarian ideology of the Age of Enlightenment, which emphasized how all men were equal, as found in the Declaration of Independence. In consequence, the Chasseurs initially deplored any assignment to perform menial labor, like digging trenches, especially when they and not the white soldiers were given such an assignment, feeling that the decision was based on color, which was the case.

In reality, however, the siege's basic requirements had changed the old racial dynamics and forced white attitudes to change. Blacks and whites needed to work closely together as one during the siege, including hauling cannon into forward positions, building gun platforms, and other related tasks. When the Chasseurs understood that everyone, regardless of color, was required to work together to ensure the siege's progress, they readily accepted their duty without complaint. The Chasseurs realized that such orders from aristocratic white officers were not due to racism, as suspected and feared, but because of the necessary requirements of the siege.

The Chasseurs joined in the hard work of menial labor that called for a united effort in the hope of choking the life out of the British garrison. Doing what would have shocked the Black workers in the sugarcane fields of Saint-Domingue, free Blacks and mulattoes of a higher class performed their patriotic duty in the trenches without complaining, with the vigor that was required by their white officers. After all, if even the elitist whites were digging and sweating under the hot rays of the Georgia sun during the afternoons as well as struggling in the cold rains that fell, then the Chasseurs needed to do the same—not only for the overall good of the allied effort, but also to demonstrate they were worthy of equality to whites, in the hope that it would translate into greater equality one day for them in the racially stratified Saint-Domingue society, after their fighting day were over.

The proud soldiers of the Chasseurs never wanted it to be said that they had not done everything in their power to ensure victory, just like the privileged white men of France. For these reasons, the Blacks and mulattoes of Saint-Domingue's free Black society engaged in the kind of labor relatively few of them had known in the past, especially if they had loving white fathers who had ensured they received only the best during their privileged upbringing.[131]

THE SYSTEMATIC DESTRUCTION OF AN AMERICAN CITY

As October (or Oktob to the Creole-speaking Chasseurs) began, knowing the prudent Prévost was not taking any chances, the British, Hessian, and Loyalist garrison was on full alert, expecting an assault at any moment. Prévost was wisely not assuming that d'Estaing would continue his unorthodox European-style siege of intimidation by terrorizing the civilian population with a harassing bombardment, knowing it would take weeks before Savannah could be sufficiently reduced to force a surrender.

In his journal, one defender wrote on October 1 that the entire garrison of alert soldiers was "[i]n hourly expectation of the Attack."[132] On the following day, one of Prévost's aides-de-camp wrote in a letter to his wife: "This morning, the 2nd of October, as we fired our Morning Gun, they opened one of the most tremendous Firings I ever heard . . . The Town was torn to Pieces, and nothing but Shrieks from Women and Children to be heard. Many poor Creatures were killed in trying to get in their Cellars, or hide themselves under the Bluff of Savannah River. The Firing lasted for some Hours, and a Flag was sent from us to Count d'Estaing, to allow Time for the Women and Children to go to an Island out of Danger. 'Twas savagely refused; and that Night they began to fire again, and heave Carcases [sic] and red [heated] Shot, which set two Houses on fire, and burnt them down; but some proper Persons being appointed to extinguish the Bombs, did it very effectively, and prevented any further Conflagration."[133]

Vice Admiral d'Estaing had hoped to break the will of the civilian population to resist, believing they would apply sufficient heavy pressure on Prévost to surrender. Because of this ill-founded strategy, the worst aspect of the siege descended upon the terrified citizens, including General Prévost's wife, Anne. The bombardment meant that citizens were deprived of sleep as well as food, once supplies of everything started to run low. Vice Admiral d'Estaing bragged about one of his key strategies that he hoped would shortly force the surrender of Savannah: "We chose to begin firing the firebombs at night in order to make them more terrifying."[134] One of Lincoln's men heartily approved of this harsh measure that targeted fellow Americans and their homes and businesses, boasting in a letter to his wife: "[T]he whole [city of Savannah] will be in flames by nightfall."[135]

But the greatest punishment to Savannah and its trapped populace was yet to come in this siege of a major port in the South. Monday, October 4, was the day that the French had finally positioned all of their guns, including siege cannon of the heaviest caliber that had been hauled from the French warships, and they were finally ready to unleash their most powerful bombardment to date.

In a letter, one British officer "of the General Hospital at Savannah" described how "On the Morning of the 4th of October, their Batteries were finished and opened with the Dawn. Their Cannon were well served, and key a severe and constant fire till 11 o'clock, a.m. The Night preceding, they opened a Bomb Battery. I counted 187 Shells thrown into Town from it, with little Effect."[136]

Artilleryman François d'Auber de Peyrelongue, who must have wondered if he would ever again see his beloved France by this time, if the intense bombardment failed to achieve its intended results, described the scene in his journal: "Everything was ready at dawn on October 4. At that time we fired forty-three bombs simultaneously . . . At first the enemy seemed surprised at the rate of our fire. Then, shortly afterwards, they responded by a salvo every quarter hour on the quarter hour, thus showing that we were superior. They pulled back their cannon from the embrasures we were firing on, put them under the cover of the ramparts, and retreated to the bastions, where they had protection . . . We then fired on the city, where we caused much disorder. Our bombs set fire to it twice. Many women and children were killed. After that all prudent folk took refuge in the cellars and did not come out anymore."[137]

The ever-critical Grenadier Séguier de Terson was appalled by the lingering disorganization and confusion of d'Estaing's malfunctioning expeditionary force in the art of siege warfare, which helped to nullify the best efforts of the French artillery. He described in his journal on October 4 how all of "our batteries [including a battery of nine mortars] finally opened fire at five o'clock in the morning . . . For two hours the cannonade was quite brisk, but we had to stop it, or rather slow it down, because our left battery collapsed due to poor construction and the great shock caused by the cannon. We completed the repairs necessary by noon; then we began firing again, but more slowly because we were afraid of running out of ordnance. That shows how disorganized our army was. We also had a mortar battery firing simultaneously, but it fired so poorly that the bombs fell into our trenches. What else could we expect? We have neither an artillery officer nor a gunner! However, if we could have prevented the unlucky mishaps to our batteries, they would have been well enough served to hasten the fall of the city."[138]

On Tuesday, October 5, fated to die in four days during the assault on the Spring Hill Redoubt, Major John Jones described his ever-increasing level of frustration to his wife Polly. He was discouraged because the British, Loyalists, and Hessians continued to defiantly hold firm, without any signs of faltering in Savannah's stubborn defense: "The enemy [is] still being obstinate . . . The time I have been absent from you appears almost an age. As soon as this important affair is over, I shall immediately return home."[139]

All the while, the French cannon continued to roar day and night, causing far more damage to the houses of Savannah than the defenders in the earthworks, especially to wooden structures. The Independent Pres-byterian Church, established in 1755, and the Christ Episcopal Church, which was founded in 1733, were repeatedly hit by projectiles. Brick structures, like the John Eppinger Tavern at 112 East Oglethorpe Ave-nue, which had been built around 1764 and was the oldest brick struc-ture in Georgia, fared much better under the pounding. On Wednesday, October 6, one defender penned in a letter how "there was another Cannonade and Bombardment as before, which shattered the Houses in Town considerably."[140] He later wrote: "It is imagined the French . . . did not throw less than 1,000 shells into the Town and Camp . . . The Carcases [sic] thrown [into the town] were in Number about twenty."[141]

Worried about the fate of his family and other civilians, General Prévost was indignant about the vice admiral's plan to deliberately ter-rorize the citizens of Savannah, writing to Lord Germain: "They throw carcasses [charges filled with flammable material] into town" to force a surrender as soon as possible.[142]

In one of the great ironies of the struggle, and to the shock of the vice admiral, the intense bombardment actually backfired, as did so many of d'Estaing's plans during this doomed campaign. Instead of breaking the morale of the defenders and the people of Savannah, they became even more determined to stand firm to sabotage d'Estaing's central strategic thinking that was based more on wishful thinking than reality. One of General Prévost's young aides-de-camp described how the Loyalists, whose faith was often unfairly questioned by the British, were emboldened to stand firm under the pounding of the French guns, writing how the "brave Tories [were] full of Spirit" and eager to defend Savannah to the last.[143]

Meanwhile, as was true for French troops in general, the morale of the lightly uniformed Black and mulatto soldiers of the Chasseurs-Volontaires de Saint-Domingue fell lower after the summer. Serving at this altitude in America, even though it was in the Deep South, was so much colder and foggier than their Caribbean homeland, and swept with cold winds, especially after the arrival of fall (or oton to the credes in blue uniform). In the words of one French officer: "The barren Sands of Georgia being *beneath our Notice* [compared to the strategic and economic importance of the sugar islands of the West Indies], having indeed found by Experience that they by no Means agree with our Constitutions."[144]

It was the sandy terrain that now saved British lives, however, as they had prudently dug holes in the sand at their encampments behind the front lines, just like at the front lines, to shelter themselves, basically living underground. One incredulous American wrote how British leaders had their men "burrowed . . . in the sand; the tops of their [white] tents being not more than on a level with the parapet, they were safe from the cannonade."[145]

All the while, the fragile relationship between the allies continued to be damaged with each passing day, spiraling to new lows. One Gallic officer held absolute contempt for the Georgians, as he did for Americans in general, writing about "these poor half starved Devils, the Anglois Georgians" of Savannah and the surrounding area.[146]

Despite all the noise of the big French guns and the wasting of tons of ammunition, most of the advantages during this showdown at long range were still enjoyed by Prévost. In his journal on September 20, Séguier de Terson of the French grenadiers revealed a fundamental truth about how thoroughly everything had changed since the first heady days of d'Estaing's arrival, when he had caught the British completely by surprise and a decisive victory had seemed inevitable to one and all: "We need reinforcements because the enemy is solidly entrenched."[147] And those much-needed reinforcements were not coming from France or anywhere else to bolster the besiegers, who were wearing down even more than the besieged with each passing day.

Séguier de Terson was unaware of how prophetic his words had been in this notation. On October 8, the day after the French began to fire incendiary shot into Savannah, he wrote about an unsettling rumor that was rapidly making the rounds through the French camp, truly alarming and against all good sense: "Rumor has it that M. d'Estaing is busy making plans for a general attack. He is forced to resort to that because the fleet has no supplies and is putting pressure on him."[148]

Indeed, when an eerie and inexplicable quiet suddenly descended over Savannah, this in fact was only the lull before the storm. Artilleryman François d'Auber de Peyrelongue, who served the guns with zeal, complained about the inactivity and the siege's lack of progress: "From October 5 to October 8 we did nothing."[149]

On October 7 Major John Jones wrote to his wife, Polly, and poured out his innermost feelings. Fated to die in just two days during the attack on the formidable Spring Hill Redoubt, and fearing that an all-out assault would have to be launched, Jones felt great sympathy for his fellow American civilians trapped inside Savannah, and lamented their sad plight of suffering, both day and night: "The enemy still continue very obstinate, and a more cruel civil war could never exist than this. The poor women and children [of Savannah] have suffered beyond description. A number of them, in Savannah, have already been put to death by our bombs and cannon . . . Count d'Estaing being determined they shall now surrender at discretion. We are expecting hourly that they will strike [in a sortie], though many, with myself, are of opinion they will not, until we compel them by storm. I think the matter so near a conclusion [at this time]."[150]

By October 8, it was quite clear to the frustrated d'Estaing that the siege had been a failure. His more patient and wiser top lieutenants felt that the siege should continue unabated to force a surrender, and they rightly feared the folly of launching a frontal assault. The French guns, especially the largest ones, were still located too far to the rear to inflict serious damage on the array of defenses that lay in a semicircle around Savannah. These sand and soft timber defenses that absorbed the iron projectiles—"works of sand," in the words of one French officer—had easily withstood the ineffective bombardment.

The vice admiral, already embittered by an agonizing frustration that had increased with each passing day, explained the overall vexing situation that he now faced: "Here then was the high point of a siege [that was reached on October 5], the moment when you fire and are not fired on, when the works are proceeding rapidly, when conquest comes almost without risk. Ordinarily it is the occasion of success and foreshadows the day of capitulation. Our position was quite different. The movements [of the British] in the trench lines told us that we had won nothing; new trenches were dug while the old ones were neither abandoned nor taken."[151]

By this time, the young Frenchmen, especially the noble-born officers of the aristocratic elite who served under d'Estaing, had become even more disgruntled and disillusioned with the ragtag Americans, especially the raw militiamen from the remote Georgia and South Carolina backcountry, and the South in general. A young and well-educated French cadet who caught the representative mood of the increasingly discouraged soldiers of his Gallic army described the Savannah Campaign as nothing more than an "ill-conceived enterprise without anything in it for France."[152] Becoming increasingly gloomy, like his men, Major General Lincoln lamented how "the desired purpose, that compelled a surrender" was not achieved, nor would it be anytime soon.[153]

Aristocratic French officers, especially those high-placed members of the infantry and artillery, blamed d'Estaing and the navy for having failed to achieve a decisive result, while mocking the vice admiral's faulty reasoning in his first major land battle: "It was believed that the noise [of the big guns] would intimidate the English, and that they were only waiting for that to surrender . . . The artillery and part of the camp blamed Count d'Estaing for having entrusted such important batteries to the navy."[154]

While the spirits of the allied soldiers continued to plummet with each passing day, with no sign of Prévost's position weakening or any desire of the Switzerland-born major general to surrender, the morale of the British, Hessians, and Loyalists continued to rise ever higher, in stark contrast to the allies. Part of the Loyalist's high motivations stemmed from the promise of an easy life in the future and rewards for having remained loyal and fighting for the king. For example, one Loyalist recruiting poster promised Americans a great deal, a life of ease on their own land with a pretty woman, if they would fight for King George III. This had proved irresistible to a good many men who had been born in America: "Such spirited Fellows, who are willing to engage [in service for the king], will be rewarded at the End of the War, besides their laurels [won on the battlefield], with 50 Acres of Land, where every gallant Hero may retire, and enjoy his Bottle and Lass."[155]

But first, what was about to erupt in full fury was destined to be one of the bloodiest and most unique battles of the American Revolution, a dramatic multiethnic showdown between "nations and races [in a bitter] struggle in which English Redcoats, Scottish Highlanders, Tories from the Carolinas, Georgia, New York and New Jersey, hired Hessians, armed slaves, Creek and Cherokee braves, all under a tough-minded Swiss-born general, were to be pitted against grenadiers of Old France, American patriots, Polish hussars, Irishmen serving under the Bourbon banner, and mulatto and black troops from the French West Indies."[156]

And in regard to the upcoming final death struggle for possession of Savannah, the stakes could not have been higher for the first major united allied effort—the Rhode Island disaster was hardly a display of unity on any level—in the history of the Franco-American alliance, which was absolutely critical to the survival of America in the end.

The strategic-minded General Henry Clinton had informed Lord Germain in no uncertain terms of what was now at stake for the overall British war effort: "Should Georgia [and Savannah was the key] be lost, I shall have little hope of recovering that Province and also of reducing and Arming South Carolina [with large numbers of Loyalists]." This was not long after he had learned of Vice Admiral d'Estaing's sudden and entirely unexpected arrival just outside Savannah, posing the danger of completely destroying Great Britain's ambitious Southern Strategy, which had been calculated to win the war and return the colonies back to the Crown, to forever alter the course of world history.[157]

CHAPTER 4

One of the War's Bloodiest Assaults: October 9, 1779

Clearly, Vice Admiral d'Estaing faced not only a most daunting military dilemma of immense proportions but also a personal one that was as vexing as it was frustrating to the revered and much-decorated man held in such high esteem by King Louis XVI. His lofty reputation in France and with the king, so severely damaged in America during the Rhode Island expedition in 1778, when seemingly every aspect of the Franco-American alliance had gone terribly wrong until the entire effort had ended in shambles, was now at stake as never before.

The vice admiral's reputation was tarnished especially among the Americans because he had abruptly sailed away from General John Sullivan's army and headed north to repair his warships at Boston, after the doomed allied bid to capture Newport ended, without delivering a decisive blow. He had even been charged with desertion by the outraged Americans, including by Sullivan, even though he had had no choice, as he was faced with the arrival of a British fleet with reinforcements and storm damage to his vessels.

Under mounting pressure, consequently, d'Estaing now realized that he had no choice but to strike a blow at Savannah. He and his men had already been mocked and charged with having been the "Heroes of Flight" by the enraged Americans, whose old anti-Catholic and anti-French prejudices had risen to the fore immediately following the embarrassing Newport disaster.

Finding himself mired in a disadvantageous position before Savannah's formidable defenses, the siege having proven ineffective, the next command decision that d'Estaing made on that ill-fated October 8, 1779, was the easiest of his long career for him, personally, but also the most foolish one professionally. It was doomed to failure, and would cost the lives of hundreds of Frenchmen and Americans. At long last, it was now time to launch a headlong assault on the most formidable of defenses in the view of the frustrated, impatient vice admiral, who had tired of the siege's slow progress without achieving significant results of any kind. Indeed, no previous decision by d'Estaing would have caused a greater loss of life or a greater disaster than this one, which was destined to be entirely in vain in the end.

D'Estaing's ill-fated decision led to the bloody disaster forever known as the Battle of Savannah. The vice admiral refused to listen to the sound logic and military advice given to him by his top lieutenants, who argued for him not to commit this ultimate folly. Somehow he felt that he had no choice but to unleash this assault on the powerful defenses, partly because of his immense pride and lofty ego, and also the fact that time was not on his side.

Major General Benjamin Lincoln only reluctantly agreed to the joint offensive effort and coordinated assault that was calculated to win the day. Although they had been constructed in record time and the allies were still not entirely convinced the British defenses had been sufficiently strengthened in such a short time, Lincoln believed this to be one of the most powerful networks of fortifications he had ever seen. Despite backgrounds that could hardly have been more different, Lincoln and d'Estaing now shared something in common: a gross underestimation of the defenders' resolve and the strength of Prévost's defensive network that lay around Savannah, at the only British-held port and toehold on the American mainland located between Canada and Florida, besides New York City.

Although d'Estaing's greatest mistake was primarily based on his inflated ego and reputation, other pressing factors called for him to undertake the risky gamble, including pride and the hope of compensating for the Rhode Island failure by winning the day at Savannah. It would now obviously take much more time to choke the life out of the Savannah garrison—an estimated ten more days at the height of hurricane season, continuing the laborious process of bombardment, and then advancing parallels ever closer to Prévost's main line in the traditional siege formula. Lacking patience by nature, the vice admiral rejected the idea of taking this additional time to reduce Savannah.

Quite simply, he was sick and tired of this siege; he was sick of America, and the ungrateful rebels who seemed more than happy with the sacrifice of French resources and lives for their gain. Most important, d'Estaing never forgot that he needed to return to the West Indies as soon as possible. The French sugar islands needed his protection, and that was his top priority—and also the top concern of King Louis XVI, since the sugar islands represented vast profits and a key foundation of the French economy.

The spirits of his men were getting lower with each passing day, including the Black and mulatto citizen-soldiers of the Chasseurs-Volontaires de Saint-Domingue, who continued to curse in Creole and suffer severely from the biting cold of early autumn and the downpours of rain, which were not the warm tropical rains they were used to in Saint-Domingue. This cold rain soaked right through their thin linen uniforms, which were only suited for tropical weather, as opposed to the British woolen uniforms that were ideal for this time of year. The Chasseurs also struggled with the scanty rations of tasteless Georgia rice (compared to the more flavorful West Indian rice), which provided the blandest of diets.

While the afternoons were still warm in the Savannah River country in early October, being so close to the Atlantic coast meant the nights were cold, and only made colder by the blustery winds. The Chasseurs could only dream about the pleasant tropical weather and the balmy nights of Saint-Domingue while they attempted in vain to keep warm on the cold Georgia nights.

Most pressing of all, d'Estaing continued to risk his fleet during this dangerous peak of hurricane season, when tropical storms often caused massive destruction along the low-lying eastern coasts of Florida, Georgia, and the South Carolina. D'Estaing was well aware that a severely damaged French fleet might never make it back to Saint-Domingue to protect their king's most valuable and profitable islands in the sun.[1]

Supplies of every kind continued to diminish at a rapid rate, which caused widespread discontent throughout the French army. The spirits of the men continued to drop even lower with each passing day, as did their energy levels during this most unproductive of sieges. An estimated thirty to thirty-five French sailors on the anchored warships were dying of disease each day, to d'Estaing's lament. The once-high spirits among the naval men of all ranks fell to new lows, almost as if they had already lost the battle. They blamed their overambitious vice admiral of sacrificing them in his relentless pursuit of glory and fame while neglecting his usual naval priorities, including the welfare of the average sailor, as he played the ill-suited part of a general experienced in fighting on land.

Meanwhile, the British, Hessian, and Loyalist defenders' spirits continued to be sky-high after Maitland's timely arrival, and continued to steadily rise like their prospects for success. They also possessed plenty of supplies for an extended siege—more than the besiegers, in a paradoxical situation not often seen in the annals of siege warfare.

At a commanders' conference that included Major General Lincoln and his top lieutenants, the vice admiral at last revealed his final decision on the evening of Friday, October 8, 1779. Bull-headed and egotistical, d'Estaing never wavered in his decision to attack, despite all of the sound arguments leveled against his decision, including the strong opinions voiced by his adjutant Viscount de Fontanges and Major General Lincoln. As emphasized by the vice admiral's top lieutenants and the American army's commander, the obvious existing evidence emphasized that the siege needed to be continued in order to be successful, and that the total number of French and American attackers would simply be too low to achieve a decisive success, because of the strength of the fortifications. These sound arguments were all simply dismissed out of hand by the stubborn d'Estaing.

The level of d'Estaing's frustration, if not anger, had reached a new high by this time, especially after Chief Engineer Antoine O'Connor informed him in no uncertain terms that it would take ten more days for the siege to be effective. O'Connor was a highly capable Irish Catholic, and at age twenty-nine had been educated at the prestigious School of Engineers in France. Ironically, the number ten was significant in d'Estaing's mind at this time. That was the number of days in his original timetable for capturing Savannah and staying in American waters before returning south to protect the valuable French sugar islands.

In his journal, artilleryman François d'Auber de Peyrelongue recorded the futile arguments made by d'Estaing's top lieutenants, which did nothing at all to change his mind, except perhaps making him even more stubborn in his arrogance. "Finally, a direct assault was decided upon [by the vice admiral], in spite of everyone's advice, especially that of M. de Noailles, who did all he could to change the general's mind. We were supposed to hit the enemy's first bastion [the Spring Hill Redoubt] on the right, although while advancing our batteries could not fire such an enormous distance." Hence, no artillery fire would be provided to support the French and American attackers, like in a traditional infantry assault, another key factor destined to seal the fate of so many unfortunate attackers on bloody October 9.[2]

Other French officers felt much like Colonel Louis-Marie, vicomte de Noailles, who was wise beyond his years and every inch a fighter. In the words of one gloomy French officer about the general fatalistic mood that had already pervaded the army against an obstinate opponent who refused to capitulate, and seemed committed to fighting to the bitter end at all costs: "We began to lose confidence upon discovering that all this heavy firing will not render the assault less difficult."[3]

Even Vice Admiral d'Estaing had lost some of his initial overblown confidence in success, in part because so many things had already gone wrong. It seemed almost as if an "evil star" hovered over the mistake-prone allied army, which had yet to encounter any measure of good fortune in this dreary, ill-starred campaign, after having initially surprised the enemy so completely and with so much ease. However, reinforced by what he had seen of French valor during his Caribbean victories over the British, the vice admiral still believed that "extreme bravery can conquer everything," as he himself had demonstrated with his great personal courage in the attack and capture of the island of Grenada.[4]

Indeed, although an aristocratic noble, the vice admiral was no coward, or typical headquarters general who stayed safely in the rear and out of harm's way while sending his men to their deaths, like sheep to the slaughter. D'Estaing sincerely meant every word that he said when he had informed his top lieutenants in no uncertain terms about his aggressive plans for Saturday, October 9: "I will march at the head and you will follow me," and act accordingly.[5]

Another demonstration of French heroics had added to d'Estaing's growing frustrations. Major Pierre Charles L'Enfant had made a bold attempt to enhance their prospects for success, but it had proved a failure. Born in Paris in 1754, young L'Enfant had been one of the first Frenchmen to volunteer his services to America in 1776, and he was destined to design and engineer the general layout of the new capital of the infant republic after the war was won, in Washington, DC. In charge of a small detail of only five men, L'Enfant had risked his life under heavy fire from the defenses in a bold attempt to light the abatis of green felled timber to turn them into a mass of roaring flames. The fact that this heroic effort had proved futile was not enough to dissuade d'Estaing from his desire to immediately launch a headlong frontal assault early on the following day.

This young Frenchman, who wore a resplendent uniform of Bourbon white, was a remarkable man by any measure. L'Enfant was impressive both on and off the battlefield, having studied the timeless beauties of art under his teacher father at the prestigious Royal Academy of Painting and Sculpture. However, despite the young Frenchman's best efforts on October 8, the tireless efforts of the British to fortify Savannah in the nick of time had paid more dividends than originally expected, thwarting L'Enfant's best efforts and leaving d'Estaing with no choice, in his mind, but to unleash an all-out assault.

Fate would not be kind to the vice admiral. On the following day of destiny, d'Estaing would go for broke as never before. He would be cut down with multiple wounds like so many of his followers when he led the attack in daring fashion, being left for dead on the body-covered field during one of the bloodiest days of the Revolutionary War.[6]

The vice admiral was less open-minded than usual at this time—partly because French honor was at stake, along with his own reputation. He now thought more like a veteran French grenadier than a career navy man, desiring most of all to strike an overpowering blow. He could not simply sail away from Georgia with a humiliating admission of defeat, like he had done at Newport. It seemed as if fate itself had ordained that he would "take sword in hand," in his own words, in leading the assault on the powerful fortifications. D'Estaing's mind was set in stone, and nothing that Colonel Noailles or anyone else could say at the headquarters conference would change his aristocratic mind.

The vice admiral's own words revealed his stubbornness and the state of his mind, which had been clouded by his growing fear of the high personal and strategic cost of any kind of failure at Savannah, especially in not leading an all-out assault on the sprawling array of fortifications. He feared this would set the stage for even more embarrassment and humiliation for him in the future, including in the court at Versailles: "Thus, if I had not attacked Savannah, I would have been considered a coward [which was] the kind of torment which was personal to me . . . Not that it would have stopped me from making the right decision, but London, America, and even Paris would have more than dishonor[ed] me."[7]

In a most ominous development when about to lead a major assault of two armies, d'Estaing had basically now changed hats. He had now become more of a naval officer, with navy priorities foremost in his mind, rather than the land commander he had been pretending to be, partly because his officers and the men of his fleet had complained of his self-serving conduct during the siege, when he had neglected the fleet and his seamen. He still feared the sudden arrival of a hurricane or a British fleet that would deliver a devastating blow, and these omnipresent risks had played a large role in his final decision-making. The vice admiral knew that his sailors were suffering from lack of food and water, and that as many as thirty-five French sailors were dying each day. Morale in the navy had reached a new low, in consequence. It is not known for certain, but it is very likely that some mutinous talk had begun to circulate in the fleet by this time.[8]

In his journal on October 8, Séguier de Terson described the fateful news of the vice admiral's final decision: "At 4 p.m. the order is issued to attack the enemy tomorrow. There will be several assaults. The feint attack [on the British left flank by General Isaac Huger will be] the signal for the assault at 4 a.m. . . . . Once the orders were issued, our entire army marched under arms at midnight to the American camp on our left and the city's right."[9]

In an optimistic letter, an American officer, a "Major Clark," described how the overall tactical "design was to force the town, if possible, without firing a gun, there to form, and commence their further operations."[10]

Going for Broke on an Ill-Fated Saturday

The experienced vice admiral, who knew the complexities of seamanship and naval warfare like the back of his hand, was about to audaciously lead the way in targeting the British right, especially the strategic Spring Hill Redoubt on the Ebenezer Road, with a headlong assault. He had chosen this strategic point, where a vast marsh and swampy rice fields on the west side of the Spring Hill Redoubt nearly reached the British works, on the premise that they would provide good cover and mask the bold forward penetration close to the strategic redoubt, which was poised on a slight elevation to dominate the open ground in front, and the low-lying marsh.

Vice Admiral d'Estaing had divided his approximately five thousand attackers into five columns in what would be a desperate bid to secure a victory from the jaws of defeat and overwhelm about three thousand defenders, especially at the formidable Spring Hill Redoubt on Prévost's right—a tactical challenge far more daunting and extensive than it appeared on paper.

Three of the assault columns, or divisions, were French, while the other two were American, during the attack that primarily targeted the key redoubt on the Ebenezer Road, despite its formidable qualities. However, the main assault rested on the performance of two French attack columns, which were led by 250 battle-tested grenadiers under Colonel Jules-Jacques-Elenore de Béthisy, who had been assigned to capture the Spring Hill Redoubt on the dusty Ebenezer Road, strategically important because it led straight into town.

The northernmost column of the two assault columns also targeted the works farther north toward the Savannah River, located between the Spring Hill Redoubt and the low-lying marsh formed from the overflow of Yamacraw Creek, which is sometimes called the Yamacraw River. Located on the western side of Savannah, this chocolate-colored river flowed north to enter the Savannah River—all part of delivering a planned knockout blow to Prévost's right, which d'Estaing had deemed vulnerable, despite his inadequate observations and hasty conclusions.

Commanding the hard-fighting Sons of Erin of his Irish regiment which served under the Bourbon colors, Colonel Arthur Dillon had been chosen to lead the right column that targeted the battery and defenses located just northwest of the Spring Hill Redoubt, while Colonel Curt von Stedingk, an aristocratic count like other French leaders of the assault columns, was to advance farther to the left, or west. However, as fate would have it, he was destined to strike on the west side of the Spring Hill Redoubt in the end, like Dillon.

To his credit, and in his wisest decision, d'Estaing also established yet another French column, the sixth in total, or the fourth of his own Gallic army—the strategic reserve that included the Chasseurs-Volontaires de Saint-Domingue. Here, near two low-walled Jewish cemeteries, these troops were placed on good ground at the edge of the mostly pine woods in an excellent elevated position in the rear and south of the Spring Hill Redoubt. It was most significant that the strategic reserve was placed on slightly higher ground to the south and within striking distance of the Spring Hill Redoubt, which was d'Estaing's primary target on the British right. If the attackers overwhelmed the redoubt on what was called Spring Hill, then the strategic reserve would be hurled north into the assault to exploit the breakthrough to achieve additional gains. Each French division possessed a special role and mission, consisting of a van-guard column, a right column, a left column, and, last but not least, the strategic reserve of which the Chasseurs were a part.[11]

D'Estaing's intricate and overly complicated battle plan was based on almost perfect timing that looked possible when staring for hours at a detailed map in the comfort of the headquarters conference tent on a quiet night without distractions. However, the fundamental truths of the realistic situation on the ground were quite different. The overall tactical plan was severely flawed, which added to the folly that seemed to have no end. In reality, d'Estaing faced the superior strength of the lengthy array of defenses that were tightly ringed around Savannah in a semicircle, as well as the high quality of the determined defenders, all while the wide, brown and deep waters of the Savannah River protected the rear of Prévost's garrison on the north.

Vice Admiral d'Estaing's poorly designed battle plan, entirely divorced from the realities that existed on the ground, was bound to fail from the beginning. No adequate reconnaissance had been conducted over the difficult terrain, for reasons that are unexplained to this day, even though the attackers would be advancing across this unfamiliar ground that would have to be crossed in darkness, before sunrise on October 9, in order for multiple columns to strike at the same time, at 4:00 a.m.

With badly misplaced confidence, the French vice admiral was about to fight his first major battle on land in a foreign country with which he was entirely unfamiliar, leading large numbers of ground troops with which he was also unacquainted. D'Estaing was shortly to discover that the first casualty of war is always a carefully conceived battle plan, even an excellent one. And d'Estaing's plan was not a good one by any measure—except for getting a good many of his men killed for nothing but a misguided sense of destiny, excessive pride, and French honor.

Ironically, many top French leaders had already found a host of flaws with d'Estaing's plan of attack. This group included young Vicomte de Noailles, who called the plan "impracticable," and Major Thomas Browne, who was fated to be killed on October 9, while second in command of Colonel Dillon's right column of the crack Dillon regiment of seasoned Irishmen who fought for Catholicism and the honor of old Ireland. They had already predicted a doomed assault that would come at a frightfully high cost in French and American lives, wasted in vain. Their words of tactical wisdom made no difference at all to the stubborn vice admiral, who was adamant about sailing his own course on land as he did on the high seas, where he truly belonged.

As the dark course of events was about to demonstrate, d'Estaing should have listened to his experienced and wiser top lieutenants, especially the young blueblood named Noailles, whose sound opinions had been curtly dismissed by d'Estaing, who lacked the open-mindedness and flexibility necessary for a good commander. D'Estaing simply expected everyone to obey orders and follow him while he led the attack with his ornate saber in hand, thinking more like a common grenadier captain than one of France's most respected and celebrated military leaders.

As could be expected for a tradition-minded commander who still fought like he was on a European battleground in a more romantic, bygone age, d'Estaing decided to rely far more on his own experienced French troops, especially his well-trained grenadiers (or regulars) and light troops, than his American allies, who were true amateurs at the deadly game of war, and certainly looked the part. Clearly, the vice admiral wanted to win glory for himself and France to impress King Louis XVI and the people of his country, so far away.

Because he had been told by deserters that it was only defended by untrained Loyalist militiamen, d'Estaing believed that the square-shaped Spring Hill Redoubt on Prévost's right at the southwestern side of Savannah's sprawling network of defenses could be easily taken, including by the two main French columns, composed entirely of grenadiers and light troops who were not burdened by heavy or excess equipment to ensure swift mobility in the attack, leading the way in the assault.

At first glance, the formidable Spring Hill Redoubt on Ebenezer Road, which ran south along the Savannah River from the town of Ebenezer, looked weaker than was actually the case. From his own insufficient reconnaissance, the vice admiral was convinced that this imposing redoubt that dominated the northern horizon was the "least fortified," or so it seemed from a long and safe distance, and hence vulnerable at the point where the Ebenezer Road reached its southwestern edge, where it was composed of a high mound of red dirt and sand. Even Prévost recognized that this was the case, to his consternation.

The redoubt was perched on a sandy elevation known as Spring Hill, whose slight height gave it a greater topographical advantage over the surrounding lower-lying terrain, especially the swamp to its west. This well-constructed defensive work of quite sizable proportions was protected by a deep ditch and a dense field of abatis lying before the deep ditch, immediately in front of the main earthwork, which was shortly to become the eye of the storm.

The Spring Hill Redoubt was made even more formidable by what lay in the bottom of the deep ditch, which could not be seen by d'Estaing or anyone on the American and French side when looking north, even with a good field glass: a single sharpened row of logs that thrust upward to impale attackers, disrupting unit organization or tactical formation if they piled into the deep ditch to escape the punishing fires pouring from the redoubt. The Spring Hill Redoubt had been named for the small spring—one of the few in the area—that seeped forth from the underground limestone to the sandy surface.

The Spring Hill Redoubt was located near the "edge" of the dusty Ebenezer Road, almost as if the British had expected an attack from the north along this dirt road that cut through the eternal pine forests of the Savannah River country. Batteries of experienced British artillerymen lay on each side of the redoubt to enfilade the attackers, making it even more formidable. Most important, Prévost's strategic reserves were positioned not far away, including behind the Spring Hill Redoubt and in the works just to the southeast, so that they could be quickly rushed forward to reinforce the defensive bastion on the Ebenezer Road if attacked.

The astute Prévost had clearly left no stone unturned in his smart defensive and tactical preparations, which were uncommonly thorough and thoughtful. He continued to be one step ahead of the haughty aristocratic vice admiral, who seemed cursed by fate on October 9, handicapped by his own narrow, entrenched views and inexperience. With one of the British army's most capable engineers by his side, and making all the right defensive decisions from beginning to end, Prévost had ensured that the Spring Hill Redoubt and its high earthen sides were incredibly strong, to anchor his sprawling defensive line that ringed Savannah in a semicircle.

In d'Estaing's mind, however, this defensive bastion was not strong enough to resist the weight of his upcoming offensive effort, primarily because a marshy hollow lay on the redoubt's west side. The vice admiral was determined to exploit this natural advantage for a stealthy approach of multiple columns, in order to gain the tactical advantage on the redoubt's west side by easing his troops through this low-lying marsh and surprising the defenders. Negating this natural advantage was the fact that the redoubt stood on higher ground that dominated the nearby lower ground of the large expanse of marsh, which was guaranteed to cause confusion and slow any attackers, especially in the dark.

D'Estaing was only partly correct in his underestimation of the overall quality and experience of the defenders at this primary target on the Ebenezer Road. They were mostly Loyalists of the North Carolina Provincials, raised by Colonel John Hamilton, a wealthy merchant, with his own considerable wealth. At another part of the defenses—the anchor of Prévost's right flank—along the river and north of the Spring Hill Redoubt, Hamilton, a popular North Carolina Loyalist leader and a veteran of the slaughter of Celtic Jacobians by the British at that terrible Scottish moor known as Culloden in April 1745, would not see the finest day of his fighting men from the Tar Heel State on October 9.

Like forgetting about the folly of headlong Scottish attacks on British troops at Culloden, d'Estaing displayed his lack of understanding about the true nature of this ever-unpredictable people's revolution in the South beyond the heady patriotic rhetoric and idealism, especially the fact that this increasingly bitter struggle was America's first civil war. He failed to realize that the North and South Carolina Loyalists in the defenses were highly motivated and excellent fighting men. After all, they had plenty of old scores to settle with the patriots from years of past bitter persecution and harassment. Most of these men had been driven from their homes and dispossessed of all that they owned, just for following their political conscience and what they believed was best for America. These key factors made them eager to kill rebels, especially their fellow staters, because of the ongoing civil war in the Carolinas.

Indeed, the South Carolina defenders who occupied the Spring Hill Redoubt had plenty of old scores to settle with the men who thought of themselves as the righteous "Sons of Liberty" in a holy cause blessed by God. They had been victimized for years by patriots like the North Carolinians and their families, because of their political beliefs, especially since they were convinced that America's destiny and best hopes lay within the old, familiar framework of the British Empire and a constitutional monarchy.

Even more, these North Carolina men of Hamilton's command were expert marksmen, especially with the deadly long rifle. For this reason, around seventy-five of the sharpest-eyed North Carolina boys had been placed along the parapet of the "Carolina Redoubt," located north of the Spring Hill Redoubt. They had been specifically directed to single out French officers in front who would be wearing their fancy white uniforms of the Bourbon dynasty and distinctive white tricorn hats laced with gold and silver silk, cutting them down once the assault was unleashed in its full fury. Unlike d'Estaing, Prévost knew exactly how to best utilize the Americans and their own unique warfighting skills that sharply deviated from European tradition and etiquette, understanding how this was a new kind of conflict in America.

General Prévost, described "as brave as Caesar" because of his outstanding leadership qualities and tactical skills, had wisely placed his best commander, Scotland's Lieutenant Colonel John Maitland, and his finest troops, the 71st Regiment of Foot (also known as the Fraser Highlander Regiment of crack Celtic fighting men), just to the southeast, for the express purpose of reinforcing the Spring Hill Redoubt. In honor of his past performances and in a well-deserved compliment, Maitland had been given command of the most critical defensive sector centered at the Spring Hill Redoubt, on Prévost's right. Leaders on both sides recognized that it was relatively weak because of its topography, especially the nearby swamp to the west, a situation which ordained that this strategic redoubt on the Ebenezer Road would be the primary bone of contention during the upcoming attack.

Captain Thomas Tawes was officially a member of the 71st Regiment of Foot but had commanded an ad hoc contingent of hard-riding dragoons since early in the Georgia Campaign. In charge of the defense of the Spring Hill Redoubt, the experienced Tawes was eager for action. The captain's dismounted dragoons were now by his side in the defenses. Lieutenant Colonel Archibald Campbell had originally selected fifty men of the Scottish regiment to serve as mounted dragoons under Tawes, whose abundant skills and fighting qualities were well known and had already paid dividends in this campaign.

The fact that a good many Loyalists defended the strategic Spring Hill Redoubt guaranteed that the upcoming showdown at this key earthen defense would be a bloody one in the forgotten civil war among

South Carolina Continental attackers and South Carolina Provincial defenders. As fate would have it, the highly capable Captain Tawes was about to take center stage in the redoubt's defense, rising splendidly to the occasion on October 9, when the stakes could not have been higher.

The dismounted dragoons under the ever-reliable Captain Tawes now stationed at the Spring Hill Redoubt were excellent fighting men. They were first formed by Campbell for his push north into the Georgia backcountry to capture Augusta. At that time, volunteers had been specifically drawn from the Scottish Highland members of the 71st Regiment of Foot and then placed under Tawes for this special service in the South, because the British were extremely short of horsemen.

Having been raised in Scotland in 1775 for service in America, the 71st Regiment of Foot was the first British command formed after the opening shots at Lexington and Concord, and no ordinary regiment. The two battalions of the 71st served as the very nucleus of not only the garrison of Savannah, but also the overall defensive effort, both in manning the Spring Hill Redoubt and being available to reinforce the defensive bastion on the Ebenezer Road by moving southwest as a hard-hitting strategic reserve, when the most decisive moment came on October 9. Prévost knew that he possessed an ace in the hole with Maitland and his fine regiment of elite Scottish Highlanders, who were well-known for their combat prowess, and the major general wisely used them accordingly.

Also located nearby, in an earthen redoubt located on the White Bluff Road—which converged on the city like the Ebenezer Road, from the outlying countryside of rural Georgia—was the highly capable New York colonel, John Harris Cruger. A die-hard Loyalist and hater of rebels, Cruger was determined to defeat "Monsieur" at any cost. He was encouraged by the growing discord that existed between the allies, growing with each passing day; he knew what harmony and unity meant for this all-important alliance and any upcoming offensive effort. He commanded a fine group of around five hundred New York Loyalists, who had exchanged their old green uniforms for red ones. This was the 1st Battalion of Oliver DeLancey's Brigade, and it was one of the best units in the entire garrison. As could be expected in a bitter civil war, these tough New Yorkers especially detested rebels.

The so-called Sailors' Battery was a strong position located northwest of the Spring Hill Redoubt. Anchoring the British right on the Savannah River, the Sailors' Battery was manned by around 117 experienced naval gunners from British warships. Clearly, Prévost had smartly utilized all of the resources and assets available to him in a desperate bid to save Savannah. Most important, the battery of British seamen was located sufficiently close to protect the Spring Hill Redoubt with a covering fire of well-aimed artillery.

Also positioned northwest of the Spring Hill Redoubt on Prévost's far right flank, anchored on the Savannah River, was Lieutenant Colonel Thomas Brown's East Florida partisans (178 men). In the nick of time, they had rushed south to Savannah from the town of Ebenezer, located on the Savannah River, when Prévost had recalled his widely scattered units in timely fashion. Perhaps d'Estaing had incorrectly believed that it was these Loyalist partisans—Americans all—who now manned the redoubt at Spring Hill, which had then caused his gross underestimation of the overall quality of these defenders, since they were not regulars.

Brown's die-hard Loyalists, including many who had been forced from their homes by patriots and now lusted for revenge, had served as mounted partisans. They were expert guerrilla fighters of the Florida King's Rangers, or the East Florida Rangers. Most important to ensure heightened motivations, these Deep South Loyalists were veterans and excellent fighting men, ensuring that they would make a fine showing on October 9, when it counted the most.

As wide-ranging horsemen who were masters of guerrilla warfare during this bitter civil war, including raids into Georgia to strike the hatred patriots, they had never before fought behind defenses or served in a major battle. Although these soldiers were Loyalist militiamen who had been exiled from mostly South Carolina and Georgia before they had found refuge in British East Florida and then joined Brown's command, they now almost looked like regulars in their new green uniforms with crimson-colored cuffs and collars. Their fighting spirit was as high as that found in the best-trained regulars in scarlet uniforms—a fact known to

Prévost, but certainly not to d'Estaing. Although they had long fought with skill as irregulars, they had smoothly made the transition to fighting in a conventional manner, which was necessary on October 9 when they faced a do-or-die situation.

Like his Florida Loyalists, the England-born Thomas Brown had departed the Albion Island for the express purpose of becoming a gentleman Georgia planter of the upper class among the gently rolling hills of the fertile piedmont. In 1775, after having landed in Savannah and settling in the upcountry, he had plenty of old scores to settle with the patriots, for a long list of past misdeeds and abuses. Brown's troubles began when he made the initial mistake of making enthusiastic speeches in the Georgia backcountry—a patriot haven—supporting the king and Great Britain, and aggressively rallying support for the Crown.

In consequence, the unfortunate Brown found himself in the wrong place at the wrong time. He had been badly crippled and partly scalped; he had suffered a fractured skull when knocked unconscious with a musket-butt; he had been tarred and feathered and then tied to a tree, where his feet were burned (he lost two toes) with glowing irons by enraged members of a patriot mob of around a hundred men—a torturous ordeal that earned the lieutenant colonel the distinctive nickname of "Burnfoot," and his ever-lasting hatred of rebels. Brown had been one of the masterminds behind the bold strategic plan of employing Native American allies, led by white Loyalists, to work in conjunction with both Loyalists in the west and British troops in the east to regain possession of Georgia, and then South Carolina.

Last but not least, Prévost had wisely decided to arm more than two hundred Blacks, who one defender merely referred to as "our armed Negroes" in his journal. Like the Loyalists, these former slaves, who had been collected from nearby Georgia rice plantations to build fortifications, also desired to wreak a measure of revenge on white patriots, especially slave owners. In addition, some of these Blacks now serving with the British had been liberated in South Carolina by Prévost, when he had marched with impunity through South Carolina and threatened Charlestown.

To his credit, because this was an emergency situation, Major General Prévost had acted on Lieutenant Colonel Maitland's wise example of arming former slaves. Among his timely reinforcements from Beaufort had been a good many armed ex-slaves. These ebony fighting men were stationed either in or near, or both, the Spring Hill Redoubt, to bolster the defensive effort, adding a measure of psychological warfare, because of their race. Nothing terrified white patriots of the South more than the sight of armed Blacks. The former slaves were even more highly motivated than the Loyalists, as they now feared a return to slavery if Savannah fell and they were captured.

The massive Spring Hill Redoubt protected Prévost's right and anchored his lengthy semicircular line of defenses that protected Savannah on all sides, except to the north, where the Savannah River had flowed on its slow-moving journey to the Atlantic since time immemorial. According to one official estimation, this defensive bastion on the Ebenezer Road was manned by 54 South Carolina Loyalists, 28 dismounted British dragoons (Tawes's horsemen), and at least 28 grenadiers of the 4th Battalion of the 60th Regiment of Foot, which consisted mostly of Germans. They were all under the command of the capable Lieutenant Tawes, who had led the only dragoons in Prévost's army with skill during prior distinguished service in Georgia. They could not have found a more capable commander in a crisis situation.

However, another account revealed that there were only 24 dismounted dragoons, and other numerical differences have been found in various estimates of the number of defenders at the Spring Hill Redoubt, partly because it was later reinforced in timely fashion when the attack was ascertained. The Spring Hill Redoubt on the Ebenezer Road was now appropriately called Tawes's Redoubt, because the hard-fighting captain was the man chosen by Prévost to command its defense. Because 349 North Carolina militiamen held the strong earthen work located just to the northwest, or on the extreme right flank, of the Spring Hill Redoubt, close to the river, it was known as the "Carolina Redoubt" in honor of its mostly North Carolina defenders—around 90 men under Colonel John Hamilton, who had been defeated at the Battle of Kettle Creek on February 14, 1779, along with 75 Georgia Loyalists.

The South Carolina Loyalists were about to face a good many South Carolina patriots at the Spring Hill Redoubt—just one of the many forgotten mini civil wars that raged among the multiethnic participants at Savannah, and a forgotten tragedy of the Battle of Savannah.

Major General Prévost possessed other key strengths, like the Loyalists, who the French and Americans had wrongly perceived as liabilities by this time. Even more, Prévost wisely maximized all of his strengths to the utmost, continuing his record of making the smartest of decisions when everything was on the line. For example, the red-uniformed grenadiers of the 60th Regiment of Foot had been augmented by around 40 Royal Marines from the British warships, and the entire regiment was located nearby in an excellent position, not far from the Ebenezer Road, ready to quickly reinforce the Spring Hill Redoubt in an emergency situation that was sure to come; it was only a matter of time.

The more than 400 tough British regulars of the 2nd Battalion, 71st Regiment of Foot, under Major McDonald, served as the primary nucleus of the defense, including for the less-trained and less-disciplined Loyalist militiamen, bestowing added confidence to these men about to engage in their first major battle, and as the strategic reserve. Major General Prévost could not have chosen a better commander in Captain Tawes, or a better strategic reserve than the tough Scottish Highlanders of the 71st Regiment of Foot, located in an adjacent redoubt, just southeast of the Spring Hill Redoubt.

The rest of the Scotsmen of the 71st Regiment of Foot (the 1st Battalion of 282 men, under Major Arthur McArthur), along with three grenadier companies of the 16th Regiment of Foot and one company of Royal Marines, of around 40 well-trained men, had been positioned on the right flank as a strategic reserve. The defenders of the Spring Hill Redoubt also knew that the rest of the 60th Regiment of Foot, with Royal Marines incorporated in the unit's ranks, was situated nearby and ready to rush to the rescue if attacked. This gave Captain Tawes and his men, positioned inside the Spring Hill Redoubt, a good deal of well-placed confidence for future success.

D'Estaing still expected an easy conquest of Savannah because both the American and French assaults had been ordered to primarily target the Spring Hill Redoubt and its immediate vicinity. After all, the confident vice admiral in his highly decorated, resplendent uniform had led the charge that had overrun the strong British fort perched on the high ground of Grenada last July, by a night attack; certainly the Spring Hill Redoubt was far less imposing by comparison.

AN ILL-FATED PLAN DOOMED FROM THE START

With his patience at an end, and not listening to any dissenting voices, d'Estaing planned to unleash a predawn attack at 4:00 a.m. in the foggy darkness of October 9. He hoped to catch the enemy by surprise, which called for attacking just before the break of dawn, to deliver a powerful blow. This type of fanciful, overly optimistic plan was always the most problematic for any commander, because of crossing a large stretch of unfamiliar terrain in the darkness.

Indeed, the possibility of multiple columns of two different armies advancing a lengthy distance across unfamiliar ground in the dark, especially crossing a wide marsh west of the Spring Hill Redoubt, and striking as one at the same time along multiple fronts was extremely slim, and far more unlikely than imagined by d'Estaing. Nevertheless, this career navy man, about to fight his first major battle on land, was not deterred in the least, when he certainly should have been extremely worried under the circumstances. The dissenting voices he had dismissed out of hand would shortly come back to haunt him.

Meanwhile, however, D'Estaing remained confident that his divergent columns of troops, who had already screwed fresh flints into the iron hammers of their flintlock muskets, could maneuver across a wide stretch of unfamiliar and rough ground in the Georgia darkness with the ease of warships gliding across a wide expanse of the Atlantic—a most dangerous illusion that was nothing short of folly. The highly respected vice admiral was fighting the war as if he was still serving back in the Caribbean, or in Europe. Because of his success in attacking the high ground at Grenada at night, it seemed logical to d'Estaing that the upcoming night attack against what appeared to be weaker defenses at the Spring Hill Redoubt—positioned on much lower ground and with level terrain—would easily succeed.

Because of the broad field of thick abatis fronting the defenses as far as the eye could see, the vice admiral had directed a vanguard of French volunteers to hack through the tangled branches of the maze of fallen trees. These volunteers included seasoned and expertly trained grenadiers and light troops who were armed with axes and other tools for the task of clearing the field of abatis. They were led by Colonel Jules-Jacques-Elenore de Béthisy, another French nobleman who possessed a bountiful amount of courage and Gallic pride. De Béthisy had gained the extremely challenging mission of clearing a path through the thick field of abatis for the initial assault column of more than one thousand French troops to strike an overpowering blow before the Spring Hill Redoubt's defenders knew what had hit them, and before the sun rose to reveal the large number of attackers in white uniforms, out in the open.

Irishman Count Arthur Dillon had long commanded the elite Dillon Regiment of hardy Green Islanders, who fought as hard for Catholic France as for Catholic Ireland, so far away. They were a fitting feisty and skilled counterpart to the Scottish Highlanders of Maitland's crack 71st Regiment of Foot, which confirmed the superiority of the Celtic fighting man. With unique distinction and in his typical daredevil style, Dillon would lead the right column, which consisted of the troops of the Irish regiment, grenadiers, light troops, and chasseurs of various French regiments. Dillon's column also included white colonial troops from Le Cap and Port-au-Prince, as well as troops from the West Indies island of Guadeloupe and numerous French companies, such as the Chasseur Company from Champagne, France.

Like his ancestors, Count Dillon knew all about the finely polished manners of the elite at the king's court at Versailles. He was an excellent leader and a hard-nosed fighter, just like his faithful followers and other members of this Irish clan of Celtic-Gaelic warriors. Although nagged by a feeling of impending death in the upcoming assault against such formidable defenses, the dashing Irish count was especially determined that he and his fellow Irishmen would distinguish themselves by an inspiring exhibition of their legendary heroism on October 9. In the end, Dillon certainly achieved his goal on that fateful day of destiny, albeit in a failed offensive effort.

Meanwhile, the left column, consisting solely of fusiliers, would be led by Baron von Stedingk. This group was made up of ordinary French line infantrymen and not a single chasseur company, and included white fusiliers from Le Cap, Port-au-Prince, and also Guadeloupe, as well as fusiliers from various regiments, such as the Walsh Regiment. Another nobleman of outstanding ability, von Stedingk was a dashing Swede—a fact that no doubt would have disturbed Major General Prévost, who was the grandson of the marshal of Frederick the Great. The aristocratic baron was to march to the left, or west, of the French vanguard, which was to be led by d'Estaing, to strike the right flank of the strategic Spring Hill Redoubt. Then, after the redoubt was overpowered, all three French assault columns—vanguard, right, and left—were to continue north and charge into the battered streets of Savannah to reap the final victory in what d'Estaing envisioned as a glorious triumph that would make him even more famous across not only France, but all of Europe.

Meanwhile, two columns of Americans—carrying forty rounds in their leather cartridge-boxes, hung over their right shoulders or in their pants or shirt pockets—were to strike after the French had attacked, in order to maximize the overall offensive effort in the form of a hard-hitting one-two punch. The first American column on the right was to be led by Lieutenant Colonel John Laurens, a Southern blueblood of Huguenot heritage, and one of the best fighting officers in the army. The privileged son of one of the wealthiest men in South Carolina, Henry Laurens, John Laurens fought for the honor of the family name, and for his beloved South Carolina.

The young and extremely capable Laurens now commanded the seasoned fighting men of the crack Light Infantry Corps of Continental troops—suitable and worthy counterparts to the French grenadiers, and the ideal soldiers for leading the American assault. Laurens's command consisted of the crack 2nd South Carolina Continentals, under Lieutenant Colonel Francis Marion; the 3rd South Carolina Continentals, under Colonel William Thompson; the 1st Virginia Continentals; and the considerably less capable, but better uniformed, Charlestown militiamen of the 1st Battalion, under Colonel Maurice Simons. Despite this being their first major battle, the Charlestown boys from South Carolina's largest and most important city were destined to rise splendidly to the occasion and fight much like regulars on October 9. During the chaos of the upcoming assault, and not by initial design or plan, Lieutenant Colonel Laurens would ultimately target the northwestern side of the Spring Hill Redoubt in still another desperate attack on the imposing defensive bastion on the Ebenezer Road.

The left (or the second) American column of around five hundred South Carolinians was to follow on the heels of the French attackers, who had been assigned by the proud d'Estaing to lead the way for their rustic allies. This second American column, consisting of the 1st, 5th, and 6th South Carolina Continental Regiments (under Colonel Charles Pinckney, Lieutenant Colonel Alexander McIntosh, and Major William Henderson, respectively), was commanded by Celtic brigadier general, Lachlan McIntosh. They were to advance behind the French left column to strike the Loyalist Carolina Redoubt located just northwest of the Spring Hill Redoubt, toward the Savannah River, while General Isaac Huger, of Huguenot and French Protestant heritage, who led around five hundred Georgia and South Carolina militiamen, was to conduct a feint against Prévost's left flank.

French feints, disguised as main assaults, were to be directed at the British center to draw attention away from the main target, which was Prévost's right, specifically the Spring Hill Redoubt. D'Estaing had chosen the latter without sufficient care as part of his complex battle plan, which may have looked good on paper but was absolutely impossible in practical reality. He had not factored in the inherent weaknesses and inevitable developments that were sure to sabotage his best laid plans. First and foremost, any kind of delay on the night of October 8–9 would throw off the extremely delicate timetable of being able to unify multiple strikes as one in the darkness just before dawn. This lofty goal of multiple assault columns successfully covering a lengthy stretch of unfamiliar ground that had not been adequately reconnoitered left absolutely no margin for error. This was especially true on a foggy night, when the ground was covered in the thick white haze so common at this time of year in coastal Georgia. Trying to catch the defenders of the Spring Hill

Redoubt by surprise at 4:00 a.m. on October 9 under these conditions would be impossible, as d'Estaing and his men would soon learn.

In addition, it seemed that d'Estaing had not thought about the difficulty the men of Colonel de Béthisy's French vanguard would have in cutting their way through the thick abatis of sharpened tree limbs with their axes. Not only would they have to contend with the darkness and the considerable time it would take to create a passageway for large numbers of troops to pass through, but the element of surprise would have long since vanished. The noise they would make would fully alert the nearby defenders, who would then open fire, decimating both them and the main assault column.

As usual in the true French style, d'Estaing would order the French drummer boys at the head of the assault column to begin beating their drums to announce the attack. Although this was according to the traditional French manner long used in a grand assault on a European field of strife, it would have been far wiser to leave the traditional drumming to the old-fashioned martial customs of a European battleground, and instead embrace a more practical battle plan containing the element of surprise, which was the key to success on October 9.

Without ever having seen the ground up close, the vice admiral's main attack on the formidable Spring Hill Redoubt, located on Prévost's alleged weak right, was also based on the premise that a nearby swamp, situated just to the redoubt's west, would provide ample cover for a stealthy approach by the attackers, almost all the way up to the redoubt's west side, and to within around fifty yards of the defensive bastion.

D'Estaing failed to understand that thousands of troops who were unfamiliar with the area, advancing in the dark, on a foggy Georgia night, through a wide, low-lying swamp, engaged in their first large-scale offensive, was simply a recipe for certain disaster.

Conversely, to the vice admiral's credit, because of this more difficult terrain, General Prévost had initially reasoned that the French and American attack would target his left and not his right—that is, until the words of deserters told him otherwise, which would change his view in a timely fashion. Unlike Prévost, Vice Admiral d'Estaing failed to see the folly of assaulting the Spring Hill Redoubt, not grasping that the extent of the difficulties his attackers would face was far greater than he had imagined.

In truth, the overly complex battle plan of the vice admiral had been designed to fail from the very beginning. Besides the main attack to be directed at the Spring Hill Redoubt, another French column would strike beyond that defense, to the north, and then push on toward the Savannah River, turning Prévost's right flank, anchored on the river by the redoubt, and held by Brown's Florida Rangers and Hamilton's North Carolina Volunteers.

Then, in the hope of confusing Prévost and his men, the French would launch a feint with another column against the British center, while South Carolina and Georgia militia, under Brigadier General Isaac Huger—who had just recovered from a wound inflicted during the Battle of Stono Ferry—would strike Prévost's left, at Lieutenant Colonel John Harris Cruger's White Bluff Road Redoubt on the southeastern edge of the defenses. It was hoped that this feint would take the enemy's mind off the main assault at the Spring Hill Redoubt.

All of these supposedly well-coordinated assaults were to somehow miraculously take place at the precise hour of 4:00 a.m. on a dark autumn morning, as conceived at headquarters by the vice admiral. Like British leaders and strategists, d'Estaing failed to understand the unique nature and complexities of the American war in the South, where men often switched sides because this was a civil war. Even Americans failed to understand how so many, playing a risky game of simple survival, could change sides on a whim, depending on which side was winning the war.

Consequently, it was almost certainly true that Prévost was fully fore-warned of the attack by one or two deserters with Loyalist sympathies, perhaps hoping to gain reward money. This proved to be the case, to Prévost's delight and advantage, which meant there would be no surprise on October 9, as planned by the vice admiral. Tradition has it that the turncoat was a sergeant major of the Charlestown militia. However, while Prévost knew that October 9 was d'Estaing's selected day of launching his desperate bid to win it all, he believed that it would be the Americans—and not the French—who would target his right, including the strategic Spring Hill Redoubt.[12]

Grenadier Séguier de Terson—who naturally always blamed the Americans, like so many other Frenchmen, who felt an absolute disgust toward their homespun and rustic ally—described how cruelly fate had turned against the allies even before the assault was launched, especially in regard to having lost the crucial element of surprise upon which d'Estaing's entire plan of assault had been devised: "The enemy, forewarned of our plan [by American deserters] and reading it well, had moved all his soldiers to that front," meaning, the Spring Hill Redoubt and nearby sectors of the lengthy line of defenses.[13]

Unfortunately for the attackers, who could not conceive how a host of unforeseen developments had already conspired against them, Lieutenant Colonel Maitland, who commanded the garrison's strategic reserve, and his elite fighting Highland men of the 71st Regiment of Foot, would be ready and waiting both inside the Spring Hill Redoubt and nearby when the French and Americans final struck. They would advanced southwest from their assigned defensive position to reinforce the embattled redoubt, just in the nick of time.[14]

Likewise, the well-trained grenadiers of the 60th Regiment of Foot, who had been strengthened by around forty highly disciplined Royal Marines from the British warships, were positioned close by, to the northeast. They were a suitable counterpart to the 71st Regiment of Foot on the redoubt's other side, just to the southwest. General Prévost again demonstrated considerable wisdom in regard to his careful and farsighted placement of elite troops, who basically acted as a strategic reserve, ready to come to the rescue of Captain Tawes and his defenders at Spring Hill in case of an assault.[15]

EARLY PROBLEMS FOR THE ATTACKERS

Prévost benefited immensely from the fact that d'Estaing's utterly unrealistic timetable was certain to fall to pieces under such disadvantageous circumstances—ultimately, too many to overcome. The French and American fighting men were not properly rested or prepared for the arduous challenge of the long late-night march to their assigned positions, followed by the attack in the cold early hours of October 9. They had been roused from their makeshift tents at midnight, and had wasted far too much precious time preparing to march toward the looming British defenses.

The weary French had finally reached the American camp far later than planned. The French vice's admiral's fragile timetable inevitably self-destructed due to the poor condition—physical and mental—of his troops; the lengthy stretches of unfamiliar ground they needed to cross; the heavy predawn fog that covered the ground like a blanket; and the blinding darkness, which led grenadier Séguier de Terson to describe the early falling apart of the "order of attack" as "rather disorder, [it] was so confusing."[16]

The American guides for the worn-out French troops, including a Frenchman named Roman who had volunteered from a Continental regiment for this all-important mission, proved less reliable than hoped. Even the guides for Lincoln's column got lost in the pitch-blackness of the autumn night, whose biting cold made the men miserable during their sojourn through dark thickets and swamps to their assigned positions.

Located on the low-lying western approaches to the strategic redoubt, the watery marsh of underbrush and high swamp grass dominated the coastal plain like a thick carpet. The vice admiral, who continued to be out of touch with reality because of his grandiose expectations, unlike when in his natural comfort zone at sea, had envisioned that this low-lying landscape would help to disguise his long advance on the Spring Hill Redoubt. On the contrary, it provided more assistance to the defenders than the French in another paradox of the vice admiral's war in Georgia. Inevitably, the Gallic fighting men became mired in the clinging mud and dark water, which felt freezing cold to the troops, throwing the advance into confusion as more precious time slipped away.

The break of day on fateful October 9 was just about to shine a pale light upon the sprawling array of silent, dark fortifications, illuminating a vast killing field in ominous fashion, before the foundering attackers had struck a blow of any kind. As if conducting an assault on a traditional European battlefield during the Hundred Years' War, when time was unimportant, d'Estaing's detailed order of advance was based on traditional French army protocol and etiquette. This had included aligning his regiments by seniority rather than combat capabilities at the last minute, when time was of the essence—still another time-consuming and costly mistake.

Upper-class French officers were obsessed not only with their inflated egos but also with outdated concepts of honor and rules of etiquette, at the wrong place and time. They were similarly focused on their elevated status as proper gentlemen, especially in regard to sensitive issues of seniority. This priority had often resulted in deadly duels with flintlock pistols or swords between aristocrats, whose inflated pride and sense of honor knew no bounds.

At Savannah, and in a tragic repeat of the French nobility at Agincourt, having argued over rights of seniority and advanced positioning in the attack, the French captains had taken their sweet time moving their companies toward the head of the assault column based on the exact dates of the issuing of their commissions, revealing the precise order of seniority and regaining more privileged positions of honor. They did this to the martial tunes of fifes and beating drums, which alerted the enemy of the attack—when d'Estaing's entire strategy was based on catching the enemy by surprise!

Then, compounding such time-consuming errors on this ill-fated Saturday morning, the fumbling vice admiral, who was already in way over his head in his first major land operation far from home, suddenly reorganized his troops to the detriment of overall cohesion, placing units under new commanders to ensure inevitable delays, as if time was not the most crucial factor at this point. If d'Estaing was a perfectionist, which seemed to be the case, this was precisely the wrong place and time to fulfill those proclivities.

For such reasons, therefore, it was not until around 5:30 a.m.—a full hour and a half later than the vice admiral's original timetable—that the crack French grenadiers finally emerged from the pine woods and muddy swamp to the open, level plain around two hundred yards south of and before the elevated Spring Hill Redoubt. Only Colonel de Béthisy's vanguard of mostly grenadiers (five companies) and also two chasseur companies, with d'Estaing at the head, were prepared to attack at this time. Despite having now finally come to his senses, having "a very poor opinion" of the attack by this time because so much had gone wrong, the vice admiral gamely, or foolishly, forged ahead with drawn saber, as if pushed forward by fate itself, while encouraging every one of his vanguard by his inspiring example.

At this moment—the point of no return—d'Estaing felt that he had no choice but to finally shout the fateful order to charge the Spring Hill Redoubt. When he heard the firing erupting from General Huger's feint attack—during which the South Carolina general from the Santee River country fell wounded—with his Georgia and South Carolina militiamen on the British left, to the east at the southeastern side of the defenses, he knew it was too late to call off the assault. If he had been prudent and called off the attack, he feared he would become the laughingstock of the court of Versailles, and all Europe. Under such pressure, and desiring to demonstrate French commitment to the fragile Franco-American alliance to compensate for the Rhode Island fiasco, he forged ahead with waving saber and shouts of encouragement to his men, sealing the fate of a large number of Frenchmen and Americans in the process. More than one thousand soldiers of the allied army were about to fall, either killed or wounded.

Despite most of his right assault column not being ready to strike as one on Prévost's southwestern defenses, and with most French troops still lingering far behind the grenadier vanguard, still attempting to get through the swamps and piney woodlands of the western approach, d'Estaing ordered the vanguard to attack across the open ground, heading north and straight for the Spring Hill Redoubt.

True to his word, the vice admiral was now at the column's head, leading the way across the broad killing field, just as he had told his top lieutenants at the October 8 conference. Because success had come so easily for him in the Caribbean, he naturally expected to win the same glory at Savannah. Whatever can be said of Vice Admiral d'Estaing in having orchestrated the folly of the assault on Savannah, it cannot be said that he lacked either determination or courage when the stakes were high. To his credit, he risked his life in leading the way, and demonstrated uncommon valor for a commanding officer.

The French grenadiers of Colonel de Béthisy's vanguard, with d'Estaing in front, demonstrating considerable bravery, came on in their usual manner, as expected by the British who had fought them before. They were aligned in a long formation across the open ground as drummer boys in their resplendent white uniforms furiously beat the charge, the white silk flags of the Bourbon kings waving in the early morning breeze.

The elite vanguard grenadiers and two chasseur companies had orders from the vice admiral not to stop to return fire during the desperate push across the wide stretch of open, level ground. He wanted to gain the west side of the earthen redoubt so as not to waste time, while the grenadiers and chasseurs surged toward the Spring Hill Redoubt and shouted the traditional French battle cry of *Vive le Roi!*

Meanwhile, when the first light of day arrived, around three thousand defenders were standing by in the sprawling array of defenses, flintlock muskets primed and ready to fire. The morning sunlight on this all-important Saturday in Georgia revealed large numbers of French soldiers aligned in a neat assault formation with a heavily decorated vice admiral at their head, moving steadily north across the open ground before the Spring Hill Redoubt. This was too good to be true for Prévost's delighted men, who could hardly believe their eyes. Representing a good mix of veteran Loyalists with seasoned regulars, the eager defenders under Captain Tawes were ready to unleash concentrated volleys from the imposing Spring Hill Redoubt whenever the order finally came to open fire.[17]

CHARGING AT THE DOUBLE-QUICK

Vice Admiral d'Estaing then ordered the vanguard troops forward at the double-quick over the open, level ground between the marsh and the slightly rising ground that led to the looming Spring Hill Redoubt, which now looked much higher and larger to French eyes. The foremost vanguard attackers of grenadiers were now moving across lower-lying terrain. D'Estaing's and Colonel de Béthisy's shouted orders finally unleashed the crack grenadiers and chasseurs of the vanguard in a desperate dash across the open terrain, out of the lingering patches of ground fog and straight toward the menacing defensive bastion before them. Neatly aligned formations were broken when the grenadiers (five companies) and chasseurs (two companies) rushed forward pell-mell, their fixed steel bayonets gleaming in the early morning sunlight.

It was now clear to the defenders that the Spring Hill Redoubt was d'Estaing's primary objective. The earlier feint on the British left under General Huger with his ragtag Georgia and South Carolina militiamen had fooled no one; Prévost already knew where the main attack was coming from, thanks to information gleaned from one or more American deserters. D'Estaing's great gamble of basing everything on catching the enemy by surprise had already failed miserably. As one British officer penned in a letter: "An Hour before Day the Attack began with a Feint [Brigadier General Huger's attack] on our Left, the main Body upon the Right."[18]

Likewise, the British cannoneers of the three batteries on each side of the Spring Hill Redoubt, who manned their guns with deadly loads of canister, fairly lusted at the incredible sight of the French regulars, grenadiers, and chasseurs advancing across the open and level ground, with a finely uniformed vice admiral leading the way as if they were on Sunday parade on the spacious lawn at the luxurious palace of Versailles, for the entertainment and amusement of King Louis XVI.

The experienced gunners and sailors of a British warship were anchored in the nearby Yamacraw Creek, a tributary of the Savannah River located just northwest of the Spring Hill Redoubt, and named after the ancient Native American tribe that had inhabited this area before the coming of the white man who had changed their world forever. They were also ready to unleash a perfect canister hell, which included cut-up chains and bolts, into the white-colored mass of French attackers, whose ragged ranks of charging men stretched across a considerable length of the plain.[19]

Keen-eyed and insightful, French artilleryman François d'Auber de Peyrelongue penned perhaps the best account of the folly and disastrous course of the assault in considerable detail: "All was to begin at dawn on October 9. On the eighth at 11 p.m. the final order still had not been given to the officers. Imagine what disorder there was! Here was our strategy. There were supposed to be two false attacks: one by 300 troops from the trenches; another by a like number from the galleys. [U]nder [Chevalier Trolong] Durumain's orders, [they] were to debark, enter the city from the rear, set it afire, and complete the assignment by penetrating as far as the lines if possible. But since no one took the trouble to synchronize the hour of this attack with the main one by way of the swamp, Durumain arrived too late and was only too happy to re-embark, having accomplished nothing. The troops from the trenches were drawn up in skirmish lines on the far side of the trench and did not march on the enemy's entrenchments. The English easily saw that this second feint attack was only a joke, which troubled them very little. And so there was no advantageous diversion from this ploy. Nevertheless it would have been much too difficult to hide our plans from them. We were sold out by a pack of Thorismonds [ancient Visigoths], which called attention to the fact that in our camp nothing was more difficult than to distinguish a Thorismond from a rebel."[20]

In a letter, one British defender described the onslaught they had been long expecting, and which should have been launched by d'Estaing long before that fateful Saturday, October 9, when it was already too late: "About daybreak on the ninth, the united forces of France and America, consisting of upwards of four thousand French, and the Lord knows how many rebels [even today, the exact numbers of militiamen is unknown], attempted to storm our lines. The principal attack was made in three columns, who intended to unite and attack the works at the [Spring Hill] redoubt upon the Ebenezer road. The count [d'Estaing], in person, began the attack with great vigor, but was soon thrown into confusion by the well-pointed fire from our batteries and redoubts."[21]

A defender of Irish heritage, Captain Kennedy, described the incredible scene when the storm erupted over Savannah in a letter: "On Saturday, the 9th, about daybreak, an Attack was made by the French and Rebels upon the Redoubt to the Right of our Lines, on the Road leading to Ebenezer, the Battery near the Spring, and on the Redoubt by Colonel Maitland's Tent, into which the Colonel, Governor [Wright] and Lieutenant Governor repaired."[22]

Nevertheless, the French just kept coming with drums beating and flags waving. In his journal, François d'Auber de Peyrelongue explained the sheer folly of the desperate attempt of the storming party of axmen to cut through the dense abatis, which made too much noise, took too much time, and alerted the British: "Each of our two columns was composed of 700 men, with a vanguard of 300 men and 60 'lost souls' armed with hatchets. They had orders to attack the same outwork [Spring Hill Redoubt] from two different sides [while] [t]he main force, with a strength of 500 men [Chasseurs-Volontaires de Saint-Domingue], was commanded by the Vicomte de Noailles . . . One thousand rebels were supposed to charge in columns, but only 600 advanced. A hundred American horse soldiers [125 finely uniformed mounted men of the Pulaski Legion] under [Casimir] Pulaski's orders joined them . . . The marsh which covered the front of the attack had not been taken into account [by d'Estaing], and we maneuvered in it awkwardly. Those who lost their shoes [in the mud and water of the swamp] were the most fortunate."[23]

However, the assaults by the French were fated to be launched in the most uncoordinated and piecemeal fashion. These attacks were led by "many of the Nobility of France" in their resplendent uniforms and stylish white-powdered wigs, the day's aristocratic fashion so dominant and beloved in cosmopolitan Paris. They lived in a privileged manner that was unimaginable to the vast majority of Americans and Frenchmen, especially the rough-hewn patriots from the remote backcountry who lived in rustic log cabins. This disastrous tactical situation meant no support would arrive in time to exploit any of the gains made by the foremost French troops, at a time when the only chance of success was to deliver a concentrated blow to maximize the attack's overall impact. Of course, this required a concentration of force to gain a permanent breakthrough of the British lines, to deliver a knockout blow—one of the most basic principles of successfully waging war throughout the ages.[24]

All the while, with Colonel de Béthisy's vanguard of grenadiers and chasseurs now unleashed, the French soldiers of the first two assault columns continued to struggle through the swampy terrain in the lowlands, drained by the dark waters of Yamacraw Creek. They would then turn right, or east, toward the western side of the Spring Hill Redoubt, while d'Estaing continued to lead the vanguard column north on the double-quick, ever closer to the Spring Hill Redoubt, while his optimistic vision of multiple columns striking at the same time steadily faded away like a summer dream.[25]

CHAPTER 4

This disastrous tactical situation had been guaranteed by d'Estaing's impatience and recklessness, which resulted in the folly of launching not simultaneous but distinct and separate assaults in an isolated fashion. These attacks could easily be met by the defenders, who would merely shift their aim at each new wave of attackers charging across the open, lower ground in a simplistic exercise that was much like shooting fish in a barrel. Vice Admiral d'Estaing, in the strange position of a highly decorated admiral leading the way for infantrymen in a land battle while on foot, waving his saber in front of his charging grenadiers, continued to demonstrate a remarkable degree of moral courage. All the while, he encouraged Colonel de Béthisy's troops in their Bourbon white uniforms onward, toward the blazing Spring Hill Redoubt.

Clearly, having prematurely ordered the charge with his vanguard of elite grenadiers and chasseurs instead of prudently waiting for the vast majority of his troops to emerge from the muddy quagmire of the swamp, the admiral's inexperience and impatience had once again gotten the better of him, which in large part explains why the assaults were launched in such an uncoordinated, or suicidal, fashion, in the first place, dooming any possibilities for success.

Major Thomas Pinckney, a fine South Carolina militia officer and future governor of South Carolina, described the folly of d'Estaing's impetuousness that was destined to cost so many young lives: "[B]y the time the first French column had arrived in the open space, the day had fairly broke [around 5:30 a.m.] when Count d'Estaing, without waiting until the other columns [including the Americans, farther to the rear than the French] had arrived at their position, placed himself at the head of his first column and rushed forward to the attack."[26]

François d'Auber de Peyrelongue continued with his revealing narrative of the fast-brewing disaster on this ill-fated Saturday morning, which was partly caused by the "scouts [or guides who] deserted us," resulting in even more confusion and the wasting of additional time in all the assault columns. This ensured that d'Estaing and his vanguard attacked on their own and in an isolated manner before everyone else in the battlefield's most crucial sector.[27] With justifiable bitterness, another French officer complained about "the scouts that they were obliged to furnish us, [but

Major General Benjamin Lincoln] could provide only one," which was entirely insufficient for seamlessly guiding the French columns to their objective, especially in navigating the thickets of the swamp.[28]

Because of the chorus of noise that had erupted from the advance troops splashing through the mire of the swamp, the thunderous sound of the pounding drums, and the enthusiasm and fighting spirit of the French soldiers—including Vice Admiral d'Estaing, who had also alerted the enemy with cries of *Vive le Roi!* ("Long Live the French King, Louis XVI"), which were then echoed by his troops—the British, Hessian, and Loyalist defenders were ready all along the lengthy defensive line. With the French sappers now busily cutting through the dense field of abatis with axes and other implements, the defenders of the Spring Hill Redoubt almost immediately opened up with a blistering fire that caught the vice admiral and his vanguard completely exposed.

In gallant style, the undaunted foremost French soldiers, led by d'Estaing, continued to head toward the western side of the blazing Spring Hill Redoubt on the double, through the storm of lead bullets and iron projectiles from roaring cannon. While bullets streamed by and dropped men around him, Vice Admiral d'Estaing, his fighting blood up as if commanding his warships in a battle with the British navy at sea, continued to shout above the din: "Advance, my brave grenadiers—kill the wretches."[29]

THE OMINOUS MOCKING SHRILL OF THE BAGPIPES

By this time, d'Estaing's bravado had been considerably diminished; he had heard another strain of martial music that echoed over the plain, and it was not the French drummer boys beating the traditional charge. The last illusions of the vice admiral had already been abruptly shattered even before the arrival of the cold dawn and his ordering of the vanguard's attack. He knew the game was up for the French—that he had already lost the all-important element of surprise when he had deployed his vanguard grenadiers in a neat line across the open ground for the assault. The haunting music that he now heard reflected the heritage of an ancient Celtic land and people, informing d'Estaing that his chances of a successful assault had early plummeted to new lows.

Even before the first fire had erupted on the left in response to General Huger's feint attack, which had failed to fool the British, d'Estaing had been shaken by the haunting sound of bagpipes, being played by the Scottish Highland musicians of the 71st Regiment of Foot. The shrill and eerie sounds from the remote "Scotch mountains" found in a breathtakingly beautiful land had openly ridiculed the vice admiral's best efforts to catch the enemy by surprise. He faced ever-diminished chances for success, as broadcast by the blaring tunes from the Scottish bagpipes. This shrill martial music from the ancient Celtic nation came not from the normally assigned position in the defenses to the northwest, but nearer to the strategic Spring Hill Redoubt. The traditional tunes from the Scottish Highlands, which were well-known for their beauty, told d'Estaing that these tough Scotsmen, Prévost's elite troops, were now acting in the all-important role of a strategic reserve that was in an ideal position to quickly reinforce the Spring Hill Redoubt.

The shocked vice admiral realized that the enemy's best troops were fully ready for action and waiting to slaughter as many Frenchmen as possible, and that the British seemed to know all about d'Estaing's battle plan, including where he had decided to concentrate his main blow. D'Estaing wrote: "Scotch Highland bagpipes [are] the saddest and most remarkable of instruments . . . it also taunted us . . . At the moment we came out of the marsh, we were given a serenade . . . I concluded that the enemy was not only forewarned, but also that he wanted to remind us that his best troops were waiting for us. Certainly when I heard the unexpected sound of these peripatetic bagpipes, I would have decided to call off the attack, if we had not been so far advanced and had not had the Americans for companions, or rather, for masters. And I could by no means call a halt to such an important undertaking, for fear that my indecision might afford an ample excuse for ridicule."[30]

A MOST MURDEROUS FIRE

Providing d'Estaing with another shock, rows of British cannon—including from one naval vessel anchored in the nearby deepwater Yamacraw Creek, just northwest of the Spring Hill Redoubt, toward the Savannah River—unleashed loads of grapeshot, canister, and homemade canister that now combined with the roaring musketry from the defenses. This British homemade canister included lengths of chain, even some that were six feet long, bolts, scissors, knife blades, and nails, which tore into the surging tide of white uniforms and turned them red as the spray of iron struck home to inflict terrible damage.

This punishing fire was most destructive as it unmercifully ripped into the flesh of the throng of attackers, who were shredded and cut to pieces in the storm of projectiles of all makes and sizes, both conventional and unconventional. In his journal, François d'Auber de Peyrelongue described the desperation of the attacking French troops, who displayed a remarkable degree of heroism in the face of a murderous fire: "The column on the right pressed on the one on the left in order to avoid the fire of a battery that was making things hot, so that the two attacks merged into one, which was a great misfortune. We had to march in the open for 425 yards. Then we intended to cross the abatis, jump down into the trench, and clamber up the redoubt. As soon as the English saw us, they set up a very stiff fire against our troops and greatly retarded our march. [There were] those who were stuck in the marsh, not being able to follow . . . the column was broken, and the first ones to reach the glacis [open plain] were easily knocked down."[31]

Gallic soldiers of Colonel de Béthisy's vanguard fell in large numbers in what was early becoming a slaughter; then, arriving French troops just emerging from the swamp and into the open ground suffered the same cruel decimation. Aristocratic officers and lowly peasants in the enlisted ranks fell like tenpins in the hail of the scorching fire. Six French soldiers of the LeBey family were cut down in short order on the bloody morning of October 9. Five brothers were killed, and the last one, Andre LeBey, was badly wounded in the rain of iron and lead that cut down Frenchmen in sickening clumps of torn and mangled bodies.[32]

Meanwhile, the Spring Hill Redoubt defenders continued to blast away, reloading their flintlock muskets as fast as possible and inflicting hundreds of casualties on the French vanguard attackers. Then they aimed at the following troops, who never had a chance on the open ground. In consequence, the onrushing vanguard troops received no timely support, which might have made a difference on this gory killing field.

One defender described the decision of Lieutenant Colonel Maitland at this moment, when he ordered the British regulars—or disciplined and well-trained grenadiers, in this case—of the 60th Regiment of Foot, which had been augmented by tough Royal Marines from the British vessels, from the defenses just to the northwest, to the rescue of the band of defenders in the Spring Hill Redoubt, before it was too late: "The French attacked us warmly on the Right, and endeavored to storm the Redoubt and Ebenezer Road Battery, [but] the Grenadiers of the 60th Regiment, under Major Beamsley Glazier, advanced to support them" in a timely manner.[33]

Describing the key turning point moment, one British naval officer in a scarlet uniform wrote how "The grenadiers of the 60th Regiment advanced to support" the Spring Hill Redoubt in the nick of time, to greatly strengthen the defensive effort before it was too late.[34]

But it was General Prévost, the one who chose and then hurled his crack strategic reserve into the escalating combat, who best described the significant role played by the hardy grenadiers of the 60th Regiment of Foot: "And at this critical moment Major Beamsley Glazier of the 60th Grenadiers and the marines, advancing rapidly from the lines, charged, it may be said, with a degree of fury."[35]

Despite being hit by the blistering fire pouring from the Spring Hill Redoubt like a volcano, Vice Admiral d'Estaing continued to demonstrate valor, as he had done during his previous successes in the West Indies, while leading his troops, both Colonel de Béthisy's vanguard troops of chasseurs and grenadiers and those soldiers coming forward to the rear, toward the fiery redoubt on the Ebenezer Road. But despite d'Estaing's best efforts, the vanguard was hurled back from the Spring Hill Redoubt that belched fire as it cut down attackers, including Colonel de Béthisy, in sickening clumps. The stunned vice admiral was forced to fall back toward the swamp with his decimated vanguard, leaving piles of grenadier and chasseur bodies in bloodstained white uniforms behind them.

Major Pinckney described how near the causeway, across the swamp, "Count d'Estaing was wounded in the arm, and [that he] endeavor[ed] to rally his men, a few of whom with a drummer he had collected" in the confusion and noise.[36]

But no amount of French sacrifice and courage could negate the bloody reality of this Saturday in hell: Each successive column, both French and later, American, would continue to strike without any coordination whatsoever. Leading the foremost grenadiers of the right column while the majority of the men were still mired in the swamp, in a repeat of d'Estaing's earlier performance in the clinging mire, Count Arthur Dillon encouraged around eighty Green Islanders onward with fixed bayonets, and they now closed in on the Spring Hill Redoubt on the double, with proud battle flags flying.

After the vice admiral and his vanguard had been repulsed, with surviving comrades carrying back the dead and wounded—including the badly injured leader of the vanguard, Colonel de Béthisy, who had been cut down with three wounds—to save them from capture, or worse, Count Dillon and his hard-hitting Irishmen in their red uniforms finally struggled through the abatis and struck the northwestern side of the Spring Hill Redoubt. Here, the Green Islanders reached the fiery parapet and engaged in savage hand-to-hand combat. Despite the heavy fire, the Sons of Erin held tight after having gained the parapet amid the swirling clouds of whitish smoke and clumps of bodies, while battling hand-to-hand with Captain Tawes's defenders and protecting their precious regimental battle flag of silk, which they planted on the works, as if signifying that they had already won the tenacious struggle on Prévost's right.

But the British and Loyalists thought otherwise, fighting back fiercely with jabbing bayonets and swinging musket-butts in the rising dust and smoke that choked their throats. More and more Irishmen were cut down by the fast-firing defenders, including Dillion, who fell with a wound that left him crippled for the rest of his life. Like in previous assaults that morning, no reinforcements were forthcoming in a timely manner, as eagerly expected by the Sons of Erin, who continued to fight gamely on their own, while sealing the fate of the hard-fighting Irishmen so far from their beloved Emerald Isle.

After having suffered severe punishment, the surviving members of this fine Celtic-Gaelic regiment, whose past battlefield performances in Europe were legendary throughout the army, and France, began to fall back into the body-strewn deep ditch, where earlier attackers of Colonel de Béthisy's vanguard had found safety as they fought to survive against the hot fire of the defenders under Captain Tawes. The Dillon Regiment lost Irish major Thomas Browne, who surged into the redoubt with a drawn sword and some of his followers. He was fated to be the highest-ranking allied officer killed in the assault; second in command, and one of the finest officers of the Dillon Regiment, he had taken command when Dillon was cut down. Another brave Irishman of the Dillon Regiment, Captain Bernard O'Neill, was killed in the savage combat.[37]

Fortunately, d'Estaing was luckier than the ill-fated Major Browne, who was a talented Irish officer beloved by his fellow Emerald Islanders, and known for his hard-fighting qualities and fondness for drink. His loss had played a role in causing the mauled Irish regiment to fall back from the hellish redoubt.

Always in the front, to his credit, the fearless career navy man and the toast of France had had numerous close calls with death, before and after he received his second wound. But all of d'Estaing's tireless efforts in attempting to overrun the Spring Hill Redoubt were in vain. He repeatedly rallied his hard-hit men, sending them forward with fixed bayonets three times against Captain Tawes's defenders, who stood firm and refused to budge. The vice admiral would eventually be "left for dead until a French officer managed to drag him to safety. In a sign of respect, the opposing British forces held their fire until the aristocratic comte [who was easily identifiable in his resplendent uniform and expensive powdered wig] could be evacuated from the field."[38]

Meanwhile, the bloody struggle for possession of the Spring Hill Redoubt continued unabated. The roar of the guns on both sides grew louder until they sounded like thunder on a summer evening. During the bloody hand-to-hand combat that swirled to new levels of intensity inside the smoke-filled redoubt, finely uniformed French grenadiers in Bourbon white uniforms and then Dillon's Irishmen in red uniforms were shocked by the sight of not only so many hard-fighting redcoat

defenders, who they knew were obviously regulars, but also South Carolina Loyalists in civilian garb. But after some of the most bitter combat
of the war, all attackers would be eventually pushed back over the parapet and into the depths of the deep ditch, where they laid low amid the
stream of projectiles and murderous enfilade fires.

While trapped in the hell of this deep ditch bordering the redoubt,
French soldiers frantically loaded and fired their muskets at Tawes's men,
who were only a few feet away, ignoring the piling up of the bodies of
their comrades at their feet and dropping around them like fallen leaves.
In his journal, one defender wrote admiringly of the Gallic enemy's courage, and of the "obstinate Resistance by the French" against a cruel fate
and odds that could not be overcome, just as d'Estaing's top lieutenants
had earlier emphasized to him at headquarters would be the case in an
all-out assault.[39]

After having gained the deep ditch of the Spring Hill Redoubt, Captain Séguier de Terson waited in vain for the expected reinforcements
that would never come, while watching in horror as even more of his
men fell around him in what had become a slaughter-pen. He wrote in
his journal about the uncoordinated attacks, negating French valor and
their best efforts to overcome a cruel fate: "With sixty men from different
regiments I stayed between the abatis and the redoubt for almost fifteen
minutes, taking all the enemy fire and waiting for reinforcements. But
many of the soldiers were already retreating. I did not know that, but
when no one came to my support, I fell back too."[40]

Séguier de Terson's anguished words were confirmed by other French
soldiers, whose beautiful white uniforms were now stained with a mixture of black powder, swamp mud, and blood. They watched helplessly
while their comrades were slaughtered like sheep in the body-clogged
deep ditch. In his journal, François d'Auber de Peyrelongue described
what had become a massacre: "Those who had overrun the trench were
not supported and practically all killed. Some of them climbed up the
redoubt from which they were soon dislodged. The troops gave way a
little, were rallied, but they advanced only very apathetically. The enemy
[at the Spring Hill Redoubt] received reinforcements [Major Glazier

and the 60th Regiment of Foot, with the Royal Marines attached to it].
[S]uddenly, his fire became stiffer, and everyone fled."[41]

THE AMERICANS BELATEDLY STRIKE

As fate would have it, it was time for the Americans to demonstrate the
same courage as the French in an inevitable march of folly in attempting
to overwhelm the formidable Spring Hill Redoubt. It was the ultimate
tragedy that both French and American valor were destined to be wasted,
negated by the mistakes of an obstinate vice admiral who thought he
would perform exceptionally well on October 9, in his first major campaign, and the first great test of allied unity of operations after the miserable failure at Newport.

The irrepressible Lieutenant Colonel John Laurens, who was wearing
his finest blue uniform, led the way for the right column at the head of
the crack Continental troops (190 soldiers) of his Light Corps. They were
followed by the less capable 200 men of the 1st Battalion, Charlestown
militia under Colonel Maurice Simons, and a company of 50 grenadiers
of the Charlestown militia, which would rise splendidly to the challenge
that morning. The Americans were about to encounter the same bloody
and tragic results that always come with uncoordinated infantry assaults
against strong defensive positions.

Even before the assault was launched, numbers of American
soldiers—like a good many French attackers—had already not only
accepted the fate of a doomed and inevitable repulse against the powerful network of fortifications, but also their own deaths in a futile effort.
Consequently, they had already said their final good-byes to their friends
with heartfelt sincerity and tears. Nevertheless, the fatalistic Americans
with their dark premonitions bravely moved forward with fixed bayonets,
heading for the formidable defenses that extended on the horizon as far
as the eye could see. [42]

But Lieutenant Colonel Laurens, leading his right column onward—
the first American column in the assault—was not the kind of officer
to admit that any task on the battlefield was impossible, or beyond his
ability—or that of his Continental troops: the 1st Virginia Regiment
(166 soldiers) under Colonel Richard Parker, and the 1st and 3rd South

Carolina Regiments under Lieutenant Colonel Francis Marion and Colonel William Thompson, respectively. To gain greater control when defeated French soldiers, in wild retreat, disrupted his ranks, and without orders to do so, the determined South Carolinian from one of the state's leading families prudently shifted his advance, with Lieutenant Colonel Francis Marion's 1st South Carolina Continental Infantry leading the way, followed by the more than 200 men of the 1st Battalion, Charlestown militia, and then the 1st Virginia Continental Regiment of more than 160 soldiers. With a flashing saber, the capable Laurens led them not toward the Carolina Redoubt, to the northwest, as originally planned. Instead, he turned to the right, or east, and straight toward the northwest side of the Spring Hill Redoubt.

To gain more of an advantage, Laurens was both wise and fortunate in his last-minute tactical decision-making as he now went for broke and fought for the honor of South Carolina, the infant republic, and patriots everywhere. The well-trained Continental soldiers of Laurens's column crossed the open ground without getting slaughtered, as the lieutenant colonel had ascertained the best way to handle this timely maneuver. Because Tawes's defenders were still busy shooting down the remaining French soldiers trapped in the deep ditch and the groups of French soldiers still advancing before the defensive bastion, after they had emerged from the swamp, there was a narrow window of opportunity that Laurens exploited to the fullest.[43]

After most French troops had been repulsed and poured rearward, and too much time had been wasted, the Americans, beginning with Laurens's right column, had struck belatedly when they should have attacked earlier, in conjunction with the French, not long before Major Glazier's hard-hitting troops had rushed to the rescue of the Spring Hill Redoubt. In his journal, one bitter French soldier complained about the small size of the first American assault column, which contained barely half of the number expected to have united with the French to strike an overpowering blow, penning how "only 600 advanced [and they only] added to the disorder."[44]

However, this was an unfair analysis of the overall American effort that was too frequently expressed by the disgruntled French, because of their prejudicial judgments and unfair assumptions regarding their unmilitary-like allies, who gave their best efforts and performed exceptionally well under the circumstances. In fact, the valor of Laurens's troops of the right column was unsurpassed on this bloody day of destiny, the attackers charging forward with enthusiasm to reach the parapet of the Spring Hill Redoubt, which was lit up with a sheet of fire. Clumps of soldiers then surged over the parapet and into the smoke-filled redoubt. Before they were cut down in a hail of lead, the courageous color bearers of the 1st South Carolina Continental Regiment raised the unit's two flags on the parapet of the northern face of the Spring Hill Redoubt, feeling that victory had finally been won.

However, all the while Captain Tawes and his defenders continued to battle back tenaciously as the surging tide of yelling South Carolinians, joined by some reenergized French and Irish soldiers of Dillon's regiment, went over the top and engaged in hand-to-hand combat inside the smoke-shrouded Spring Hill Redoubt. The hard-fighting Tawes, who cut down more than one attacker with his own hand, and his men rose splendidly to the challenge. The defenders then hurled these determined attackers rearward and out of the body-strewn redoubt, after the most bitter combat seen on bloody October 9.[45]

For the better part of an hour, the fighting raged in and around the deep ditch of the Spring Hill Redoubt, where the intermingled soldiers—Americans, French, and Irish—of four assault columns, which had all arrived in piecemeal fashion at different times, contrary to d'Estaing's best-laid plans, battled as one in front of the body-strewn redoubt. However, in the end, the tragic results of these disjointed and uncoordinated offensive efforts of one allied command after another were as predictable as they were inevitable. The late-arriving Americans, who had reinforced the remaining French, trapped in the deep ditches before the Spring Hill Redoubt, had not been enough to overpower the defenders on this day of slaughter. To escape the slaughter-pen, the Americans had fallen back, but this was long after hundreds of French had already retired or found refuge in the shelter of the deep ditch. As could be expected, the French naturally blamed the Americans for having fled first. They had become the favorite Gallic scapegoat for practically everything that had gone awry during this campaign, but in this case, it was not true, and the Americans blamed the French for the same failing.

An embittered Séguier de Terson wrote in his journal: "Although the [French] troops were badly beaten, it was not their fault that Savannah was not taken; rather, it was the responsibility of those who commanded us. At the beginning the whole command knew how the [assault] columns were to advance, but at the critical moment these same persons lost their heads so that we could find no one to lead us. That is why the columns were mixed up from the beginning"—a recipe for disaster.[46]

Contrary to the traditional and most pervasive French view, one eyewitness recorded how the Americans "showed the greatest courage, remaining at the foot of the ditch exposed to the enemy's fire without wavering [while the British] deliver[ed] their fire with their muskets almost touching our troops [during the] Slaughter."[47] The fighting was so close across the parapet that insults were traded back and forth, while some defenders of the Spring Hill Redoubt yelled: "Kill the Rascles French docks [dogs], God save the King of Great Britaine!"[48]

Boldly defending the entrance of the Spring Hill Redoubt, Lieutenant Tawes not only saved the day by inspiring the most tenacious resistance at the embattled defensive bastion, but also by turning the tide of battle, when the combined might of Laurens's attackers, with some rejuvenated French soldiers and Emerald Islanders of Count Dillon's regiment, had surged across the parapet with fixed bayonets. All the while, and even after the color bearers had been cut down, the two South Carolina battle flags still waved from the parapet, which was covered in bodies, and a dense layer of battle smoke hung over the defenses like a whitish cloud.

In a letter, one British officer described the key turning point of the bitter struggle for possession of the Spring Hill Redoubt: "A choice body of [French] grenadiers [and then Americans] came on with such spirit to attack the old redoubt upon the Ebenezer road, that if Tawse [Tawes], with a number of his men had not thrown himself in very opportunely, it must have been carried; upwards of fifty them. It is almost incredible the trifling loss we sustained; the only killed was poor Tawse [Tawes]," who was cut down during the bitter hand-to-hand combat in defending the main entry to the redoubt.[49]

In his journal, another defender described the nightmarish struggle for possession of the Spring Hill Redoubt, where both French and Americans fought together in the vain hope of overcoming the defensive bastion on the Ebenezer Road, but eventually "they drove them back with great Slaughter. Their Loss is reported to be 600 or 700 killed, wounded, and Prisoners; our Loss, Captain Tawes, of the Dragoons, who died nobly fighting on the Parapet of the Redoubt; 7 of the 60th killed and wound, and 2 Marines killed and 4 wounded."[50]

In his report to Lord Germain, and because many believed that the Spring Hill Redoubt would have certainly fallen without the heroic efforts of Captain Tawes and his defenders, who fought with great courage and tenacity, General Prévost praised Lieutenant Tawes for his magnificent defense of the redoubt, when everything was at stake: "And it is but justice to mention to your Lordship those troops who defended it. They were part of the South Carolina Royalists [Loyalists], the light dragoons dismounted, and the battalion men of the 4th Battalion of the 60th, in all about 100 men commanded (by a special order) by Captain Tawse [Tawes] of the dragoons (lieutenant in the 71st), a good and gallant officer, and who nobly fell with his sword in the body of the third he had killed with his own hand."[51]

In a letter, a British officer described the repulse at the Spring Hill Redoubt that was very much a slaughter, in which "the best blood of Europe" was freely shed and ran like water after a Georgia thunderstorm in July: "They stormed twice, but were repulsed with great Loss. Repulsed by whom? By 349 South Carolinians, and 24 [Scottish] dismounted Horsemen [former members of the 71st Regiment of Foot]! The whole under the Command of the immortal Capt. Tawse [Tawes], to whole sacred Memory, while my Recollection of his unequalled Merit lives, I'll pay an anniversary Tribute. The Peace of Heaven be with him."[52]

But the offensive effort was far from over, despite the extent of the surreal bloodletting on this ill-fated Georgia morning, when the Gods of War had seemingly cursed the best French and American offensive efforts that had all been in vain to this point. Leading the left column,

Count von Stedingk's troops, which consisted of fusiliers, had belatedly toiled through the stinking swamps of dark, stagnant water and then were slowed by a throng of retiring French troops, who had no more fight left in them. Von Stedingk and his Frenchmen struck like the other columns on the western side of the Spring Hill Redoubt, after having swung too far to the left, coming under the fire of the men at the Carolina Redoubt to the northwest.

Unfortunately, von Stedingk's determined efforts would come far too late. Although these attackers achieved significant gains, with a great loss in lives and seemingly on the threshold of victory, the non-arrival of reinforcements doomed von Stedingk's best efforts in a tragic repeat of the previous failed assaults.

Count von Stedingk suffered a painful contusion to his leg while bravely planting a fallen American flag (evidently one of the South Carolina banners had been shot down) on the parapet. He had early believed that the assault was doomed to failure, but then had changed his mind upon gaining the earthen works and seeing allied battle flags flying proudly on the smoke-laced parapet. He remained in the relative shelter of the deep ditch, awaiting the arrival of the expected reinforcements. Instead, he received the order from d'Estaing to retreat, while his command continued to be cruelly decimated by the blazing close-range fires pouring from the Spring Hill Redoubt. The aristocratic count wrote of how d'Estaing's order came as a shock: "[W]ith the cries of our dying comrades piercing my heart, [it] was the bitterest of my life, [and I] wished for death. Of nine hundred I led into action, four hundred men and thirty-nine officers were dead and wounded."[53]

As cruel fate would have it, American fortunes were no different from the tragic French fortunes. Far too much had already gone wrong. However, Von Stedingk's chances for success had been improved for a short time when Brigadier General Lachlan McIntosh belatedly struck with the second, or left, American column after Laurens's right column had struck. In uncoordinated fashion, he had also pushed too far left, to the right of the Carolina Redoubt, striking the northwestern side of the Spring Hill Redoubt. His approximately four hundred troops of the 1st, 5th, and 6th South Carolina Continental Regiments had joined the previous attackers, including von Stedingk's men, who were trapped in the hell of the deep ditch. Although the ditch offered some safety from the scorching fires, it would prove murderous to soldiers who were crowded close together, making them easy targets. Sadly, these reinforcements were not enough to turn the tide throughout this bloody Saturday.[54]

Once again, Lieutenant Colonel Maitland rose magnificently to the occasion during this emergency situation, when it appeared that the Spring Hill Redoubt was about to fall, having ordered Major Beamsley Glazier to counterattack in a fierce bayonet charge that was as hard-hitting as it was desperate. The last French and Americans were finally hurled from the deep ditches by the arrival of Major Glazier and the grenadiers of the 60th Regiment of Foot, known as "the old Royal American Regiment," and the around forty Royal Marines assigned to the regiment, which struck with "a degree of fury . . . In an instant the ditches of the [Spring Hill] redoubt and a battery to its right were cleared, the grenadiers charging headlong into them" to force the surviving French and American soldiers rearward.[55]

The combined French and American assaults can perhaps best be described as the bloody playing out of a Greek tragedy on Georgia soil, when fate and the gods of war were determined to wreck the best-laid plans of the attackers. In his journal, Massachusetts-born James Thacher, a skilled physician of Washington's army, described how the French and American attackers had advanced "with the most signal firmness and intrepidity, and faced their fire for about fifty-five minutes, when they were repulsed with considerable loss. Count d'Estaing received two slight wounds; more than six hundred of his brave troops, and about one hundred and seventy continentals were killed or wounded. Count [Casimir] Pulaski, a brigadier-general in our service, at the head of two hundred horsemen, was in full gallop, with the intention of charging the enemy in the rear, when he received a mortal wound. This gentleman was a Polander [who had] offered his services to our Congress, who appointed him to the rank of brigadier-general. He has [made a name for himself] by his active and enterprising service to our army, and his death is universally lamented."[56]

As if battling for his native homeland's liberation, Poland-born Casimir Pulaski daringly led the Pulaski Legion, which had been detached from Washington's army for service in the South. It had originally served as the vanguard for the right column under Laurens, in an advance position, to exploit any opportunity at the first sign of the breaking of British, Loyalist, or Hessian troops. It is said that Pulaski had a dark premonition of his impending death.

In regard to the forgotten role of the finely uniformed 125 cavalrymen of the Pulaski Legion, this kind of a tactical concept could only have been written by a career navy man masquerading as a field general in his first land battle, entirely out of his element. D'Estaing had possessed the crazy idea—one that would get Brigadier General Count Pulaski killed, for no gain, like the tragic fates of hundreds of his men—that a "very superior cavalry would create fear by charging through the streets [of Savannah] at open rein, after the way was opened for it; it could outflank foot soldiers and cut them down from behind."[57]

It's likely the gallant Brigadier General Count Pulaski, born in cultural Warsaw to an aristocratic family, and a single man totally dedicated to liberty, had reconciled with the fact that he would almost certainly be killed on October 9. Nevertheless, he had bravely charged ahead in stoic fashion across the open plain before the flaming Spring Hill Redoubt to carry out d'Estaing's orders at any cost.[58]

Thirty-year-old Count Pulaski was Washington's first cavalry commander, and was now leading the Pulaski Legion's lancers, who had been recruited mostly from Baltimore, Maryland, far from his Polish homeland. The traditional version of his death, as told by Surgeon Thacher and others, has become a popular myth, embellished over time: the headlong charge of the dashing Pulaski in his finely tailored Hussar uniform, astride his splendid black charger, dashing forth in a suicidal effort, almost on his own and far ahead of his men, when he saw that the assaults on the Spring Hill Redoubt were failing.

The tragic death of Count Pulaski could have been avoided if prudence and wisdom had been applied to the battle plan, rather than d'Estaing's misguided strategy that paid no honor to the dead, who were sacrificed in large numbers for no gain. The vice admiral did not appreciate Pulaski's last desperate effort, just as he did not appreciate American offensive efforts in general. Not to his credit, he was even critical of Pulaski's heroics, seeing them as too late to assist the ever-diminishing number of attackers, who were barely maintaining their slim toehold on the embattled redoubt on the Ebenezer Road. However, it was Pulaski's assigned role to exploit any breakthrough, and he had perceived one that had sent him and his men forward in a thundering charge.

Falling from his horse, the resplendently uniformed Polander was not killed outright, as long thought; rather, he was only wounded by an iron canister ball to the groin and upper thigh during the attack on the Spring Hill Redoubt. Count Pulaski remained conscious during the extremely painful removal of the iron canister by Surgeon James Lynah, chief surgeon of the South Carolina Light Dragoons. Although Pulaski was evacuated on the vessel *Wasp* for transport to a decent hospital in Charlestown, he was fated to die two days later of gangrene before reaching the port city to the north.[59] In one soldier's words, Pulaski's "corpse was carried to Charlestown, and there interr'd with great military funeral pomp."[60]

In every defensive sector surrounding Savannah, the British regulars, Hessians, Loyalists, and "the gallant Tars of old England" stood firm to ensure that the slaughter had been complete, and that they had thoroughly decimated d'Estaing's attackers.[61] One British soldier described in a letter what was nothing less than a massacre of some of the best fighting men of both France and the infant United States: "The enemy's loss was astonishing. I never saw such a dreadful scene, as several hundreds lay dead in a space of a few yards, and the cries of many hundreds of wounded was still more distressing to a feeling mind."[62]

In a letter to his wife, Major T. W. Moore wrote about the surreal horror that he saw all around him: "[S]uch a Sight I never saw before. The Ditch was filled with Dead, and in Front, for 50 Yards, the Field was covered with Slain. Many hung dead and wounded on the Abattis [*sic*]; and for some hundred Yards without the Lines, the Plain was strewed with mangled Bodies, killed by our Grape and Langridge [small iron bars]."[63]

Like other British, Hessian, and Loyalist writers, Moore also emphasized the casualties among the top allied leadership on the darkest and most tragic day in the history of the Franco-American alliance during its second offensive effort, after the first one at Newport, Rhode Island: "D'Estaing is wounded in two Places very badly. Pulaski was thought dangerously so, now dead. I saw my old Friend, Charles Mott, a Major [among American forces], among the Dead, but recollected no other quondam [former] Acquaintance."[64]

The redcoat victors of the Spring Hill Redoubt captured the bullet-riddled blue silk colors of the 1st South Carolina Continental Regiment, after the flag-bearers had been cut down in the storm of lead. This beautiful flag, with a distinctive gold-embroidered regimental insignia in the center, had been presented by Mrs. Bernard Elliott to the 1st South Carolina on July 1, 1776, in honor of its successful defense of Fort Sullivan, which had saved Charlestown against General Henry Clinton's best efforts during the first British attempt to conquer the South.[65] The flag-bearers of these two colors, one blue and the other red, of this fine South Carolina regiment of Laurens's right column had boldly planted them on the parapet of the Spring Hill Redoubt, before they were cut down in the carnage.[66]

British flags now flew in triumph from the parapet of the smoke-laced and body-strewn Spring Hill Redoubt, which had stood firm largely because the French, and then the American, assaults were launched in piecemeal fashion, and had lacked coordination and timeliness from beginning to end. If only d'Estaing had been so aggressive and "keen to land his forces quickly and go on the attack at once [upon his arrival], he would have caught Prévost with inadequate defensive fortifications, especially artillery positions, and short of manpower . . . [Instead, d'Estaing] display[ed] the timidity and unwillingness to take bold risks that unfortunately characterized so many French naval commanders of the period."[67]

The great combined effort of the French and Americans to take Savannah by storm had turned into an unprecedented disaster, destroying the flower of the French expeditionary force and the American army, to a lesser degree. Meanwhile, the architect of the bloody fiasco, Vice Admiral d'Estaing, was carried by his men to the rear, all the way to the main Jewish cemetery, located several hundred yards south of the Spring Hill

Redoubt, known as the Levi Sheftall Hebrew Cemetery. Here, the vice admiral, who had demonstrated far more physical courage than tactical wisdom and good sense, was placed behind a stone crypt for protection.[68]

Located a good distance south of the Spring Hill Redoubt, the well-laid-out, walled main Hebrew cemetery had never flooded because it was located at a higher elevation than the surrounding terrain. It was here that d'Estaing had smartly placed his strategic reserves, including the more than five hundred men of the Chasseurs-Volontaires de Saint-Domingue, in an ideal reserve position to meet the growing crisis just to the north, which would be the most severe of the day.

It is not known for a fact, but some of the mulattoes in the ranks of the Chasseurs might have been fathered by Hebrew planters, or French plantation owners in Saint-Domingue with various amounts of Jewish blood. The white volunteers from Saint-Domingue, only sixty-six men of the Volunteers Grenadiers, were also part of the strategic reserves along with the relatively few men from other units, and bolstered by small-caliber artillery.[69]

For the most part, one of the most nightmarish repulses of the war had resulted from d'Estaing squandering the crucial element of surprise. The garrison was now simply too strong and well-prepared for the attacks in a powerful network of defenses, especially after the timely arrival of Lieutenant Colonel Maitland and his troops from Beaufort. After looking in disbelief at so many of his men lying dead in the deep ditch of the Spring Hill Redoubt, a distraught and sickened Lieutenant Colonel Laurens had thrown his saber to the ground in disgust, cursing loudly, and lamenting: "Poor fellows, I envy you!"

Not long after the battle, a Southerner from Charlestown listed the primary reasons for such a costly defeat in the December 8, 1779, issue of the *New Jersey Gazette*: "The Enemy having a much more numerous Garrison [around 5,000 men under d'Estaing and 3,000 men under Prévost] than had been represented; being said to consist of 1,700 effective Regulars, and a great Number of Sailors, Marines, Militia and armed Blacks."[70]

This was a significant mention—one of the very few—about the most forgotten defenders of Savannah, the armed former slaves, who have been as totally ignored as the Blacks and mulattoes on the other side, the men of the Chasseurs-Volontaires de Saint-Domingue. These former slaves who fought under the Union Jack had played their part with distinction, standing firm in defying the attackers, avenging innumerable injustices and sins against humanity inflicted because of the color of their skin.

While the exhilaration among the defenders could not have been greater at the sight of the vast throng of d'Estaing's routed soldiers fleeing across the open plain, so was the British contempt for their vanquished Gallic enemy. One jubilant defender, who targeted the much-touted French grenadiers for his unbridled contempt, wrote about the magnificent stand made by the troops under Captain Tawes stationed at the Spring Hill Redoubt: "They attempted to carry by Storm a square Redoubt, consisting simply of a Ditch and Sand Parapet, without a Pallisade [sic] or Fraise [sharpened wooden stakes placed in the earthen slopes of redoubts and pointing outward to frustrate attackers] on it! The vaunting Grenadiers de France Sabre a la Main, took French Leave by a precipitate Flight, leaving Heaps of their martial Comrades in the Ditch, and immortal GLORY WITH THE GARRISON."[71]

Not only were the French soldiers in flight all across the field, but the Americans were also falling back in extreme disorder, in what was a total rout that consumed the fortunate survivors of both allied armies. In his journal, one Frenchman described the extent of the rout among the Americans, who always presented the most convenient target for seemingly unlimited Gallic contempt that seemed to have no end. These professional military men truly despised the amateurish rebels, who hardly looked or acted like the stereotypical heroes of republicanism and the Age of Enlightenment. According to this Frenchman, the Americans "looked like a crowd leaving church," because of the widespread confusion and disorder of their panicked withdrawal. This only encouraged the opportunistic British to hurriedly align for a counterattack, in preparation for taking the offensive to exploit the most advantageous of situations.[72]

Sickened by the gory sights of the slaughter, a saddened grenadier, Séguier de Terson, penned in his journal: "Our attack cost us dearly; our losses amounted to 564 men killed and wounded and 40 officers, 12 of whom were killed. M. d'Estaing was wounded twice; he conducted himself as a brave grenadier but [a] poor general in the affair."[73]

In a letter, one astonished British officer described with disbelief "the trifling loss we sustained, [as] there were not twenty privates killed and wounded. The enemy's loss was astonishing. I never saw such a dreadful scene, as several hundreds lay dead in a space of a few yards, and the cries of many hundreds wounded [were] still more distressing to a feeling mind."[74]

In his revealing journal, François d'Auber de Peyrelongue wrote about the extent of not only the rout, but also the extreme danger that continued to exist for the rapidly retiring French troops at this time. They had been badly routed, like the Americans, losing even more men and a great deal of Gallic dignity in the process: "We continued to be hit by artillery as far as 425 yards from the [Spring Hill] bastion. We had to run away from grapeshot" fired from the cannon of the Spring Hill Redoubt.[75]

Fortunately, at this point, when the day's crisis was reaching its height and it appeared that all was lost, the French army's strategic reserve was positioned on the slightly higher ground at the walled Jewish cemetery, including the largest unit of the reserve, the men of the Chasseurs-Volontaires de Saint-Domingue. They were in good shape at this time and ready for action, the ideal situation for a strategic reserve, especially in a crisis situation such as the one that had now emerged.

Even Vice Admiral d'Estaing was amazed by the fact that the men from Saint-Domingue were in excellent shape, far better than even the finest French troops: "It is extraordinary that there were so few sick among 3,000 men [the majority of the expeditionary force] who came from the islands [of the West Indies] and Saint-Domingue, who were constantly under arms for nearly a month, most of them without tents, dressed only in linen [tropical uniforms], suffering from heat in the daytime, and freezing to death at night."[76]

These Black and mulatto soldiers of the Chasseurs, who had never before engaged in battle as a unit, were now all that stood between the confident, resurgent enemy, now on the offensive and sensing complete victory, as they were the only large force among the strategic reserve capable of delivering an offensive impact of significance in this crisis situation. Thanks to Maitland's "comprehensive eye" and keen tactical mind, the counterattacking grenadiers of the 60th Regiment of Foot and its assigned Royal Marines continued to pour forth across the open plain with fixed bayonets to crush the French and American soldiers in wild retreat, in what was seemingly a complete disaster for the allied army.

D'Estaing put forth his version of why this shocking disaster had just occurred, which now placed the very future of both the American and French armies and the Franco-American alliance at risk. Predictably, d'Estaing targeted the Americans for his abuse: "The action did not last longer than an hour; it was very violent. The enemy, almost as numerous as we, as we learned later, had gathered the greater part of their force around the Spring Hill redoubt; and it appears certain that two American deserters alerted them about the point of attack the day before. That no attention at all was paid to the two feint attacks from the trenches is even more reason for thinking so. The diversion that 500 Americans were to attempt on the enemy's left did not take place. They got lost. The two American galleys caused the attack from the river to fail . . . [In consequence] the enemy was not surprised . . . Everything depended on it, in my opinion."[77]

In truth, Vice Admiral d'Estaing had only himself to blame for the endless errors and misjudgments that had led to possibly one of the greatest and most one-sided British victories of the American Revolution. This was especially the case if the now-existing supreme advantage could be properly exploited in full by Maitland's counterattacking forces; they possessed the lethality to destroy the routed allied armies now in disorganized flight, and wreck the fragile Franco-American alliance, which had seen its most disastrous and bloodiest day on October 9.[78]

CHAPTER 5

The Chasseurs-Volontaires de Saint-Domingue Save the Day

After the bloodiest single hour of the eight years of the American Revolution, centered at the vortex of the storm that had roared with a fury over the Spring Hill Redoubt, the rout of thousands of defeated American and French soldiers was as complete as it was thorough. More than one thousand men had fallen in a slaughter, including the bravest soldiers who had advanced the farthest and top officers who had led the way, encouraging their troops onward all the way into the depths of the embattled Spring Hill Redoubt, in some cases. This number also included the three-times-wounded d'Estaing, who had left the French army officially under the command of Irish count Arthur Dillon, before the hard-fighting Emerald Islander was likewise cut down in the holocaust.

The full extent of the defeat of the two allied armies that had turned into a fiasco of unprecedented proportions was shockingly evident to the men of the Chasseurs-Volontaires de Saint-Domingue, who were positioned on the slightly higher ground near the Levi Sheftall Hebrew Cemetery. From this vantage point, they could view the astonishing sight of the rout across the plain in full, and it shocked them to the core. A good many wounded American and French soldiers were also scattered in wild flight across the level ground as far as the eye could see, running or limping rearward in desperate attempts to escape the sweeping British counterattack.

While the Saint-Domingue soldiers left no written descriptions of the stunning sight of hundreds of defeated American and French soldiers streaming across the open and level field, they must have been thoroughly shaken by the extent of the rout. At this time, the young and inexperienced mixed-race and Black Chasseurs included the two grandsons (René and Maturin Olivier) of Captain Vincent Olivier, who had been a member of the 1697 Cartagena expedition. They were likely most astounded at the sight of the two badly defeated armies, as many of the Chasseurs had fully expected to achieve victory in the battle. No doubt, the white officers of the Chasseurs might have taken some necessary action to steady the ranks to some degree in such a crisis situation, although paradoxically, these defeated and routed white soldiers, both French and Americans, had long felt they were vastly superior to the Chasseurs in every way possible, because of the color of their skin.[1]

The young men in the finely uniformed and disciplined ranks of the Chasseurs-Volontaires de Saint-Domingue now faced the most daunting of challenges in their first battle together as a command. They possessed uncommon confidence partly because a good many of them had already served in the Saint-Domingue militia and had fought maroons in the past. Veteran soldiers like Joseph Pellerin, Mathieu Blaise, Alloun, Jean One, Jean-Louis Cassagne, Paul Doue, Joseph Pyracmour, Jean-Baptiste Lagarde, Etienne La Rivière, Fabien Gentil, Jean-Baptiste Riché, Pierre Augustin, Jacques Le Roy Gautier, Jean-François Edouard L'Eveille, François Felix, and others would stand firm in the face of the shocking defeat of not one but two armies.

In part, this situation explained why these Blacks and mulattoes from Saint-Domingue had been chosen as the strategic reserve by d'Estaing, who had been entirely correct in having accurately measured the overall quality of these men and placing confidence in them to rise to the occasion, much to his credit. Their level of experience ensured that they would stand firm, even as thousands of panicked and demoralized Americans and Frenchmen were now streaming around them and heading rearward in the panicked flight south. Despite the unnerving sight of a complete rout taking place in front of them to a shocking degree, the men of the Chasseurs-Volontaires de Saint-Domingue, including Daniel Castanet, the mulatto son of white planter and merchant Denis Castanet, were ready for the key role they were about to play in reversing the fortunes of war.[2]

Clearly, a great challenge lay ahead for the soldiers of the Chasseurs, because the ever-opportunistic and tactically astute Maitland had thrown in his strategic reserve to exploit the crushing defeat to the fullest, in a bid to completely destroy the allied command that was in a shambles after the bloody repulse. As he had done in the past, Lieutenant Colonel Maitland continued to prove he was a master at getting the most out of any situation, especially on the battlefield.

As if the rout of two armies was not enough, Major Beamsley Glazier of the 60th Regiment of Foot was determined to take full advantage of the tactical situation that now offered the distinct possibility of not only winning glory, but also completely destroying the disorganized and reeling allied force. Major Glazier was merely obeying the orders of the astute Lieutenant Colonel Maitland, ready to reap the dividends of the most thorough repulse of any attackers he had ever seen.

The experienced team of Maitland and Glazier knew this was the most "critical moment" of the battle. The golden opportunity had been bestowed upon them to annihilate the vanquished and routed allied army. On Maitland's earlier directive to deliver a devastating blow, Glazier had "ordered a bayonet charge that threw the French and Americans into even greater confusion."[3] Historian Theophilus Gould Steward described this key turning point: "As the army began its retreat, lieutenant-colonel Maitland with the grenadiers, and marines who were incorporated with the grenadiers, charged the rear with the purpose of accomplishing its annihilation."[4]

General Prévost wrote of how Glazier and his grenadiers and marines charged with abandon, striking "with a degree of fury" that routed the last remaining attackers in the deep ditch of the body-strewn Spring Hill Redoubt. They then pushed onward in a sweeping counterattack that promised to achieve far more important gains: the complete destruction of the allied army.[5]

As ordered by Maitland at exactly the right time, this hard-hitting counterattack by the men of the 60th Regiment of Foot and the Royal Marines swept all before it to ensure the permanent reclaiming of the Spring Hill Redoubt, and then continued the charge over the defenses with victory cheers. Sensing that they were about to achieve a decisive victory, the counterattackers then swarmed through the abatis, made easier because the French and American troops had torn paths through the fallen timber to allow their own hasty retreat, across ground that was strewn with the bodies of Frenchmen in white uniforms and Americans in Continental blue and civilian garb.

General Prévost described the devastating impact of the British counterattack of revenge-seeking redcoats, who had hit their reeling opponents exceptionally hard: "the grenadiers charging headlong into them, and the enemy drove in confusion over the abatis and into the swamp."[6]

This was the most serious threat of the day to the very existence of the routed French and American armies. It became even more serious when additional troops were ordered by the ever-opportunistic Maitland to move forward and attack behind the counterattacking grenadiers and Royal Marines of Major Glazier's 60th Regiment of Foot, who had already charged forth from the Spring Hill Redoubt. Spying a golden opportunity with the rout of both allied armies, Maitland knew they were in no condition to resist an attack of elite troops at this time.

General Prévost described the growing strength and momentum of the counterattackers, who steamrolled onward with flags flying and victory cheers that echoed over the plain: "On the advance of the grenadiers [of the 60th Regiment of Foot and the Royal Marines attached to the command], three companies of the 1st Battalion of the 71st were ordered [by Maitland to advance southwest from the nearby defenses to the Spring Hill Redoubt] to sustain them, but tho' these lay [where Prévost had positioned them, for just such an eventuality] at an inconsiderable distance, and advanced with the usual ardour of that [Scottish Highland] corps, so precipitate was the retreat of the enemy, they could not close with them."[7]

The redcoat grenadiers of the 16th Regiment of Foot of the Light Corps, under Major Colin Graham, were now likewise part of the steamrolling counterattack by Lieutenant Colonel Maitland, who was determined to not only exploit the golden opportunity to the fullest, but also to destroy the allied army with a powerful blow that he envisioned would achieve the most decisive victory yet won by England in the South.[8]

As demonstrated throughout this campaign, which was all about the conquest of the entire South and restoring the thirteen colonies back into the king's fold, the tactically astute Maitland was just the man for the job.

He was naturally aggressive and exceptionally cagey, ideal for exploiting this golden opportunity to the fullest. At the Battle of Stono Ferry on June 20, 1779, for instance, he had rushed his crack Scottish Highlanders of the 71st Regiment of Foot to plug a gap in the lines at the most critical moment—lines which were broken after the Hessians on the far left flank had withdrawn in panic after being hit hard by attacking Continentals. Maitland had rallied the reeling Germans in a timely manner and then counterattacked with his Highlanders to restore the line, which seemed about to be rolled up like a carpet.

All in all on this bloody Saturday, everything was shaping up for the counterattacking British to inflict a decisive blow and destroy the French and American armies, which seemed inevitable and only a matter of time. However, General Prévost had overlooked a key factor that was destined to stop the sweeping counterattack, acquiring more momentum with each passing minute and threatening to destroy both allied armies: the last line of resistance, the finely uniformed troops of the Chasseurs-Volontaires de Saint-Domingue, and d'Estaing's ace in the hole.[9]

It's likely that Prévost never knew the exact details of what was happening on the other side at this decisive moment, as the battlefield was obscured with clouds of whitish smoke and dust when the fate of the French and American armies hung in the balance. Clearly, the overall tactical situation was now ripe for the counterattacking British troops to deliver a death blow to the vulnerable French and American armies, placing Maitland in the enviable position of achieving one of the greatest British victories of the war. One dismayed defender, Captain Kennedy, felt a degree of embarrassment for the disastrous state of the vanquished foe, now in wild flight. He was shocked by the extent of the disastrous rout, writing how the defeated French and Americans "most shamefully retreated with great Precipitation."[10]

Historian Norman Desmarais, an expert on France's role during the American Revolution, described what was now at stake, and how the Blacks and mulattoes of Saint-Domingue were about to rise magnificently to the challenge: "The Fontanges Legion [the Chasseurs-Volontaires de Saint-Domingue], stationed as a reserve in the rear guard [at the Jewish cemetery] [were about to accomplish the impossible when they rose to the supreme challenge], prevented the annihilation of the allied force."[11] Historian Theophilus Gould Steward wrote about this decisive moment, when the existence of the French and American armies, and the overall Franco-American alliance, hung in the balance and seemed doomed: "It was then that there occurred the most brilliant feat of the day," on bloody October 9.[12]

To his credit, D'Estaing had wisely placed the primary force of the French army's strategic reserve south of the Spring Hill Redoubt on the higher ground at the Levi Sheftall Hebrew Cemetery, where it was bolstered by four four-pounder guns situated just to its right-rear. It was now time for the Chasseurs-Volontaires de Saint-Domingue to play a leading role, not only as the vanquished army's last remaining guardians and protectors, but also as saviors in the face of the slashing British counterattack that now threatened to destroy all before it, after having skillfully "maneuvered to save the remnants of the retreating army."[13]

Indeed, despite the many errors he made earlier, Vice Admiral d'Estaing had employed excellent foresight and made his best tactical decision of the day by having stationed the Chasseurs-Volontaires de Saint-Domingue at exactly the right place. In his own words: "The reserve corps, commanded by M. le vicomte de Noailles, [had] advanced as far as an old Jewish cemetery" to protect the two vanquished armies in the worst-case scenario, which was exactly what was happening now.[14]

But who ordered the bold forward movement of the Chasseurs at this most critical moment, to meet the British counterattack head-on? It was not the vice admiral, who had been wounded multiple times and carried rearward by his aides. It was not Dillon, who had taken over command after the vice admiral was twice wounded, but then had also been cut down in the utter confusion and chaos of the rout. It was left up to Colonel Louis-Marie de Noailles, just twenty-three years old, the brother-in-law of the Marquis de Lafayette, and a young nobleman of France's elite, to rise to the challenge in the day's greatest crisis situation. Based on his own judgment and initiative, he made the most important tactical decision in a timely manner at this point on bloody October 9.

Fortunately for the American and French armies, the aristocratic Vicomte de Noailles was a gifted officer and natural leader of men, despite his pampered upbringing of extreme privilege and wealth. With close family connections to more than one French king, and from one of France's leading families, Noailles had been recommended for the prestigious Croix de Saint-Louis medal for valor because of what he had demonstrated while leading the attack of French marines up "Hospital Hill" to capture Grenada. While d'Estaing took credit for the taking of the Caribbean island of Grenada, the victory might not have been won without Noailles.

A remarkable individual both on and off the battlefield, Noailles was a true Renaissance man. His love of liberty stemmed from his enlightening experiences in America, like so many other Frenchmen who served in the Savannah Campaign, and would later translate directly to his role in the French Revolution and in the Age of Napoleon. He had received a splendid education in the finest schools in France and was musically talented, often with a violin in his hands when he was not carrying the expensive and ornate saber that represented one of France's leading families, and a noble tradition.

Thanks to the strategic reserve troops, especially the Chasseurs-Volontaires de Saint-Domingue, which was the largest unit by far, Colonel Noailles was now in the best position to save the day in a classic case of do or die. This was an ironic development, considering he had been the most outspoken officer against the attack when the leaders discussed it at the October 8 commanders' conference at headquarters, when d'Estaing made his final ill-fated decision, ignoring the sound advice and wiser tactical views of Noailles and other top lieutenants.

One French officer described what happened when Noailles decided to act on his own when it mattered the most, without orders, recognizing this was now a true emergency situation when only bold and desperate action could possibly save the day: "When the Viscount de Noailles perceives the disorder reigning in the columns, he brings his reserve corps up to charge the enemy; and when he hears the retreat sounded, advances in silence, at a slow step and in perfect order, to afford an opportunity to the regular troops to reform themselves in his rear."[15]

With sword in hand and white Bourbon flags waving, Colonel Louis-Marie de Noailles led the way over the open, high ground from the strategic reserve position at the Jewish cemetery, straight north toward the Spring Hill Redoubt and the onrushing formation of redcoat counterattackers, who had triumphantly charged beyond the abatis by this time. The Black and mulatto soldiers of the Chasseurs, in neat navy blue uniform coats and tricorn hats of the same dark color, advanced with precision and spirit across the open plain from the slightly higher ground of the Levi Sheftall Hebrew Cemetery.

With fixed bayonets, the neat, disciplined ranks of the Chasseurs headed straight north for the Spring Hill Redoubt and the lengthy scarlet formations of Glazier's and Maitland's counterattacking troops, now advancing rapidly south across the open plain, respectively in that order of alignment from south to north. The Black and mulatto attackers of the Chasseurs steadily advanced toward the smoke-filled redoubt in a desperate effort to save the day by coming to the timely rescue of the two routed armies. They were the only troops standing between the counterattacking British, who were convinced they were on the verge of a great victory, and the routed American and French troops, who were now all but helpless, and could not have been more vulnerable at this time.[16]

The well-trained soldiers of the Chasseurs-Volontaires de Saint-Domingue were about to play their most distinguished role ever in the battle, which became a legend in Haiti, unlike in the United States and France. Very few, if any, commanders ever expected they would successfully perform their crucial mission in this key battlefield situation, including perhaps Vice Admiral d'Estaing himself, since they had not had much experience in conventional warfare during past campaigns, especially on American soil.

What has been most forgotten is the fact that more than any other fighting men on either side at Savannah, these young mixed-race and Black soldiers from the West Indies possessed the highest of motivations, of a complex nature. They had a great deal to prove for a wide variety of reasons, especially racial, and were highly motivated. In addition, these men of the Chasseurs, so far from home and the warm breezes of the Caribbean, were extremely proud to not only represent Saint-Domingue, but also France, which also played a role in ensuring they would rise to the ultimate challenge. And, of course, pride in their color was also a major factor for performing above and beyond the call of duty.

Unfortunately, Blacks in the United States throughout history have faced discrimination and all manner of racism. As recently as the 1950s and 1960s, they lived in a segregated and discriminatory society and faced legal discrimination from state and national governments, especially in the South. So, too, had the Blacks and mulattoes of the Chasseurs-Volontaires de Saint-Domingue, who now had their eyes on the greatest prize for the future: the winning of complete equality with whites, which they believed would come from displaying exceptional courage on the battlefield. They hoped that success here in Savannah would lead to the systematic dismantling of the legal system of racism and discrimination, based on a toxic mixture of prejudice, racism, and ignorance, which had kept them second-class citizens all their lives, despite their free status and high standing in Saint-Domingue society mostly as coffee plantation owners. As noted, the vast majority of the Chasseurs were of mixed race, and most of them were the sons and grandsons of white French planters and women of color, both enslaved and free. They were fully aware that they also represented with considerable pride their large class of free Blacks, including their family members and friends so far away in the tropics.

Consequently, for the free Blacks and mulattoes of the Chasseurs, the quest for full equality was not only a lifelong passion and a great dream that never died, but also a lifelong struggle against the odds in a discriminatory society dominated by the ruling planter-class elites, including some who had their own mixed-race children—the most abusive slave regime in the Americas. These largely successful men of color who now served in the Chasseurs' ranks had long detested the unlimited power of the rich white planters and government officials who had long relegated them to inferior second-class stature, undeserving of full rights as French citizens and any kind of respect, even from whites of the lowest ranks. Ironically, the greatest abusers of the free Black population were French-born whites who were transplants from the mother country, while the Chasseurs were Creoles who spoke an eloquent Creole had been born in Saint-Domingue, their native homeland, unlike those of a lighter color who looked down and hated them for superficial reasons of skin color. In this sense, it was truly symbolic that these men of a darker shade now represented their home colony with such pride, willing to sacrifice their lives, even for the whites who detested them, if it meant it would better the lives of their family members back home.

The overall deplorable racial situation in Saint-Domingue that had led to a long list of "injustices and tyrannies" was a major reason why these young Black and mulatto men had joined the Chasseurs-Volon-taires in the first place. Most of all, it also led to the key role they would now play as they struggled toward their goal of winning full equality for themselves, their families, and the entire class of free Blacks and mixed-race people. It was a new, rare opportunity to fully demonstrate their equality and the content of their character by way of valor in a key situation on the battlefield, in their idealistic, hopeful belief that such proven valor and equality in combat on behalf of their colony and nation would prove decisive in changing their discriminatory world forever.

Black and mulatto courage demonstrated on the battlefield would finally allow all whites, especially high-ranking military and political leaders, the opportunity to see fundamental racial truths that would, in their overly optimistic minds, automatically translate into complete equality for them in Saint-Domingue society. Once they took off their neat blue uniforms after an impressive victory at Savannah, and if they succeeded in demonstrating superior valor and commitment to France and their colony, they believed everything would change for the better.

As a result of these fondest hopes and beliefs, the upcoming chal-lenge to save both shattered armies could not have been more formida-ble and significant for the Chasseurs. These idealistic young men had convinced themselves that they would be able to now rise higher in Saint-Domingue society and gain the ever-elusive racial equality they had long dreamed of—if they could just manage to thwart the British counterattack that was now pushing toward them from the north like a steamroller. They sincerely believed that their upcoming starring role on the battlefield in the most desperate of situations would convince whites to stop their overt racism and discrimination, setting the stage for a bright new day of greater equality for all free Blacks and mulattoes in

Saint-Domingue—an intoxicating vision for men who had faced endless racial discrimination all their lives.

As future events would demonstrate in full, this burning desire of the young, idealistic Chasseurs for future racial harmony was nothing more than a pipe dream and an illusion, however. Whites would never change their racist views, engendered in their hearts and minds since childhood, no matter what these Black and mulatto soldiers achieved on the battlefield, including at Savannah. Even in the current crisis situation, in which their role was that of savior to two battered armies, even if they sacrificed their own lives for God and country—it would not happen in their lifetime, or even for their future descendants. The ugly reality of French racism was deeply ingrained in society, both in Saint-Domingue and in France, at every possible level. Indeed, racism was permanently fixed in the very psyche and fiber of white French society, including within the culture and government of Saint-Domingue, which were based on the concept that all whites were superior to Black and mixed-race people on every imaginable level.

Of course, in truth, Blacks and whites are fully equal in the eyes of God, and according to the fundamental truths of human nature, history, and existence since time immemorial, as the Chasseurs realized and had been long taught. In this sense, there was nothing for the Black and mulatto men from Saint-Domingue to prove to whites. It was only prejudiced, man-made rules and discriminatory laws written by narrow-minded, upper-class elitists out of overt racism and a shockingly high level of ignorance that had deemed otherwise.

Nevertheless, the young soldiers of the Chasseurs-Volontaires de Saint-Domingue embraced two great ambitions and enlightened visions at this moment in time: They were now determined to prove their worth and fundamental equality to the most aristocratic and elitist of Frenchmen on the battlefield, including counts and noblemen, in the hope of not only saving the day for the French and American armies, but also, it was hoped, that their courage and sacrifice would at long last change the mindless French racism that had made their lives miserable and hampered their fondest hopes and ambitions for so long.

In consequence, these mulatto and Black men in navy blue uniforms were now more than ready to give their all, including their lives, if necessary, in the hope of changing the hardened hearts of racist whites in Saint-Domingue, while striking a blow for the equality of all men on Georgia soil, as had been proclaimed in America's Declaration of Independence just over three years before, and in accordance with the high-minded philosophies and egalitarian spirit of the Age of Enlightenment. Perhaps their crucial mission of rescuing the American and French armies and preserving the existence of the all-important Franco-American alliance—the very key to American independence—would extend to safeguarding the life of the infant republic in America. This is now what was at stake for the five hundred relatively inexperienced Chasseurs as they boldly advanced to face the British counterattack with fixed bayonets and flags flying in the Georgia sunshine.[17]

Even more than fighting for the honor of Saint-Domingue and France, the highest personal motivation of these free Blacks and mulattoes of the Chasseurs was to win the recognition and laurels on the battlefield that would translate to the freeing of family members who were still slaves on Saint-Domingue. In this regard, the Chasseurs were battling for freedom not only in America, but also in Saint-Domingue, where the meaning of liberty had a much more intimate and personal connection for them, when their beloved family members were shackled in the bonds of man's most evil institution.[18]

The bloody morning of October 9 was therefore a special day of destiny for the Black and mulatto soldiers of the Chasseurs-Volontaires de Saint-Domingue on a variety of levels. They now suddenly found themselves in the most serious crisis of any soldiers on either side during the entire Savannah Campaign: an imposing and extremely heavy burden of responsibility for young men in their first major battle, hundreds of miles from home, especially after their Gallic army had already been vanquished. As never before, the futures of the two allied armies were now at stake, as more than one thousand men, both Frenchmen and Americans, had been killed and wounded in the bloody assault.

Whatever self-doubts, fears, and anxieties now nagged at the men in the advancing ranks of the Chasseurs, they were put aside as they marched with discipline over the open, level ground with flintlock muskets on their right shoulders, pushing ever closer to the sweeping counterattack of the charging redcoats, whose long steel bayonets glistened in the morning sunlight before the Spring Hill Redoubt.

Indeed, all that was now standing in the way of Lieutenant Colonel Maitland and his counterattacking troops of the Royal Marines and the 60th Regiment of Foot, troops of the 16th Regiment of Foot, and the three Scottish companies of the 71st Regiment of Foot immediately to their rear were the young men of the Chasseurs-Volontaires de Saint-Domingue and the equally young Colonel de Noailles, who continued to lead the way across open ground with sword in hand.

At this crucial moment, these Black and mulatto soldiers clearly saw that they were in the most critical of tactical situations that could possibly exist on the battlefield for strategic reserve troops. They had suddenly been thrown into the vortex of the storm—a classic case of do or die, not only in regard to themselves, but also in regard to the future existence of the two armies and, most important, the existence of the Franco-American alliance, upon which America's future rested. After d'Estaing's miserable 1778 failure in Rhode Island and, as noted, deep divisions had formed in this increasingly fragile alliance, which was later impacted by newly emerging rivalries, mistrusts, and animosities of a deep-seated nature. All of this had proven extremely detrimental for the allied armies in this current campaign.

If the Chasseurs-Volontaires de Saint-Domingue now failed to rise to the ultimate challenge in accomplishing what expert military men deemed impossible in such a dire situation, when so much was at stake, then the most crucial alliance in the annals of American history would be destroyed, useless thereafter to forever change the course of the American Revolution and world history.[19] Indeed, if Maitland's vigorous counterattack was allowed to tear into the shattered remains of the two routed armies, then the already extremely delicate alliance, upon which the young republic's future now depended, would fall apart and be no more. Quite simply, the very life of America was now at stake, like on no other field of strife during the course of the American Revolution before the final showdown in the Virginia tidewater at Yorktown two Octobers in the future.

CHAPTER 6

Black and Mixed-Race Soldiers Strike a
Decisive Blow for America's Liberty

When the Chasseurs-Volontaires de Saint-Domingue had been formed
in the tropics during the spring and summer of 1779, the command's
top officer had wanted the enthusiastic young men joining the new unit
to reflect on the harsh and disadvantageous racial situation in Saint-
Domingue and what was needed to force a change in their society. He
had spoken to them using the first person, to express the ultimate and
most passionate objective of the Black and mixed-race soldiers of d'Estaing's expeditionary force: "I must make the whites blush for the scorn
they have heaped on me in my civic status, and for the injustices and
tyrannies they have continually exercised over me with impunity. I must
prove to them that as a soldier I am capable of at least as much honor
and courage and of even more loyalty."[1]

Now on the bloody field of Savannah, at this key moment in
time when they viewed the rout of both allies' armies with astonishment during an unprecedented disaster, the Chasseurs-Volontaires de
Saint-Domingue were about to magnificently rise to the challenge,
performing in an especially distinguished manner that would certainly
make the haughty and racist whites of both Saint-Domingue and France
"blush for the scorn they have heaped" on these young Black and mulatto
fighting men.[2]

This golden opportunity had finally arrived because Lieutenant Colonel "Maitland, whose men held the British right at the Springhill [*sic*]
redoubt, [had] immediately [put his best troops] in pursuit of the fleeing
French and Americans," threatening the existence of both the French and
the American armies.[3]

As mentioned, Maitland had prudently ordered three companies of
the crack 71st Regiment of Foot of elite Scottish fighting men to join

Major Glazer's counterattack, which also had been bolstered by Light Corps troops of the 16th Regiment of Foot. By this time, these confident British attackers had pushed well beyond the Spring Hill Redoubt, through the abatis, and into the open plain beyond in a hard-hitting counterattack: not a one-two, but a three-way punch that could not be resisted by either the badly defeated Americans or the French, after the bloody repulse that had cut down hundreds of men for no gain.[4]

As the strategic reserve that now served as the army's only and last principal guardians, in the supreme emergency situation that was the day's greatest crisis, the young men of the Chasseurs realized the importance of their role, as the largest organized, unbloodied unit left on the field for the allies at this crucial moment.

Indeed, this was the climactic moment of the largest and most important battle in the South to date during the course of the American Revolution. If the Chasseurs failed in their crucial mission, then all would be lost for the all-important Franco-American alliance. If the Chasseurs failed to turn the tide of this battle, then there would be no glorious allied success at Yorktown. Lord Cornwallis would never surrender his army in October 1781 to ensure the independence of the infant United States of America. The first revolution of a colonial people against a powerful mother country and king-led monarchy in Europe would fail, meaning no bright new day for people around the world.

If the day was not saved by the young men from Saint-Domingue at this key moment, then the enlightened idea of establishing the new system of government by and for the common people, a republic, would die an early and ugly death. A long life for the infant republic would affect hundreds of thousands of peasants and common people in the future across Europe, including in France—one based on the novel concepts of the worth of the average man and his God-given equality and personal merit. None of this would not be realized if the Black and mixed-race Chasseurs were not able to meet the greatest challenge of their lives on this gory battlefield in Georgia.

At the head of the surging ranks of the Chasseurs, meanwhile, young Louis-Marie, Vicomte de Noailles, the brother-in-law of the Marquis de Lafayette, who had basically become Washington's surrogate son by this time, continued to lead the steady advance of his strategic reserve troops. They had left from the high ground around the Levi Sheftall Hebrew Cemetery at a good pace because of their prior militia experience and the thoroughness of their training back in Saint-Domingue during the summer. The smooth movements of the lengthy formation of Chasseurs revealed that the men in the ranks were highly disciplined and motivated.

After the stunning sight of the American militiamen in their ragtag uniforms and the civilian clothing of the common people, which revealed that they were merely fighting farmers, the foremost British attackers were now shocked to see through the drifting clouds of whitish battle smoke some of the most finely uniformed troops in the French army now advancing straight toward them, with fixed bayonets and colorful banners waving in the breeze.

These Black and mixed-race soldiers were wearing navy blue uniforms made by some of the finest tailors in Cap-Français. The long-tailed uniform jacket was topped with high yellow trim, and their overall martial look was distinguished by white cross belts that presented an extremely smart appearance on the battlefield. These steadily advancing soldiers from Saint-Domingue also wore tricorn hats of blue, which matched their natty uniform coats. To the British, this disciplined formation of fresh soldiers in some of the finest uniforms seen in the allied army almost certainly made them think they were being attacked by French regulars, who the British had not expected to suddenly appear like magic out of nowhere, when decisive victory seemed well within their grasp. By this time, Major Glazier and his men almost certainly realized they were not facing Americans, because of their splendid uniforms, and especially since the Chasseurs continued to advance in a neat, tight formation with fixed bayonets, like French regulars, moving forward with discipline and determination.[5]

The young men of the Chasseurs-Volontaires de Saint-Domingue were fortunate to be led by the irrepressible Colonel Noailles, who was a hard-fighting nobleman. Despite his youth, at just twenty-three, he was a dashing officer and renowned ballroom dancer who enchanted the ladies of Paris. By any measure, the handsome and well-built young aristocrat was one of the most remarkable and talented leaders in d'Estaing's expeditionary force, determined to maintain the honor of the family name by reaping glory for France and the king during his most crucial mission.

Noailles was about to prove his worth to both allied armies, while fulfilling the military legacy of his noble family, whose fame and achievements extended back to the days of the Middle Ages, when crusades were launched from France and all the way to the Holy Land. Both on and off the battlefield, French troops, especially the Chasseurs, were devoted to the inspirational Noailles, who led the way in the spirited counterattack in a relentless advance that rolled forward across the open ground with a will of its own.[6]

Colonel Noailles was shocked at the extent of the rout of two altered armies, the terrible losses suffered in barely an hour's time. It was clearly a slaughter of some of the best and brightest of both nations during some of the worst carnage of the American Revolution. This was the most tragic and saddest day for the Franco-American alliance, bound together largely by fate and circumstances in an alliance of convenience. The young French nobleman with such a bright future continued to lead the Chasseurs onward during the most unexpected French advance of the day. He knew this most aggressive and drastic action was needed in order to save the vanquished French and American armies, which were on the brink of destruction, especially if they were additionally decimated by the oncoming counterattack that would hit extremely hard, like a knife cutting through butter.

After having advanced a good distance north over the open terrain, within sight of the Spring Hill Redoubt, Colonel Noailles now took center stage at the head of the Black and mixed-race soldiers. Knowing what had to be done, he ordered them to charge with the bayonet, sending the Chasseurs forward across the level ground on the double-quick and charging north through the drifting battle smoke that covered the ground like a thick shroud.

The finest troops of D'Estaing's strategic reserve was now fully unleashed on the most desperate offensive effort of the day, turning the tables by endangering the British counterattack that was caught in the open, well beyond the field of abatis before the Spring Hill Redoubt.

Having caught the British by surprise, this timely and aggressive tactic proved highly effective. Noailles's aggressiveness convinced the hard-hitting but prudent team of Major Glazier and Lieutenant Colonel Maitland to order their troops to halt their counterattack in its tracks and prepare to meet this new threat that had suddenly appeared out of nowhere, when least expected.

Still maintaining a neat formation, more than five hundred Black and mixed-race soldiers from Saint-Domingue charged with abandon and fixed bayonets just south of the Spring Hill Redoubt, in the face of the neat formations of the British, who thought the day had already been won. The unit's colors proudly waved overhead, reminding the Chasseurs that they were fighting for the honor of Saint-Domingue, and France. But the determined Colonel Noailles was not content with having unleashed his own counterattack; he was not taking any chances when so much was at stake. Knowing that aggressiveness and momentum was the key to any kind of offensive success, Noailles was going for broke as never before.

At some point during the third charge on the Spring Hill Redoubt, Major General François, Vicomte de Fontanges, who officially commanded all the troops, including the white Volunteer Grenadiers from Saint-Domingue, had been hit. He had been seriously wounded while leading the way, dropping with an iron canister ball in the thigh to receive a life-threatening injury. This situation had helped to set the stage for the highly capable Noailles to take center stage and exploit the tactical situation to the fullest.

Therefore, with the dramatic and daring flair for which he was noted, Colonel Noailles had now shouldered even more responsibility by leading his counterattack on his own, with sword in hand and with his typical aggressiveness. Noailles wanted to do much more than just simply force the halting of the British counterattack, which had stopped by this time, in preparation for meeting the Chasseurs on a level and open battlefield, just like on the famous fields of strife in Europe through the ages. In the words of a disbelieving French officer, the Vicomte de Noailles then made "a demonstration to penetrate within the entrenchments," all the way to the Spring Hill Redoubt and perhaps even more, if the opportunity was presented and exploited in full.[7]

At least one rolling volley was ordered by Colonel Noailles and then delivered by the Chasseurs-Volontaires de Saint-Domingue, after he briefly halted his charge and hurriedly formed the Black and mulatto soldiers into a lengthy line. The close-range volley shocked Major Glazier's and Lieutenant Colonel Maitland's counterattackers that had poured well beyond the Spring Hill Redoubt and the abatis and into the open plain that was now covered with fallen French and American soldiers by this time, before they had halted upon spying the formation of the advancing Chasseurs.

However, in the swirling dust and smoky chaos of the battlefield, it had taken more than the sight of Noailles's attacking force and the unleashing of a single volley for the Chasseurs to convince Lieutenant Colonel Maitland to order his troops to retire back to the safety of the Spring Hill Redoubt—especially when the hard-fighting Scotsman felt that he was about to reap a great victory by destroying the enemy, as no organized French or American force had been in sight before the sudden arrival of the Chasseurs.

Before Maitland and Glazier had ordered the retreat back to the Spring Hill Redoubt, with the Chasseurs now advancing more rapidly, as again ordered by Noailles, the Scotsman had ordered a volley fired in a last desperate attempt to stop the unexpected French counterattack. In response, Noailles then ordered the Black and mixed-race soldiers to return fire—a second volley—to ensure the elimination of the day's most serious threat, and to guarantee that Maitland retired back to the redoubt, where the Union Jack now fluttered from the parapet strewn with French and American bodies.

Colonel Noailles's tactical aggressiveness when least expected by the British proved decisive in a true turning point of the battle. The attacking Chasseurs were able to push Major Glazier and his men rearward before they were joined by the three 71st Regiment of Foot companies of the army's elite soldiers, dispatched by Maitland in the hope of achieving greater gains with his counterattack. It is very likely that the British counterattack could not have been stopped by the Chasseurs if this timely reinforcing of Glazier's counterattack with the best fighting men in the British army had been allowed to proceed, and had not been thwarted by the volleys and attack of more than five hundred Chasseurs. The timeliness of Noailles's aggressiveness in ordering the charge to continue so close to the Spring Hill Redoubt after the British began to fall back, to exploit the tactical advantage, could not have been more important in ensuring that the British counterattack failed to gain the strength that it would have needed to sweep all, including almost certainly the Chasseurs, before it.

Sensing greater success, Colonel Noailles fully exploited his tactical gains—and Maitland's and Glazier's withdrawal back to the Spring Hill Redoubt—by advancing farther north and ever closer to the strategic redoubt, in a French officer's words, "in case the enemy should leave them, and prepare to cut them off in that event." Noailles brilliantly succeeding in having prevented "the total destruction of our army" with his aggressiveness and tactical skill, while the Chasseurs rose to the challenge beyond all expectations.[8]

As they neared the strategic redoubt on the Ebenezer Road, the charging Chasseurs came under the fire of the defenders, including close-range artillery fire from a spray of canister. The Spring Hill Redoubt was once again lit up with a ring of fire after Maitland's men had slipped out of harm's way by gaining the redoubt's safety. This was the time when "many Haitians" fell wounded and others were killed in the attack.[9] As they neared the Spring Hill Redoubt and a concentrated fire erupted from the earthen bastion, Colonel Noailles's capable adjutant and top lieutenant, M. Calignon, fell mortally wounded by the nobleman's side, at the height of the spirited counterattack that saved the day.[10]

The battered French troops finally ceased running for their lives, from both the British counterattack and the artillery fire, upon ascertaining the significant gains achieved by the counterattacking Chasseurs-Volontaires de Saint-Domingue, and determining that Noailles's aggressiveness had achieved significant impressive tactical gains, and far more than anyone had expected possible. François d'Auber de Peyrelongue wrote in his journal about how the battered French army had rallied upon sight of the charging Black and mixed-race soldiers of the Chasseurs-Volontaires de Saint-Domingue: "Our troops began to reassemble in small platoons behind the reserves," rallying upon the sight of a job exceptionally well done by Noailles and his men.[11]

In his 1995 book entitled *The Price of Folly*, historian William Seymour briefly described how the British counterattack had gone "in pursuit of the fleeing French and Americans, but a stout rearguard action, fought mainly by the volunteer regiment of Haiti Chasseurs, kept the British at bay."[12]

Although wounded, Vice Admiral d'Estaing saw the last part of the action of the day after having been carried to the Levi Sheftall Jewish Cemetery, from where he had ordered the retreat of his vanquished forces. In his journal, Chief Engineer Antoine O'Connor, who had "distinguished himself greatly at the capture of Grenada," described the important role of the Chasseurs-Volontaires de Saint-Domingue, although his account was understated, as he had not seen the precise tactical situation or the extent of the impressive results of the Chasseurs' charge: "M. le general, wounded a second time by a ball through his leg and witness of the confusion which began again, ordered the retreat. M. le vicomte de Noailles covered it at the head of the reserve. Our troops suffered greatly in the retreat. M. le vicomte de Noailles formed the rear guard, and the enemy, who came out of their abatis, did not dare a sortie when they saw the determination and discipline of our rear guard, exposed to their cannon loaded with grapeshot."[13]

One thankful French officer said it best in regard to the timely counterattack of the Chasseurs, who had saved the day by abruptly thwarting the British charge that almost certainly would have "caused the destruction of our army."[14]

Philippe Girard, today's leading French historian of Haiti and an authority on Haitian and French sources, wrote of the stirring role of the Chasseurs: "Only during the final French assault on Savannah were they able to prove their mettle: the British counterattacked, and the Chasseurs successfully defended the French camp."[15]

This is actually an understatement by Girard, who is more of a social historian than a military one, to be fair to him, which has been a central weakness of the majority of modern historians on both sides of the

Atlantic to this day. Exact details of the dramatic story of the Chasseurs and their timely contribution to save the day have long been obscured, handicapping generations of historians when it comes to the specifics of the crucial role they played on October 9. In fact, the true story of the significant contributions of the Chasseurs has come from the French soldiers who were on the field and saw exactly what happened, rather than from what is recorded in most official reports; hence, the supreme importance of French soldiers' words from primary accounts, especially in the absence of accounts, letters, and diaries from the Chasseurs.

The Chasseurs-Volontaires de Saint-Domingue launched their own counterattack, which "prevented the annihilation" of the French and American armies, when it appeared that no hope remained and they were about to be destroyed, along with the Franco-American alliance.[16] In the words of one French officer who saw what happened and knew exactly where full credit belonged, the Chasseurs saved the day, accomplishing the impossible by mounting the timely charge that "prevented the total destruction of our army" by a sudden reversing of the tide of battle when it appeared that all was lost.[17]

Equally important and as noted, the sight of the counterattacking Chasseurs-Volontaires de Saint-Domingue rallied the shattered army when it had been on the verge of destruction. As continued in the most revealing narrative of this same officer of the French army: "The frag-ments of the army hastily form . . . behind the reserve corps, and [are] march[ed] to our camp [while Colonel] Noailles constitutes the rear guard and retires slowly and in perfect order," to the great credit of the Chasseurs.[18]

One historian emphasized how the "Noailles-led retreat avoided even more carnage in the French-American ranks," a conclusion that is right on target, but still another understatement that has obscured and devalued the overall role and performance of the Chasseurs, which has so often been the case.[19] In his journal, François d'Auber de Peyrelongue described the importance of the spirited and timely performance of the Chasseurs-Volontaires de Saint-Domingue under the excellent leader-ship of Noailles, who reversed the day's fortunes when they could not have appeared darker, unleashing his Chasseurs on the tactical offensive to achieve the most significant and meaningful French gains is the saving of the day: "The Vicomte de Noailles took sole charge of the retreat, which was well executed. The enemy, seeing his resolution, did not dare pursue us."[20]

Grenadier Captain Philippe Séguier de Terson, as penned in his journal, gave full credit where it was due—to the Chasseurs-Volontaires de Saint-Domingue and their aggressiveness when it was most needed by the reeling allied armies. He wrote an on-target analysis with no exaggeration whatsoever, about one of the most remarkable battlefield performances of not only the war in the South, but the entire American Revolution: "[T]he entire army plunged into the marsh during the retreat. The retreat order had to be given several times . . . the troops were badly beaten . . . [Therefore] we were fortunate in the whole business that our reserve corps preserved good discipline and so impressed the enemy that they did not dare pursue us," saving the mauled allied armies from destruction.[21]

This accurate and on-target analysis gives full credit where it is due and is no exaggeration, as has been claimed by generations of white historians who have long overlooked the Chasseurs and their invaluable contribution. To be fair, some Black historians, in general, and especially scholars from Haiti, learned the truth from firsthand oral accounts never heard by white scholars in the United States and in France. In one of the official reports about the Battle of Savannah, now located in historical archives in Paris, France, these descriptive words of the white French soldiers ring true, revealing what can no longer be denied by historians as they have been denied in the past: "This legion [the Chasseurs-Volontaires de Saint-Domingue] saved the army at Savannah by gravely covering its retreat."[22]

Perhaps because he had not ordered Colonel Noailles's hard-hitting counterattack that would save the day, Vice Admiral d'Estaing, known for petty jealousy, was not complimentary about one of the most heroic French actions of the day. This was a striking paradox and a miscarriage of justice, partly because d'Estaing was talking about troops who were not white—always the most convenient scapegoat for any failure of white French troops. The vice admiral's post-battle behavior was all about laying blame for the debacle. Even more bizarre, d'Estaing actually had the nerve to shamelessly condemn the tactical astuteness and aggressiveness of young Colonel Noailles, who had employed his own initiative and aggressiveness in masterful fashion to save the defeated allied armies: "Our corps of reserves by being a little less impetuous would have better received those who were retiring than by going out to look for them . . . His excess of vigor and courage (respectable fault) have increased the loss" among the Chasseurs.[23]

THE ENDURING MYSTERY OF CHASSEUR LOSSES

Unfortunately, because of incomplete documentation—due to the fact that reports about the Black and mixed-race command were sent back to the governor of Saint-Domingue, and not to Paris, where they would have been preserved, as well as the lack of letters, diaries, and memoirs from the Chasseurs—the exact losses of the Chasseurs-Volontaires de Saint-Domingue are not known to this day, and almost certainly will never be known with any degree of certitude.

What we do know from the very little existing information is the fact that casualties were widespread among the Chasseurs, and higher than generally thought by generations of historians. For one, Noailles's capable adjutant, Calignon, fell mortally wounded, representing the highest-ranking officer to go down during the counterattack on the Spring Hill Redoubt. Like others in the front rank of the Chasseurs, drummer Henri Christophe was hit, suffering "a dangerous gunshot wound" during the counterattack. This was just a fraction of the cost of advancing across a lengthy distance of open, level ground and then charging north, so close to the Spring Hill Redoubt, falling under the fire of both cannon, loaded with canister, and musket-fire, to add to the loss total of one of the three bloodiest battles of the American Revolution.[24]

Gifted historian Tom Shachtman, who is fluent in French, wrote the fine 2017 work, *How the French Saved America*. He tells how former commander of the Chasseurs, Major General François, Vicomte de "Fontanges was also grievously wounded [earlier in the fight], along with many Haitians."[25] But Shachtman fails to mention that the Viscount de Fontanges—who was acting as d'Estaing's chief of staff, and most likely was hit around the time that the vice admiral was wounded—was cut down before the Chasseurs launched their counterattack, and was not part of the final offensive effort that saved the day.[26]

For a variety of reasons, Vice Admiral d'Estaing never revealed the losses suffered by the Chasseurs-Volontaires de Saint-Domingue during the siege, and on October 9. He did indicate that they suffered far higher losses than has been commonly believed by historians: "An excess of valor and courage [by Noailles and the Chasseurs] was a mistake and increased our losses."[27]

The only surviving official French report known to exist today has maintained that only one Chasseur was killed and another seven wounded on October 9, but these figures are far too low, and reveal the French government's attempt to minimize losses, or even to downplay the role of Black and mixed-race soldiers in saving the day for white troops, including the elite fighting men of France. The French government certainly did not want these disturbing facts to become common knowledge in its Caribbean empire based on slavery, and founded on the premise of Black inferiority on every level, especially in regard to character and courage.[28]

Indeed, these low official losses for the Chasseurs-Volontaires de Saint-Domingue in this single French report represent an inconceivable total. This impossibly low figure of only eight men killed and wounded is much too low given the unit's role in launching the counterattack against the British army's best troops, nearly all the way to the Spring Hill Redoubt, and especially considering the fact that it was the Chasseurs who "prevented the total destruction of our army" in what was a daring offensive role that turned the tide.[29]

One modern white historian emphasized how a large number of men of the Chasseurs-Volontaires de Saint-Domingue became casualties during the assault, and his words align with the key role they played in the overall tactical situation and in their attack that saved the day on October 9. In general, Haitian historians have more willingly embraced the higher figures of sacrifice of the Chasseurs-Volontaires de Saint-Domingue at Savannah than white historians, because of their closeness to a greater amount of source material—a classic case of racial politics in regard to minimizing the losses suffered by this unsung Black and mulatto command, also mirrored in different views about the Chasseurs saving the day, largely because of racial, social, and political reasons.[30]

The distinct possibility exists that the French and Saint-Domingue governments deliberately lowered the number of Chasseur losses for fear that the example of Black and mulatto valor in a major battle on American soil in which they demonstrated equality with white soldiers might have a negative impact on not only the Franco-American alliance but also on a Caribbean colony whose economy, safety, and future rested solidly upon slavery and the concept of white supremacy, in general, especially its racially rigid social strictures.

Unprecedented Autumn Disaster in Georgia

As could be expected, the astonishing news of the remarkable and totally unexpected British success at Savannah sent London into wild celebration. London's cannon at the Tower and Park were fired in honor of the one-sided victory in faraway Georgia, which brought new hopes for a successful bid to end the brash life of the young, upstart United States of America and the collapse of the Franco-American alliance, which was now key to the infant republic's survival.[31]

In the end, the day's only allied success and shining bright spot on an exceptionally dark day was the splendid performance of the Chasseurs-Volontaires de Saint-Domingue, when they rose to the ultimate challenge in saving the day for thousands of routed Americans and Frenchmen.[32]

Like other South Carolina militia officers and their men, an embittered Major Thomas Pinckney of South Carolina described the extent of the tragedy and then fingered who was to blame for the unprecedented disaster: "Thus was this fine body of troops [Americans and Frenchmen] sacrificed by the imprudence of the French general, who, being of superior grade, commanded the whole. If the French troops had left their encampment in time for the different corps to have reached their positions, and the whole attacked together, the prospect of success would have been infinitely better, though even then it would have been very doubtful on account of the strength of the enemy's line, which was well supplied with artillery. But if Count d'Estaing had reflected a moment, he must have known that attacking with a single column before the rest of the army could have reached their position, was exposing the army to be beaten in detail. In fact the enemy, who were to be assailed at once on a considerable part of their front, finding themselves only attacked at one point [the Spring Hill Redoubt], very deliberately concentrated their whole fire on the assaulting column, and that was repeated as fast as the different corps were brought up to the attack."[33]

To his credit, and to justify the faith that General Washington and Congress had in him, Major General Benjamin Lincoln did not want to give up the struggle for possession of Savannah, like d'Estaing. He wanted to renew the assaults on Savannah upon the correct premise that the enemy had been severely weakened and ammunition was low. It is not known, but the major general from Massachusetts might well have been encouraged in his thinking by the excellent battlefield performance of the Chasseurs-Volontaires de Saint-Domingue, which had confirmed that the fighting spirit of the French was certainly alive and well, as well as the fact that the French troops had rallied upon viewing the Chassuers's amazing success.

However, Vice Admiral d'Estaing had had enough of Savannah, the dreary siege, the high loss of life, and Americans in general. He wanted to end it all by just sailing away and heading for the French West Indies, like he had done at Newport. Therefore, Lincoln's appeals to continue offensive efforts to capture Savannah were immediately rejected by the battle-weary vice admiral, without any serious consideration whatsoever.[34]

In hindsight, this sudden ending of the siege of Savannah was still another mistake committed by d'Estaing, who had suddenly given up, like at Newport. A good opportunity had still existed for victory at Savannah, which vindicated Major General Lincoln. Loyalist Elizabeth Lichtenstein—who was connected with top leadership inside the city, and as such, in the know—revealed the ultimate tragedy and irony of the bloody showdown at Savannah, in which so many Frenchmen and Americans had died in vain: "Had the enemy not apprehended danger to the fleet by remaining, in all probability they would have renewed their attack, and it was not thought possible we could have had strength to defeat them again."[35]

The brilliant Scottish lieutenant colonel, John Maitland, had saved the day twice: first, by reaching Savannah from Beaufort in a timely manner, after a lengthy trek that was not thought possible; and second, by playing a key role in the defense of the Spring Hill Redoubt, and then counterattacking with Major Beamsley Glazier and his elite troops of the 60th Regiment of Foot, known as the "old Royal American Regiment," elements of the 16th Regiment of Foot, and seasoned Royal Marines, who were reinforced by several companies of the elite 71st Regiment of Foot. In a letter that paid an appropriate tribute, Lieutenant Colonel von Porbeck, who led the Hessians of the von Wissenbach Regiment of disciplined German troops, wrote: "Lieutenant Colonel Maitland of the 71st Scots Regiment won from the affair of this day [October 9] great honor and much thanks from his Britannic Majesty."[36]

By any measure, Lieutenant Colonel Maitland was truly a remarkable Celtic officer, as he had demonstrated in full throughout the course of the Savannah Campaign, especially in crisis situations. Although he was from Scotland's upper-class elite and an Old World aristocrat, a member of the House of Commons, and possessed a hefty family fortune, Maitland served with such outstanding distinction because of his uncommon abilities and skills. He considered it his duty to serve until the final victory was won in America, refusing to retire from the army even after the loss of his right hand in battle and bouts with serious illness.[37]

In a letter, Captain Kennedy praised the other two primary British heroes for saving British Savannah in its darkest hour: "Great Honor is due to General Prévost for his steady, cool, and moderate Manner, in which he gave his Orders during the Siege, particularly on the Day of Attack. Our Chief Engineer, Capt. Moncrieffe [*sic*], has immortalized himself by his indefatiguable Perseverance in erecting and strengthening the Batteries, Redoubts, &c."[38]

Loyalist Elizabeth Lichtenstein, who had been trapped inside Savannah like hundreds of other citizens, laid more credit to God for the unexpected victory than Maitland, writing how the besieged soldiers of the seemingly doomed garrison were "not daring to anticipate a victory with such fearful odds . . . The Almighty and Gracious God did, however, assist us, and we conquered, though no men could have behaved more gallantly than the French."[39]

Georgia's royal governor, James Wright, felt much the same, believing that a Divine Providence had intercepted in a timely manner on behalf of the British. He issued a stirring proclamation to officially observe the saving of Savannah and Georgia "as a Day of public Thanksgiving to Almighty God, for his very signal Mercies vouchsafed us during the Siege of this Town, by the united Forces of the French and Rebels."[40]

Praise to God was almost without end from the thankful British, Hessians, and Loyalists. Anthony Stokes, who was the chief justice of Georgia, penned in a letter to his wife: "Many who did not think so much of religion before now acknowledge that our deliverance was miraculous, and arose from the immediate interposition of God in our favor. Had the French marched up to town immediately, or had they prevented Colonel Maitland joining us with the troops under his command, I will leave you to judge what the consequences must have been."[41]

British victory had come at a high cost on their side—not in lives, but in massive destruction to the picturesque city on the river. Elizabeth Lichtenstein described Savannah's devastation from the days of the siege: "[T]he town [now] offered a desolate view. The streets were cut with deep holes by the shells, and the houses were riddled with the rain of cannon balls . . . and many houses were not habitable."[42]

In a letter to his wife, Major T. W. Moore, who served on Major General Prévost's staff, described his own personal losses that were considerable: "Poor Pollard, my assistant, was killed on the 4th of October by an 18-Pounder, my fine valuable Negro Carpenter the 7th, and a beautiful Mare that cost me 20 Guineas; my Store of Wine, all broke by Shot and Shells, and my Quarters torn to Pieces; but this is Neighbor's Fate, and the whole Town is in the same State."[43]

In the end, it was Vice Admiral d'Estaing who reaped the lion's share of blame for the Savannah disaster, and deservedly so. In his official report—as could be expected, given his personality and ego, and knowing that it would be read by King Louis XVI—he blamed everyone for the defeat except himself. In the greatest paradox of the Battle of Savannah, and to his ever-lasting shame, d'Estaing even blamed the soldiers of the Chasseurs-Volontaires who had saved his army, and the day, by fostering the outrageous lie that he had lacked an adequate number of French regulars, which had forced him to rely on "seven hundred mulattoes and two hundred men lifted from the ranks of vagabonds at Saint-Domingue."[44] Clearly, the vice admiral was disguising the fact that it had been Black and mixed-race soldiers who had saved his army; he could not admit that it had been on the verge of destruction until the unleashing of the successful counterattack of the Chasseurs-Volontaires de Saint-Domingue.[45]

Clearly, both on the field and off, what happened at Savannah and shortly thereafter was not Vice Admiral d'Estaing's finest hour, unlike the case of the Black and mulatto Chasseurs, who had proved to be the army's saviors when its life had been at stake, like that of the Franco-American alliance in general.[46]

Vice Admiral Estaing was only worried about departing ill-fated Georgia and America as soon as possible, leaving behind the humiliation, tragedy, and disgrace, like some bad dream that had proved to be a living nightmare. The end of the Savannah Campaign for the Chasseurs-Volontaires de Saint-Domingue ended when they and their comrades boarded the French warships with other troops and departed America's shores forever.

Like the V-shaped formations of Canada geese flying south with the gradual encroachment of winter in the lower Savannah River country, so Vice Admiral d'Estaing was determined to head south to a much warmer climate, by returning to the comfort and safety of the West Indies. Captain Kennedy wrote a letter revealing that the British knew all about their darker-skin opponent, who had saved the day: "Sunday, the 17th, we were informed that the French Mulatto and Black Brigade had marched to Col. [John] Mulryne's [Plantation and wharf] to embark."[47]

Indeed, the British fully realized that the French invasion force contained "some Hundreds of free Blacks and Mulattoes, taken on board in the West Indies."[48] Survivors of d'Estaing's seemingly endless folly were the fortunate ones, having escaped the greatest and most monumental disaster in the history of the Franco-American alliance, which had seen its darkest day on October 9—the low point in the history of the crucial alliance so vital to America's existence.

Not as fortunate as d'Estaing's departing troops, including the Chasseurs, were a good many young French and American soldiers who now lay in shallow graves in the wind-blown sands of Savannah. They had become victims of the bloodiest day of the war in the South for a single side. Major John Jones, the faithful aide-de-camp to Scotland-born General Lachlan McIntosh, had been buried so shabbily and in such haste that a friend recognized Jones's hand sticking up from his final resting place in the shifting sands, blown by the cold autumn winds howling off the Atlantic.

In Jones's last letter home to his beloved wife Polly, on October 5, the deeply religious and thoughtful major had placed his abiding faith in God and the righteousness of the struggle for liberty, while battling beside the American army's Catholic allies against a Protestant enemy. Major Jones wrote just before meeting his Maker at Savannah: "We have the prayers of the [Protestant] Church & I hope from the justness of ours that God will decide in our favor." But her husband's solemn commitment to God and country came at a frightfully high cost for him and so many of his comrades, who had been lost forever in the doomed assaults on the Spring Hill Redoubt. The determined major had ignored Polly's sage warning in one of her letters to him: "Consider you have two dear children and a wife whose whole happiness depends on yours. May heaven guard you, and give me once more a happy sight of you"—a much-desired sight that would never become a reality for this average American family of the South.[49]

Teenager Paul Hamilton was sickened by the terrible "slaughter of my countrymen," like Major John Jones and so many others who had died in vain, including the tragic "loss of some of my particular friends and school fellows" who were no more.[50] For no gain, hundreds of young men from both sides of the Atlantic had died far from glory and laurels at an obscure place—in the words of Anthony Stokes, Savannah "rendered famous a sickly hole, which was in the [pine] woods, and had only one white man in it at the time General [James] Oglethorpe landed" there, on an obscure pine-covered bluff overlooking a sluggish river of a brownish hue, which had endlessly flowed into the Atlantic since time immemorial.[51]

Partly because of his tireless exertions in one of the most tenacious defensive stands of the American Revolution, Lieutenant Colonel Maitland, the hero of the successful defense of Savannah, died of disease on October 26, 1779, after having made his most important contributions to British victory in this war—especially in regard to saving Savannah—as if his usefulness had come to an end.[52]

Ironically, as cruel fate would have it, Maitland's name and "fame was soon forgot. His has been the fate of most British heroes of the American Revolution—unrecognized in this country, forgotten at home. No marble tomb commemorates his memory, not even a tablet. No stone marks his burial place . . . There is no record of Colonel Maitland's burial . . . [S]omewhere in a nameless grave this great but forgotten soldier of the Empire sleeps the long and dreamless sleep" forever.[53]

HARD-EARNED LESSONS

In the end, the primary lessons stemming from the Savannah disaster were very much like the ones that had already been learned by Vice Admiral d'Estaing at Newport, Rhode Island: To be successful, the French fleet needed an unhampered and lengthy stay in American waters, especially without being threatened by the British navy, allowing the allies to work smoothly together to win on land. It was this combined land and sea superiority that would guarantee decisive victory for the Franco-American alliance in this war. After all, it was this winning formula—the close coordination of allies working together—that led to the dramatic victory at Yorktown during the autumn of 1781.[54]

Far too late, French officers realized that it would have been wiser to have ordered Major General Lincoln and the Americans to attack Maitland at Beaufort instead of focusing on Savannah; d'Estaing could then have easily forced Prévost to surrender Savannah, which could not have been successfully defended without the arrival of Maitland and his sizable body of reinforcements who arrived in the nick of time.[55] As revealed in the pages of the *Maryland Gazette* to readers across America: If only Major General Benjamin Lincoln "had been properly supported with men, [then] he would long ago have taken Prévost and all his plundering adventurers."[56]

Knowing that the entire Southern Strategy was at stake during the crucial showdown at Savannah, the royal governor of Georgia, James Wright, perhaps said it best about the importance of the Savannah Campaign, which has long been ignored by generations of historians, along with the overall importance of the war in the South, where the conflict was ultimately won in the end: "I clearly saw that if this Province then fell, America was lost, and [it was General Prévost and his feisty garrison who] have preserved the Empire."[57] The Chief Justice of New York was also right on target when he correctly emphasized the supreme importance of the British victory at Savannah: "In my opinion [this remarkable success] preserved the Empire."[58]

But what happened during the high-stakes showdown at Savannah was destined to have a much further reach in the overall story of the expansion of human liberty and progress. It would prove to be significant in another people's revolution barely a decade later, in Saint-Domingue, which became the Republic of Haiti on January 1, 1804. The young Black and mixed-race soldiers of Saint-Domingue who fought at Savannah left behind a distinguished record and enduring legacy in America, which fortunately was never forgotten by these same men, who then served as inspirational and experienced leaders during the Haitian Revolution—the key connection between two people's republics and their respective revolutions, and a most distinguished legacy that has been largely forgotten today.

In the on-target words of historian Philippe Girard: "Although it was a military failure, the Savannah expedition served an important long-term political purpose. Free people of color, who already served in the rural police (*maréchaussée*) and the militia (*milice*) in Saint-Domingue, learned in Savannah that they could be a fighting force equal to any white army, [and this] lesson was not lost on the various Savannah veterans who later participated in the Haitian Revolution."[59]

Indeed, a good "many of the Chasseurs were destined to become famous in the Haitian Revolution," leading the way toward decisive victory for tens of thousands of Black and mulatto people of Saint-Domingue (Haiti). They would then boldly proclaim a new people's republic, when tens of thousands of Napoleon's ruthless invaders were finally driven away forever—the epitome of the true meaning of egalitarianism, universal emancipation, and liberty for the common people of a darker hue, and far more than in the case of the American Revolution: one of the most forgotten realities, hidden facts, and dirty little secrets about America's excessively glorified and romanticized struggle for liberty, long shrouded in seemingly endless layers of myth and legends.[60]

Epilogue

In their fine work entitled *The World of the Haitian Revolution*, David Patrick Geggus and Norman Fiering summarized how the impressive battlefield performance of the Chasseurs-Volontaires de Saint-Domingue on October 9, 1779, had long-term implications in the expansion of liberty and human progress in the Western world: "During the War of American Independence, two free colored battalions had seen service overseas which provided military experience to several future revolutionary leaders. The experience encouraged some of the wealthiest men of color to lobby the colonial ministry [before the Haitian Revolution] about reforming the regime of racial discrimination."[1]

For the young mixed-race and Black men of the Chasseurs-Volontaires de Saint-Domingue, even in the midst of the greatest defeat for allied armies and the Franco-American alliance of the American Revolution, glory had been won at Savannah, where they demonstrated their worth as men and how they were truly deserving of equality as citizens of Saint-Domingue and France. In fact, in a striking paradox, they actually had been too successful on the bloody battlefield of Savannah for their own good. After what they had achieved at Savannah, these veterans were viewed by the white elites of Saint-Domingue as a potential threat to their own power and the overall racial stability of their colony.

In consequence, the Chasseurs were dispatched on various obscure assignments and remote locations after the Savannah Campaign. Unfortunately, they were denied the social and economic benefits that would have increased their status and that of their family members in society, like the ones received by other free Black and mulatto militiamen of Saint-Domingue in the past, especially the notable case of Captain

Vincent Olivier, who had won laurels and pensions for heroism against enemies on behalf of both Saint-Domingue and France since the 1690s.

If the soldiers of the Chasseurs-Volontaires "were hoping French officials or white colonists would take them seriously as civic-minded patriots [after Savannah], their expedition was a disaster. Upon their return [to Saint-Domingue] in 1780, officials in Cap-Français tried to conscript them into a permanent unit [to be dispatched overseas if necessary, and far from Saint-Domingue], nearly producing a revolt."[2]

Today, despite its location in a major American city, the battlefield of Savannah is a largely forgotten one, with most of the ground where so many men fought and died covered with the sprawl of modern development, businesses, and city blocks of houses. Very little remains of the original natural setting, including the long line of defenses and series of powerful redoubts, which were either leveled by citizens or worn down by time and erosion. Congress and the National Park Service, which has long maintained well-preserved and beautiful historic sites all across the South, and even at nearby Fort Pulaski, located just outside Savannah, has failed to designate the Savannah site as a battlefield park worth purchasing and preserving.

Today's visitor will see little of the heart of the Savannah battlefield; they will see no stately monuments or statues dedicated to the French, Americans, British, Loyalists, or Hessians. They will see the modern reconstruction of the Spring Hill Redoubt, which is much smaller than the original, in today's Tricentennial Park, a recent creation by the Coastal Heritage Society that purchased the land from the Norfolk Southern Railroad. It almost seems as if thousands of men never fought at this little-known place atop a sand bluff in Chatham County, Georgia, during an extremely important showdown of the American Revolution that was absolutely critical for a host of strategic reasons. In fact, except for the recently reconstructed Spring Hill Redoubt—only about one-third the size of the original—within the sprawl of the City of Savannah, it very much appears today that no battle was ever fought for possession of the strategic port during America's life-or-death struggle so long ago.

THE FORGOTTEN DEAD IN HALLOWED GROUND

Not long after the angry guns of Savannah had ceased to roar, claiming the lives of young victims from both sides of the Atlantic and the Caribbean, the survivors of the slaughter focused on what had to be done in the time-honored tradition of Christian soldiers. They turned to the grim task of burying the hundreds of dead who had been cut down in a living nightmare that saw the second-highest rate of losses by the patriots in any battle of the American Revolution, and the bloodiest day in the history of the Franco-American alliance. One British soldier wrote in a letter: "Soon after a [white] Flag came from d'Estaing for Liberty to bury their Dead, and requested their Wounded. 'Twas granted. Another [white] Flag came from General Lincoln, who commanded the Rebels, for the same Purpose, which was also granted; and that whole day [October 10] was taken up in this Service."[3]

In fact, it took two days to bury so many dead allied soldiers, whose bodies seemed to be everywhere. They were situated in remote places, like the dark waters and snarled thickets of the fatal swamp that lay just west of the Spring Hill Redoubt, which had so hampered the attack to help sabotage Vice Admiral d'Estaing's best-laid offensive plans. In the joyous words of a British officer, who worked at the main hospital in Savannah, attempting to save the multitude of wounded men who had been cut down in a terrible day of slaughter: "I never began, my dear Tom, to write a Letter in better Humor . . . The French lost 67 Officers killed, and 594 Privates, killed and wounded. The Rebels lost 633 [and] we were two Days employed in burying their Dead . . . believe me, Tom, I never was happier in my Life than upon this Occasion."[4]

In his journal on October 11, also bestowing an extremely rare compliment to patriot valor, one defender of Savannah penned with equal joy how "their Loss in the Attack is much more than we imagined. The Rebels miss 1,300 and the French Loss uncertain, but greater than the Rebels, as they fought like Soldiers."[5]

Major General Prévost wrote to Lord Germain, the primary orchestrator of the Southern Strategy that had been calculated to win it all for Great Britain in this war, describing the grim body count in and around the Spring Hill Redoubt: "[A] truce was desired by the enemy and leave to bury the dead and carry off the wounded . . . Those within or near the abatis [before the Spring Hill Redoubt] are buried, number 203 on the right [the northwestern side of the redoubt], on the left 28 [on the southwestern side of the redoubt], and delivering 116 wounded prisoners, greatest part mortally. A good many were buried by the enemy, many more self-buried in the mud of the swamp, and no doubt many were carried off."[6]

As a tragic fate would have it, more French and American fighting men were killed at Savannah than during the siege of Yorktown, that would force Lord Charles Cornwallis to surrender his entire British-Hessian-Loyalist army on October 19, 1781, changing the war's course and ensuring the winning of American independence: the zenith of the Franco-American alliance, which had matured since the dark days of its seemingly endless fumbling and costly mistakes at Savannah.[7]

Wearing a scarlet uniform, Captain Kennedy described the grim harvest that had been reaped by the fury of the guns of the British, Hessians, Black defenders, and Loyalists on October 9: "After the retreat of the Enemy from our Right, 270 Men, chiefly French, were found Dead; upwards of 80 of whom lay in the Ditch and on the Parapet of the [Spring Hill] Redoubt, first attacked, and 93 were within our Abattis [sic]. Since the Attack, we have learnt from French Officers, Deserters and others, that they lost in killed and wounded 700 Men, some say 1,000, and others 1,800, reckoning 3 Officers, in the List of Slain."[8]

No official local, state, or national cemetery for the hundreds of dead Americans (a total loss of 312 casualties) and Frenchmen (a total loss of 821 casualties) has ever been dedicated or even preserved, because the final resting places of these young men and boys are not known to this day. In a compliment to the highly capable team of Prévost and Maitland, the defenders had suffered the loss of barely 100 men in the determined defense of the city on the river. To this day, the precise number of those killed is known only to God. In "one of the bloodiest [battles] of the American Revolution . . . Only Bunker Hill exceeded it in casualties sustained by a single side" during the eight years of war, the grim harvest of young French and American soldiers was reaped in gory fashion in barely an hour's time.[9]

Evidently, no modern seismic ground study or investigative survey of the ground has been conducted around the Spring Hill Redoubt in an attempt to ascertain the location of any abnormalities or disruptions of the soil that would indicate the location of a burial pit or trenches.

However, two fine modern historians of Savannah, Preston Russell and Barbara Hines, in their excellent book *Savannah: A History of Her People Since 1733*, have recently speculated that the French and American dead were buried to the right, or east, of the reconstructed Spring Hill Redoubt, where Savannah History Museum and Visitor Center on Martin Luther King Boulevard is now located. This theory has been based on the fact that some human remains were discovered during the construction of the large museum complex.

Since the original redoubt was larger than the modern reconstructed one (which is only about one-third of its original size), then it is more likely that the burial place of so many Frenchmen and Americans would be located just to the northwest of the Savannah History Museum, and just south of where the northernmost point of the Spring Hill Redoubt was located at the time (farther south than the northernmost point of today's reconstructed redoubt of a much smaller size).

Years ago, one worker of the Central of Georgia Railway described how when the railroad depot was enlarged, some "thirty skeletons" were discovered in a location around three feet underground, near the foot of Liberty Street, which runs east–west and parallel to the Savannah River, which flows just to the north and eventually into the sea. Here, along with relics such as brass military buttons from the battle, the workers found "[skeletons] buried in a Row with what was decided to be the Hessian [of the von Trumbach Regiment] uniform."[10]

The distinct possibility exists that these discovered bodies were not the dark-uniformed Hessians, as long assumed, including by historians. What everyone has overlooked or forgotten is the possibility that some of these bodies were men of the Chasseurs-Volontaires de Saint-Domingue. After all, the Black and mulatto soldiers wore navy blue uniform coats, a distinctive style all their own, and different from any other unit at Savannah. These could have been easily mistaken for Hessian uniforms by non-experts, because they wore their traditional Prussian navy blue uniforms.[11]

In one of the many mysteries about the Battle of Savannah, the final resting place of hundreds of American and French soldiers has remained unknown to this day, although some feel it is located somewhere southwest of the center of Savannah, near the reconstructed Spring Hill Redoubt, at some point on the level ground just to the south. Indeed, all evidence has indicated that the burial ground is located under or near the Georgia State Railroad Museum, in today's Tricentennial Park.

Here, just south of the original Spring Hill Redoubt, on the level ground of the old Georgia railroad and its depot—which is now a National Historic Landmark operated by the Coastal Heritage Society—the skeletons of hundreds of both Frenchmen and Americans have remained undisturbed to this day. What little is left of the bodies—of course, only bones at this point—of young men from both sides of the Atlantic and the Caribbean rest in peace in the sandy soil atop the long river bluff that overlooks the wide Savannah River not long before it flows into the sea.[12]

No memorial from the people of two ungrateful nations has ever been erected to the dead of Savannah, in one of the sad paradoxes of the American Revolution, especially in regard to one of the most important battles of America's struggle for liberty. No statue or even a marker has been established on this forgotten field of strife, to honor the dead from either America or France during the long struggle for the existence of the infant United States of America.

Because of the general obscurity of the Battle of Savannah, which has faded from popular memory for generations of Americans, the people of France have lost a heroic chapter of their own nation's history, like the people of today's Republic of Haiti. Few people in France today have heard anything about the Battle of Savannah and what happened to hundreds of the best fighting men at this faraway place atop a bluff that overlooks the dark waters of the Savannah River.

Ironically, more than a century after the Battle of Savannah raged in all its savage fury, the people of France kindly donated the funds for the creation and installation of the famous copper-covered Statue of

Liberty, distinguished in its distinctive and symbolic neoclassical style, on Liberty Island in New York Harbor, instead of making any contribution whatsoever toward recognizing the Savannah battlefield site in honor of the large number of French soldiers who died there on October 9, 1779. But in the end, perhaps this was appropriate, because the true and most lasting memorial to the French who fought for America at Savannah is actually the long and prosperous life of America itself, which would have died an early death without the invaluable French aid stemming from the Franco-American alliance of 1778, an alliance that evolved and strengthened from the painful and bloody lessons learned at Savannah to ensure victory in the end.

Of course, this would have been of very small consolation to the many grieving families across France who lost their loved ones at an obscure place in faraway America called Savannah, Georgia. The people of France never knew the full details of exactly what happened at Savannah on October 9, 1779, and how thoroughly France and a revered vice admiral had seriously blundered, ensuring the deaths of so many young men who would never again see their homes or their families.

The dark tragedy of October 9 was the ultimate irony, because an amazing amount of French courage and Saint-Dominguan valor was fully demonstrated on the field at Savannah, more than at any other place during the American Revolution, including the final showdown at Yorktown, where the French lost far fewer troops than they had at Savannah. Although not realized at the time, the impressive example of French valor on October 9 would have provided a great measure of pride and consolation to those family members across France who were grieving the deep personal loss of so many courageous fathers, sons, and brothers. It is a great shame that the people and governments of both the United States and France have basically forgotten the bravery of their sons at Savannah.

This inexcusable negligence in regard to the lack of an appropriate and dignified honoring of the American dead at Savannah has been a most ironic development, as the nation's military dead have long received tributes on battlefields of the past, including in foreign lands far away. As early as 1851, for instance, the US Congress officially established the US

National Cemetery, now known as the Mexico City National Cemetery, located in the capital of the Republic of Mexico. Three years after the end of the Mexican-American War in 1848, the bodies of hundreds of dead Americans who had fallen in the final 1847 drive of General William Scott's army on Mexico City were collected and placed in the one-acre national cemetery, located today in the heart of Mexico City.

A stone memorial has long honored this hallowed ground in the midst of the Mexican capital atop the mass grave of 750 unidentified American soldiers, who died on foreign soil far from home in 1847. Located nearly six hundred miles south of the lengthy international border between Mexico and the United States, this sacred ground in Mexico City has marked the heroics of these young American soldiers forevermore in an impressive tribute not afforded to the Americans from across the South who gave their lives at Savannah in 1779.

Likewise, the battlefield of Savannah is not recognized today, the place where American and French valor reached a high point seldom seen in any battle of the American Revolution, during their suicidal assault on a powerful network of well-engineered fortifications. Although the average visitor to Savannah would not be able to realize as much, given the almost total obscurity of the battlefield of Savannah today, it is nonetheless hallowed ground to three people's republics born of violent revolutions, the United States, France, and Haiti, whose contributions to the Western world and Western civilization have been all-important. In some unknown location yet to be ascertained or memorialized by anyone, for nearly 250 years, "hundreds of French and Americans lie together in mass graves lost to history."[13]

Of course, among the heroic men who sacrificed their lives and lie today in the ground at Savannah were Black and mixed-race fighting men of the Chasseurs-Volontaires de Saint-Domingue. An unknown number of free mulatto and Black families of the Caribbean colony lost their sons, brothers, and fathers at Savannah. When the Chasseurs were formed during the spring and summer of 1779, a mulatto father had brought his two young sons and presented them to the unit's colonel with pride and a sense of self-sacrifice. Despite needing as many men in the ranks as possible, the colonel, a mature white man of means, was moved by the patriotic gesture and supreme self-sacrifice. Consequently, he emphasized to the mixed-race father that he should keep one of his sons at home for fear that both young men might never return from the upcoming expedition to this distant land yet unknown to either man at this time. In response, the father had spoken with emotion: " 'Eh Monsieur,' [he] tearfully replied, 'what better can a mulatto do with his life than get himself killed'" for his country.[14]

The Forgotten Enduring Racial Legacy

The most forgotten but enduring lesson and legacy of the Battle of Savannah is a racial one that is still relevant to this day. While the men who fought at Savannah have been forgotten and the battle has become little more than a footnote in most Revolutionary War history books, the enduring racial legacy and lesson of the importance of the united interracial bond that existed between Black and white as brothers in liberty, battling for America, lives on. It was this special bond and comradeship that helped to make America: a representative example of a shared history between Blacks and whites, and how it took two distinctive people of two different races to make the America that we know today, a fundamental truth in the creation of America over the course of centuries. It is this forgotten but important story from the American Revolution—a success achieved by both Black and white patriots, united together as brothers in arms, with common goals—that needs to be remembered and celebrated today, even at this late date in the Age of the Internet.

The bloody showdown at Savannah on October 9, 1779, was much more than just another battle of the American Revolution in the traditional sense. Its broader racial dimensions and the enduring racial lessons—of how Black and white unity has long played a key role in the making of America—remain important and meaningful to this day, for the overall betterment of America's future and for the understanding of today's Americans, Black and white, about their shared history.

First and foremost, the men of the Chasseurs-Volontaires de Saint-Domingue represented the largest number of Black and mixed-race soldiers who ever fought together as one for the independence of America, on any battlefield, during the eight years of the American

Revolution. Black and white fighting men served together in the name of liberty and a righteous cause that they considered sacred and holy, while risking and giving their lives, in many cases, for the fulfillment of the great egalitarian dream of America and its lofty promise of equality and freedom for all men.

Without realizing it at the time, the mulattoes and Blacks from Saint-Domingue were also battling for another essential part of the American Dream, which remains unrealized and even less appreciated today in the racially divided and polarized America of the twenty-first century: a racially blind nation of one equal people, Black and white, united in racial harmony and bonded together by the common pursuit of fulfilling the American Dream, including equality for all. These young Chasseurs risked their lives for the same lofty and idealistic objective—a free and just society of a people's republic that would provide ample opportunities for *everyone*, regardless of color, to fulfill their egalitarian ambitions and aspirations. Far more than glory or battlefield laurels, they desired equality for all men, Black and white, and their families, regardless of background, class, and wealth.

Of course, Saint-Domingue's mixed-race soldiers, who were products of Black mothers and white fathers, were the closest symbolic representation of the most idealistic and hardest-to-obtain of social concepts and constructs in the course of American history: the complete unity of Black and white as one people with a shared heritage, true brothers and sisters—an idealistic and utopian vision of America in the future. At Savannah, they battled as one and risked their lives for each other, for the fulfillment of a beautiful dream, because America's historical racial dilemmas and racism—then and now—can only be permanently solved by Blacks and whites truly becoming one people in the United States, by working more closely together for the achievement of common goals and understanding the positive aspects of their shared history and not just the negative, which have been endlessly emphasized in modern America, especially in the twenty-first century.

After the Chasseurs-Volontaires de Saint-Domingue fought in the American Revolution, the next-largest contingent of Black and mulatto troops who battled on American soil in the name of freedom for all

Blacks was not seen in America until the Civil War. It was not until President Abraham Lincoln's famous Emancipation Proclamation of January 1, 1863, even before the midpoint of the Civil War, that Black troops, or the so-called United States Colored Troops (USCT), were officially authorized in large numbers to serve in Northern armies. This was at a time when Union manpower was desperately needed during a lengthy war of attrition, when war weariness and a long list of battlefield defeats had taken a severe toll on the Northern people and white recruitment had fallen to new lows—nearly a century after the distinguished role of the Blacks and mulattoes of the Chasseurs-Volontaires de Saint-Domingue in the Battle of Savannah.

On bloody October 9, 1779, and then in the Civil War, Blacks and whites were united and bonded together as one in the pursuit of common republican goals for the good of the republic. This was a far cry from today's deep racial divisions and polarization that have created a dysfunctional society and torn America apart at the seams in racial terms, on a scale not seen since the turbulent 1960s. In the context of today's unfortunate national environment of racial disunity and antagonism, the story of the Chasseurs at Savannah provides us with hope for the future, for the kind of unity between Black and white that is necessary today for the fulfillment of America's core egalitarian values and the very meaning of the nation, as revealed in the inspiring words of the Declaration of Independence. Only when Blacks and whites come together as one will America truly become a unified nation in the future and fulfill its destiny by way of an elusive racial harmony.

In many ways, what was most forcefully demonstrated by the Chasseurs-Volontaires de Saint-Domingue on the gory field of strife at Savannah on October 9, 1779, was a most revealing glimpse of the most idealistic future promise of America—the true equality of both Blacks and whites, which America has long struggled to make into a meaningful reality, and is even now still struggling to fulfill with great difficulty at this late date, nearly two hundred and fifty years later. By way of their courage and sacrifice at Savannah, Black and white soldiers, both French and American, demonstrated to the world that it was well worth fighting and dying for this most beautiful of egalitarian promises—unprecedented in world history, and as defined by Thomas Jefferson in the Declaration of Independence—and in larger numbers than on almost every other battlefield of the American Revolution and any conflict until the Civil War of 1861–1865.

This rather remarkable distinction in both racial and egalitarian terms made the Battle of Savannah the most unique major battle of the Revolutionary War in both real and symbolic terms. This is why it is a great shame today that the battlefield of Savannah, along with the battle and those who fought in it, has become one of the most obscure and forgotten hallowed grounds of the American Revolution. No memorial or statue has been erected to the Franco-American alliance and the notable example of patriotic unity of the Black and mulatto men of Saint-Domingue and the white Frenchmen and Americans—a forgotten racial bond of brotherhood and shared sacrifice—partly because the fundamental truths about race had to be silenced by Southerners, especially in the Deep South, to give meaning to ugly racial stereotypes and myths that have endured to this day. At the time, the unity between Black and white that had been demonstrated on the Savannah battlefield represented the most dangerous of examples to a race-based society and culture. America's brutal system of racial apartheid, which included ugly Jim Crow realities imposed by the nation and the states, would last well into the twentieth century.

Coming more than a century and a half before the official integration of the US military, not long after the end of World War II, what the stirring battlefield performance of the Chasseurs-Volontaires de Saint-Domingue revealed in full on October 9, 1779, was a fundamental truth: the undeniable equality of Blacks and whites, demonstrated in dramatic fashion in a key battlefield situation, where valor and content of character was revealed in full by the Blacks and mulattoes from the French colony of today's Republic of Haiti. Courage and character were indeed color-blind for these brothers in liberty, battling for America and the great dream of equality for all men.

These forgotten brothers in liberty—white Americans, white Frenchmen, and the Blacks and mulattoes of the Chasseurs-Volontaires de Saint-Domingue, bonded together as one in overall egalitarian and racial terms—were indeed "brothers from another mother," in today's popular vernacular. During the fall of 1779, when so much was at stake for the future of America, these brothers in liberty fought, sacrificed, and died together at Savannah with a passion best articulated by Virginia's Patrick Henry, when he famously declared on March 23, 1775, "Give me liberty or give me death!"

In much the same way, so the mothers and sisters, both Black and mulatto, had kissed their young, beardless sons' heartfelt good-byes and shed tears when they went off to war and left Saint-Domingue far behind, with high hopes and idealistic visions of reaping martial glory in mid-August of 1779. These forgotten sisters in liberty of today's Haiti made their own personal sacrifices on the home front. Like the males, these free Black and mulatto women (and some who were still slaves) of Saint-Domingue also believed in the egalitarian dream of a brighter day in the future, and therefore selflessly made personal sacrifices in sending their menfolk forth in the name of liberty, which has also been forgotten and overlooked.

Here, on the hard-fought field of Savannah, America's egalitarian vision was revealed when Blacks and whites fought by each other's side as one, largely for the same reasons, demonstrating for the world to see the rare unity of brothers in liberty of different colors. Color no longer made any difference to men on both sides of the Atlantic on the bloody morning of October 9, 1779, quite unlike on any other battlefield on the US soil before the Civil War, which erupted because of race, and slavery, more than three-quarters of a century later, at Fort Sumter in Charleston harbor, a relatively short distance from Savannah.

What has been most overlooked about the story of the dramatic showdown at Savannah is the fact that the Black and mixed-race soldiers had journeyed more than 1,600 miles from their homes in Saint-Domingue to risk everything for America and its lofty egalitarian vision, despite the fact that the New World was still a tarnished land of slavery with an ugly racial heritage and dark legacy that continues to exist in the United States to this day. In this sense, the Black and mulatto soldiers fought not only for the unfulfilled promise of America, but also for the same hopeful promises for a better life and a brighter future for themselves and their families in Saint-Domingue and France.

The young men of the Chasseurs-Volontaires de Saint-Domingue overlooked the fact that they had basically sided with large numbers of American slave owners in the hope and belief that America would one day, after independence had been won, live up to its core revolutionary values and idealistic promise, that "all men are created equal, that they are endowed by their Creator with certain unalienable rights, that among these are life, liberty and the pursuit of happiness." This great egalitarian dream came alive and rose to the fore in dramatic fashion on October 9, 1779, as demonstrated by the Chasseurs, when everything was at stake for two armies, the Franco-American alliance, and America itself. For this reason, "the colored sons of Haiti fearlessly shed their blood for the independence of the United States."[15]

This shedding of blood by young Black and mixed race soldiers from Saint-Domingue was part of a vital link in the overall evolution of progress toward achieving human freedom in the world, far beyond America's shores. In the 1899 words of one historian, Theophilus Gould Steward: "It was this legion [from Saint-Domingue] that formed the connecting link between the siege of Savannah and the wide development of republican liberty on the Western continent [achieved by] a remarkable body of men" from today's Haiti.[16]

It was only on January 7, 1780, that the people of Paris and all of France learned from the pages of the *Paris Gazette* that "The coloured troops consisted of 545 Volunteer Chasseurs, Mulattoes and Negroes, newly raised in Saint-Domingue" to serve the country against the nation's ancient Protestant enemy.[17] But ironically, there was no mention of the Chasseurs-Volontaires de Saint-Domingue having saved the day at Savannah, which of course played a role in the general obscuring of what they accomplished against all odds for success on October 9, 1779, which has lingered to this day, including among the vast majority of today's historians.[18]

And the fact that one company of the Chasseurs-Volontaires, a total of sixty-two men, escorted the wounded men of the French army who had been cut down at Savannah to hospitals in Charlestown was also never mentioned, revealing the fact that the Chasseurs continued their faithful service in America for some time after the Battle of Savannah.[19]

The high level of sacrifice among French, American, and Saint-Dominguan soldiers at Savannah was absolutely necessary for the fulfillment of the Franco-American alliance's promise of future decisive victory, finally achieved at Yorktown, where they finally worked together like a team rather than as rivals, as they had during the fall of 1779. In this regard, Vice Admiral D'Estaing was correct in his strategic analysis of the necessity of an assault on October 9, 1779, upon which the future destiny and fate of the United States of America rested in full. He explained he had no choice but to order the doomed allied attack because of the urgent need to maintain the continued unity of an ever-so-fragile Franco-American alliance, since "London, America, and even Paris . . . would have supposed that I had secret orders [from King Louis XVI] not to assist the Americans. It would have created an inexhaustible source of complaint, of suspicion between two nations; perhaps even a rupture of relations would have been the result [to ensure that there would be no great victory at Yorktown] . . . This justification was important, but the only truly decisive one was the likelihood of success."[20]

ULTIMATE GRIM IRONY: THE GUILLOTINE DOOMS FRENCH LEADERS OF SAVANNAH

In a classic case of history's unintended consequences that are inevitable in the twisting contours of history, there would have been no French Revolution without the American Revolution. This was not only because of the spread of republican ideology, but also the huge amount of expenditures and borrowing of the French government to support what was then a failing American war effort. There was also a global war going on, especially in defense of the precious French sugar islands in the Caribbean: the strategic and logical situation that ultimately drove France deeply into debt and bankrupted the monarchy of King Louis XVI, setting the stage for the hardships that led to social collapse and the common people rising up to initiate the French Revolution, in the summer of 1789.

However, like all revolutions once unleashed and unable to be controlled or manipulated by any leader or people, so the French people shortly learned to their horror that their revolution had a life of its own, devouring its own creators during the infamous Reign of Terror, despite their best intentions of allegedly attempting to save the revolutionary republic, in the name of unattainable idealistic goals that were far too utopian to be practical or realistic.[21]

A true French hero of bloody October 9, for leading the daring counterattack of the Chasseurs-Volontaires that saved the day, Louis-Marie de Noailles was one of the French noblemen who suffered at the hands of the original concept of *Liberté, égalité, fraternité* ("Liberty, equality, fraternity"), which became twisted and perverted beyond recognition during the nightmarish Reign of Terror. The radical Jacobin revolutionaries orchestrated the state-initiated genocide of thousands of members of its aristocracy and royalty, purging the nation of its upper-class elite who were viewed as the enemies of republicanism.

The dynamic violin-playing aristocratic hero who led the timely counterattack of the Chasseurs-Volontaires de Saint-Domingue at Savannah lost not only his wife to the unfeeling steel blade of the guillotine, but also both parents and even his grandmother, in the bloody year of 1794, at the height of the Reign of Terror. Luckily for him, by this time Noailles had already escaped to America and settled in Philadelphia, in the infant republic, far from the chaos and horrors of the Old World.[22]

Ironically, in attempting to purify French society according to the republican virtues of ancient Roman society, Maximilien Robespierre's Reign of Terror relied on the guillotine in a systematic effort to eliminate perceived enemies of the state. First utilized in 1792, it was widely advertised as a humane killing machine, and was used to end the threat of an alleged royalist counterrevolution, as opposed to the king's more torture-based methods of killing French citizens. As cruel fate would have it, Robespierre—a former lawyer and a lover of the ancient classics, who had abolished slavery in France and its colonies, which was a high point of the egalitarianism of the French Revolution—himself went to the guillotine in July of 1794.[23]

In addition, Irishman Count Arthur Dillon, who had been second in command of the French army and then took over when d'Estaing fell wounded, before he himself was cut down on bloody October 9, 1779, also became a victim of the cruel excesses of the French Revolution. Like other French officers who had served with distinction and courage during the assault on the Spring Hill Redoubt, the unlucky Dillon was also beheaded at the guillotine.

Ironically, the hard-fighting Irishman's premonition of death had been narrowly avoided on that bloody October day in Georgia, as he somehow escaped slaughter by the murderous volleys pouring from the Spring Hill Redoubt. Like on the hellish field of Savannah, the gentlemanly and chivalric Irishman remained gallant to the very end. At the high wooden scaffold of the guillotine, an aristocratic French woman about to be executed by the massive sharp blade glistening in the sunlight asked the chivalric Irishman: "Oh! Monsieur Dillon, do you wish to go first?" With only minutes to live, he responded by bowing to the ill-fated woman, doffing his stylish hat, and ascending the steps to the guillotine: "What would I not do for a lady!" Dillon's last words, shouted to the jeering crowd of elated onlookers from the scaffold of the guillotine in 1794, echoed the battle cry of the attacking French soldiers going for broke at Savannah: "*Vive le Roi!*"[24]

Other aristocratic members of the legendary Irish Regiment, which had performed magnificently at Savannah during "a very brilliant moment" when gaining the fiery parapet of the Spring Hill Redoubt, and nearly succeeding in doing the impossible by capturing the defensive bastion, also became victims during the bloody abuses of the French Revolution. One of Dillon's finest Irish officers and a son of County Roscommon, Ireland, Captain James O'Moran, who had carried d'Estaing's surrender summons to Major General Prévost when it seemed as if a capitulation was inevitable, was also sent to the guillotine in the same heartless manner, killed on March 6, 1794, at the hands of his adopted Catholic country in a classic case of revolutionary utopianism gone badly awry.[25]

Like his tireless efforts to ensure that America won its independence, Vice Admiral d'Estaing's bad luck, fully displayed to one and all in his orchestrated fiasco at Savannah, continued in the years ahead, as if ordained by a cruel destiny. He made the great mistake of being too vocal in his support for the royal family, especially Marie-Antoinette, who was particularly despised by the French people, and he was entirely too well respected by King Louis XVI, who also literally lost his head in January 1793, on the phony charge of treason to the French nation.

In a truly tragic ending, like the Savannah disaster, Count d'Estaing became still another aristocratic victim to the insanity of the Reign of Terror. He was fated to go to the guillotine, like Marie-Antoinette, who went through a mock trial and was charged with crimes by the radical Jacobians against the state that were never committed. She was later beheaded after her husband, largely for political and domestic reasons, to garner continued support from the French people for the revolution, and to satisfy the desire of a vindictive leader of the Committee of Public Safety, who had demanded "the head of Antoinette." As a cruel fate would have it, the courageous d'Estaing met an untimely death despite having spent most of his life battling courageously for France, and also for America, as he had demonstrated at Savannah, where he had suffered multiple wounds on October 9, 1779.

On the fateful day of April 28, 1794, two years after the grim innovative instrument of death known as the guillotine was introduced as a "humanitarian means" of eliminating state enemies as neatly and quickly as possible, the sixty-four-year-old d'Estaing bravely walked up the executioner's steps to the uplifted steel blade in stoic fashion, with the same courage he had shown while leading the charge of his vanguard in the attack on the Spring Hill Redoubt at Savannah, less than fifteen years before.

What the unruly crowd of French onlookers and millions of Frenchmen and Americans had forgotten at this time was the significant fact that the American Revolution was the ideological and inspirational mother of the French Revolution. America's war might not have been won without d'Estaing's contributions at Savannah, despite the campaign having ended in a humiliating failure. What has often been overlooked is the fact that d'Estaing had enthusiastically urged King Louis XVI to dispatch a powerful second expedition, including siege artillery, to America under Comte de Rochambeau, who then basically led Washington to his greatest victory at Yorktown in October 1781.

The vice admiral had correctly realized that he had to launch an almost suicidal attack and sacrifice a good many of his best men at Savannah on October 9, in order to demonstrate the future viability of the Franco-American alliance, which was literally hanging in the balance because of the ever-rising tide of national rivalries, pride, jealousy, and pettiness that existed between the often-feuding allies of convenience. Going to his grisly death at the guillotine with stoic courage, still thinking like a veteran French grenadier, and in a classic case of employing humor in the face of death, d'Estaing's last bitter words on the high, wooden scaffold were "After my head falls off, send it to the British; they will pay a good deal for it."[26]

When in his prime, and when he was fully committed to the great dream of American independence, d'Estaing had correctly guaranteed that by attacking Savannah, in his own words, there would now be no fatal "rupture of relations" between allies, which might well have resulted in the complete collapse of this all-important alliance upon which America's fate and future depended.[27] If the vice admiral had been successful at Savannah on October 9, 1779, then his name would still be celebrated today in America, comparable to that of the idolized Marquis de Lafayette, who emerged as one of the greatest heroes of the American Revolution.[28]

But it was not to be, as fate would have it. Instead, d'Estaing has been forgotten today in America, and even in France. His headless body was buried with contempt by his own people in a common mass grave without markers or headstones, like other decapitated French aristocrats, including the king and queen, and just as the bodies of his dead soldiers had been tossed into mass burial pits at Savannah: an ironic and tragic ending for one of France's most distinguished and famous military men.

A cruel fate also awaited one of the most dynamic French leaders who led the Chasseurs to glory in Savannah, the Vicomte de Noailles. As noted, he was spared the horrors of the guillotine by luck and good fortune. The talented Noailles fell at the head of still another courageous charge, this time while leading French grenadiers with his usual valor in Cuba in 1804, instead of the Black and mixed-race soldiers from Saint-Domingue.[29]

Other Frenchmen at Savannah were more fortunate, including a sixteen-year-old corporal who worked as an apprentice to a silk merchant in more peaceful days, named Jean-Baptiste Jourdan. He served in the Auxerrois Regiment, which had been first created in 1692, and was named for the Auxerre region of Burgundy, in north-central France. Despite being hampered by a chronic disease that had struck him while serving under d'Estaing in the Caribbean, Jourdan rose to lofty heights in the years ahead, battling for France and becoming a marshal under Napoleon Bonaparte.[30]

A Beautiful Dream Deferred

In the end, the long-coveted equality that the men of the Chasseurs-Volontaires de Saint-Domingue had so eagerly anticipated as a reward for their solemn commitment, fidelity, and heroics at Savannah proved to be a cruel illusion and an outright betrayal. While they did receive official recognition and praise from the leaders and people of Saint-Domingue in the short term, what they most desired and had long prayed for was not forthcoming, from either the government of France, or Saint-Domingue. As mentioned, the primary reason for some of these young men to join the unit in the first place was in part to win the freedom of enslaved family members, including mothers and sisters who were vulnerable to all manner of abuse and the sexual whims of white slave owners. This did not happen, which was a tragic betrayal of trust.

For the vast majority of these Blacks and mulattoes of the Chasseurs, despite having earned "the respect of French officialdom," no social gains, especially against an entrenched racism, or positive steps toward winning greater equality, were forthcoming. Such imagined gains would never come from an ungrateful nation and colony led by upper-class white men, who felt no obligation toward the free Blacks and mulattoes of the Chasseurs, largely because of their color, despite their significant contributions at Savannah.

Therefore, after having won their greatest success at Savannah, the young men of the Chasseurs-Volontaires de Saint-Domingue had their most heartfelt dreams and visions of equality shattered and crushed, just as the desperate French and American assaults on the formidable Spring Hill Redoubt had been crushed—wasted dreams and dashed heartfelt wishes when it came to the eagerly anticipated social gains that were never forthcoming.[31]

However, some individual gains were achieved by way of invaluable training and experience, which helped lead to the rise of leadership in the revolutionary army to free Saint-Domingue (Haiti) from French rule and domination during the Haitian Revolution. Fabien Genty (or Gentil dit Tollo) had been freed in mid-April 1780 by his master, Captain Antoine Augustin Aubert Defoix Seigneur Dupetithouars, who led one of the ten companies of the Chasseurs-Volontaires de Saint-Domingue, after the return from saving the day at Savannah. Genty then became "a substantial landowner and 'big man' among the Cap [Cap-Français] military leader group, and later he was an officer in the revolutionary Army of Saint-Domingue" during the Haitian Revolution—still another example of the important and direct link that existed between the Savannah Campaign and the Haitian Revolution.[32]

AMERICA FINALLY ON THE RIGHT ROAD TO YORKTOWN

The sparkling victory won by the British at Savannah that preserved the key southern flank of British operations and made East Florida and the sugar islands of the British West Indies safer convinced strategists and King George III in London that the Southern Strategy was working as planned, and that it would succeed in the future. After all, thanks to the sparkling Savannah success, the British now continued to retain control of a vital Southern port and had negated the threat of the French navy, ensuring the continuation of the Southern Strategy that was calculated to win the war. If Savannah had fallen to the allies in October 1779, then so would have the Southern Strategy, leaving New York City as the only port in British possession and saddling the increasingly war-weary British with a failed plan for the conquest of America.

To fulfill their ambitious Southern Strategy—because a British-controlled Savannah and Georgia pointed "like a dagger at the back of South Carolina"—the victorious British now cast their eyes to the north, where Charlestown and South Carolina lay open to conquest. This would fulfill the next logical step in their ambitious plan for conquering the South, and eventually winning the war—or so it seemed in faraway London. As fate would have it, the British continued to embrace the belief that this increasingly bitter war of attrition could be won not only in the South, but also by conventional means. This was entirely the wrong strategic lesson, and certainly not the case, as would be demonstrated by future events in the South.[33]

Despite having been the sharpest of setbacks, the combined offensive effort of the French and Americans at Savannah proved to be important in overall political, symbolic, and psychological terms. Quite simply, the Franco-American alliance was finally sealed in blood at Savannah, like a dark Faustian bargain. This would later pay immense dividends, paving the way for decisive success in the final showdown at Yorktown, when the allies performed together flawlessly and with perfect unity—the antithesis of the dreadful Savannah experience. This decisive success was partly born of the bitter lessons learned by the fiasco at Savannah, and d'Estaing's savvy political understanding that the necessary price—in the form of a high sacrifice in French and American lives—had to be paid at Savannah in order for the troubled Franco-American alliance to gain any possible future success. The alliance had very nearly fallen apart before it was eventually revitalized to perform miracles during the Yorktown Campaign and what happened at Savannah was the key. In this regard, d'Estaing had proved prophetic and right on target, to his credit. Without the Savannah disaster, no glory would have been reaped by the alliance in October 1781 at Yorktown, which ensured the winning of the war and the independence of the newest republic on Earth.

As it fueled the core egalitarian concepts of the French Revolution, the American Revolution also helped to pave the way for the Haitian Revolution, in which America's egalitarian visions and aspirations were combined with the Age of Enlightenment's highest and most refined level—freedom and equality for all regardless of color—by the former slaves and free men of color when they defeated Napoleon's expeditionary force to establish the world's first Black republic, based on the day's most enlightened concept of universal emancipation, on January 1, 1804.

The great dream of winning complete freedom and equality had never died for the Chasseurs-Volontaires, who had survived in the intense combat at Savannah. It lived on in their hearts and minds, and would be resurrected and bloomed to full flower in Haiti. In the words of one Haitian historian: "These men who contributed their mite toward American independence, had still their mothers and sisters in slavery; and they themselves were subject to humiliating discrimination. Should not France have expected from that very moment, that they would soon use in their own cause, those very arms which they had learned so well to use in the interests of others?"[34]

Although the blue silk flag of the 1st South Carolina Continental Regiment was long thought to have been housed somewhere in London, the exact location of this tattered silk banner was not known for more than two centuries. Of course, it would have been most appropriate if the US government had long ago officially requested the return of this blood-stained banner, which had been lost on October 9, 1779. Fortunately, and much to their credit, the Smithsonian Institution in Washington, DC, has recently come to the rescue. The flag had been located in England, with the descendants of General Augustine Prévost, who had taken the 1st South Carolina's flag back to England as a war trophy. The Smithsonian purchased the precious banner, which was only recently returned to the United States, after so many years.[35]

Symbolically, in regard to the Haitian Revolution, the proud legacy and spirit of the Chasseurs-Volontaires de Saint-Domingue was also resurrected in dramatic fashion in the next war against Great Britain, at the famous Battle of New Orleans on January 8, 1815, during the War of 1812. At that time, Major General Andrew Jackson, who had been born in South Carolina of Irish immigrant parents, relied on the free Black and mulatto militiamen, exiles and the sons of exiles from the Haitian Revolution, who had doubled the size of New Orleans during a three-month period in 1809, to help defend the thin line of earthworks at Chalmette, Louisiana, against a powerful British army on another day of destiny.

Much like Napoleon Bonaparte, who had planned to use Saint-Domingue as a strategic staging base for the creation of a vast

New World Empire in French Louisiana and farther north up the Mississippi Valley—which would have blocked the epic westward movement of generations of Americans—the British also possessed visions of a New World Empire, if New Orleans had been captured by victory at Chalmette. Napoleon's mighty French expeditionary force was defeated by the Haitian revolutionaries in 1802–1803, and likewise, the ambitious British plan developed in London died along with hundreds of British soldiers during the frontal assaults on Chalmette, including against the Black and mulatto militiamen, or "the Men of Color." As noted, these citizen-soldiers of both African and white blood had originally fled with their families from Saint-Domingue because of the massive slave revolt in August 1791 and then the bloody revolutionary upheaval, in an overall historical process that helped to give "birth to Louisiana," and then ensuring its ultimate survival with Jackson's victory at the Battle of New Orleans.

Here, on the plain of Chalmette just south of New Orleans, the Black and mulatto refugees from Saint-Domingue had plenty of old scores to settle with France's archenemy, England. The British were partly responsible for the instability of Saint-Domingue during the revolutionary years, caused by their direct military intervention in an effort to possess Saint-Domingue for their own. Major General Andrew Jackson described the New Orleans second battalion of free men of color as America's "adopted children."[36]

In the end, Haiti—perhaps the most despised nation in the world and people, long maligned in the American memory because of their color, voodoo, poverty, and AIDS—played two pivotal roles in the making of America during times of national crisis: the free Blacks and mulattoes of Saint-Domingue at Savannah in 1779, where they saved the day, and the Franco-American alliance; and at New Orleans in 1815, where the men from Saint-Domingue fought with "noble enthusiasm" and "ardor," in Jackson's complimentary words, as America's "adopted children," in long-overlooked and forgotten roles as saviors of America during key turning points in American history.[37]

At both Savannah and New Orleans, Black and mulatto men from Haiti indeed risked their lives and fought with their hearts, not only as proud West Indians, but also as freedom fighters on American soil. This was more so the case at the Battle of Savannah than the Battle of New Orleans, when the Black and mixed-race soldiers from faraway Saint-Domingue saved the day with the tactical offensive (the tactical defensive was successfully employed at Chalmette) during "one of the Revolution's three bloodiest battles—the one nobody remembers, if indeed they ever heard of it."[38]

Even more, the former freedom fighters of the American Revolution and the Haitian Revolution played key roles in the struggle for human freedom on two continents, North and South America: "Haitian arms, money, and men turned [Simón] Bolívar's disasters [against the Spanish in South America] to victory; and the spirit of Western liberty marched on to the redemption of South America. The liberation of Mexico, and all Central America, followed as a matter of course . . . The black men of the Antilles who fought in the siege of Savannah, enjoy unquestionably the proud historical distinction of being the physical conductors that bore away . . . the sacred fire of liberty to rekindle it in their own land; and also of becoming the humble but important link that served to unite the two Americas in the bond of enlightened independence."[39]

For such reasons, an impressive Haitian Monument has recently been dedicated to the courage and sacrifice of the Chasseurs-Volontaires de Saint-Domingue, and it proudly stands today in Franklin Park, in the north part of Savannah, Georgia. This stately monument was created by artist James Mastin, and the six bronze statues of Haitian soldiers include young drummer boy Henri Christophe, who served at Savannah. Christophe who would rise up to play a leading military role in the Haitian Revolution, becoming the president of Haiti after independence had been won with the defeat of Napoleon's expeditionary force.

This impressive monument was dedicated in 2007 and 2009 by the Haitian-American Historical Society, the first ever to honor the mixed-race and Black men who fought with distinction at Savannah on October 9, 1779, and one of the most distinguished memorials that stands today on any American Revolutionary War battlefield in America.

It is not known how many Haitian soldiers were killed and buried in a shallow pit in the sand, but the Haitian Monument has bestowed belated recognition and honor to the Black and mulatto soldiers from Saint-Domingue, including those who fell in one of the bloodiest battles of the American Revolution. Today, hundreds of miles away from where the reconstructed Spring Hill Redoubt (much reduced in size) now stands, on sacred ground, descendants of the Chasseurs who served with distinction in Savannah and currently live in the natural disaster–prone Republic of Haiti do not know exactly what happened to their Black and mixed-race ancestors in faraway Georgia—only that their ancestors departed the tropical French colony on the sailing ships of Vice Admiral d'Estaing, who commanded a mighty fleet on a far-flung expedition, and that some of them never returned to their tropical homeland under the sun.

The stately Haitian Monument at Franklin Park in Savannah is significant for a variety of reasons. As noted, the capture of Savannah would have meant the end to Great Britain's Southern Strategy, which was calculated to win it all. It came very close to succeeding, and failed only by the narrowest of margins. As mentioned, the Franco-American defeat at Savannah helped to pave the way for the ultimate British disaster at Yorktown, when Lord Charles Cornwallis surrendered his entire British, Hessian, and Loyalist army on October 19, 1781, to ensure the winning of America's independence.

Despite its failure and the dismal performance of the allies, the Savannah Campaign created a new awareness among the Black and mixed-race colonists of Saint-Domingue, not only about their own courage that rose to the fore on October 9, 1779, but also the inevitable and frightful cost of liberty that they would eventually pay when they battled to regain their own homeland, when the greatest of all challenges was posed by the Haitian Revolution and Napoleon's mighty invasion that planned to restore slavery in the colony.

Because of what they had learned at Savannah, the next war for the Chasseurs would be the loftiest in egalitarian terms, in regard to battling for the fulfillment of their greatest dream—the most enlightened concept of all, which was universal emancipation for all slaves and equality for all men, regardless of color, unlike what proved to be the case with the American Revolution. Thanks partly to what had been learned at

Savannah, the Haitian Revolution led to the establishment of the Republic of Haiti on January 1, 1804, which was nothing less than a bright, shining new day in the course of human liberty and the history of human progress in the Western world.

The long-overlooked Battle of Savannah during the autumn of 1779 and the saving of both the French and American armies by the Chasseurs-Volontaires de Saint-Domingue on October 9 was a forgotten turning point in not only American history, but also world history, the course of human progress, and the evolution of human freedom in the Western world. The long road that led from the body-strewn Spring Hill Redoubt on the strategic Ebenezer Road significantly increased the desire for equality among Blacks and mulattoes, which helped to pave the way for the ultra-egalitarian Haitian Revolution and the establishment of the first Black republic in history, which was declared on a memorable and historic Sunday—appropriately, the Holy Sabbath Day.

The young Chasseur drummer boy at Savannah, Henri Christophe, would become the president of the Republic of Haiti because of his vital leadership role in the Haitian Revolution, during which he served as the capable top lieutenant and right-hand man of Toussaint Louverture. He would be the only survivor of the trio of the nation's three greatest revolutionary heroes, after the deaths of Toussaint Louverture, who died in a prison in France, thanks to Napoleon's treachery, and Jean-Jacques Dessalines, who had led his people to the final victory over the French expeditionary force in late 1803.

Ironically, the color-obsessed white officials of Saint-Domingue and the aristocratic officers throughout the French army had fully believed, in their casual arrogance and deep-seated racism, that the Black and mixed-race soldiers of the Chasseurs-Volontaires de Saint-Domingue were simply "not capable of being employed for more than trench work." Consequently, it came as a great shock to whites in both Saint-Domingue and France that the men of a darker hue held in such unquestioned contempt were the ones who "prevented the total destruction of our army" on October 9, 1779, at Savannah.[40]

In the overall context of the Haitian Revolution, based on the earth-shaking concept of universal liberty, the death of slavery, and the emancipation of all slaves, the bloody showdown at Savannah and the unforgettable performance of the free Blacks and mixed-race soldiers from Saint-Domingue on October 9 "had a wider bearing upon the progress of liberty in the Western world than any other battle fought during the [eight years of the American] Revolution."[41]

Given the worldwide repercussions of the Battle of Savannah and its significance in dictating the course of the American Revolution—which eventually led to the little Virginia tobacco port on the York River named Yorktown, and in providing key players in the Haitian Revolution—it is a central paradox that it has been forgotten for so long, just like the Black and mixed-race soldiers of the Chasseurs-Volontaires de Saint-Domingue. Realizing as much, in regard to the remarkable British, Hessian, and Loyalist victory and dramatic results that stemmed from saving Savannah from capture, General Henry Clinton proclaimed without hesitation: "I think this is the greatest event that has happened in the whole war."[42]

The overall importance of telling the long-forgotten story of the Chasseurs-Volontaires de Saint-Domingue in *Brothers in Liberty* has been primarily to provide a significant example of the kind of Black and white unity that played a key role and was necessary in the winning of the American Revolution, and in the overall making of America. What also has been forgotten is the importance of racial unity in 1779 mirrored the pre–Revolutionary War experience of Blacks and whites, including in the South, when these two groups of divergent people were forced to band together as one on the frontier, from New England to Georgia, to face external threats, especially in fending off the attacks from Native Americans during not only the French and Indian War, but also other prior bitter colonial conflicts long before the American Revolution. All of this was at a time when whites still debated (actually, there was no debate at all in most white minds, because of racism) whether Blacks were even human beings, which of course was the greatest of all racial myths, and one that had to disproved by them on the battlefield, like at Savannah and during the Civil War, to expose the greatest of all racist lies.

In this sense, hundreds of Blacks, both slaves and free men, and whites of the South Carolina militia had together bravely defended the colony. (More than a half-century before the Battle of Savannah, the colony incorporated Black slaves as soldiers into the militia during its brutal Indian Wars, including against the Yamasee, Cherokee, and Tuscarora, when Black and white together marched deep into Indian territory. In fact, this was very likely the vital margin for victory, since a full half of the militia sent to fight against the colony's Native American enemies in 1715 during the Yamasee War were Black, and officially formed all-Black companies of slaves that were part of an expeditionary force the South Carolina militia sent against the Cherokee.) Blacks and whites long worked closely together on the remote frontiers of the thirteen colonies in both the North and South, long before the American Revolution's outbreak, helping to ensure the survival of their remote frontier settlements and vulnerable colonies at a time when both white and Black blood was spilled on American soil for the common good, and for simple survival.

This historical lesson should not be forgotten today, by either Black or white Americans in a racially divided America, especially in regard to the close connections between the American Revolution, the French Revolution, and the Haitian Revolution, as exemplified by the vital role played by the Chasseurs-Volontaires de Saint-Domingue at Savannah.[43] Indeed, it was these most forgotten soldiers of the American Revolution who "established a vital link between the American and the Haitian revolutions," in the insightful words of one modern historian.[44]

No wonder one of today's leading historians has asked a legitimate question, appropriate and right on target, in regard to an undeniable reality long ignored by generations of Americans and long considered utterly unimaginable: "Did Haiti save the United States?"[45] Indeed, the forgotten contributions and sacrifices of hundreds of thousands of Haitians, including the young men of the Chasseurs-Volontaires de Saint-Domingue, and especially in regard to the winning of the Haitian Revolution that resulted in Napoleon's sale of the vast Louisiana Territory to the United States, doubling the republic's size and ensuring its future dominance on the world stage, "greatly contributed to the rise of the economic and military colossus to the north."[46]

It is certainly a striking paradox that a disciplined command of fighting men of a darker hue—who through no fault of their own represented the most unfortunate and despised people on Earth, from an allegedly cursed land—played such a key role in history and in the shaping of America's creation story. They not only saved the day in a major battle of the American Revolution, while representing a key link between the American Revolution and the Haitian Revolution, but also played an equally forgotten role in ensuring the successful continuance of the crucial Franco-American alliance, which led to a decisive victory at Yorktown that guaranteed American independence and changed the world forever.

NOTES

CHAPTER 1

1 Philippe Girard, *Haiti: The Tumultuous History—From Pearl of the Caribbean to Broken Nation* (New York: Palgrave Macmillan, 2010), 17–23; Stewart R. King, *Blue Coat or Powdered Wig: Free People of Color in Pre-Revolutionary Saint-Domingue* (Athens: University of Georgia Press, 2001), 268; Carl A. Brasseaux and Glenn R. Conrad, eds., *The Road to Louisiana, The Saint-Domingue Refugees, 1792–1809* (Lafayette: University of Louisiana at Lafayette Press, 1992), 3, 8–10; Donald R. Wright, *African Americans in the Colonial Era: From African Origins through the American Revolution* (Wheeling, IL: Harlan Davidson, Inc., 2010), 108–09.

2 Bernard Moitt, *Women and Slavery in the French West Antilles, 1635–1848* (Bloomington: Indiana University Press, 2001), xiv–xv, 4–5, 9–12, 16–17; Girard, *Haiti*, 25–26, 34; David Patrick Geggus and Norman Fiering, eds., *The World of the Haitian Revolution* (Bloomington: Indiana University Press, 2009), xi–xii, xiv, 3; Douglas Botting, *Rio de Janeiro* (New York: Time-Life Books, 1977), 73, 83, 105; Brasseaux and Conrad, eds., *The Road to Louisiana*, 4, 11–12.

3 Bertrand, Jost, *Life and Death of a French Soldier in the American War of Independence, 1778–1781* (Coppell, TX: Private printing, 2020), 70.

4 Philippe Girard, *Toussaint Louverture: A Revolutionary Life* (New York: Basic Books, 2016), 46.

5 Girard, *Haiti*, 34–35, 38, 62–64; Geggus and Fiering, eds., *The World of the Haitian Revolution*, 9–10, 14, 56–57; King, *Blue Coat or Powdered Wig*, 267–69, 271–72; Brasseaux and Conrad, eds., *The Road to Louisiana*, 10, 13.

6 Christopher Leslie Brown and Philip D. Morgan, *Arming Slaves, From Classical Times to the Modern Age* (New Haven: Yale University Press, 2006), 3, 14–34; Phillip Thomas Tucker, *Blacks in Gray Uniforms: A New Look at the South's Most Forgotten Combat Troops, 1861–1865* (Gloucestershire, UK: Fonthill Media Publications, 2018), 7–8.

7 Geggus and Fiering, eds., *The World of the Haitian Revolution*, 49–55; Brasseaux and Conrad, eds., *The Road to Louisiana*, 9; John D. Garrigus, "Catalyst or Catastrophe? Saint-Domingue's Free Men of Color and the Battle of Savannah, 1779–1782, *Revista/Review Interamericana*, vol. 22 (1992), 112–14; Moitt, *Women and Slavery in the French Antilles, 1635–1848*, 4–5.

8 Jost, *Life and Death of a French Soldier*, 71.

9 Geggus and Fiering, eds., *The World of the Haitian Revolution*, 56.

10 Garrigus, "Catalyst or Catastrophe?," 109, 114–16.

11 King, *Blue Coat or Powdered Wig*, xv; Norman Desmarais, *America's First Ally: France in the Revolutionary War* (Philadelphia: Casemate Publishing 2019), 201; Garrigus, "Catalyst or Catastrophe?," 116.

12 King, *Blue Coat or Powdered Wig*, xv, 267; Girard, *Toussaint Louverture*, 71.

13 King, *Blue Coat or Powdered Wig*, 28; Girard, *Toussaint Louverture*, 71; Jacques Nicholas Leger, *Haiti: Her History and Her Detractors* (New York: Neale Publishing Company, 1907), 42, note 4, 161; Girard, *Haiti*, 65–66; Desmarais, *America's First Ally*, 201; Alexander Lawrence, *Storm Over Savannah: The Story of Count d'Estaing and the Siege of the Town in 1779* (Athens: The University of Georgia, 2021), 18.

14 Desmarais, *America's First Ally*, 201.

15 Tom Shachtman, *How the French Saved America: Soldiers, Sailors, Diplomats, Louis XVI, and the Success of a Revolution* (New York: St. Martin's Press, 2017), 197; Preston Russell and Barbara Hines, *Savannah: A History of the People Since 1733* (Savannah, GA: Frederic C. Beil, 1992), 70.

16 Norman Desmarais, ed., *The Road to Yorktown: The French Campaigns in the American Revolution, 1780–1783, by Louis-François-Bertrand du Pont d'Aubevoye, Comte de Lauberdière*, annotated (El Dorado Hills, CA: Savas-Beatie, 2021), xiii, note 3; Desmarais, *America's First Ally*, 201.

17 Geggis and Fiering, eds., *The World of the Haitian Revolution*, 56–57; King, *Blue Coat or Powdered Wig*, 269.

18 Jost, *Life and Death of a French Soldier*, 77–78; Girard, *Haiti*, 54; Girard, *Toussaint Louverture*, 97.

19 Jost, *Life and Death of a French Soldier*, 79.

20 Ibid.

21 Light Townsend Cummins, *Spanish Observers and the American Revolution, 1775–1783* (Baton Rouge: Louisiana State University Press, 1991), 64, 67–69; Girard, *Haiti*, 54.

22 Jost, *Life and Death of a French Soldier*, 74, 76.

23 Garrigus, "Catalyst or Catastrophe?," 110–12.

24 Ibid., 110.

25 Geggus and Fiering, eds., *The World of the Haitian Revolution*, 56–58; Russell and Hines, *Savannah*, 70.

26 Garrigus, "Catalyst or Catastrophe?," 109–10.

27 Ibid., 109–13; King, *Blue Coat and Powdered Wig*, 69, 226–28, 253.

28 Garrigus, "Catalyst or Catastrophe?," 67, 110.

29 Garrigus, "Catalyst or Catastrophe?," 116; Russell and Hines, *Savannah*, p. 70.

30 Don Cook, *The Long Fuse: How England Lost the American Colonies, 1760–1785* (New York: Atlantic Monthly Press, 1995), 317–18; Girard, *Toussaint Louverture*, 69–71; Desmarais, *America's First Ally*, 200; Shachtman, *How the French Saved America*, 172–73, 177, 181; Scott Martin and Bernard F. Harris Jr., *Savannah 1779: The British Turn South* (Oxford, UK: Osprey Publishing, 2017), 12, 28–31, 77, 79; William Seymour, *The Price of Folly, British Blunders in the War of American Independence* (Washington, DC: Brassey's Ltd., 1995), 138; Lawrence, *Storm Over Savannah*, 14–17, 131;

Benjamin Kennedy, ed. and trans., *Muskets, Cannon Balls & Bombs: Nine Narratives of the Siege of Savannah in 1779* (Savannah, GA: Beehive Books, 1974), viii–ix, xii.

31 King, *Blue Coat or Powdered Wig*, 67, 69, 226–28, 272; Geggus and Fiering, eds., *The World of the Haitian Revolution*, 57–58; Lawrence, *Storm Over Savannah*, 55; Girard, *Toussaint Louverture*, 71; Christopher M. Church, *Paradise Destroyed: Catastrophe and Citizenship in the French Caribbean* (Lincoln: University of Nebraska Press, 2017), 13; Martin and Harris, *Savannah 1779*, 19, 24, 28–31.

32 Geggus and Fiering, eds., *The World of the Haitian Revolution*, 57–58; King, *Blue Coat or Powdered Wig*, 66, 68.

33 Geggus and Fiering, eds., *The World of the Haitian Revolution*, 56–57.

34 Desmarais, *America's First Ally*, v–vi.

35 Garrigus, "Catalyst or Catastrophe?," 118; King, *Blue Coat or Powdered Wig*, 73.

36 Garrigus, "Catalyst or Catastrophe?," 118.

37 King, *Blue Coat or Powdered Wig*, ix–x, xii–xiii, 66, 69–70, 154, 226–27; Girard, *Toussaint Louverture*, 71.

38 King, *Blue Coat or Powdered Wig*, xii–xxi; Girard, *Toussaint Louverture*, 71, 73; Brasseaux and Conrad, eds., *The Road to Louisiana*, 10, 13; Russell and Hines, *Savannah*, 70.

39 King, *Blue Coat or Powdered Wig*, 67.

40 Ibid.

41 Lawrence, *Storm Over Savannah*, 65; Russell and Hines, *Savannah*, 70; Girard, *Haiti*, 11, 14–16.

42 Church, *Paradise Destroyed*, 44–45, 59; Brasseaux and Conrad, eds., *The Road to Louisiana*, 14–17.

43 King, *Blue Coat or Powdered Wig*, ix–x, xvi–xxiii, 67–69, 142–57, 228–69, 272; Girard, *Haiti*, 64; Church, *Paradise Destroyed*, 44; Brasseaux and Conrad, eds., *The Road to Louisiana*, 5; Russell and Hines, *Savannah*, 70.

44 King, *Blue Coat or Powdered Wig*, 277–78; Russell and Hines, *Savannah*, 70.

45 Garrigus, "Catalyst or Catastrophe?," 117–18.

46 Shachtman, *How the French Saved America*, 177, 181–82, 197; Kennedy, ed. and trans., *Muskets, Cannon Balls, & Bombs*, vi–vii, 28–29; King, *Blue Coat or Powdered Wig*, 68; Russell and Hines, *Savannah*, 70.

47 Kennedy, ed. and trans., *Muskets, Cannon Balls & Bombs*, vii, 28–29; Martin and Harris, *Savannah 1779*, 12, 28–31.

CHAPTER 2

1 Shachtman, *How the French Saved America*, 9, 94–95, 98–99, 302–03; Desmarais, *America's First Ally*, vi–vii; Martin and Harris, *Savannah 1779*, 6; Phillip Thomas Tucker, *Ranger Raid: The Legendary Robert Rogers and His Most Famous Frontier Battle* (Guilford, CT: Stackpole Books, 2021), 23–38; Seymour, *The Price of Folly*, 115–31; Esmond Wright, ed., *Causes and Consequences of the American Revolution* (Chicago: Quadrangle Books, 1996*)*, 294–96, 298; Girard, *Haiti*, 54.

2 Dan L. Morrill, *Southern Campaigns of the American Revolution* (Baltimore, MD: Nautical & Aviation Publishing Company of America, 1993), 38.

3 Holger Hoock, *Scars of Independence: America's Violent Birth* (New York: Crown, 2017), 302; Desmarais, *America's First Ally*, 66.
4 Edward J. Cashin, *The King's Ranger: Thomas Brown and the American Revolution on the Southern Frontier* (New York: Fordham University Press, 1999), 99–100.
5 Shachtman, *How the French Saved America*, 182.
6 Ibid.
7 Stanley D. M. Carpenter, *Southern Gambit: Cornwallis and the British March to Yorktown* (Norman: University of Oklahoma Press, 2019), 63.
8 Mills Lane, *Savannah Revisited, A Pictorial History* (Savannah, GA: Beehive Press, 1977), 7, 12, 52, 57; Russell and Hines, *Savannah*, 3–8, 11–12, 61; Lawrence, *Storm Over Savannah*, 1; Martin and Harris, *Savannah 1779*, 5; Bruce Edward Twyman, *The Black Seminole Legacy and North American Politics, 1693–1845* (Washington, DC: Howard University Press, 2001), 58–59; Medora Field Perkerson, *White Columns in Georgia* (New York: Bonanza Books, 1956), 98.
9 Lane, *Savannah Revisited*, 11, 53, 57; Russell and Hines, *Savannah*, 29–31; Martin and Harris, *Savannah 1779*, 6–7.
10 Russell and Hines, *Savannah*, 17, 36, 39, 44, 61; Lane, *Savannah, Revisited*, 7.
11 Russell and Hines, *Savannah*, 61; Wright, ed., *Causes and Consequences of the American Revolution*, 49.
12 Russell and Hines, *Savannah*, 62.
13 Twyman, *The Black Seminole Legacy*, 59–60; Lawrence, *Storm Over Savannah*, 1.
14 Russell and Hines, *Savannah*, 15–17, 44–45; Lane, *Savannah Revisited*, 15.
15 Martin and Harris, *Savannah 1779*, 13; Lane, *Savannah Revisited*, 16, 20.
16 Lane, *Savannah Revisited*, 23; Martin and Harris, *Savannah*, 47–57.
17 Carpenter, *Southern Gambit*, 3–8, 28, 41–42, 44–45; Henry Lumpkin, *From Savannah to Yorktown* (New York: toExcel Press / iUniverse.com, 2000), 9; Morrill, *Southern Campaigns of the American Revolution*, 39; Robert Stansbury Lambert, *South Carolina Loyalists in the American Revolution* (Clemson, SC: Clemson University Press, 2010), 55–56; Martin and Harris, *Savannah 1779*, 5, 13; Shachtman, *How the French Saved America*, 171–72.
18 Morrill, *Southern Campaigns of the American Revolution*, 38–39.
19 Ibid., 38, 42; Carpenter, *Southern Gambit*, 3–8, 17–18, 41–42, 44–45, 50–51; Lumpkin, *From Savannah to Yorktown*, 8; Morrill, *Southern Campaigns of the American Revolution*, 42; Shachtman, *How the French Saved America*, 172–73; Martin and Harris, *Savannah 1779*, 5.
20 Carpenter, *Southern Gambit*, 48–49; Lumpkin, *From Savannah to Yorktown*, 28; Shachtman, *How the French Saved America*, 172–73.
21 Martin and Harris, *Savannah 1779*, 13.
22 Carpenter, *Southern Gambit*, 51; Lumpkin, *From Savannah to Yorktown*, 27.
23 Morrill, *Southern Campaigns of the American Revolution*, 40.
24 Michael C. Scoggins, *The Day It Rained Militia: Huck's Defeat and the Revolution in the South Carolina Backcountry May-July 1780* (Charleston, SC: History Press, 2005), 34–35; Martin and Harris, *Savannah 1779*, 27.
25 Russell and Hines, *Savannah*, 59–60.

26 Cook, *The Long Fuse*, 312–13; Cashin, *The King's Ranger*, 83; Martin and Harris, *Savannah 1779*, 22, 33, 36–37, 45, 47; Lumpkin, *From Savannah to Yorktown*, 28; Carpenter, *Southern Gambit*, 53–54; Franklin Benjamin Hough, *The Siege of Savannah* (Albany, NY: J. Munsell, 1866), 13–14; Morrill, *Southern Campaigns of the American Revolution*, 46; Shachtman, *How the French Saved America*, 172.
27 Russell and Hines, *Savannah*, 61.
28 Morrill, *Southern Campaigns of the American Revolution*, 46–47.
29 Cashin, *The King's Ranger*, 85; Carpenter, *Southern Gambit*, 54; Lumpkin, *From Savannah to Yorktown*, 29; Martin and Harris, *Savannah 1779*, 14–15, 45.
30 Carpenter, *Southern Gambit*, 55; Martin and Harris, *Savannah 1779*, 10.
31 Carpenter, *Southern Gambit*, 56–57, 61; Cashin, *The King's Ranger*, 1, 85, 88–92, 98; Martin and Harris, *Savannah 1779*, 14–15, 48, 52–53, 56; Seymour, *The Price of Folly*, 141.
32 Cashin, *The King's Ranger*, 92–94; Carpenter, *Southern Gambit*, 60; Martin and Harris, *Savannah 1779*, 14, 50–52.
33 Morrill, *Southern Campaigns of the American Revolution*, 54–55; Cashin, *The King's Ranger*, 85, 96–97; Donald M. Londahl-Smidt, *German Troops in the American Revolution, Hessen-Cassell* (Oxford, UK: Osprey Publishing, 2021), 9–10; Carpenter, *Southern Gambit*, 58–59, 61–62; H. W. Brands, *Andrew Jackson: His Life and Times* (New York: Anchor Books, 2005), 11, 24; Andrew Burstein, *The Passions of Andrew Jackson* (New York: Alfred A. Knopf, 2003), 8; Lumpkin, *From Savannah to Yorktown*, 31–32; Lawrence, *Storm Over Savannah*, 28; Martin and Harris, *Savannah 1779*, 14–15, 21–22, 57, 62–63, 66.
34 Cashin, *The King's Ranger*, 99; Martin and Harris, *Savannah 1779*, 14; Morrill, *Southern Campaigns of the American Revolution*, 54–55; Seymour, *The Price of Folly*, 138, 140.
35 Lawrence, *Storm Over Savannah*, 131; Morrill, *Southern Campaigns of the American Revolution*, 55–56.
36 Hoock, *Scars of Independence*, 300–03.
37 Carpenter, *Southern Gambit*, 63; Cashin, *The King's Ranger*, 99; Morrill, *Southern Campaigns of the American Revolution*, 41.
38 Kennedy, ed., and trans., *Muskets, Cannon Balls & Bombs*, 44.
39 Ibid., 114.
40 *Maryland Gazette*, Annapolis, Maryland, October 1, 1779.
41 Martin and Harris, *Savannah 1779*, 67.

Chapter 3
1 Ibid.; Kennedy, ed. and trans., *Muskets, Cannon Balls & Bombs*, vii; Morrill, *Southern Campaigns of the American Revolution*, 55–56; Martin and Harris, *Savannah 1779*, 29–30; Lawrence, *Storm Over Savannah*, 65–66, 81; Desmarais, *America's First Ally*, 200.
2 Carpenter, *Southern Gambit*, 64; Girard, *Toussaint Louverture*, 71; King, *Blue Coat or Powdered Wig*, 59–77, 277–78; Lawrence, *Storm Over Savannah*, 64–65; Martin and Harris, *Savannah 1779*, 19; Desmarais, *America's First Ally*, 200.

3 Lawrence, *Storm Over Savannah*, 21; Wayne C. Temple, ed., *Campaigning with Grant by General Horace Porter* (New York: Bonanza Books, 1961), 196.

4 Kennedy, ed. and trans., *Muskets, Cannon Balls & Bombs*, 3, 7.

5 Ibid., 28.

6 Ibid., 8.

7 Ibid., 40, 43.

8 Lawrence, *Storm Over Savannah*, 21.

9 Kennedy, ed. and trans., *Muskets, Cannon Balls & Bombs*, vii, 40; Cashin, *The King's Ranger*, 99; Desmarais, *America's First Ally*, 200; Morrill, *Southern Campaigns of the American Revolution*, 56; Shachtman, *How the French Saved America*, 182; Lawrence, *Storm Over Savannah*, 14–16.

10 Kennedy, ed. and trans., *Muskets, Cannon Balls & Bombs*, 32.

11 Desmarais, ed., and annotated, *The Road to Yorktown*, 7.

12 Lawrence, *Storm Over Savannah*, 22.

13 Shachtman, *How the French Saved America*, 173; Claude Manceron, *The Wind from America: Age of the French Revolution*, 4 vols. (New York: Touchstone Publishing, 1978), 142–43; Kennedy, ed. and trans., *Muskets, Cannon Balls & Bombs*, 44–45.

14 Desmarais, *America's First Ally*, 201.

15 Shachtman, *How the French Saved America*, 193; Carpenter, *Southern Gambit*, 64; Lawrence, *Storm Over Savannah*, v, 65.

16 Kennedy, ed. and trans., *Muskets, Cannon Balls & Bombs*, 9–10; Lawrence, *Storm Over Savannah*, 64, 105; Braden Phillips, "Cannons in the Savannah: A Blast from Georgia's Past," *National Geographic History* (July-August 2022), 6-7.

17 Kennedy, ed. and trans, *Muskets, Cannon Balls & Bombs*, 10–11; Lawrence, *Storm Over Savannah*, 31.

18 Lawrence, *Storm Over Savannah*, 31.

19 Ibid., 58.

20 Ibid.

21 Ibid.; Carpenter, *Southern Gambit*, 64.

22 Cashin, *The King's Ranger*, 98, 100; Philip Katcher, *The American Provincial Corps 1775–1784* (Oxford, UK: Osprey Publishing, 1973), 19–20, 39; Lumpkin, *From Savannah to Yorktown*, 33; Morrill, *Southern Campaigns of the American Revolution*, 57; Martin and Harris, *Savannah 1779*, 24, 67–68; Lawrence, *Storm Over Savannah*, 26, 39; Russell and Hines, *Savannah*, 61.

23 Martin and Harris, *Savannah 1779*, 15; Lawrence, *Storm Over Savannah*, 26–27.

24 Katcher, *The American Provincial Corps*, 20; Martin and Harris, *Savannah 1779*, 52, 57–58, 62, 66; Lawrence, *Storm Over Savannah*, 150.

25 Katcher, *The American Provincial Corps*, 34.

26 Kennedy, ed. and trans., *Muskets, Cannon Balls & Bombs*, 90; Martin and Harris, *Savannah 1779*, 15.

27 Carpenter, *Southern Gambit*, 64–65; Morrill, *Southern Campaigns of the American Revolution*, 65–66; Russell and Hines, *Savannah*, 63; Kennedy, ed. and trans., *Muskets, Cannon Balls & Bombs*, 21, 29, 67, 101, 128; Shachtman, *How the French Saved America*,

193; Lawrence, *Storm Over Savannah*, 1–2, 38; Martin and Harris, *Savannah 1779*, 68, 70.

28 *Rivington's Gazette*, New York, New York, December 29, 1779.

29 Kennedy, ed. and trans., *Muskets, Cannon Balls & Bombs*, 90.

30 *Rivington's Gazette*, November 20, 1779; Morrill, *Southern Campaigns of the American Revolution*, 57–58; Russell and Hines, *Savannah*, 66; Martin and Harris, *Savannah 1779*, 61, 70.

31 Elizabeth Lichtenstein Johnston, *Recollections of a Georgia Loyalist* (New York: Bankhead Press, 1901), 57.

32 *Rivington's Gazette*, December 11, 1779.

33 Shachtman, *How the French Saved America*, 194, 197; Martin and Harris, *Savannah 1779*, 70.

34 Kennedy, ed. and trans., *Muskets, Cannon Balls & Bombs*, 95.

35 Shachtman, *How the French Saved America*, 194; Kennedy, ed. and trans., *Muskets, Cannon Balls & Bombs*, 40, 91.

36 Martin and Harris, *Savannah 1779*, 67, 72.

37 Lawrence, *Storm Over Savannah*, 36.

38 Johnston, *Recollections of a Georgia Loyalist*, 61.

39 Kennedy, ed. and trans., *Muskets, Cannon Balls & Bombs*, 12; Lawrence, *Storm Over Savannah*, 36.

40 Carpenter, *Southern Gambit*, 64–65; *Rivington's Gazette*, November 20, 1779; Manceron, *The Wind from America*, 142–43; Lawrence, *Storm Over Savannah*, 41; Russell and Hines, *Savannah*, 62–63.

41 Lawrence, *Storm Over Savannah*, 36–37.

42 Ibid.; Martin and Harris, *Savannah 1779*, 72.

43 Martin and Harris, *Savannah 1779*, 24; Lawrence, *Storm Over Savannah*, 58.

44 Lawrence, *Storm Over Savannah*, 65–66.

45 Morrill, *Southern Campaigns of the American Revolution*, 57; Lawrence, *Storm Over Savannah*, 26, 52; Shachtman, *How the French Saved America*, 194.

46 Kennedy, ed. and trans., *Muskets, Cannon Balls & Bombs*, 13.

47 Martin and Harris, *Savannah 1779*, 73; Lawrence, *Storm Over Savannah*, 52.

48 Lawrence, *Storm Over Savannah*, 52.

49 Kennedy, ed. and trans., *Muskets, Cannon Balls & Bombs*, 30.

50 Ibid.; Lawrence, *Storm Over Savannah*, 9–10.

51 Lawrence, *Storm Over Savannah*, 12–13, 89; Edward P. Hamilton, edited and translated, *Adventure in the Wilderness: The American Journal of Louis Antoine de Bougainville, 1756–1760* (Norman: University of Oklahoma Press, 1964), xi–xii, xvii–xviii.

52 Hamilton, ed. and trans., *Adventure in the Wilderness*, 333.

53 Lawrence, *Storm Over Savannah*, 17–18.

54 Ibid., 64–67.

55 Ibid., 35.

56 Ibid., 58.

57 Johnston, *Recollections of a Georgia Loyalist*, 59.

58 Shachtman, *How the French Saved America*, 195; Lawrence, *Storm Over Savannah*, 8; Kennedy, ed. and trans., *Muskets, Cannon Balls & Bombs*, 21, 47, 61.

59 Carpenter, *Southern Gambit*, 63–64; Shachtman, *How the French Saved America*, 193–94; Martin and Harris, *Savannah 1779*, 12, 28–31.

60 Kennedy, ed. and trans., *Muskets, Cannon Balls & Bombs*, 11; Martin and Harris, *Savannah 1779*, 10.

61 Martin and Harris, *Savannah 1779*, 57, 59.

62 Lawrence, *Storm Over Savannah*, 22–23.

63 Kennedy, ed. and trans., *Muskets, Cannon Balls & Bombs*, 30.

64 Lawrence, *Storm Over Savannah*, 24–25; Martin and Harris, *Savannah 1779*, 24.

65 Martin and Harris, *Savannah 1779*, 10.

66 *Rivington's Gazette*, December 11, 1779; Carpenter, *Southern Gambit*, 64; Russell and Hines, *Savannah*, 65–66, 70, 73; Morrill, *Southern Campaigns of the American Revolution*, 59; Lawrence, *Storm Over Savannah*, 8, 27–28, 30, 41, 45–46, 49–50, 52, 54–55, 150; Martin and Harris, *Savannah 1779*, 15, 23, 56.

67 *Maryland Gazette*, November 5, 1779.

68 Johnston, *Recollections of a Georgia Loyalist*, 61–62.

69 *Rivington's Gazette*, December 11, 1779.

70 Kennedy, ed. and trans., *Muskets, Cannon Balls & Bombs*, 30.

71 Ibid., 41, 47; Martin and Harris, *Savannah 1779*, 74; Edith Hall, *Introducing the Ancient Greeks: From Bronze Age Seafarers to Navigators of the Western Mind* (New York: W. W. Norton, 2014), 5; Erich Lessing, *The Voyages of Ulysses* (Vienna, Austria: Herder Freiburg, 1965), 238–39.

72 Lawrence, *Storm Over Savannah*, 49.

73 Kennedy, ed. and trans., *Muskets, Cannon Balls & Bombs*, 35; Martin and Harris, *Savannah 1779*, 75.

74 Lawrence, *Storm Over Savannah*, 65–68.

75 Russell and Hines, *Savannah*, 61, 63–64; Martin and Harris, *Savannah 1779*, 23–24, 58; Lawrence, *Storm Over Savannah*, 22.

76 Hough, *The Siege of Savannah*, 23; Russell and Hines, *Savannah*, 64.

77 Martin and Harris, *Savannah 1779*, 25–27; Perkerson, *White Columns in Georgia*, 104.

78 *Rivington's Gazette*, December 15, 1779.

79 Ibid., December 29, 1779.

80 Ibid., January 12, 1780.

81 Kennedy, ed. and trans., *Muskets, Cannon Balls & Bombs*, 28–29.

82 Ibid., 44.

83 *New-York Mercury*, New York, New York, December 10, 1779.

84 Kennedy, ed. and trans., *Muskets, Cannon Balls & Bombs*, 45.

85 Ibid., 47.

86 Ibid., 49.

87 Ibid., 51.

88 Ibid., 90.

89 Ibid., 55.

90 Ibid., 30.

91 Martin and Harris, *Savannah 1779*, 16–22.

92 Lawrence, *Storm Over Savannah*, 74.

93 Kennedy, ed. and trans., *Muskets, Cannon Balls & Bombs*, 9–22, 32.

94 Ibid., 49.

95 Ibid.

96 Lawrence, *Storm Over Savannah*, 61.

97 Johnston, *Recollections of a Georgia Loyalist*, 57; Shachtman, *How the French Saved America*, 196; Morrill, *Southern Campaigns of the American Revolution*, 60–61; Kennedy, ed. and trans., *Muskets, Cannon Balls & Bombs*, vi; Theophilus Gold Steward, "How the Black St. Domingo Legion Saved the Patriot Army in the Siege of Savannah 1779," American Negro Academy, Occasional Papers, Number 5, Washington, DC, 1899, 4; Lawrence, *Storm Over Savannah*, 61; Martin and Harris, *Savannah 1779*, 15, 24, 70, 74–75.

98 Russell and Hines, *Savannah*, 64; Martin and Harris, *Savannah 1779*, 24.

99 Morrill, *Southern Campaigns of the American Revolution*, 60.

100 Shachtman, *How the French Saved America*, 196.

101 Kennedy, ed. and trans., *Muskets, Cannon Balls & Bombs*, 32–33.

102 Shachtman, *How the French Saved America*, 196.

103 Lawrence, *Storm Over Savannah*, 75.

104 *Maryland Gazette*, November 5, 1779.

105 Johnston, *Recollections of a Georgia Loyalist*, 57–58.

106 *Rivington's Gazette*, December 11, 1779; Lawrence, *Storm Over Savannah*, 159.

107 Lawrence, *Storm Over Savannah*, 158; Kennedy, ed. and trans., *Muskets, Cannon Balls & Bombs*, 98; Martin and Harris, *Savannah 1779*, 75.

108 Kennedy, ed. and trans., *Muskets, Cannon Balls & Bombs*, 17.

109 Ibid.

110 Lawrence, *Storm Over Savannah*, 62–63.

111 Kennedy, ed. and trans., *Muskets, Cannon Balls & Bombs*, vii.

112 Ibid., 61–63.

113 Ibid., 129–30.

114 Katcher, *The American Provincial Corps*, 4.

115 Hoock, *Scars of Independence*, 300; Kennedy, ed. and trans., *Muskets, Cannon Balls & Bombs*, 30; Martin and Harris, *Savannah 1779*, 24.

116 Hoock, *Scars of Independence*, 299–300.

117 Ibid., 301.

118 Ibid., 300–01.

119 *Maryland Gazette*, November 5, 1779.

120 Lawrence, *Storm Over Savannah*, 81.

121 Ibid., 81–82.

122 Hoock, *Scars of Independence*, 301.

123 John U. Rees, *'They Were Good Soldiers': African-Americans Serving in the Continental Army, 1775–1783* (Warwick, UK: Helion and Company, 2019), 135–36.

124 Shachtman, *How the French Saved America*, 196–97; Lawrence, *Storm Over Savannah*, 85; Russell and Hines, *Savannah*, 70.
125 Kennedy, ed. and trans., *Muskets, Cannon Balls & Bombs*, 31.
126 Ibid., 132.
127 Ibid., 52.
128 King, *Blue Coat or Powdered Wig*, 72; Russell and Hines, *Savannah*, 70.
129 Garrigus, "Catalyst or Catastrophe," 119; Lawrence, *Storm Over Savannah*, vi.
130 Lawrence, *Storm Over Savannah*, 157.
131 Lawrence, *Storm Over Savannah*, 9–10, 16–19; Garrigus, "Catalyst or Catastrophe," 119; King, *Blue Coat or Powdered Wig*, 1–196.
132 *Rivington's Gazette*, December 15, 1779; Lawrence, *Storm Over Savannah*, 61.
133 *Rivington's Gazette*, December 29, 1779.
134 Kennedy, ed. and trans., *Muskets, Cannon Balls & Bombs*, 61; Martin and Harris, *Savannah 1779*, 76.
135 Martin and Harris, *Savannah 1779*, 76.
136 Hough, *The Siege of Savannah*, 80.
137 Ibid., 34–35.
138 Kennedy, ed. and trans., *Muskets, Cannon Balls & Bombs*, 18–19; Lawrence, *Storm Over Savannah*, 61.
139 Kennedy, ed. and trans., *Muskets, Cannon Balls & Bombs*, 129, 131.
140 *Rivington's Gazette*, December 11, 1779; Lane, *Savannah Revisited*, 27; Perkerson, *White Columns in Georgia*, 99, 105.
141 *Rivington's Gazette*, December 11, 1779.
142 Kennedy, ed. and trans., *Muskets, Cannon Balls & Bombs*, 99; Lawrence, *Storm Over Savannah*, 78.
143 *Rivington's Gazette*, December 29, 1779.
144 Ibid., January 12, 1780.
145 *Maryland Gazette*, December 3, 1779.
146 *Rivington's Gazette*, January 12, 1780.
147 Kennedy, ed. and trans., *Muskets, Cannon Balls & Bombs*, 14.
148 Ibid., 19–20; Martin and Harris, *Savannah 1779*, 76.
149 Kennedy, ed. and trans., *Muskets, Cannon Balls & Bombs*, 36.
150 Ibid., 129–30, 132.
151 Lawrence, *Storm Over Savannah*, 83; Kennedy, ed. and trans., *Muskets, Cannon Balls & Bombs*, 62–63.
152 Lawrence, *Storm Over Savannah*, 72–74.
153 Ibid., 83.
154 Ibid., 83–84.
155 Katcher, *The American Provincial Corps*, 4.
156 Lawrence, *Storm Over Savannah*, 100.
157 Ibid., 100; Martin and Harris, *Savannah 1779*, 12, 28–31.

CHAPTER 4

1 Desmarais, *America's First Ally*, 204; *Rivington's Gazette*, December 11, 1779; Morrill, *Southern Campaigns of the American Revolution*, 61; Carpenter, *Southern Gambit*, 66; Kennedy, ed. and trans., *Muskets, Cannon Balls & Bombs*, viii–ix, 14–20, 31; Lawrence, *Storm Over Savannah*, 60, 85–87, 100; Martin and Harris, *Savannah 1779*, 28, 30–31.

2 Kennedy, ed., and trans., *Muskets, Cannon Balls & Bombs*, 36; Lawrence, *Storm Over Savannah*, 85–88, 165, note 9; Martin and Harris, *Savannah 1779*, 74, 77.

3 Lawrence, *Storm Over Savannah*, 84.

4 Ibid., 15, 101, 103; Martin and Harris, *Savannah 1779*, 31, 77.

5 Martin and Harris, *Savannah 1779*, 77.

6 Pierre Charles L'Enfant Biography, Brittanica.com; Lawrence, *Storm Over Savannah*, 147; Martin and Harris, *Savannah 1779*, 77.

7 Lumpkin, *From Savannah to Yorktown*, 38; Kennedy, ed. and trans., *Muskets, Cannon Balls & Bombs*, 44–45; Lawrence, *Storm Over Savannah*, 91.

8 Martin and Harris, *Savannah 1779*, 75, 77.

9 Kennedy, ed. and trans., *Muskets, Cannon Balls & Bombs*, 19–20.

10 *Maryland Gazette*, November 12, 1779.

11 Martin and Harris, *Savannah 1779*, 77–78; Lawrence, *Storm Over Savannah*, 96–97.

12 Manceron, *The Wind from America*, 142–43; Morrill, *Southern Campaigns of the American Revolution*, 62–63; Hough, *The Siege of Savannah*, 138; Cashin, *The King's Ranger*, 6–7, 17–18, 26–29, 98, 100; Desmarais, *America's First Ally*, 203–05; Russell and Hines, *Savannah*, 63; *Rivington's Gazette*, December 11, 15, 29, 1779; Lumpkin, *From Savannah to Yorktown*, 37; Kennedy, ed. and trans., *Muskets, Cannon Balls & Bombs*, xi, 30, 86, 89, note 7, 101, 114; Hough, *The Siege of Savannah*, 70, 81; Lawrence, *Storm Over Savannah*, 17–18, 72, 74, 91–94, 97–99, 101, 104, 120, 137, 168, note 3; Martin and Harris, *Savannah 1779*, 11, 19–22, 24, 70, 77–79, 82–83.

13 Kennedy, ed. and trans., *Muskets, Cannon Balls & Bombs*, 20; Lawrence, *Storm Over Savannah*, 97, 101.

14 Russell and Hines, *Savannah*, 66–67, 70; Lawrence, *Storm Over Savannah*, 107.

15 *Rivington's Gazette*, December 15, 1779; Kennedy, ed. and trans., *Muskets, Cannon Balls & Bombs*, 101; Lawrence, *Storm Over Savannah*, 101, 107.

16 Kennedy, ed. and trans., *Muskets, Cannon Balls & Bombs*, 20; Lawrence, *Storm Over Savannah*, 100–01.

17 *Rivington's Gazette*, December 11, 1779; Shachtman, *How the French Saved America*, 197; Martin and Harris, *Savannah 1779*, 77–79; Morrill, *Southern Campaigns of the American Revolution*, 62–63; Lumpkin, *From Savannah to Yorktown*, 38; Martin and Harris, *Savannah 1779*, 24, 82–83; Lawrence, *Storm Over Savannah*, 15, 101–04; *Rivington's Gazette*, December 15, 1779; Juliet Barton, Agincourt, Henry V and the Battle that Made England (New York: Little Brown and Company, 2005), 264-266.

18 Hough, *The Siege of Savannah*, 80; Lawrence, *Storm Over Savannah*, 91, 97–98, 104; Martin and Harris, *Savannah 1779*, 24, 79.

19 Morrill, *Southern Campaigns of the American Revolution*, 63; Martin and Harris, *Savannah 1779*, 24, 79.

20 Kennedy, ed. and trans., *Muskets, Cannon Balls & Bombs*, 36.

21 *Rivington's Gazette*, November 20, 1779; Carpenter, *Southern Gambit*, 66.

22 *Rivington's Gazette*, December 11, 1779.

23 Kennedy, ed. and trans., *Muskets, Cannon Balls & Bombs*, 36–37; Martin and Harris, *Savannah 1779*, 23.

24 Morrill, *Southern Campaigns in the American Revolution*, 63; *Rivington's Gazette*, December 29, 1779.

25 Martin and Harris, *Savannah 1779*, 24, 79.

26 Henry Steele Commager and Richard B. Morris, eds., *The Spirit of Seventy-Six: The Story of the American Revolution as Told by Participants* (New York: Bonanza Books, 1983), 1096; Morrill, *Southern Campaigns of the American Revolution*, 63; Russell and Hines, *Savannah*, 65; Martin and Harris, *Savannah 1779*, 24.

27 Kennedy, ed. and trans., *Muskets, Cannon Balls & Bombs*, 37.

28 Ibid., 67.

29 *Rivington's Gazette*, December 15, 1779; Lawrence, *Storm Over Savannah*, 102; Martin and Harris, *Savannah 1779*, 79; Cashin, *The King's Ranger*, 100; Russell and Hines, *Savannah*, 67.

30 Lawrence, *Storm Over Savannah*, 101, 103; Kennedy, ed. and trans., *Muskets, Cannon Balls & Bombs*, 73.

31 Kennedy, ed. and trans., *Muskets, Cannon Balls & Bombs*, 37.

32 Russell and Hines, *Savannah*, 67.

33 *Rivington's Gazette*, December 15, 1779; Lawrence, *Storm Over Savannah*, 91, 104–05, 107; Hough, *The Siege of Savannah*, 138.

34 Kennedy, ed. and trans., *Muskets, Cannon Balls & Bombs*, 86.

35 Ibid., 101; Lawrence, *Storm Over Savannah*, 107; Martin and Harris, *Savannah 1779*, 20.

36 Commager and Morris, eds., *The Spirit of Seventy-Six*, 1096; Martin and Harris, *Savannah 1779*, 24; Lawrence, *Storm Over Savannah*, 105.

37 Martin and Harris, *Savannah 1779*, 79–80; Lawrence, *Storm Over Savannah*, 105–06.

38 Carpenter, *Southern Gambit*, 66; Lawrence, *Storm Over Savannah*, 69, 105.

39 *Rivington's Gazette*, December 15, 1779; Lawrence, *Storm Over Savannah*, 92–93.

40 Kennedy, ed. and trans., *Muskets, Cannon Balls & Bombs*, 20.

41 Ibid., 37, 101.

42 Lawrence, *Storm Over Savannah*, 95, 97; Martin and Harris, *Savannah 1779*, 80.

43 Martin and Harris, *Savannah 1779*, 23–24, 80.

44 Kennedy, ed. and trans., *Muskets, Cannon Balls & Bombs*, 36–37, 101.

45 Martin and Harris, *Savannah 1779*, 80.

46 Kennedy, ed. and trans., *Muskets, Cannon Balls & Bombs*, 20–21, 37; Martin and Harris, *Savannah 1779*, 80–81.

47 Russell and Hines, *Savannah*, 67.

48 Ibid., 70.

49 *Rivington's Gazette*, November 20, 1779; Lumpkin, *From Savannah to Yorktown*, 38; Martin and Harris, *Savannah 1779*, 80.

50 *Rivington's Gazette*, December 15, 1779; Kennedy, ed. and trans., *Muskets, Cannon Balls & Bombs*, 102.
51 Kennedy, ed. and trans., *Muskets, Cannon Balls & Bombs*, 102; Lawrence, *Storm Over Savannah*, 104.
52 Hough, *The Siege of Savannah*, 81; Lawrence, *Storm Over Savannah*, 105; Martin and Harris, *Savannah 1779*, 80.
53 Russell and Hines, *Savannah*, 67; Kennedy, ed. and trans., *Muskets, Cannon Balls & Bombs*, 68.; Martin and Harris, *Savannah 1779*, 24; Lawrence, *Storm Over Savannah*, 93, 105–09.
54 Martin and Harris, *Savannah 1779*, 24, 87; Lawrence, *Storm Over Savannah*, 106–09.
55 Kennedy, ed. and trans., *Muskets, Cannon Balls & Bombs*, 101; Lawrence, *Storm Over Savannah*, 107; Martin and Harris, *Savannah 1779*, 24.
56 James Thacher, *Military Journal during the American Revolutionary War, 1775 to 1783* (Cranbury, NJ: The Scholar's Bookshelf, 2005), 183; Lawrence, *Storm Over Savannah*, 96; Martin and Harris, *Savannah 1779*, 11–12, 78.
57 Kennedy, ed. and trans., *Muskets, Cannon Balls & Bombs*, 66; Martin and Harris, *Savannah 1779*, 23.
58 Lawrence, *Storm Over Savannah*, 96.
59 Thacher, *Military Journal during the American Revolutionary War*, 183; Russell and Hines, *Savannah*, 64; Martin and Harris, *Savannah 1779*, 12, 81; Lawrence, *Storm Over Savannah*, 109–10, 118.
60 *Maryland Gazette*, November 12, 1779.
61 *Rivington's Gazette*, December 29, 1779.
62 Ibid., November 20, 1779.
63 Ibid., December 29, 1779.
64 Ibid.
65 Stuart Reid and Marko Zlatich, *Soldiers of the Revolutionary War* (Oxford, UK: Osprey Publishing, 2002), 42; Martin and Harris, *Savannah 1779*, 80.
66 Martin and Harris, *Savannah 1779*, 80.
67 Carpenter, *Southern Gambit*, 67.
68 Russell and Hines, *Savannah*, 69.
69 Kennedy, ed. and trans., *Muskets, Cannon Balls & Bombs*, 68; Martin and Harris, *Savannah 1779*, 24.
70 *New Jersey Gazette*, Burlington, New Jersey, December 8, 1779; Lawrence, *Storm Over Savannah*, 111.
71 *Rivington's Gazette*, November 4, 1780.
72 Seymour, *The Price of Glory*, 142; Kennedy, ed. and trans., *Muskets, Cannon Balls & Bombs*, 37.
73 Kennedy, ed. and trans., *Muskets, Cannon Balls & Bombs*, 21.
74 *Rivington's Gazette*, November 20, 1779.
75 Kennedy, ed. and trans., *Muskets, Cannon Balls & Bombs*, 37.
76 Martin and Harris, *Savannah 1779*, 78; Kennedy, ed. and trans., *Muskets, Cannon Balls & Bombs*, 32, 63, 67.

77 Lawrence, *Storm Over Savannah*, 107; Kennedy, ed. and trans., *Muskets, Cannon Balls & Bombs*, 68–69, 101; Martin and Harris, *Savannah 1779*, 24.
78 Lawrence, *Storm Over Savannah*, 100–12.

CHAPTER 5

1 King, *Blue Coat or Powdered Wig*, 69, 253; Lawrence, *Storm Over Savannah*, 105–06; Russell and Hines, *Savannah*, 67, 69; Martin and Harris, *Savannah 1779*, 87.
2 King, *Blue Coat or Powdered Wig*, 74, 277–78; Russell and Hines, *Savannah*, 70.
3 Morrill, *Southern Campaigns of the American Revolution*, 63; Lawrence, *Storm Over Savannah*, 107, 111; Lumpkin, *From Savannah to Yorktown*, 39; Russell and Hines, *Savannah*, 70; Kennedy, ed. and trans., *Muskets, Cannon Balls & Bombs*, 101; Desmarais, *America's First Ally*, 204–05.
4 Steward, "How the Black St. Domingo Legion Saved the Patriot Army," 8–10; Russell and Hines, *Savannah*, 70.
5 Kennedy, ed. and trans., *Muskets, Cannon Balls & Bombs*, 101; Russell and Hines, *Savannah*, 70.
6 Lawrence, *Storm Over Savannah*, 107, 111; Kennedy, ed. and trans., *Muskets, Cannon Balls & Bombs*, 101; Russell and Hines, *Savannah*, 70.
7 Kennedy, ed. and trans., *Muskets, Cannon Balls & Bombs*, 101; Lawrence, *Storm Over Savannah*, 107, 111; Russell and Hines, *Savannah*, 70.
8 Lawrence, *Storm Over Savannah*, 107, 111; Russell and Hines, *Savannah*, 70; Lumpkin, *From Savannah to Yorktown*, 39; Martin and Harris, *Savannah 1779*, 24.
9 Russell and Hines, *Savannah*, 70; Lawrence, *Storm Over Savannah*, 107, 111; Martin and Harris, *Savannah 1779*, 63, 66.
10 *Rivington's Gazette*, December 11, 1779; Lawrence, *Storm Over Savannah*, 111.
11 Desmarais, *America's First Ally*, 204–05; Kennedy, ed. and trans., *Muskets, Cannon Balls & Bombs*, 67.
12 Steward, "How the Black St. Domingo Legion Saved the Patriot Army," 8–10; Lawrence, *Storm Over Savannah*, 111.
13 Kennedy, ed. and trans., *Muskets, Cannon Balls & Bombs*, 36, 67; Russell and Hines, *Savannah*, 69–70; Lawrence, *Storm Over Savannah*, 111.
14 Kennedy, ed. and trans., *Muskets, Cannon Balls & Bombs*, 67; Russell and Hines, *Savannah*, 70.
15 Kennedy, ed. and trans., *Muskets, Cannon Balls & Bombs*, 67; Russell and Hines, *Savannah*, 69–70; Lawrence, *Storm Over Savannah*, 87, 105–06; Shachtman, *How the French Saved America*, 181; Wright, ed., *Causes and Consequences of the American Revolution*, 300, 302–03.
16 Russell and Hines, *Savannah*, 69–70; Lawrence, *Storm Over Savannah*, 111; Kennedy, ed. and trans., *Muskets, Cannon Balls & Bombs*, 67, 101.
17 King, *Blue Coat or Powdered Wig*, ix–xxiii, 52–77, 226–72; Garrigus, "Catalyst or Catastrophe?," 110–11, 117; Martin and Harris, *Savannah 1779*, 19; Russell and Hines, *Savannah*, 70.
18 King, *Blue Coat or Powdered Wig*, 67; Russell and Hines, *Savannah*, 70.

19 Russell and Hines, *Savannah*, 70; Lawrence, *Storm Over Savannah*, 107, 111; Martin and Harris, *Savannah 1779*, 81.

CHAPTER 6

1 King, *Blue Coat or Powdered Wig*, 67; Garrigus, "Catalyst or Catastrophe?," 117; Lawrence, *Storm Over Savannah*, 107; Russell and Hines, *Savannah*, 70.

2 Garrigus, "Catalyst or Catastrophe?," 117; Lawrence, *Storm Over Savannah*, 111; Russell and Hines, *Savannah*, 70.

3 Seymour, *The Price of Folly*, 142; Lawrence, *Storm Over Savannah*, 111; Russell and Hines, *Savannah*, 70.

4 Martin and Harris, *Savannah 1779*, 81–87.

5 Ibid., 19; Russell and Hines, *Savannah*, 70; Lawrence, *Storm Over Savannah*, 70, 111; Garrigus, "Catalyst or Catastrophe?," 117–18.

6 Lawrence, *Storm Over Savannah*, 16–17; Martin and Harris, *Savannah 1779*, 77, 79; Russell and Hines, *Savannah*, 70.

7 *Rivington's Gazette*, December 11, 1779; Steward, "How the Black St. Domingo Legion Saved the Patriot Army," 8–10; Shachtman, *How the French Saved America*, 181, 197; Russell and Hines, *Savannah*, 69–70; Seymour, *The Price of Folly*, 142; Lawrence, *Storm Over Savannah*, 106; Kennedy, ed. and trans., *Muskets, Cannon Balls & Bombs*, 21, 67, 101, 128, note 4.

8 Russell and Hines, *Savannah*, 69–70; Kennedy, ed. and trans., *Muskets, Cannon Balls & Bombs*, 101; Shachtman, *How the French Saved America*, 197; Martin and Harris, *Savannah 1779*, 81, 87.

9 Russell and Hines, *Savannah*, 69–70; Kennedy, ed. and trans., *Muskets, Cannon Balls & Bombs*, 68; Shachtman, *How the French Saved America*, 197.

10 Lawrence, *Storm Over Savannah*, 111; Russell and Hines, *Savannah*, 70.

11 Kennedy, ed. and trans., *Muskets, Cannon Balls & Bombs*, 37; Russell and Hines, *Savannah*, 70.

12 Seymour, *The Price of Folly*, 142.

13 Kennedy, ed. and trans., *Muskets, Cannon Balls & Bombs*, 42, 68.

14 Lawrence, *Storm Over Savannah*, 111.

15 Girard, *Toussaint Louverture*, 73; Russell and Hines, *Savannah*, 70.

16 Desmarais, *America's First Ally*, 204–05.

17 Russell and Hines, *Savannah*, 70.

18 Ibid.

19 Ibid.; Shachtman, *How the French Saved America*, 197.

20 Kennedy, ed. and trans., *Muskets, Cannon Balls & Bombs*, 37.

21 Ibid., 20–21.

22 Steward, "How the Black St. Domingo Legion Saved the Patriot Army," 8–10; Russell and Hines, *Savannah*, 70.

23 Lawrence, *Storm Over Savannah*, 111; Russell and Hines, *Savannah*, 70.

24 Russell and Hines, *Savannah*, 63, 69–70; Kennedy, ed. and trans., *Muskets, Cannon Balls & Bombs*, 68; Shachtman, *How the French Saved America*, 197; Steward, "How the Black St. Domingo Legion Saved the Patriot Army," 8–10; "Henri Christophe,

1767–1820," Encyclopedia.com; Lawrence, *Storm Over Savannah*, 111; Martin and Harris, *Savannah 1779*, 87–89.

25 Shachtman, *How the French Saved America*, 197.

26 Lawrence, *Storm Over Savannah*, 106; Russell and Hines, *Savannah*, 70; Kennedy, ed. and trans., *Muskets, Cannon Balls & Bombs*, 21, 128.

27 Kennedy, ed. and trans., *Muskets, Cannon Balls & Bombs*, 71.

28 Garrigus, "Catalyst or Catastrophe?," 119; Russell and Hines, *Savannah*, 70.

29 Russell and Hines, *Savannah*, 70.

30 Ibid.; Shachtman, *How the French Saved America*, 197.

31 Lawrence, *Storm Over Savannah*, 113.

32 Russell and Hines, *Savannah*, 70.

33 Commager and Morris, eds., *The Spirit of Seventy-Six*, 1097.

34 Shachtman, *How the French Saved America*, 197.

35 Johnston, *Recollections of a Georgia Loyalist*, 62–63.

36 Russell and Hines, *Savannah*, 70; Kennedy, ed. and trans., *Muskets, Cannon Balls & Bombs*, 101; Lawrence, *Storm Over Savannah*, 107; Martin and Harris, *Savannah 1779*, 79, 81.

37 *Rivington's Gazette*, December 15, 1779.

38 Ibid., December 11, 1779.

39 Johnston, *Recollections of a Georgia Loyalist*, 62.

40 *Rivington's Gazette*, December 11, 1779.

41 Kennedy, ed., and trans., *Muskets, Cannon Balls & Bombs*, 115–16.

42 Johnston, *Recollections of a Georgia Loyalist*, 63.

43 *Rivington's Gazette*, December 29, 1779.

44 Shachtman, *How the French Saved America*, 198; Russell and Hines, *Savannah*, 70.

45 Russell and Hines, *Savannah*, 70.

46 Ibid.

47 *Rivington's Gazette*, December 11, 1779; Lawrence, *Storm Over Savannah*, 89; Russell and Hines, *Savannah*, 70.

48 Hough, *The Siege of Savannah*, 145–46.

49 Lawrence, *Storm Over Savannah*, 114.

50 Ibid., 116.

51 Lawrence, *Storm Over Savannah*, 113.

52 Ibid., 150.

53 Ibid., 153; Russell and Hines, *Savannah*, 70.

54 Kennedy, ed. and trans., *Muskets, Cannon Balls & Bombs*, xii–xiii.

55 Martin and Hines, *Savannah*, 70; Lawrence, *Storm Over Savannah*, 126.

56 *Maryland Gazette*, December 3, 1779.

57 Lawrence, *Storm Over Savannah*, x.

58 Ibid., 113.

59 Girard, *Toussaint Louverture*, 73.

60 Ibid., 55, 71; Girard, *Haiti*, 48–55.

EPILOGUE

1 Geggus and Fiering, eds., *The World of the Haitian Revolution*, 14; Russell and Hines, *Savannah*, 70.

2 Geggus and Fiering, eds., *The World of the Haitian Revolution*, 58; Garrigus, "Catalyst or Catastrophe?," 109–13; Russell and Hines, *Savannah*, 70.

3 Hough, *The Siege of Savannah*, 86; Martin and Harris, *Savannah 1779*, 87.

4 *Rivington's Gazette*, December 15, 1779; Hough, *The Siege of Savannah*, 80–81.

5 *Rivington's Gazette*, December 15, 1779.

6 Kennedy, ed. and trans, *Muskets, Cannon Balls & Bombs*, 102.

7 Ibid., v.

8 *Rivington's Gazette*, December 11, 1779.

9 Lawrence, *Storm Over Savannah*, 116, 160; Martin and Harris, *Savannah 1779*, 87.

10 Lawrence, *Storm Over Savannah*, 175, note 7; Martin and Harris, *Savannah 1779*, 21–22, 71; Russell and Hines, *Savannah*, 70.

11 Martin and Harris, *Savannah 1779*, 19.

12 Lawrence, *Storm Over Savannah*, 175, note 7.

13 Russell and Hines, *Savannah*, 66; Mexico City National Cemetery, American Battlefield Monuments Commission.

14 Garrigus, "Catalyst or Catastrophe?," 117; Shachtman, *How the French Saved America*, 197.

15 Leger, *Haiti: Her History and Her Detractors*, 42; Hines and Russell, *Savannah*, 70; Edwin S. Redkey, ed., *A Grand Army of Black Men* (Cambridge, UK: Cambridge University Press, 1993), 1–8; Girard, *Haiti*, 48–55.

16 Steward, "How the Black St. Domingo Legion Saved the Patriot Army," 8–10; Shachtman, *How the French Saved America*, 197.

17 *Paris Gazette*, Paris, France, January 7, 1780.

18 Hines and Russell, *Savannah*, 70.

19 Garrigus, "Catalyst or Catastrophe?," 119.

20 Kennedy, ed. and trans., *Muskets, Cannon Balls & Bombs*, p. 45.

21 Desmarais, *America's First Ally*, 233–34; Shachtman, *How the French Saved America*, 173; Wright, ed., *Causes and Consequences of the American Revolution*, 298–99.

22 Russell and Hines, *Savannah*, 69–70; Lawrence, *Storm Over Savannah*, 87, 138.

23 Colin Jones, *Paris: The Biography of a City* (New York: Viking, 2004), 232.

24 Russell and Hines, *Savannah*, 67, 70–71; Lawrence, *Storm Over Savannah*, 137.

25 Lawrence, *Storm Over Savannah*, 105, 138; "James O'Moran," Dictionary of Irish Biography.

26 Shachtman, *How the French Saved America*, 308, 311; Martin and Harris, *Savannah 1779*, 12; Jones, *Paris*, 232; Lawrence, *Storm Over Savannah*, 101; Antonia Fraser, *Marie Antoinette: The Journey* (New York: Anchor Books, 2002), 424–25.

27 Kennedy, ed. and trans., *Muskets, Cannon Balls & Bombs*, 45.

28 Lawrence, *Storm Over Savannah*, 131.

29 Shachtman, *How the French Saved America*, 312; Russell and Hines, *Savannah*, 70.

30 Martin and Harris, *Savannah 1779*, 90; Lawrence, *Storm Over Savannah*, 19.

31 Garrigus, "Catalyst or Catastrophe?," 67, 109–24; King, *Blue Coat or Powdered Wig*, 66, 77; Russell and Hines, *Savannah*, 70.

32 King, *Blue Coat or Powdered Wig*, 66; Russell and Hines, *Savannah*, 70.

33 Carpenter, *Southern Gambit*, 67–68; Lawrence, *Storm Over Savannah*, v, x–xi, 5; Russell and Hines, *Savannah*, 62.

34 Steward, "How the Black St. Domingo Legion Saved the Patriot Army," 9; Lawrence, *Storm Over Savannah*, v, x–xi, 59–60.

35 Lawrence, *Storm Over Savannah*, 108–09, 199; Russell and Hines, *Savannah*, 68.

36 Andrew Burstein, *The Passions of Andrew Jackson* (New York: Alfred A. Knopf, 2003), 113, 115; Brasseaux and Conrad, eds., *The Road to Louisiana*, vii–30, 279–80; Girard, *Haiti*, 48–55.

37 Burstein, *The Passions of Andrew Jackson*, 113; Russell and Hines, *Savannah*, 70.

38 Russell and Hines, *Savannah*, 63, 70; Desmarais, *America's First Ally*, 204–05.

39 Steward, "How the Black St. Domingo Legion Saved the Patriot Army," 10.

40 Garrigus, "Catalyst or Catastrophe?," 119; Hines and Russell, *Savannah*, 70; Lawrence, *Storm Over Savannah*, v; Girard, *Haiti*, 48–76; Shachtman, *How the French Saved America*, 197.

41 Steward, "How the Black St. Domingo Legion Saved the Patriot Army," 8–10; Russell and Hines, *Savannah*, 70.

42 Martin and Harris, *Savannah 1779*, 88.

43 Roger Wilkins, *Jefferson's Pillow: The Founding Fathers and the Dilemma of Black Patriotism* (Boston: Beacon Press, 2001), 51, 87; Russell and Hines, *Savannah*, 70; Tucker, *Ranger Raid*, 52–54; Girard, *Haiti*, 51–58; Wright, ed., *Causes and Consequences of the American Revolution*, 298–303; Gary B. Nash, *Red, White and Black: The Peoples of Early America* (Upper Saddle River, NJ: Prentice-Hall, 2000), 125, 311–12; Charles M. Hudson, ed., *Red, White, and Black: Symposium on Indians in the Old South* (Athens: University of Georgia Press, 1971), 106.

44 Sylvia R. Frey, *Water from the Rock: Black Resistance in a Revolutionary Age* (Princeton, NJ: Princeton University Press, 1991), 96.

45 Russell and Hines, *Savannah*, 70; Girard, *Haiti*, 1–55.

46 Girard, *Haiti*, 55.

ABOUT THE AUTHOR

Phillip Thomas Tucker, PhD, is a writer and historian who has gained recognition as "the Stephen King of History" for having authored more than 80 books in many fields of history. His previous books include *Pickett's Charge: A New Look at Gettysburg's Final Attack* (Skyhorse, 2016), which historian William C. Davis praised as "thoughtful and challenging . . . fresh and bold," and *Death at the Little Bighorn: A New Look at Custer, His Tactics, and the Tragic Decision Made at the Last Stand* (Skyhorse, 2017). For Stackpole, Tucker has written *Cathy Williams* (2002), *Custer at Gettysburg* (2019), and *Ranger Raid* (2021). He lives in Central Florida.